New Directions in Project Management

BEST PRACTICES SERIES

New Directions in Project Management

Editor

Paul C. Tinnirello

CRC Press
Taylor & Francis Group
Boca Raton London New York

CRC Press is an imprint of the
Taylor & Francis Group, an **informa** business

AN AUERBACH BOOK

Chapter 30, "Outsourcing as a Means of Improving Process Maturity: An Approach for More Rapidly Moving up the Capability Maturity Model," © 1998 by Keane, Inc. Used by permission.

CRC Press
Taylor & Francis Group
6000 Broken Sound Parkway NW, Suite 300
Boca Raton, FL 33487-2742

First issued in paperback 2019

© 2002 by Taylor & Francis Group, LLC
CRC Press is an imprint of Taylor & Francis Group, an Informa business

No claim to original U.S. Government works

ISBN-13: 978-0-8493-1190-1 (hbk)
ISBN-13: 978-0-367-39692-3 (pbk)
Library of Congress Card Number 2001046081

Library of Congress Cataloging-in-Publication Data

New directions in project management / edited by Paul C. Tinnirello.
    p. cm. — (Best practices)
Includes bibliographical references and index.
ISBN 0-8493-1190-X (alk. paper)
    1. Project management. I. Tinnirello, Paul C. II. Best practices series (Boca Raton, Fla.)

T56.8 .N49 2001
658.4'04--dc21
                                          2001046081

**Visit the Taylor & Francis Web site at
http://www.taylorandfrancis.com**

**and the CRC Press Web site at
http://www.crcpress.com**

Contributors

LAYNE C. BRADLEY, *Information Technology Management (Retired), Arlington, Texas*

JANET BUTLER, *Senior Editor, Auerbach Publications, New York, New York*

EDWARD G. CALE, JR., *Professor, Information Systems, Babson College, Babson Park, Massachusetts*

TOM CHAUDHURI, *Project Director, Canadian Imperial Bank of Commerce, Toronto, Ontario, Canada*

PAUL CULE, *Assistant Professor of Management, Marquette University, Milwaukee, Wisconsin*

PAUL CULLEN, *IS Technical Consultant, Norwest Audit Services, Inc., Minneapolis, Minnesota*

SUSAN PHILLIPS DAWSON, *CIM Development Manager, Microprocessor and Memory Technologies Group (MMTG) Final Manufacturing, Motorola, Austin, Texas*

KEN DOUGHTY, *Manager, Disaster Recovery, Colonial Bank, Cherry Brook, New South Wales, Australia*

GINGER H. EBY, *Director, Data Administration, Computer Sciences Corporation*

DANA T. EDBERG, *Assistant Professor, Computer Information Systems, University of Nevada, Reno, Nevada*

CHRIS GANE, *President, Rapid System Development, Inc., New York, New York*

HAL H. GREEN, *Director, Manufacturing Systems Division, SETPOINT Inc., Houston, Texas*

J.W.E. GREENE, *Managing Director, Quantitative Software Management (QSM) Europe, Paris, France*

LEIGH HARDY, *Project Management Office Leader, Newcourt Credit, Toronto, Ontario, Canada*

WARREN HARKNESS, *Principal Consultant, Product Development Consulting Inc., Boston, Massachusetts*

LINDA G. HAYES, B.B.A., C.P.A., M.S., J.D., *Chief Executive Officer, WorkSoft, Inc., Dallas, Texas*

DOUGLAS B. HOYT, *Consultant and Writer, Hartsdale, New York*

BRIAN JEFFERY, *Managing Director, International Technology Group, Mountain View, California*

Contributors

JEROME KANTER, *Director, Center for Information Management Studies (CIMS), Babson College, Babson Park, Massachusetts*

BRIAN KEANE, *Information Services and Healthcare Services, Keane, Inc.*

MARK KEIL, *Georgia State University, Atlanta, Georgia*

RALPH L. KLIEM, *President, Practical Creative Solutions, Inc., Redmond, Washington*

POLLY PERRYMAN KUVER, *Consultant, Boston, Massachusetts*

RICHARD B. LANZA, *Process Manager, Business and Technology Integration Team, American Institute of Certified Public Accountants, Lake Hopatcong, New Jersey*

CHANG-YANG LIN, PH.D., *Professor, Computer Information Systems, Eastern Kentucky University, Richmond, Kentucky*

IRWIN S. LUDIN, *Principal, Practical Creative Solutions, Inc., Redmond, Washington*

KALLE LYYTINEN, *University of Jyväskylä, Finland*

JAMES L. MATER, *Executive Vice President and General Manager, Services Division, QualityLogic, Inc., Beaverton, Oregon*

ULLA MERZ, PhD, *Principal Consultant, P2E, Boulder, Colorado*

NANCY BLUMENSTALK MINGUS, *President, Mingus Associates, Inc., Buffalo, New York*

JOHN P. MURRAY, *Consultant, Madison, Wisconsin*

JEANETTE R. NEWMAN, *President, Newman Consulting, Inc., Minneapolis, Minnesota*

ROGER S. PRESSMAN, PH.D., *President, R.S. Pressman & Associates, Inc., Orange, Connecticut*

ANDY ROQUET, *Systems Development Integration Manager, CUNA Mutual Group, Madison, Wisconsin*

TOM ROSE, *Director, Consultant, SMS, Inc., Hanover, Massachusetts*

HUGH W. RYAN, *Partner, Accenture, Chicago, Illinois*

ROY SCHMIDT, *Bradley University, Peoria, Illinois*

NANCY SETTLE-MURPHY, *Founder, Chrysalis International, Boxborough, Massachussetts*

CHRISTOPHER SLEE, *Senior Partner, Consulting and Systems Integration Unit, Computer Sciences Corp. (CSC), Waltham, Massachusetts*

MALCOLM SLOVIN, *Principal, Consulting and Systems Integration Unit, Computer Sciences Corp. (CSC), Waltham, Massachusetts*

DONNA B. STODDARD, *Assistant Professor, Information Systems, Babson College, Babson Park, Massachusetts*

CHRISTINE B. TAYNTOR, *Director, Application Maintenance Co-Sourcing, Honeywell International, Morristown, New Jersey*

CAROLINE THORNTON, *President and Founder, NADUM, Inc., Toronto, Ontario, Canada*

RAY WALKER, *Senior Consultant, Process Control Initiative, DuPont Engineering, Wilmington, Delaware*

Contents

Contents

Contents

Introduction

Project management remains one of the most crucial endeavors to the successful delivery of enterprise computing activities. The diversity of business globalization and electronic commerce combined with the unceasing pace of technical change continues to challenge the efforts for more proficient project management techniques. Organizations that rely on the benefits of computing technology for business survival realize more than ever the critical importance of managing projects in meeting strategic goals and objectives. This ongoing recognition of project management's important role was integral to the success of the original edition of *Project Management* and has prompted this second book to help those who are responsible for meeting the delivery of multifaceted technical projects.

To be effective in project management requires formidable effort, and in comparison to other IT related tasks, it is frequently shrouded with perceptions rather than viewed as a set of adjacent management principles. It is still surprising to find that many IT professionals often ignore basic concepts in an attempt to formalize a single approach that can handle the various facets associated with technical projects. In recognition of such perceptions, this book has been organized into six sections that cover a large spectrum of issues that traditionally exist within the project management framework.

Successful delivery of most IT applications requires a solid understanding of principles that are germane to the project management process. **Section 1, Essentials of Project Management,** provides the important background information to establish the necessary link between concepts and practice. Experienced IT professionals have learned how to apply the basic concepts regardless of the project. At the same time, it is equally important to acknowledge differences in project scope without blind adherence to the rules. The cost of ignoring sound management principles is typically disastrous and, in many cases, occurs well into the schedule of a given project. Many professionals who fail at project management are either victims of rigid discipline or reckless experimentation. Still, there are many professionals who acknowledge the fundamental concepts but have difficulty in implementing the principles into daily practice. In this regard, incremental application of the basic guidelines can yield better results than attempting a massive change to an organization's development culture. I recommend that this section of the book be read initially, and then read again after completing the other sections.

Recognition of quality initiatives has not been limited to engineering and manufacturing practices. Recently, there has been better acknowledgement of the value of quality as applied to management of software technology projects. In particular, the success of ISO 9000 and Six Sigma have been extremely useful when applied to the software development process. **Section 2, Critical Factors for Project Quality,** has been added to the book in order to offer additional information to ensure successful project management. Many IT professionals assume that quality is a guaranteed byproduct of proficient project management techniques. While quality is more likely the result of good project management methods, it cannot be guaranteed without special focus and attention. As such, this section of the book should also be reread since the principles described herein can be applied across the entire scope of all project management endeavors.

One of the crucial components of project management is the ability to utilize human resources in meeting application goals. **Section 3, Managing Business Relationships,** offers numerous insights that can leverage the knowledge held by business experts and technical professionals. Historically, acquiring the skills needed to manage people had been less emphasized than having the skills to handle technical details. Although this may explain why IT professionals struggled with human relationships, it is no longer acceptable to remain as merely the technical agent. Clearly, the most successful project managers have mastered the art of working with diverse organizational types, including vendors, contractors, and consultants. These important skills are not easily acquired and often need years of experience to cultivate. However, the information in this section of the book can provide good insight and lessen the traditional time required to become proficient.

Continuous shortages of skilled professionals, as well as the need to focus on core competencies, has prompted many, if not all, organizations to seek expertise beyond traditional boundaries. **Section 4, Effectively Managing Outsourced Projects,** describes the unique challenges when using external resources to fulfill project objectives. While the promises of outsourcing have been well identified, there are many issues that still require the experience of project management. Merely outsourcing technical tasks does not guarantee successful completion, nor does it automatically ensure that the best interests of the project will be accomplished. Unfortunately, some IT professionals abdicate their responsibilities when using external resources. This has caused numerous organizations to re-evaluate procedures when engaging in outsourcing activities. However, outsourcing will likely remain as a strong complement to internal resources needed in applications development. Understanding the appropriate risks and rewards for using outsourcing is now a mandatory part of any project management strategy.

Some projects are the function of unusual circumstances or occur less frequently than most other computing activities. These types of applications are described in **Section 5, Managing Special Projects,** and include various discussions on topics such as knowledge management, and return on investment strategies. Managing these unique types of projects can challenge even the most experienced and seasoned professional. Sometimes, there is a tendency to administer similar procedures as with more conventional projects and the results can be less favorable than expected. The most important aspect to remember in these situations is that project management should not be exercised with such regulation that it ignores the peculiar attributes of such one-time projects. Examining the different projects described in this section can improve those project management skills required for future projects that may have less definable characteristics.

Project management should not be viewed as a solitary management activity but rather as a set of dynamic principles that can be cultivated and improved through practical experience. Ignoring the need for continuous improvement would be as detrimental as ignoring the basic principles for applying project management itself. **Section 6, Measuring and Improving Project Management Success,** is offered as the last segment in the book. In some respects it could be considered the most significant portion. On the other hand, it is yet another facet of the intricate process that defines the overall manner of project management. Despite the obvious need for managing projects and the necessity to improve the process, many organizations continue to fail in the consistent and repeatable application of project management principles. This may be due, in part, to the overwhelming difficulties of technical projects, partial success, or misunderstanding the evolution of the project management life cycle. Nevertheless, without a commitment to measurement, further improvements to project management efforts will stagnate and organizations will rely on ineffective techniques to manage computing activities. This section does not constitute the only recommendations for management growth, but it does focus on the specifics that apply to the development of hardware and software systems.

As in the past, to use this book effectively I recommend that the reader complete Section 1 before proceeding to other areas. Several sections may examine the same topic but from a different perspective. Some concepts can also be applied differently depending on the circumstances, so the reader is advised to evaluate the situation from various viewpoints, including those provided in the book. It is also suggested to reread several of the chapters in Section 1 in order to fully absorb the content of the underlying basic principles.

The successful planning of project management activities for the challenges of today's business environment will remain difficult, but not unachievable. Ongoing opinions and predictions about future computing technology or shifts in economic direction should be viewed cautiously, especially since many predictions tend to confuse rather than aid in project management endeavors. For those of us who have earnestly pursued the rigors of managing projects, it has demanded the best of our skills, including the dedication to succeed. From my own experiences as a senior IT executive, I appreciate the challenges that project management poses in a time of rapid, yet exciting technical change. I am confident that this new version of the book will provide you with many important concepts that add knowledge to your existing expertise, as well as provide you with the tenacity to improve your management skills. Much success to your project management endeavors.

PAUL C. TINNIRELLO

Section 1
Essential Concepts of Project Management

Chapter 1
Ten Ways to Improve Project Performance

Ralph L. Kliem

It is a sad fact that despite all the formal methodologies, wider adoption of project management disciplines, and more powerful tools, such as World Wide Web technologies and project management software, most projects fail to complete according to the three elements of project management's iron triangle: cost, schedule, and quality. The record gets even more dismal as a project moves into the high-technology arena.

At first, the tendency is to throw one's hands into the air and ask, "What is the use?" Such resignation, however, only maintains the status quo.

Fortunately, there are ten ways to improve project performance if enterprises in general and project teams in particular implement them:

1. Bypass an obstacle
2. Cause people to stretch, not break
3. Focus on the goal
4. Follow a standardized process
5. Learn from the past
6. Maintain ongoing communications
7. Record the work being done
8. Reuse previous work
9. Seek buy-in from all involved
10. Seek simplicity, not complexity, in goal and path

1. BYPASS AN OBSTACLE

Many projects come to a standstill because an obstacle appears in the path toward achieving their goals. It is akin to a military unit being ambushed by sniper fire, so everyone hugs the ground. People are unwilling to raise their heads to determine the direction of the fire, and yet, as long as they stay down, no progress can happen. Often, any progress that was gained is lost.

0-8493-1190-X/02/$0.00+$1.50

The worst thing that the unit can do is to sit idle. It must move forward, retreat, or lose everything.

Many projects, unfortunately, sit idle. The results can become devastating. People become frustrated, the team loses momentum, and indecisiveness eats away morale and esprit de corps. People may focus on issues unrelated to the project, or insignificant issues related to the project become significant, as people look for meaning in their work.

This circumstance often arises because team leaders and members subscribe to an either/or or black/white perspective. When that happens, everything becomes significant and, when an obstacle arises, all work halts.

Instead, team leaders and members must distinguish between what is and is not important. This determination is best achieved by focusing on the ultimate objective, and asking how a particular situation will impact achievement of this final goal. If there is an effect, the team must determine the most appropriate action.

The team must remember that the best action is rarely, if ever, simply standing still. The objective is to move forward by handling an obstacle. If it cannot be dealt with head-on, the team should go around it on the left or right, or go over or underneath it. Progress can continue if coupled with some resilience, perseverance, creativity, and leadership.

2. CAUSE PEOPLE TO STRETCH, NOT BREAK

So many projects are given unrealistic deadlines that it is amazing any of them get done at all. These deadlines are not based on work to do, but by the whim of individuals having little knowledge about the effort required to meet the deadline. A good analogy is trying to place ten pounds of groceries in a five-pound bag; with enough weight and pressure, the bag will burst.

Naturally, there are many consequences. The psychological effects often manifest themselves as burnout, turnover, and conflict. Additionally, the team is set up to fail because constraints are not considered when setting the deadline. Performance and productivity begin to wane as reality confronts unrealistic expectations. Team members compete for scarce resources and start trade-off analyses of what is and is not important.

When making unrealistic demands, management and leadership must realize the impact of their decisions on individual and group performance. Promulgating an unrealistic date or goal may provide a nice exhibition of dominance and decisiveness; however, it can also cause dysfunctional behavior. It is imperative to take time to recognize the talents, knowledge, and skills of people performing the tasks; to identify the cost, schedule, and qualitative constraints; and to apply sound estimating techniques to complete the project. Only then can a realistic plan be put in place to encourage people to stretch, rather than break.

3. FOCUS ON THE GOAL

It is easy to overlook the purpose of a project when administering its details. It is similar to the saying that, when fighting alligators, it is easy to forget that the main purpose is to drain the swamp. Team leaders and team members become so wrapped up in details that they lose sight of the entire purpose of their project. People get so engrossed in the details, due to their immediacy or finiteness, that they lose sight of the big picture and forget to ask if what they are doing is contributing toward accomplishing the final goal.

Keeping focus on the goal offers several advantages. First, it enables people to be proactive rather than reactive. People can choose what to respond to, rather than jumping at each situation like one of Pavlov's dogs. Second, it helps in distinguishing between what is and is not significant. Obviously, not everything is equally important, although some team members might think so. Naturally, these people become overburdened with work. Third, focusing on the goal provides an objective standard of evaluation. The significance of a particular effort is determined by the degree to which it helps to achieve a final goal.

Unfortunately, teams rely too heavily on numbers to determine significance, which can lead to dysfunctional behavior. While numbers tell only part of the story, in some projects they become more important than accomplishing a mission. Hence, the team performs considerable work, and the metrics reflect that increase in effort. However, the fundamental question may remain unanswered: Is what is happening furthering the achievement of the final goal?

It is important, therefore, to perform three actions. The first is to constantly query about progress, asking if what people are doing is furthering goal achievement. The second is to establish a consistent, standard "yardstick" for measuring progress, keeping in mind, of course, that the importance of the yardstick is to measure the right factors in order to determine the value of the current work. The bottom line is to remove any blinders leading to myopic decision-making and performance. While such decisions and performance might appear significant, in reality they do nothing, and perhaps even impede actual accomplishment.

4. FOLLOW A STANDARDIZED PROCESS

A common set of tools, procedures, and jargon can help a project progress efficiently and effectively toward its goal. Unfortunately, people often strongly resist following a standardized process. They fear that it stifles creativity and the empowerment of people. As a result, many projects become a cacophony of tools, procedures, and techniques, requiring extensive effort to make them compatible. Naturally, this wastes time and effort, and actually hinders progress toward a goal.

Contrary to popular belief, a standardized process actually encourages creativity and furthers empowerment, rather than impeding both. It encourages creativity by allowing people to work with a given set of tools and techniques; for example, to complete a task. Through standardization, people can anticipate and understand job requirements. Less conversion and relearning are required to complete tasks. People can operate autonomously, knowing the standards to follow during decision-making. When standards do not exist, people are often stymied because everything is unclear.

Standardization, therefore, offers several benefits from a project management and technical perspective. First, it enables the efficient and effective execution of project activities through consistency. Second, it enables better integration of activities because team members can see the interrelationships of their work with that of others. Third, it reduces rework because it enables the use of output developed on earlier projects. Finally, it improves communications because team members are playing from the "same sheet of music."

For projects, standardization involves two distinct areas; one is project management. Standardization involves using tools and executing activities to build plans and manage according to those plans. The other area is technical. Standardization involves identifying requirements and specifications, and constructing a product that satisfies both.

There are many options for moving toward standardization when managing projects. People can join professional organizations, thereby exposing them to what has and has not worked in similar environments. The organization can also purchase or develop a standardized process for managing projects. Regardless of how the organization obtains a standardized process, the key is to develop or adopt one that people can agree to and that is compatible with the company's culture.

5. LEARN FROM THE PAST

The great philosopher Santayana once said that he who fails to study history is destined to repeat it. Unfortunately, because few people learn from the past, history often repeats itself on projects. In fact, many projects are dismal reminders that nothing changes.

Contrary to Henry Ford, who once commented that all history is bunk, learning from the past offers several benefits. It helps organizations avoid costly mistakes that occurred on similar projects in the past. In addition, it helps companies capitalize on previous successes. It also builds confidence and reduces risks for people who have worked on earlier projects.

Learning from the past involves learning both from oneself and from others. Of the two learning levels, learning from oneself is more difficult because it requires introspection. While learning from others can also be difficult, it is less so because there may be documentation or people may be available to provide an oral history or insights.

From personal experiences, team members can visualize the current project in the context of one from the past, identifying similarities and dissimilarities, and determining what worked and what did not work. This requires considerable introspection and objectivity. From the experiences of others, team members can also identify similar projects from the past, and then interview the participants, or read audit reports and "lessons learned," if they exist. Of course, the challenge is to obtain knowledge about the projects and gain access to their information.

6. MAINTAIN ONGOING COMMUNICATIONS

More projects have probably failed due to poor communications than from any other factor. Ironically, while everyone recognizes the contribution of good communications to success, it still remains in a dismal state.

One reason is that people confuse the medium with communication. A medium is the *vehicle* for communicating, acting as an *enabler* of communication, rather than a substitute for it. With the growing presence of e-mail, videoconferencing, and World Wide Web technologies, many people assume that they will be good communicators. All too often, the medium simply gives a poor communicator a louder voice. At least from a project management perspective, the medium is not the message.

The other reason for poor communications is the lack of team members' distinction between data and information. While data is unprocessed, information is data that is converted into something meaningful. When team members confuse the two, they send data rather than information, whereupon the recipient must go through the data to derive the information. Because this confusion manifests in electronic as well as paper format, many project team members generate countless data files and e-mails, and build innumerable Web pages replete with data but not information.

By contrast, good communication is providing the right information at the right time in the right amount to the right person. When that occurs, people operate on the "same wavelength." They take part in better dialog, reducing the number and magnitude of misunderstandings. As a result of good communication, team members are also better able to adapt to change.

To realize the benefits of maintaining good communications, team members can perform three actions. The first is to concentrate on generating information rather than data. This requires focusing on the needs of the audience, in terms of format and level of content. The second way team members can improve communications is to ensure that data and subsequent information are current and relevant. In fact, all too many projects produce data and information that are outdated and irrelevant. The third method of improving communications is to use the chosen medium as the principal means of communication to obtain the necessary data and information. For example, while a project might establish a Web site for this purpose, some people might be intimidated by the technology. In such cases, good communications cannot occur, despite the best technology.

7. RECORD THE WORK BEING DONE

On most projects, team members perform considerable work in management and development. Unfortunately, the work often goes unrecorded, and the knowledge and expertise is lost due to turnover and time constraints. This is a tremendous loss to companies that could have saved this knowledge and expertise, applying it on future, similar projects.

If companies made an effort to record the knowledge and expertise of what went well on a project, they would gain several benefits for future projects. Such a history improves performance among team members, because people can focus on issues not dealt with previously, which may not be "showstoppers." It also forces people to think about their actions, and determine where and when to spend their effort and time. In addition, a recorded history tells people what has worked in the past, enabling them to predict with reasonable accuracy the impact of their actions on the current project.

On an existing project, team members see the value in creating a trail of activity and auditing previous performance; they thereby gain an understanding of what was done and how, and why things were done a certain way. Finally, sharing the recorded information with everyone fosters good communications among team members.

If recording offers many benefits, why is it not done more thoroughly and more often? For one, it easier to react and see some tangible, immediate results than to take a proactive approach, which produces long-term rather than immediate results. In addition, such a process requires administrative overhead. Finally, even if it is done, it often gets buried, so it is overlooked and eventually lost.

Obviously, these are monumental challenges. However, organizations can take steps to ease the burden. First, they can see the time and effort to record activities as a necessary activity, establishing it as a requirement rather than an option. Second, they can establish an agreed-upon format and approach before the project begins. Waiting until after the project starts only slows momentum, frustrates people, and often becomes a futile attempt at reconstruction.

8. REUSE PREVIOUS WORK

While it is good for team members to feel creative on a project, unfortunately, their desire for creativity often leads to reinventing the wheel. There are major consequences when that occurs, including wasted effort due to repeating work, slowing of the project's momentum, a failure to capitalize on the success of the past, and extension of the project's life cycle. In other words, it is nonproductive.

Reuse enables organizations to use what was done before again, in a similar situation. The benefits include expediting the project life cycle, allowing team members to focus on more important issues, increasing the product's reliability, and enabling team members to make modifications quickly. Because plans and products are built modularly, reuse also reduces complexity. Finally, it allows more accurate planning.

Reuse occurs on both the project management and technical development levels. For project management, teams may reuse sections of schedules from similar projects, segments of files loaded into automated scheduling packages, report formats and contents, and forms. Examples of reuse related to technical development include code, models, files generated from software tools, and specifications.

Teams can take several actions to maximize the benefits of reuse. They can acquire knowledge of what occurred previously on other projects, enabling them to "cannibalize" what was done well. To obtain information about previous work, team members can review the documentation of earlier projects, interview participants on those projects, and read case histories in professional journals of similar projects.

Team members can also rely on personal experience to maximize the benefits of reuse. Wide exposure to many projects in different environments results in a greater breadth of experience from which the team can learn. That knowledge, in turn, makes it easier to determine what to reuse. In addition, teams can use professional and business organizations as a source of contacts with individuals who can provide, for free, insight on what worked well on similar projects. These organizations can also provide materials for reuse, such as forms and checklists.

9

9. SEEK BUY-IN BY THOSE INVOLVED

Perhaps the most powerful way to get a project to progress rapidly is through commitment by the people doing the work. Because buy-in provides people with ownership and a sense of empowerment, it generates a greater sense of responsibility and accountability. In turn, less effort is required to follow up on tasks. Buy-in also encourages initiative.

Unfortunately, because many projects become one-man shows, there is little commitment. As a result, estimates are often unrealistic, representing scientific wildly assumed guesses (swags), rather than being based on reliable, statistical calculations. There can also be a lack of commitment to the schedule, with team members filling in to be determined (TBD), rather than actually estimating task schedules. As time moves on and such consequences become aggravated, the lack of commitment can affect the project's potential success. Then, while it becomes costly in terms of time, money, and effort to resolve these problems, there is still little commitment.

To help generate commitment, team managers can take an inventory of team members, learning not only about their knowledge, expertise, and experience, but also about their maturity and follow-up. This allows the manager to seek their counsel appropriately. Managers can also use public disclosure to attain and sustain commitment. When team members' input is visible, regardless of perspective, there is less likelihood of their denying input or reducing commitment. Finally, and this is tied to the last point, team managers should not only gauge a person's ability to do a task, but also his or her enthusiasm. While team members might have the requisite background, they may lack the corresponding level of excitement for doing a good job. Commitment comes from the heart — not the head.

10. SEEK SIMPLICITY, NOT COMPLEXITY, IN GOAL AND PATH

Simplicity easily yields to complexity. That is, it is always tempting to make a situation or a solution as complex as possible. People make a refinement here and a slight alteration there, and before anyone realizes it, the result is totally different from what was originally envisioned.

Simplicity, of course, is not the same as being simple. While simplicity means identifying the shortest path, with a style that says "that's it," simple is merely paint-by-the-numbers and lacking in sophistication. Ironically, simplicity can appear the same as being simple because they both share the common characteristic of clarity. Complexity, however, is quite different. It is sophistication gone amuck, whereby confusion rather than clarity is the guiding rule. And a lot of confusion can drown clarity.

In distinguishing between simplicity and complexity, simplicity is recognizable when seen, but not definable. While projects always tend toward complexity, good projects result in simplicity when completed. These are usually the projects that satisfy the criteria for success in regard to cost, schedule, and quality.

In determining whether a plan is simple or complex, the symptoms are quite obvious. In the latter, many people request additions, changes, removals, or repositioning, so that the plan becomes full of exceptions and contingencies. Because this complexity makes it difficult to follow the plan, few ultimately do so. In another symptom of complexity, product developers must repeatedly explain their intent or meaning. In yet another indicator, the plan must be continually revised to accommodate different situations. The end result is similar to a rat following a path in a maze.

By contrast, simplicity forces clarity of thought, demonstrating clarity in destination and the path to take. It also requires less time and people resources to execute a plan, and gives people confidence because they know their mission and what must be done.

To encourage simplicity in project management, team members can first try to attain as much experience as possible in different environments; this provides insight on what works well. Also, they can capitalize on the experience of others to gain further insight.

Second, if team members determine that something can be done in two steps rather than four, they should choose the former, ignoring the tendency to believe that because something looks simplistic it must be wrong. More often than not, the correct solution is simplistic.

Third, project teams should ensure that all elements of a plan contribute toward accomplishing the final goal; otherwise, they should remove it. After all, it merely embellishes the plan, and might well increase complexity and confusion, either now or later. Finally, teams should remove biases from a plan. Thus, they should avoid treating an assumption as fact, and blatantly affecting approaches that have no basis in reality. Biases in fact and data only add to complexity.

NO COMPLICITY WITH SIMPLICITY

Typical high-technology firms seldom apply more than a few of the principles cited this chapter. Instead, their staff moves about "helter skelter," trying to solve a problem with a complex solution that is likely a reinvention of what was been done earlier on another project. However, while few team members agree with the solution, they concede at least temporarily, either because it eases the problem or someone important felt it was the right answer. If the problem remains unsolved, they might wait for someone to do something, all the while looking busy doing insignificant work. As this occurs, the schedule slides, the budget is exceeded, and quality deteriorates.

Team members both fear and hope that the unsolved problem is caught during testing.

Even if half the ideas in this chapter are implemented on a project, performance will improve. The dismal track record of project success and failure, however, attests to the fact that few use such suggestions. The challenge is to get project managers and team members to embrace the recommendations.

Chapter 2
Nine Factors for Project Success

John P. Murray

The successful design, development, and implementation of information technology (IT) projects is a very difficult, complex, and, at times, daunting process. However, although developing IT projects can be difficult, the reality is that a relatively small number of factors control the success or failure of every IT project, regardless of its size or complexity. There is nothing esoteric about those factors. The problem is not that the factors are unknown; it is that they seldom form an integral part of the IT development process.

Of course, the recognition and management of these factors does not ensure IT project success. Understanding the factors and the part they play in successful project management is one thing; appropriately managing them is something else. In addition, there is a high potential for project failure in not recognizing the part these factors play, or failing to appropriately manage them.

If these factors are so clearly important and well-known, why do they not form an integral part of every IT project? The short answer is that they should. The issue here is that because they are not used, too high a number of IT projects suffer some degree of failure.

The phrase "IT project failure" often raises a specter of some colossal failure. For example, the project never goes operational, or it is abandoned in midstream after considerable expense. In addition, there are other, qualified IT failures, such as projects that exceed their development time and expense estimates, but ultimately become operational. There are also many projects that move to production status, but do not meet the expectations of internal customers as defined in the project specifications. And projects may be considered failures if the applications take too long to process the data, or if they regularly fail in the operational environment.

0-8493-1190-X/02/$0.00+$1.50
© 2002 by CRC Press LLC

In short, many organizations do not have a particularly good track record in IT project success. However, many IT project failures can be eliminated or mitigated by understanding and managing the nine project failure factors described in this chapter. These factors should be recognized for the strength they can bring to every project, and accorded the attention they deserve.

THE NINE FACTORS

The following nine factors can and do make or break IT projects:

1. Appropriate senior management levels of commitment to the project
2. Adequate project funding
3. A well-done set of project requirements and specifications
4. Careful development of a comprehensive project plan that incorporates sufficient time and flexibility to anticipate and deal with unforeseen difficulties as they arise
5. An appropriate commitment of time and attention on the part of those outside the IT department who have requested the project, combined with a willingness to see it through to the end
6. Candid, accurate reporting of the status of the project and of potential difficulties as they arise
7. A critical assessment of the risks inherent in the project, any potential harm associated with those risks, and the ability of the project team to manage those risks
8. The development of appropriate contingency plans that can be employed should the project run into problems
9. An objective assessment of the ability and willingness of the organization to stay the project course

The reader will realize that none of the factors has anything to do with technology. In addition, all the factors are straightforward, and can be easily understood by anyone with a business background.

Organizations that recognize and work to appropriately include the nine factors in IT project development are taking an important step in moving to more consistent IT project success. However, they will have to do more than recognize the factors' importance. They must also understand the interlocked nature of the factors, which together form a mosaic of strong project management. If IT project success is to improve, the role and importance of each factor must be understood. A discussion of each of the factors will provide information about how they affect IT projects.

1. SENIOR MANAGEMENT COMMITMENT

When it is clear that a particular IT project has the interest, the support, and the commitment of the organization's senior management, everyone involved in the project will have a sharper focus. Almost all IT projects are expensive. In addition, these projects present opportunities — some of them significant — that foster organizational success. Poorly done projects can hamper the organization's success; some can even put the organization in jeopardy. Therefore, it is imperative that the senior managers responsible for the areas affected by a particular project become and remain involved. If, as often happens, the process is completely left to the IT department, the project is in trouble.

There are numerous examples of IT projects that have considerably benefited an organization. There are also many examples of IT project failures that have seriously disrupted an organization's business. Beyond the issue of total IT project failures, there are IT projects that are not true failures, but are less than successful. Those projects never deliver what was originally promised and are sometimes simply abandoned.

IT projects are sometimes conceived, funded, and built without appropriate senior-level review and involvement. This should not be seen as a failure on the part of senior management to *approve* a given IT project. In virtually all organizations, senior management approval is mandatory when a project reaches a certain funding level. In the majority of failed IT projects, such approval was undoubtedly granted at a high organizational level. Therefore, the issue is not that IT projects go forward without appropriate approval, but rather that the approval is too often automatic.

All too often, senior management approves IT projects that carry potentially serious consequences for the enterprise, without clearly understanding the organization's exposure or risk. Of course, one can argue that IT management is obliged to properly inform senior management of the project's potential downside. However, in the euphoria of getting the project approved, the project's risks may be ignored or glossed over. In fact, some organizations have a repeated pattern of project proposal and subsequent failure, yet senior management remains aloof.

There is an important distinction between approval of and commitment to an IT project. In IT projects that encounter difficulty, there is usually some point at which members of senior management become involved, and their attention and commitment are in place. However, this often happens at the wrong end of the project.

IT projects beyond a set funding level, which varies by organization, should never be seriously considered without senior management's clear understanding of the project's perceived difficulties, risks, and benefits. Too many IT projects gain approval based upon hype and an unrealistic calculation of the potential benefits. Thus, senior management, with or without an IT background, should probe for the facts. The project should be abandoned, or at least halted, until their questions can be satisfactorily answered.

2. ADEQUATE PROJECT FUNDING

IT projects often require heavy financial investments if they are to be successful. However, ample project funding is not in and of itself a panacea; access to large sums of money does not ensure IT project success. Conversely, inadequate project funding will lead to delivery of less than promised, if not outright failure.

Organizations must recognize that the time, hardware, software, and people components that make up an IT project are expensive. They should therefore devote ample time and attention at the project's beginning to analyze and apply realistic costs to the components. Although good project expense analysis may not produce complete figures, the process should provide a reasonable understanding of the expense associated with the project. Once a set of realistic figures is produced, the organization should also build a reasonable amount of contingency funding into the estimated project cost.

IT project funding should be seen as a continuing and flexible process. While a reasonable estimate of project expense must be made to obtain initial approval, this figure should not be considered the final project cost. After all, changes will be incorporated into the project plan as it goes forward. These will undoubtedly involve added functionality, which will in turn translate into increased project cost.

As the project moves forward, its implications will be better understood. As the true scope of the project is revealed, the project manager can more accurately identify project expenses. Therefore, costs must be recalculated at several checkpoints in the project life cycle, and the new figures communicated to senior management.

Senior management should view the changing project costs in a positive light, although they are more likely to rise than to fall. This is because a discussion of the changing expense offers senior management an opportunity to probe why the estimates changed. For example, the project sponsors might have requested additional functionality, which increased the cost. At this point, senior management has an opportunity to decide whether or not they want to fund these additional project expenses or forego the added functionality. Otherwise, there is often *de facto* approval of increased functionality (and project expense), without senior management involvement.

Without interim project expense reviews, additional functions are often added, raising project expense, but such additions are not revealed until the project is completed, if ever. In addition, interim estimates provide an opportunity to reduce the project scope, if necessary, to bring the cost to a more desirable level. This might entail extending the project's installation date, abandoning parts of the project, or curtailing some of the features. Whatever the result of the project review, it presents an opportunity to make project-expense-related adjustments in a businesslike manner.

3. WELL-DONE REQUIREMENTS AND SPECIFICATIONS

It is absolutely critical to the success of any IT project that the organization develop a clear understanding of what will be delivered and what will not be delivered within the project's scope. In fact, it is not unusual for the people who requested the project to raise issues part way through it about functions that are not to be delivered.

This sparks arguments between the project sponsors and the members of the IT department, who both seek to assign blame for the apparent oversight. It represents poor development work to make assumptions about inclusion or exclusion of items in an IT project, and is bound to create confusion and disappointment, if not serious project disruption.

Even if there are well-thought-out and documented project requirements and specifications, unforeseen events will arise as the project moves forward. Sometimes, minor additions can be made to the applications, requiring little time and expense. However, the lack of inclusion of major items can render the project inoperable. When this happens, there are two unattractive options. The project can be reworked to include what was overlooked, which is likely expensive and time consuming, and shows the IT department in an unfavorable light, even if it was not responsible for the oversight. The other option is to abandon the project.

Not only must the project-related requirements and specifications be complete, they must be reviewed by people familiar with the business issues the project is to support. This review must be careful and thorough, to avoid subsequent IT development difficulties.

All too often, when it is found that additions must be made to the requirements and specifications in the later stages of the project, a workaround is attempted. In addition to the time and expense of such a solution, it often does not work, or does not work well. And, while strong project management requirements and specifications do not ensure project success, they add considerably to the probability that the project will succeed.

4. A COMPREHENSIVE PROJECT PLAN

IT project planning is not a waste of time, although many believe it is. In fact, there is a very strong correlation between the length of time allocated to project planning and the project's ultimate success. Granted, IT planning can be overdone, but IT installations seldom exhibit excessive attention to planning.

There are three benefits to be gained from strong project planning. First, planning allows the planners to present a clear, well-documented, properly focused understanding of the project. Second, the planning process raises questions that would not otherwise be considered. There is often a rush to begin the project without an adequate understanding of what will be done or the ramifications of the work.

The third planning benefit is that it builds confidence in the project and its processes. As a result, when planning is finished, it is easier to confidently begin the project. In a well-done versus a poorly planned project, then, the transition from project concept to delivery will be easier and faster. Appropriate project planning is a function of an organization's strong IT project discipline. To succeed, IT management must make it clear that planning is an important component of project management, and that the required planning must be completed and approved before the project moves forward.

5. COMMITMENT OF STAKEHOLDERS

The track record is poor in organizations where responsibility for IT projects rests with the IT department. In fact, IT projects are, with limited exceptions, developed and operated to meet the organization's *business* needs and interests, rather than those of IT. The organization is poorly served when people outside the IT department can dissociate themselves from projects in which they have a vested interest.

Sometimes, IT projects of significant size are completed with virtually no internal customer involvement. Their attitude might well be, "Show me the results when the project is done." If and when projects of this type are finally installed, they rarely meet internal customers' needs.

IT department managers should realize that IT has a vested interest in developing a process that ensures strong internal customer involvement in its projects. A lack of customer involvement virtually ensures eventual customer dissatisfaction with some project aspect. If IT managers cannot get customers to share project ownership, they set themselves up for eventual customer criticism.

Therefore, IT should not initiate or install any projects without the complete support, involvement, and attention of the appropriate internal customers. It represents a failure on the part of senior management if internal customers take no project responsibility, yet complain about the project's content and performance once it moves into production.

Because business projects warrant the investment of large sums of IT time, effort, and money, they should warrant a comparable investment on the part of the internal customers who requested the project. It is senior management's responsibility to make certain that everyone affected by a particular IT project has a share in the project's ownership.

It will require fortitude on the part of the IT management team to halt development of an IT project due to a lack of internal customer involvement. However, this is the correct approach; otherwise, IT is exposed to excessive risk.

6. PROJECT STATUS REPORTING

It is not enough to simply provide regular project status updates; these updates must be accurate. In fact, IT project status reports are often overly optimistic. While it might be more comfortable for departments to believe that steady project progress is being made, it is more important that the reported status is realistic. IT projects routinely fall into difficulty. One cause is in the failure to accurately report the real project status in a timely fashion.

IT might provide inaccurate project reporting in the usually mistaken belief that lost ground will be regained as the project moves forward. After all, no one will be the wiser when the lost ground is made up and the project is back on schedule. However, it is almost universally true that once a project falls behind, the situation will only get worse without high-level involvement. And senior management will not provide the needed help as long as it thinks things are going well.

As early in the project as possible, project status reporting should identify adverse issues, as well as recommend how the difficulties can be overcome. Of course, candid project reporting can create tension for both the project team and the customer areas. Some degree of tension is desirable, because it will cause people to consider issues early on which otherwise might not arise until later in the project. And, while dealing with IT project problems and tensions can be difficult, ignoring them will only make them more difficult.

Members of IT projects typically postpone the delivery of bad news, such as a delay. When this happens, senior management might be alerted to the problem by some other area, or the project manager might have to reluctantly admit to the project's delayed status. Both scenarios have a negative effect on senior management, on everyone involved in the project, and on the project itself.

7. CRITICAL RISK ASSESSMENT

An organization's senior management should complete and publish a careful analysis of the project's risks before it seriously considers approval. It is not enough to recognize that the project has some risk, or to have a vague idea of some of the possible project-related risks. Risk, as it applies to a particular IT project, must be well-understood. More importantly, those who will suffer from the project-related risks must be made as aware of them as promptly as possible.

Identification of project risk falls into two categories: the more usual and obvious risks, and the risks that will be generated based upon the functions and requirements of the particular project.

Usual and obvious project risks include:

- The use of software that is new, or at least new to the organization.
- The organization's level of IT skill and knowledge. Obviously, a seasoned, well-trained group of IT professionals will be more likely to master the project development than less experienced people.
- The track record of the IT department in successfully managing IT projects. IT departments that have a strong development track record bring less risk to a project, regardless of its size and complexity, than an organization with a poor development record.
- The size and complexity of the proposed project.
- The willingness of the organization to properly fund the project.
- The level of trust and respect between the IT members of the project team and the internal customers on the team.

Risks associated with the particular project's functions include:

- The perceived importance of the project to the business of the organization. Obviously, an IT project that carries heavy business implications will present a considerably higher risk level than upgrading an existing system.
- The ability and willingness of those outside the IT department who have requested the project to become and remain involved throughout the life of the project. In projects where the assistance of outside vendors is required to bring the project to a successful completion, the level of dependency on that vendor must be calculated and managed. The willingness and ability of the vendor to perform as expected must be seriously considered. In addition, circumstances within vendor organizations change. For example, part way through the project, the vendor might decide to abandon the line of hardware the project is using. Alternatively, a competitor might buy out the vendor, lowering the vendor's level of project support. Finally, the vendor might just go out of business.

- The quality of the project requirements and specifications. The higher the quality of that work, the more probable the project will be a success.
- The possibility of the loss of a key person on the project, either from IT or from the internal customer side. If that person alone has knowledge critical to the project's success, his or her loss could deal the project a fatal blow.

Every IT project presents its own set of risks. A businesslike approach to project management requires carefully considering and addressing these risks with internal customers and senior management as part of the project's approval process. If the risk analysis leads to a decision not to move forward, it is much better for everyone involved that the decision is made sooner, rather than later.

8. PROJECT CONTINGENCY PLANS

As a project moves forward, difficulties might well arise. Although the organization might be highly confident that the project will succeed, it is prudent to consider the possibility of some type of failure. Because such a possibility exists, the organization should put a plan in place to overcome difficult situations if they should arise.

Some examples of IT project contingency planning include:

- Recognition that the planned level of hardware resources to support the project may prove inadequate when it is moved into production. One of the common failings of IT projects, particularly in client/server environments, is disappointing processing performance when the applications move to the production environment. Although the hardware plan might seem adequate, that might not be the case. Therefore, the project plan should have a provision to increase hardware resources should the need arise. In addition, senior management should be advised of this possibility.
- Anticipation of "surprise" additions to the project's functionality as it moves forward. Too often, part way through a project, the project must incorporate items that were overlooked, or changes in the business needs associated with the project. This means schedule delays (with talk of "phase two"), and additional project expense. In addition, other projects may be delayed, and business initiatives dependent upon the successful completion of this project may be delayed.

Project surprises are always a possibility, despite a strong set of project requirements and specifications. It should therefore be a mandatory part of the development process to recognize this possibility and raise the issue with the appropriate people.

When an IT project is of paramount importance to an organization, it makes good business sense to consider the possibility of delay. In addition, an attempt should be made to construct a plan to work around this eventuality.

Developing a project contingency plan should be linked to the issues of project planning and project funding, as addressed earlier in this chapter. However, while appropriate planning will identify many of the issues that may arise and that should be built into the project, no amount of planning will anticipate everything that might happen. If funding is flexible, senior management will already realize the possibility of additional expense.

Obviously, the ideal is to generate a plan, the first time around, that is absolutely precise with regard to expense and functions. However, that is virtually impossible in a project of any magnitude. Believing that such a process is viable represents one of the fundamental causes of IT project difficulty.

9. A WILLINGNESS TO STAY THE COURSE

All IT projects face some level of difficulty, and much of it can be mitigated through sound management approaches. However, problems must be anticipated. As they arise, people will try to find ways to reduce the pain associated with the project. At this point, pressure will likely build to modify the project.

Some of the suggestions for doing so include:

- A reduction in the features to be delivered. A phased approach to the project can be introduced, designed to shift parts of the project from the current schedule to some (often poorly defined) future date.
- An approach that proposes that flaws or problems in the system be fixed by some workaround process. This process offers a solution to the current problem, but will often do less than what was specified in the original project plan. The idea is that the problem should be fully and correctly repaired, but there is no time to do that work now. The workaround is usually accompanied by a promise to return to the problem at some later date and make things right. When this occurs, the chance of correcting the problem at some later date will be close to zero.
- A willingness to reduce testing standards and controls to meet project deadlines. Again, the stance is to wait to fix testing-related problems so that the schedule is met.
- Abandonment of the project.

Obviously, if a project is in difficulty, some steps must be taken to correct the situation. These steps, and their ramifications on the entire project, should be carefully thought out and considered. It is important that everyone involved in the project realize that if there are project difficulties, there may be pressure to adjust the original plan. The plan should be flexible enough to allow adjustment, if needed. Organizations must avoid overreacting to problems and adapting the wrong approach to solving them.

Those responsible for the project's ultimate success within the IT department should ensure the continuing support of the organization's senior management for the project. If the project is of sufficient importance to be initiated, it should be adequately supported if things should go wrong. In obtaining senior management support, project managers must be willing to present an accurate picture of the potential difficulties inherent in the project. Insofar as is practical, senior management must be given a realistic assessment of the potential for difficulty and be willing to stay the course if things go wrong.

CONCLUSION

It is impossible to identify and manage all the potential difficulties and ramifications associated with IT development projects. The larger the project, the greater the probability of unforeseen difficulty. In large IT development projects, it can become a massive task to coordinate the various teams working on the project.

If organizations attempted to find and resolve all project difficulties and potential difficulties, it would keep projects from moving forward; this is sometimes referred to as "analysis paralysis." This chapter does not strive for perfection. Rather, it tries to raise the awareness in IT installations and with the internal customer community, that the better prepared everyone is going into a given project, the greater the likelihood of a successful project.

While no one wants to be involved in an IT project that is less than successful, virtually every organization has project failures. If available, methods should be implemented to alleviate some of the difficulties and, as a result, improve the levels of IT service and customer satisfaction.

Of course, the nine factors outlined here create more work. However, this additional workload need not be a burden if the factors are understood and realized. When an organization incorporates the nine factors into the normal IT project development processes, the work required becomes less of a burden. If a relatively small amount of extra time and effort can improve IT projects and increase internal customer satisfaction, it is a small price to pay.

Chapter 3
Managing Project Management

Nancy Blumenstalk Mingus

As more organizations move to formal project work, it becomes critical to capably manage those projects. The best way to do so most effectively is to establish standards for project management that are corporatewide, or at least span the information systems (IS) department. These standards include project management methodologies and life cycles, as well as software packages for project management, process management, and time accounting.

This chapter discusses project management methodologies and life cycles, reviews some of the more common features of each, and explains the three types of software commonly used to support corporate project management systems.

PROJECT MANAGEMENT METHODOLOGIES AND LIFE CYCLES

Although managers can manage projects without a formal methodology, having one can be a big help. This section explains what project management methodologies are and why they are important, and gives a brief history of project management methodologies. It also defines life cycles, describes some common IS life cycles, and explains how life cycles relate to methodologies.

Project management methodologies have been around for decades, but first started to become popular in IS in the early 1970s. These methodologies usually have two components. The first is an overall process for doing things, while the second consists of templates or forms required at specific portions of that process. While the process itself is the true methodology, most project managers consider the templates and forms to be part and parcel of the methodology. However, most project managers also agree that templates alone do not a methodology make.

0-8493-1190-X/02/$0.00+$1.50
© 2002 by CRC Press LLC

Project management methodologies are important for two reasons. First, they standardize the way in which an organization manages its projects. This allows people from anywhere in the organization to talk with one another using the same terms and the same definitions for those terms. Presenting a consistent approach to project management via standards also allows project managers to cover for one another when the need arises. The second reason that methodologies are important is that they provide novice project managers with the tools to manage projects, without requiring a long learning curve.

Project life cycles generally go hand in hand with project methodologies. Such life cycles break a project's life into a series of phases or stages. The end of each phase provides a convenient project review point for senior management to institute go or no-go decisions, and also allows project managers to plan the next phases in more detail. While project life cycles can have many phases, the majority have three to five. They include some type of project start-up or initiation, a project construction or implementation stage, and, finally, a project evaluation or post-implementation review.

SELECTING PROJECT MANAGEMENT METHODOLOGIES

For organizations that do not have a methodology or are looking for a new one, this section explains what to look for in project management methodologies. It discusses the benefits and drawbacks of in-house versus vendor-supplied methodologies, as well as canned versus customized methodologies. It then describes the most popular vendor methodologies.

First, an exploration of the benefits and drawbacks of vendor methodologies is in order. The greatest benefit of a vendor methodology is that the work is already done, which can save an organization literally years of developing an internal methodology. The vendor methodology has also been tested and proven to work, saving both the time and headaches involved in smoothing out process wrinkles.

On the downside, however, purchased methodologies require an organization to change its existing practices to match those of the methodology. If it does not, then the organization must customize at least some of the methodology. These customizations can vary from minor tweaks of the process, to customizations so severe that the original purchased methodology is virtually obliterated.

Another drawback of purchased methodologies is their price. Many vendor-supplied methodologies cost $50,000 or more for a perpetual license. In addition, some vendors charge thousands of dollars annually.

Some of the more popular methodologies for IS projects include Dynamic Systems Development Method (DSDM) from Computer Associates and PRIDE from Computacenter.

IMPLEMENTING PROJECT MANAGEMENT METHODOLOGIES

This section explains how to implement a project management methodology. It covers how to establish project work breakdown structures (WBSs), as well as estimating, tracking, change control, quality control, and communication standards. It then explains how to conduct IS departmental and client training regarding both the methodology and the standards.

Once an organization has either selected a vendor methodology or developed one in-house, it is ready to start the long, often tedious process of creating project standards. While some of the purchased methodologies come with standards for various project components, organizations will need to develop standards for those that do not have them.

Creating WBS, Estimating, and Tracking Standards

The first standard to be established is how project WBSs will be created. Many organizations develop project templates for the most common types of projects developed in the organization, and then specify that project managers work from these templates. The advantage of this is that project managers are not "reinventing the wheel" on each project. In turn, this speeds up planning, and allows better project tracking.

After WBS standards are established, the organization must decide how estimates will be created. Estimates can be determined from expert opinions, weighted averages, statistics from previous projects, or from techniques such as function point analysis. If organizations track their projects accurately and religiously, they can use statistics from previous projects to provide the most accurate estimates. This highlights the need for standards in tracking projects.

Most organizations use some type of automated time-keeping package to track time against projects. Time tracking has three project-related purposes. The most critical is to accurately judge where a current project stands. However, other reasons that are almost as important are the uses of time tracking for project cost accounting, and for data collection — in order to better estimate the next project.

To provide the best database for estimating future projects, these packages should allow tracking against each task in the WBS, reinforcing the desirability of standard WBSs.

27

Change Control, Quality Control, and Communications Standards

Standards for change control, quality control, and communications are equally important to project success. Change control in this context does not refer to changes in functioning production systems, but rather to changes in the project itself. The most common modifications to be managed are scope changes, generally expressed as a need for increased or different functionality. Because estimates are based on functionality as originally conceived, changes to initial functionality will obviously impact the project's cost and schedule. To minimize this effect, change control policies outline the project manager's range of discretion for approving changes, and spell out escalation levels and procedures. While these two standards can be negotiated at the beginning of each project, general guidelines can prove helpful.

Quality standards in an IS department tend to address how the department handles testing and production turnover. Some examples include how unit testing, system testing, and user acceptance testing will be performed.

Communications standards are also important to successful projects. The main reason that projects change as often as they do is that someone misunderstood a communication, be it the systems person or the client. The organization can significantly reduce the number of changes to a project in its later stages by setting clear communication guidelines during planning, and then constantly updating everyone involved in the project as it progresses, and doing so in a standard manner.

Methodology Training

While it is attractive to start training employees on the new methodology as soon as it is selected, this 'jumping the gun' can be hazardous to the ultimate success of methodology implementation. Certainly, the methodology will evolve as employees start using it, but there should be a base of standards in place prior to training, lest employees, at a minimum, require retraining. In some organizations, employees have actually revolted and chosen not to use the methodology at all — until standards have been established.

With at least tentative project tracking, estimating, change control, quality control, and project communication standards in place, the organization is ready to conduct IS departmental and client training. This training can be performed in three ways: using outside consultants, who often develop the training as well; via internal employees; or using a combination of consultants and employees. If the organization chooses the combination approach, external consultants often develop the training, whereupon they train the internal employees regarding how to deliver the training.

Since both project managers and project participants must understand the new methodology, it often makes sense to have two separate classes. The more in-depth class, for project managers and project leaders, ideally provides case studies, so they can actually practice the critical portions of the methodology. Although this type of training initially takes longer, the learning curve is less steep when project managers and leaders start following the methodology on "real" projects.

The training for project participants can be less detailed, focusing on their roles in the new methodology. It need not specifically train them to use all the pieces of the methodology.

IMPLEMENTING PROJECT MANAGEMENT SOFTWARE PACKAGES

While selecting appropriate software packages is important, it is more critical to successfully implement these packages. This section discusses the differences between project management software, process management software, and time accounting software, and then examines various methods for implementing these packages. It also discusses the benefits and drawbacks of each approach, and outlines a process for successful implementation.

Although there are various software tools on the market today to help project managers manage their projects, having these tools does not a project manager make. Project managers must still perform the nine basic competencies of project management set forth by the Project Management Institute, an international project management professional association. Still, having these packages certainly can make performing these functions less arduous.

Package Types

Project management-related software tools are generally divided into the three categories of project management software, process management software, and time accounting software. Project management software packages perform scheduling, as well as limited project tracking. They do this by allowing project managers to enter project WBSs, assign inter-task dependencies, allocate resources, and assign effort/work estimates for each task. Once these basics are entered, the tool calculates and displays the project schedule, often graphically, via either Gantt charts or PERT/CPM (program evaluation and review technique/critical path method) network charts.

After initial project schedules have been created, the tools allow project managers to baseline the original schedule, and track the project's progress against that schedule. Since some of the project management tools are better at such tracking than others, organizations must weigh how important the tracking feature is to them when analyzing and selecting a particular software package. Evaluation of this feature is particularly important because tracking is critical to future project planning.

Low-end project management packages include MS-Project from Microsoft and SureTrak from Primavera. Low-end packages cost approximately $500 and have adequate scheduling features, but tend to have less robust tracking features.

Mid-range project management packages include Project Scheduler from Scitor and CA-SuperProject from Computer Associates. Mid-range packages generally have better schedule-modeling features, better tracking, and better output capabilities, but the purchaser pays for it. They range in price from $1000 to $2000.

High-end project management packages include Primavera Project Planner, usually called P3. The high-end packages include the features of the mid-range products, but also feature better multi-project handling capabilities.

Rather than focusing on project scheduling and tracking, *process* management packages allow project managers to more easily *plan* their projects. Typical process management packages come with standard, yet customizable, templates for a wide variety of information systems projects. However, unlike the templates that come with some project management packages, these templates suggest dependency relationships between tasks, suggest the type of skills needed to perform each task, and generally also provide a variety of estimating techniques and metrics. Process management packages include Process Continuum from Computer Associates, which includes Process Engineer.

The third type of project management-related software is time accounting software. These packages allow individuals and project managers to charge actual hours back to project tasks. They do so by creating online and hardcopy time sheets, listing each team member's tasks. The team member then keeps track of the hours spent on each task, and, usually, the date that each task was started, as well as the date that each task was completed. This information is then transferred to whatever project management package in use at the organization. While time accounting software can be used without integration with project management packages, when integrated, it can greatly simplify the sometimes difficult tracking functions in project management packages.

An example of time accounting packages is TimeSheet Professional from Timeslips.

Implementing Packages

Certainly, it helps project managers manage their projects more effectively if they break projects down into phases, activities, and tasks. Similarly, software package implementation tends to be more effective when phased in. Unfortunately, however, in their zeal to "get current," organizations often try to implement too many changes at once. Thus organizations that formerly had no tools at all might acquire three or more. The acceptance of those tools, and sometimes even the methodology, plummets.

For organizations starting from scratch with project management-related software tools, the following order can help tremendously in implementation:

- Time accounting packages. These packages should be introduced first because they affect the largest number of people. When using these packages, everyone on a project team has to track his or her time, and it is often quite a shock to people who have never had to track time before. When a time accounting system is implemented, it is critical that people understand that the purpose is not to police their work. Rather, the goal is to collect accurate data on how a current project is going, and to build an accurate database for estimating future projects.
- Project management packages. The organization will be ready to standardize on a project management software package three to six months after it introduces a time accounting package. Project managers should be involved in the selection of this standard. Otherwise, implementing the tool will be more difficult because managers feel they were not included, or do not understand the rationale behind the selection of a specific tool. Having a core group of project managers supporting the selected tool enables the company to include them in pilot testing of the system, and in system training. This also forms a core advocacy group for the new tool.
- Process management packages. In another three to six months after the project management package is introduced, project managers will be ready to further hone their project management skills. With a few projects under their belts using the time accounting and project management tools, they will be able to more fully integrate the new process management tools into their project planning process. If, however, process management tools are introduced too soon, project managers might not have enough real project experience to appreciate the benefits of the somewhat complicated process management tools.

CONCLUSION

Successful projects are critical to the success of not only project managers, but to the whole IS department — and even to the company. Selecting appropriate project management methodologies and life cycles, and supporting them with the proper software tools, can help immeasurably with project success.

Chapter 4
Strategies for Heading Off IS Project Failure

Paul Cule
Roy Schmidt
Kalle Lyytinen
Mark Keil

Information systems software projects must be considered as risky undertakings. The very nature of software contributes to this riskiness in that it consists of intellectual concepts without physical substance. For example, Brooks[1] describes software, the output of the project, as "pure thought-stuff, infinitely malleable" and "invisible and unvisualizable." The effects of these risky characteristics are manifest in the frequent reports of IS projects that are late and over budget. Furthermore, many systems do not meet the needs of the business when they are delivered and have a low user satisfaction rating. This set of truisms seems to surround information systems projects. A Standish Group study found that over 50 percent of IS projects were late or over budget.[2] This was estimated to amount to $59 billion in cost overruns and another $81 billion in canceled software projects. The ultimate extension of the late and over-budget condition occurs when projects become victims of escalation — the condition of continuing, even increasing, expenditure on a project that to the onlooker is clearly a failure.[3] Why does this happen and what, if anything, can managers do about it?

This chapter develops a behavioral model and concomitant strategies that include strategies for executives and user managers that are as fundamental to IS project success as are the strategies for IS project managers. In addition, a particular case[4] is discussed that has already been published and discussed elsewhere to illustrate how these strategies can be used to identify where, and why, an IS project is going off track and how these strategies might be used to avoid IS project failure.

RISKS AND RESPONSIBILITIES

IS project failure is not a new problem. It has existed since information systems moved beyond simple automation. Historically, the responsibility for IS project failure has been laid squarely on the shoulders of the IS project manager. The project is defined and the IS project manager is charged with the responsibility of delivering a system that meets the requirements, is on time, and is on budget. This chapter shows how reality may be somewhat more complex. Developing strategies for IS project managers alone is insufficient and requires moving beyond the typical IS-centric view of the traditional literature.

Traditionally, in books and articles, IS project managers have been advised to follow a structured approach to managing risk: identify individual risks, assess their impact, and develop coping strategies for each risk. However, as is shown later in this chapter, this approach rapidly becomes completely unwieldy as the number of risks to be managed increases. Therefore, the authors break with this tradition by showing that risks can be classified into four major types according to their sources, and then managed by dealing with the sources rather than with the individual risks. This approach yields strategies that are manageable as opposed to the unwieldiness of trying to contain each risk individually.

What Is Meant by Risk

Before proceeding any further in this exploration it is necessary to discuss what is meant by risk in the context of this chapter. In the management domain, risk is defined as negative outcome and the size of the risk is the loss incurred if the outcome should occur. Positive outcomes are not seen as risk. Thus, in management terms, there are upside potential and downside risk. Furthermore, managers differentiate between risk-taking and gambling. Gambling is seen as accepting the odds — passive management — whereas risk-taking is seen as managing the odds to achieve a favorable outcome.[5] This chapter uses this management definition of risk, and all of the following discussions are framed by this definition.

That a risk may have a low probability of occurrence does not negate the need to manage it at some level. If an event occurs that causes the derailment of a project, that event is a risk prior to its occurrence. Such an event is frequently unforeseen — an unrecognized risk. Had it been foreseen, it would have been treated as a risk to be managed. An unforeseen risk is like an invisible "sword of Damocles" waiting to fall upon the unwary, hence the literature's emphasis on the identification of risk. Identifying the risk and then managing it does not make this sword go away, it merely postpones its falling, preferably forever. From this perspective, the purpose of managing a given risk is to defer indefinitely the occurrence of the undesired outcome. Thus, management of a risk is continuous.

For example, obtaining top management commitment to a project, a condition regarded as essential by many, even beyond IS project literature, may not be sufficient. The risk always exists that the project manager will lose that top management support for one reason or another. To manage this risk requires that the project manager work actively to maintain the support. The risk outcome is defined as occurring if the project manager loses that support. Once the project manager has reestablished top management support, the potential of losing it becomes a risk once again. This is but one risk of many to be managed.

In getting to the roots of IS project risk, new dimensions of risks are disclosed beyond those usually considered to be the responsibility of the project manager. These new dimensions also impinge upon the responsibilities of the investing executive. Although some project risks are under the control of the IS project manager, others are only partially, or not at all, under his or her control. If the investment is to be adequately protected and the expected outcomes achieved, management of these shared risks must be a joint responsibility of the investing manager, user management, and the IS management. Thus, even though the proposals in this chapter are derived from a study of IS project managers, the implications are as important to non-IS managers as they are to the IS community.

Prior Approaches: Individual Risk

In the literature on IS project failure and the management of risks, there are two approaches to achieving IS project success. Both these approaches seek to establish discrete risk elements to be separately managed. One of the approaches recommends managing IS project risks through the identification and control of individual risk items, the risk management approach. A second approach is based on contingency theory: project success is contingent upon the presence of some set of factors. The second approach is predominant in the IS implementation literature.[6]

Several distinctions can be drawn between these two approaches. First, it can be argued that the contingency factors are framed as positive elements that affect the success of a project, whereas risk factors are framed as negative elements that cause failure. These two streams can be further differentiated in that the stream dealing with contingency factors represents a static view of projects, with the implicit assumption that once a factor is present (e.g., top management support) it remains present. In contrast, the risk management perspective represents a more dynamic view, suggesting that risk factors (e.g., the possibility of a lack of top management support) represent a constant threat and must be managed actively for the entire duration of the project and thus lends itself to the discussion of management processes and strategies more than do event-based contingency factors. The remaining discussion is built upon the ideas of managing risk.

A number of authors[7] have sought to propose ways of managing IS project risk. Anecdotal prescriptions have been offered but, like many such prescriptions, they smack somewhat of the "silver bullet."[8] However, one thing these authors have in common is their suggestion that if risk is to be managed, it must first be identified. In prior literature,[9] the management strategy proposed has been to develop checklists of risks and then to manage each risk as a distinct entity. However, complex projects may have many risks, and managing such a multiplicity of risks, some undefined or unrecognized, as unique items on a checklist is impractical. Managers need a means of reducing long checklists to some manageable form without discarding any of the risk items. A possible solution to this problem is now discussed.

Proposed Approach: Categorizing Risk

In contrast to prior approaches, the authors propose an integrative approach that enables risks to be consolidated into categories. Each category requires a different managerial behavior together with concomitant risk mitigation strategies. Using this integrative approach, risk becomes more manageable and managers need not concern themselves with failing to identify every risk item or contingency factor.

This new model of an IS project is grounded in the data from a study of IS project risk undertaken by the authors. In this study, 41 experienced, practicing IS project managers defined, and reached consensus on, a list of 53 risk items. A detailed description of the study that developed this risk list is found elsewhere.[10]

The approach taken to developing the model in Exhibit 1 was to look for patterns in the risk items in the above-mentioned study that show some risks as being similar to each other but different from other risks. In developing mitigation strategies for managers, the patterns sought were those that indicated differing behavioral perspectives. The process of pattern recognition was through repeated inspection of the data from the above study.

The first pattern to emerge from this inspection process was that some of the risk items were totally under the control of the project manager and others were not. The resulting division is characterized as *Inside* and *Outside* risks (i.e., risks totally within the project manager's purview, or risks outside that purview). However, there was still considerable variation amongst the risks within each group. Further inspection resulted in the

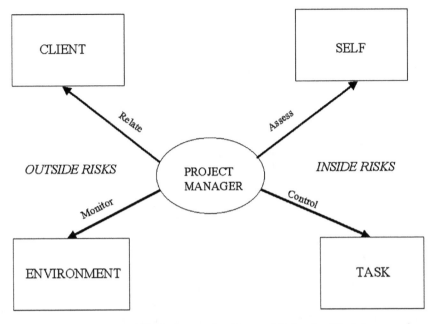

Exhibit 1.   A Risk Categorization and Behavior Model

recognition of two subgroups of Inside risks which are called *Task* and *Self*, and two subgroups of Outside risks that are called *Client* and *Environment*.

The Task classification refers to those risks that were the subject to the active direction of the IS project manager (e.g., *Poor team relationships*). These are the risk management elements typically found in the classic project management literature. The risks in the Self category reflect the characteristics of the project manager himself or herself, and are related to the understanding and capability of the project manager (e.g., *Lack of effective project management skills*).

The risks classified as Client are risks that cannot be controlled by the project manager but are risks over which the project manager may exert some influence (e.g., *Failure to manage end user expectations*). The Environment risks are external to the project and can be neither controlled nor influenced by the project manager (e.g., *Unstable corporate environment*).

Because the risks thus identified are from the project manager's perspective, the different classes can be linked to the project manager views, as shown in Exhibit 1. Each of the 53 risk items from the study was segmented into one of these four categories. It should be noted that the categories into which the risks have been put are a result of the authors' perspectives based on their own project management experiences. The results of this categorization are shown in Exhibit 2.

INSIDE	RISKS
SELF	**TASK**
• Not Managing Change Properly • Lack of Effective Project Management Skills • Lack of Effective Project Management Methology • Improper Definition of Roles and Responsibilities • Misunderstanding the Requirements • Poor or Non-Existent Control • Poor Risk Management • Choosing the Wrong Development Strategy • Lack of " People Skills" in Project Leadership • Project Not Based on Sound Business Case • No Planning or Inadequate Planning	• Bad Estimation • Lack of Effective Development Process/Methodology • Trying New Development Method/Technology During Important Project • Lack of Required Knowledge/Skills in the Project Personnel • Poor Team Relationships • Insufficient Staffing • Excessive Use of Outside Consultants • Lack of Available Skilled Personnel • Introduction of New Technology • Stability of Technical Architecture • Multi-Vendor Projects Complicate Dependencies
OUTSIDE	**RISK**
CLIENT	**ENVIRONMENT**
• Lack of Top Management Commitment to the Project • Failure to Gain User Commitment • Conflict Between User Departments • Failure to Get Project Plan Approval From All Parties • Failure to Manage End User Expectations • Lack of Adequate User Involvement • Lack of Cooperation from Users • Failure to Identify All Stakeholders • Growing Sophistication of Users Leads to Higher Expectations • Managing Multiple Relationships with Stakeholders • Lack of Appropriate Experience of the User Representatives • Unclear/Misunderstood Scope/Objetives • Number of Organizational Units Involved • Lack of Frozen Requirements • New and/or Unfamiliar Subject Matter for Both Users and Developers • Under Funding of Development • Under Funding of Maintenance • "All or Nothing" • Artificial Deadlines	• A Climate of Change in the Business and Organizational Enviroment that Creates Instability in the Project • Mismatch Between Company Culture and Required Business Process Changes Needed for New System • Project that Are Intended to Fail • Unstable Corporate Enviroment • Change in Ownership or Senior Management • Changing Scope/Objetives • "Preemption" of Project by Higher Priority Project • Staffing Volatility • External Dependencies Not Met • Lack of Control Over Consultants, Vendors, and Sub-Contractors

Exhibit 2. Categorized Risk Items

As may be seen from Exhibit 2, there is homogeneity within each category and difference between categories. However, there may be some borderline cases in which the reader feels that a particular risk may belong in another category. We believe this to be appropriate in that some risks may have a contextual element. For example, it may be that in one project, a risk such as *Bad estimation* may be classified as Self and in another, Task. Bad estimation as a result of no estimating methodology could be seen as falling in the Self category. On the other hand, where an estimating methodology exists but is poorly executed, this risk could belong in the Task category. The purpose of the model is to develop mitigation strategies relevant to the category rather than to each individual risk in isolation. Thus the risk will be managed in accordance with the category in which it falls within a given context. However, such contextual capabilities within the model may add to its applicability in both the general and the specific case, because any so-called borderline risk will be subsumed into a category and managed according to the strategy relevant to that category.

BEHAVIORS AND STRATEGIES

Given the links between the four risk classes and the project manager, it is appropriate to now explore the possibility of differing behaviors being required of the project manager in dealing with each of the four categories. The following section proposes a set of behaviors appropriate to each link. Each of these links has been named in Exhibit 1 to capture the associated behaviors.

Self Assessment

The link between project manager and the class of risks called Self suggests a behavior that can be called *Assess*. Because the risks in the Self category concern the project manager's abilities, capabilities, and knowledge regarding the management of IS projects (e.g., *Lack of project management skills*), the project manager needs to continually assess her capabilities against the project needs. The project manager can then handle any recognized shortfall in capability herself. Assessment also may need to be done by others — for example, the project manager's manager or outside auditors — to identify any shortfalls not recognized by the project manager herself. The Assess behavior requires of the project manager that she periodically ask questions of herself that are aimed at surfacing the risks in the Self category. Unfortunately, it is difficult to get an accurate answer when people ask themselves such questions as "Am I managing change properly?" "Do I lack effective project management skills?" "Do I lack an effective project management methodology?" Yet these are the first three risk items in the Self category shown in Exhibit 2.

The same problem exists for each of the risk items when phrased by individuals as a question of themselves. Nonetheless, a project manager must ask these questions of herself and answer to the best of her ability. However, there are strategies that can make a project manager more effective in answering these questions. One way is to use independent auditors. This is a viable proposition where there are knowledgeable experienced project managers in-house who can execute an unbiased audit. A second form of audit is to use assessment mechanisms such as those offered by the Software Engineering Institute and its Process Maturity Model.[11] A third way of handling these questions is for the project manager to benchmark other projects and other organizations to compare and learn. These three different, but complementary, strategies may greatly enhance the project manager's ability to exercise the Assess behavior.

Task Control

The risk factors classified as Task (e.g., *Insufficient/inappropriate staffing*) imply a *Control* behavior by the project manager in dealing with the risks. It is the task of the project manager to take care of these, thus calling for a task management approach. It is generally this behavioral link that is the subject of project management texts and education and should be ingrained in any experienced project manager. Thus, Assess and Control describe the behaviors required of project managers in handling inside risks. Now, the outside risks need to be addressed.

Environmental Monitoring

The risks that fall under the environment class are those about which the project manager can do little. Some risk items might even be granted the sobriquet "Act of God." However, should an event represented by such a risk occur, the project manager needs to maximize her lead-time to react. The other type of environmental risk is rooted in the industry environment, competition, and government action. These types of risk require that the project manager be cognizant of them even if she can do nothing to prevent their occurrence. Thus we suggest the behavior *Monitor* to represent keeping abreast of the environmental risks in order to maximize the possibilities for response. The monitor behavior is relatively straightforward. Unfortunately, it can also be time consuming. Under the Environment risks (see Exhibit 2) we see those things that relate to the industry, the company, and the company's position in the industry. This monitoring responsibility requires the project manager to be knowledgeable about what is going on "out there" and how it might affect the company and hence the project. For example, the IS project manager should be aware of the potential of a corporate takeover, assess possible impacts, and establish strategies to deal with those impacts. One way of gaining this knowledge is to read the industry trade press rather than the computer trade press. Industry conferences are another excellent source of monitoring information. Many companies have internal industry and marketing seminars. If a project manager can understand the product and market from the perspective of the company's own marketing force, it will enhance the project managers understanding of the environment at large.

Client Relationships

Relate is the behavior required to handle that category of risks denoted Client. The Client project risks are those associated with the people internal to the company with whom the project manager deals. These are the people who are essential to the successful outcome of the project. They are also the people who define what constitutes a successful outcome. It is essential that the project manager establish relationships with these individuals and groups, preferably before the project is initiated.

The term Client is used here advisedly. It encompasses that group of people who fund, as well as that group who will use, the system and, therefore, such groups may be defined as the project manager's market. A key marketing philosophy propounded by both practitioners and academics is that of Relationship Marketing, or Relationship Management. This philosophy espouses building and maintaining long-term relationships with clients (customers) regardless of any current sales activity. In other words, the sale is made within the relationship, as opposed to the traditional approach of building the relationship around the sale. For a particular project, top management commitment and user involvement are easier to obtain if there has been a strong relationship between the parties built up over time.

It is not the purpose of this chapter to describe relationship marketing and relationship management; there is a wealth of material available elsewhere. The important lesson for project managers is to realize that marketing themselves and their departments in the context of long-term relationships is a fundamental responsibility of IS management. It is equally important that the client community also subscribes to building strong relationships with IS management.

The activities discussed under Monitor now acquire an additional role. To establish this relationship with a group (e.g., top management), the project manager must demonstrate an interest in, and knowledge of, those things that interest the group. Monitoring will provide the project manager with the initial knowledge to gain access to each group that constitutes a target market. The relationship can be enhanced by information sharing and establishing bonds of common interests. However, this act of sharing is not solely the responsibility of the project manager. It requires the active participation of the investing executives, as well as the user management, to ensure that the IS project manager is fully cognizant of the effects that the changing environment is having on the organization as a whole, and the resulting potential impacts on the needs the system is supposed to fulfill.

Clients may also be considered to have different levels of sponsorship of the project. In many studies, including that by Keil et al., failure to gain top management commitment is seen as a key determinant of project failure. Top management commitment represents the active sponsorship of the project. This notion of sponsorship however, extends beyond top management. It is needed throughout the ranks of management and users affected by the project. It is here that the IS project manager can look to the sponsorship strategies and processes of sponsor-dependent sports such as motor racing, events such as the Olympic Games, or sponsor-dependent organizations in the arts. These organizations must actively seek sponsors and continuously work at maintaining that sponsorship. The IS project manager must do the same.

To many, the strategies outlined may seem obvious but, obvious or not, they do not seem to get executed effectively. As a case in point, consider now Sullivan's dilemma, using the proposed model as a vehicle for discussion.

SULLIVAN'S DILEMMA: A CASE IN POINT[12]

A brief synopsis of the case follows. In this case, a CIO, Sullivan, has "fulfilled to the letter the role of CIO that Bennet [CEO and president] had described." In particular, for our analysis, Sullivan was charged with developing an information system called Lifexpress that was supposed to provide the company's insurance agents with a competitive advantage. The system took three years to develop and is being rolled out at the time of the case. Unfortunately, the company's competitors have launched similar systems. Moreover, these competitor systems seem to be better than Lifexpress. Thus, the multi-million dollar system will not have the hoped-for impact, which is a great concern to the company's executives. "To Sullivan's distress, her boss was clearly trying to hold her accountable for more than the creation and implementation of the system — he was putting her on the hook for the results of the system, too." The case further notes: "She had delivered the system on time and on budget, and had met all the specifications that Bennett and the other senior managers had agreed to." Sullivan had been trying to explain to her boss what she could control and what she could not. This merely resulted in her boss's becoming impatient. Bennett tells Sullivan: "We have to figure out how to get this thing fixed and back on track fast. We're losing a lot of momentum. I don't think you have kept us properly informed." Here we have a case of a project manager delivering on what she thought were her commitments and yet the project is clearly falling into the "failing" category. Sullivan has done an excellent job of risk management within the traditional confines of IS project management.

She has delivered a project according to her "contract." It met the agreed specifications for the agreed price and the agreed schedule and yet it is, for all intents and purposes, a waste of money. After all the time and expense, the system does not meet the needs of the business.

Perhaps the first thing to note is that Sullivan was trying to establish that there were things over which she had control and things over which she did not. In the proposed model, the things over which she had control are have described as Task (e.g., schedule, budget, process, and technology). She exercised the appropriate behavior: control. Now, consider Sullivan's behavior regarding Self, the other Inside risk category.

Sullivan is described as "wondering how she could begin to separate what she was responsible for from she wasn't (sic)." On the one hand, Sullivan wishes to be evaluated only on that which she can control, and on the other, her management wants her to take responsibility for the project's outcome. Furthermore, she failed to understand the true requirements of the project. She understood the technical requirements as described to her three years ago, but failed to realize that the real requirement was for a "first-to-market" system that would give the company's agents a competitive advantage over all other agents of all other companies. These characteristics, responsibility and misunderstanding the requirements, fall into the category Self. The act of "wondering" to which the case refers is an example of Assess behavior. It is only now that she is becoming aware of the Self that is needed. It is only at this point that she is becoming aware of the true requirements. Lack of the proper assessment behavior has put both the project and her career in jeopardy.

The model uses two other risk categories: Client and Environment. Had Sullivan been properly monitoring the Environment, she would have been cognizant of the activities of the competition. She would have known how the competition was forcing changes to the scope and objectives of the project. Again, failure to monitor the environment and act accordingly placed the project at risk.

Finally, there is the client category of risk. Here is a case that had top management commitment, but the project still failed in the eyes of senior management. The case tells us that Sullivan started with a good relationship with Bennett, the CEO. He had high hopes for her. The case also tells us she obtained an initial management commitment to Lifexpress. It appears she then reverted to focussing on task risks, the ones she could control. In so doing, she ignored maintaining, and further strengthening, her relationships with her clients, the company executives. As a result, executive concerns, even displeasure, come as a complete surprise to her. Had she exhibited relationship management behavior, she would not have been surprised and the executives would not have been surprised. In fact, she probably could have delivered a successful project in the first place, because she would have had executive guidance as to evolving needs, and furthermore, she could have managed client expectations of what could be delivered and when. Failure to actively seek and maintain sponsorship from her client community was a major contributor to her failure.

Sullivan managed this project correctly, given the traditional approach of limiting project management to the elements she could control. These are the task-centered items that project managers learn to manage in project management classes and literature. However, once it becomes clear that the expectation of Sullivan is that she must be responsible for the outcome of the project, the scope of what it means to be an IS project manager becomes larger and much more complex. Sullivan's management lexicon had limited her to identifying only one category of risk and thus exhibiting a single behavior. As discussed, exhibiting the other three behaviors might have enabled her to achieve the desired outcome.

The fault is not entirely Sullivan's, however. Some of the blame must go to Bennett. Bennett abdicated his responsibility in that he never checked that the system being developed by Sullivan would meet his company's changing needs. He never took it upon himself to keep Sullivan abreast of the changing environment and changing needs. Similarly, Sullivan's boss "was clearly trying to hold her accountable for more than the creation and implementation of the system — he was putting her on the hook for the results of the system, too." In so doing, he was raising Sullivan's awareness of the risks in the Self category. This raising of awareness should have been done at the beginning of the project and should have been regularly assessed throughout the duration of the project. It is too late now to tell Sullivan that she failed to assess, and manage, these risks. Thus, the behavior of her executives contributed to Sullivan's project failure.

CATEGORIZED RISK AND PREEMPTIVE STRATEGIES

Brooks[13] tells us that projects fail one day at a time. This would suggest that failure is dynamic and its opportunities for occurrence are both ever-present and cumulative. Sullivan's project did not fail on the day management first expressed dissatisfaction, it had been steadily failing for some time. Other well-known software failures, such as the California State DMV project,[14] support this. The DMV project failure did not happen on the day before the state auditors arrived on the scene. As the audit report showed, this project had been on a failure track for some time. If we look at most IS project failures we find the seeds of failure sown earlier in the project and they mature in the soil of ignorance. This ignorance comes from inability to identify, and then manage, all IS project risks.

The IS Project Management Perspective

The IS project manager's strategic behavior starts even before the project is initiated. Instead of having to execute individual risk strategies every day, the project manager now has four behaviors he or she must continually exhibit. The *control* behavior should already be ingrained in any practicing project manager. However, the other three, *assess, relate, monitor,* may not be so familiar to many IS project managers. For the IS project manager, this model provides a new way of viewing the responsibilities he or she has. For example, in the case under discussion, had Sullivan had this behavioral model and acted accordingly she probably would not have been surprised by the expected scope of her responsibilities. She would have developed self-awareness. Furthermore, having established the requisite relationships, it is unlikely that Sullivan would have been unaware that the system she was delivering no longer met the needs of the business. This model gives IS project managers new insights into risk and mitigation behaviors that may help them avoid the apparent fate of Sullivan and her project.

The Senior Management Perspective

Use of this model by project managers in isolation will not be enough, as is clear from the discussion of Sullivan. The responsibility for the successful outcome of an IS project cannot lie with the IS project manager alone. The model also lays open the need for active participation and proactive responsiveness from the group of stakeholders called Clients. The need for the IS project manager to undertake relationship building and management has been asserted. However, the whole concept of relationships and their management requires the active participation of multiple parties. Success cannot be achieved unless those with whom the project manager must establish the relationship are willing to actively participate in that relationship. There may be a temptation for the executive to turn over responsibility to the IS project manager with an attitude of "leave it to the nerds." Succumbing to this temptation results in the executive's abdicating, not delegating, responsibility. The executive who stimulates the relationship with the IS community will probably be less prone to being victim of the Client set of risks than a counterpart who cuts off the Relate behavior.

The model, strategies, and behaviors can also be used in audit mode, as in the Sullivan case. They can be used, at any point in a given project, to evaluate which risk classes have the highest potential for project exposure, thus enabling management to focus on the behaviors necessary to minimize occurrence. Just as the project manager must continually assess and manage the risks in the Self category, there must also be those charged with the responsibility for external assessment, counseling, and training to ensure that these Self risks are being appropriately managed.

STRATEGIES OR TACTICS

Some strategies for preempting IS project risks have been presented; they are strategies, however, and, as such, they must be tailored to the project context, the circumstances surrounding the individuals, and the environment of the project. Because an IS project is dynamic, this context can change rapidly. One such case could be where the incumbent project manager, who has a real grasp of the strategies and behaviors, is replaced by a new project manager exhibiting some of the shortfalls discussed under Self. This would require an immediate focus on the Assess behavior by both the IS project manager and the responsible company management.

The temptation to convert these generalized strategic behaviors into some set of tactics to be executed by all project managers should be resisted. For example, there may be a temptation to identify approaches such as Object-Oriented (OO) Development as a strategy. The use of OO is more of a tactic than a strategy. In the risk items in Exhibit 2, use of OO is a tactic within *Lack of effective development methodology*. On the negative side, it could be viewed as a tactic that results in increasing risk due to *Trying new development method*.

Each IS project is unique and dynamic. Each has its own changing context of environment, people, and relationships. The tactics developed for each project, therefore, are unique to that project context and relevant to some specific point in time. Even though we have developed the model from the project manager's perspective, the development of these project specific tactics must be a shared responsibility. What is consistent between projects is the need for IS managers to acquire and exhibit each of the strategic behaviors along with the active participation and guidance of senior management.

The model developed herein is based on categorizing IS project risks as seen from the IS project manager's perspective. As a result, different behaviors and mitigation strategies by the IS project manager are suggested, one set for each of the four resulting categories. The model also shows the need for executives, investing managers, and managers who will use the system to share in the management of the IS project risks. Although this chapter is useful to different stakeholders, executives, user management, and IS project managers, it may be many times more useful when shared among these stakeholders. The implications of IS project failure are far too great to abdicate responsibility to the technologists.

Notes

1. Fred P. Brooks, Jr., 1987, "No Silver Bullet: Essence and Accidents of Software Engineering," *IEEE Computer* vol. 20 (4) pp. 10–19.
2. J. Johnson, 1995, "Chaos: The Dollar Drain of IT Project Failures," *Application Development Trends* vol. 2 (1), p. 47.
3. For example, Mark Keil, 1995, "Pulling the Plug: Software Project Management and the Problem of Project Escalation," *MIS Quarterly* vol. 19 (4), pp. 421–447. From another perspective: M. Lynn Markus & Mark Keil, 1994, "If We Build It, They Will Come: Designing Information Systems That People Will Use," *Sloan Management Review,* vol. 35(4): pp. 11–25. Also, State of California, Bureau of State Audits. California State Auditor, 1994, *The Department of Motor Vehicles and the Office of Information Technology Did Not Minimize the State's Financial Risk In the Database Redevelopment Project.*
4. Byron Reimus, 1997, "The IT System That Couldn't Deliver," *Harvard Business Review,* vol. 75(3) pp. 22–26. This case is discussed by various luminaries in the ensuing pages of the same issue of the *HBR.*
5. J.G. March and Z. Shapira, 1987, "Managerial Perspectives on Risk and Risk Taking," *Management Science,* vol. 33 (11). See also Z. Shapira, 1995, *Risk Taking: A Managerial Perspective,* New York: Russell Sage Foundation.
6. For example, T.H. Kwon and R.W. Zmud, "Unifying the Fragmented Models of Information Systems Implementation," in R.J. Boland and R.A. Hirschheim (eds.), 1987, *Critical Issues in Information Systems Research,* New York: John Wiley & Sons.
7. Barry Boehm, 1989, *Software Risk Management Tutorial,* Washington, D.C: IEEE Computer Society Press; Barry Boehm, 1991, "Software Risk Management: Principles and Practices," *IEEE Software,* vol. 8 (1) pp. 32–41.
8. Brooks, Note 1.
9. For example, Boehm, 1989, 1990, note 7.
10. Mark Keil, Paul Cule, Kalle Lyytinen, and Roy Schmidt, 1998, "A Framework for Identifying Software Project Risks," *Communications of the ACM,* vol. 41 (11) pp. 76–83.
11. Watts S. Humphrey, 1995, *A Discipline for Software Engineering,* Reading, MA: Addison-Wesley.
12. Reimus, note 4.
13. Fred P. Brooks, Jr. 1995, *The Mythical Man-Month: Essays on Software Engineering,* Reading, MA: Addison-Wesley.
14. California, note 3.

Chapter 5
Six Myths about Managing Software Development in the New Millennium

Linda G. Hayes

With widespread frustration over slipping schedules or outright runaway development projects, the dawning of a new millennium is an auspicious time to call into question the most basic assumptions regarding management of software development and adopt a strategy that reflects reality. This chapter reviews and debunks these assumptions, outlines an alternate view that takes into account the quantum changes that have occurred in software development within the last decade, and positions managers to succeed into the future.

MYTH 1: REQUIREMENTS EXIST

That requirements exist is the fundamental assumption of all software development projects. At first they exist in the minds of the users, in documented form from which the design proceeds, and then form the basis for acceptance of the finished project.

As logical and hopeful as this may sound, it is generally not proven true. Although users know what they want, it is not unlike the Supreme Court's understanding of pornography: they know it when they see it. Until then, requirements are inchoate: inarticulate needs that do not, of themselves, describe the features and functions that would satisfy them.

What is widely attributed to scope creep, or the continuous expansion of the project requirements, is really just the natural process of distilling user needs into objective expression. For example, a requirement for a banking application might be to maximize the profitability of each customer.

Once understood, this requirement spawns new requirements: the need to maximize the number of services sold to a single customer, which leads to the need for a unified database of all customers and services, and relational access among them.

Once the implementation begins, these requirements metamorphose into yet more: users realize that what appear to be many separate customers and accounts are often managed by a single individual, such as a parent creating trust accounts for children, and the requirement arises to define and associate subaccounts, followed by the need to present consolidated statements and reports ... and so forth, and so on.

Therefore, if the project manager assumes the requirements can be expressed coherently and completely before development commences, and the entire project plan and schedule is based on that assumption, subsequent changes wreak havoc. Scope creep, then, is really the inevitable realization that requirements are living, growing things that are discovered instead of defined.

Reality: Seek Problems, Not Solutions

Instead of asking users to describe requirements and solutions, ask them to describe their problems. If this is a new system, find out why it is being created — what is being done today and how will it change with the system? If this is a rewrite of an existing system, ask what is wrong with the old one. What problems will be solved?

This is a radically different approach than asking for requirements. A commonly told illustration of this involves the building manager whose tenants complained about slow elevators. After rejecting a series of costly elevator upgrade or replacement scenarios, the manager hired a problem-solving expert.

This expert interrogated the manager. What was wrong with the elevators? The tenants, he said, were complaining about waiting for them. Why did that matter, the expert asked? Because if they are unhappy they may move out, the manager responded, and I may lose my job. The expert promised a solution.

The next day, mirrors were installed outside the elevators on all floors. The tenant complaints subsided. The expert explained: the tenants were complaining about waiting, not about the elevators. The solution was to make the wait more pleasant, and mirrors offer the most popular pastime of all: admiring ourselves. This solution, of course, cost a tiny fraction of the time and money to speed up the elevators.

The point is, if one focuses on the real problem, one will arrive at the best solution. If starting with a solution, the wrong problem may be solved.

MYTH 2: DESIGNS ARE DOCUMENTS

The next assumption proceeds from the first. If requirements can be captured and subdued into a static state, then the design can be based upon them and reduced to a written document from which development flows. This assumption fails not only because the first is flawed, but also for an independent reason. It is difficult, if not impossible, to adequately express functionality in words and pictures. Software is interactive; documents are not.

There are at least two levels of interactivity of a design. The first is external, at the user interface level: what the user sees and does. A perfectly plausible screen design on paper may prove to be impractical when created. What appear to be trivial matters, such as using the mouse to position focus on a field or object, may render the application awkward and unworkable to a high-speed data entry clerk, trained in touch-typing, whose fingers never leave the keyboard.

The second level of interactivity is internal: the hardware platform, operating system, development language, database, network topology, and other decisions that affect how processing occurs and data is managed. An otherwise elegant database design may fail due to response time of the underlying network access protocol, or sheer volume demands.

Reality: Go with the Flow

Instead of expressing the design as a series of static artifacts — data elements, screens, files, reports — describe it in terms of business processes. What will the user do with it?

Users do not think about customer information databases or order entry screens. They think about adding a new customer as the result of an order, answering customer questions about their orders, shipping the orders and sending out invoices, and making sure invoices are paid. They think in terms of processes, information, and workflow: they know their job.

Understanding the system as a set of processes as a user experiences it, beginning to end, will lead to a much different design than approaching the subject as a set of disparate entities. It forces the consideration of the flow and purpose of information — not how it is stored, but when and why it is used.

Another important aspect of what is done is, how many and how often? Will there be 100 customers or one million? What happens most frequently — entering new customers or checking on orders? Are dozens of orders received daily, or thousands? These numbers will greatly influence the internal design of the system, including not just the amount of storage but the throughput rates. The external design is also affected: screens are designed to support the way they will be needed. Frequently needed information will be readily accessible, and high volume transactions streamlined for heads-down entry instead of heads-up aesthetics.

Do not ask the users what they want to see. Ask them what they need to do.

MYTH 3: DEVELOPMENT IS LINEAR

If the foundation of requirements was coherent and complete, and the structure of the design solid and stable, development would indeed be a simple, predictable matter. In the traditional, linear development life cycle, coding is a segment that begins after design and ends with test.

Yet everyone knows this is not how it is. Our budgets tell us so. Sixty to 80 percent of corporate IT budgets are consumed by maintenance, which is a euphemism for development on existing systems — systems that have already been "released," sometimes decades ago. There is not an application alive — that is, being used — that does not experience constant development. Whether called modifications or enhancements, the fact is that 25 percent of even a so-called stable application undergoes revision each year.

This indicates that software systems reflect the business, and successful businesses are in a state of continuous change and improvement. Change can be a good thing, but only if it is planned.

Reality: The Schedule Rules

Once ready to start creating the system, set a schedule that provides for the earliest possible release of the least possible amount of functionality. In other words, deliver the system before it is ready. Do not come up with the design and then the schedule: come up with the schedule first and design as you go. Do not target for error-free completion; attempt to have something that does something.

Sometimes called "time-boxing," this approach focuses on rapid-fire releases where the amount of functionality in a given release is based on the amount of time, not the other way around. One can think of this as rapid prototyping — it is and it is not. Rapid prototyping usually means throwing together a mock-up that is used as a model for the real thing. Instead, this is the real thing, it is just successively refined. Today's development technologies make it only incrementally more difficult to create a screen that works than one that does not.

In the early stages one might use a "toy" or personal database while nailing down the actual contents, then later shift to an industrial strength version when the tables settle down. The point is to get users to use it right away. The sooner they use it, the faster will be their feedback. Make sure everyone knows this is a moving target, and do not get painted into any corners until necessary. Stay out of the critical path at first, and let the users report when it is ready for prime time.

Expect changes and problems and plan for them, which means not only releasing early but repeatedly.

MYTH 4: DEVELOPERS DEVELOP AND TESTERS TEST

The mere fact that there is a title or job description of tester does not mean that testing is only done by testers. Quite the contrary: a major component of the test effort occurs in development.

The fact is, only the development organization has the knowledge and information essential for unit, integration, and system testing: testing the individual units, their interaction with each other, and their behavior as a whole. Developers are responsible for creating the software, and they not only *should* test it — they *must*.

The assumption that only testers test is especially insidious, because it shifts responsibility for software quality to those least able to affect it. The testers are not there to check up on development; they are there to protect the business. When development operates under the assumption that they have a safety net, the odds are higher that the system will crash.

The real and only reason for having an independent test organization is to represent the users: not to assure that the software does not break, but that it does what the business needs.

Reality: From the End of the Line to the Front

In this new paradigm, testing moves from the last line of defense for development to the front line of defense for the business users. It changes from testing to make sure the software runs to making sure the business does. Developers test software; testers test business processes.

This means the test cases and conditions are derived from the processes that have replaced the requirements. Testers do not verify that the order entry screen pull-down list of items is sorted alphabetically; they try to enter 100 orders in an hour. Granted, the sorting of the list may dramatically affect productivity if it is not alphabetized, but the focus is on how well the job gets done, not how well the development was done. The design has no meaning outside of its purpose: to support the process.

In this scenario, testers are not baby programmers hoping to graduate to real development. They are expert users, making sure that the business needs are served. Developers are not creative, temperamental artistes;

they are professionals delivering a working product. The purpose of testing is not to break the system, it is to prove it.

MYTH 5: TESTERS DETERMINE QUALITY

Test organizations generally find themselves in an impossible position. They are asked to determine when or whether the software is "ready." This is impossible because the testers usually cannot control the quality of the software provided by development or the rate at which problems are corrected. They cannot control what end users expect of it or will do with it. To say that the schedule is out of their hands … well, that should go without saying.

The uncomfortable truth is that testers are often approached as impediments to release, as though they somehow stand in the way of getting the software out the door. This is a dangerous idea, because it puts testing in a no-win situation. If they find too many problems, the release to production is delayed; but if they do not find enough, the release fails in production.

Reality: Ask, Do Not Tell

In the millennium, the business decides when the software is ready, based on what the test group discovers. The rolling release strategy provides for a constant flow of functionality, and the test organization's role is to constantly measure and report the level of capability and stability of the software. However, it is the business user's decision when it is acceptable. In other words, the user may elect to accept or waive known problems in order to obtain proven functions. This is a business decision, not a test criteria.

This does not absolve development from creating working product or test from performing a thorough analysis. It does mean that it is not up to them to decide when it is ready. This can work either way; the developers may be satisfied with a design that the users reject, or the users may decide they can live with some bugs that drive the testers up the wall.

The key is to remember that the system belongs to those who use it, not those who create it.

MYTH 6: RELEASES ARE FINAL

The initial release of an application is only the first of many, perhaps over decades. Mission-critical applications are frequently revised monthly, if not more often, throughout their entire lives. The idea that everything the system will ever do must be in the first release is patently untrue.

This belief drives schedule slip: that one must hold up or delay the system because it does not do one thing or another, or because it has bugs.

The truth is that it will never do everything and it will always be imperfect. The real question is whether it can provide value to the business today and, especially, in the future.

Thus, a software release is not an event; it is a process. It is not a wall; it is a step.

Reality: The Rolling Release

The concept of a release as a singular, monolithic and, often, monster event is an anachronism. Software that truly serves the business is flexible and responsive, supporting competitive agility and rapid problem resolution. Releases are like heartbeats: if they are not happening regularly, the system is dying.

Therefore, instead of a one-year development project with a vacuum after that, plan for four quarterly releases followed by monthly ones. During test, make weekly builds available. While this may sound like a pressure cooker, and using traditional methods it would be, it can be properly positioned as a safety valve.

Design defects are more easily corrected the earlier they are identified. Additionally, errors or inconsistencies are less annoying if they will be corrected in weeks instead of months. Emotion over missed requirements subsides considerably if they will be coming sooner rather than later. Value is perceived faster, and the potential for runaways is all but eliminated.

All of this, of course, drastically changes the nature of testing.

RECOMMENDATIONS

With a development process based on assumptions that are consistently demonstrated to be untrue, it is no wonder one misses schedules and budgets. The answer, of course, is to throw out the existing process and define a new one based on reality.

The accelerating rate of new technology and techniques aimed at improving the development process can address the technical hurdles but not the organizational ones. In order for this rapid-fire, rolling release strategy to work, several things have to happen.

Code Speed

Although it sounds good to say that developers need to slow down and get it right, the fact is they need to speed up and get it perfect.

A case in point is the no longer simple process of creating a build, or executable. The build process involves assembling all of the individual components of an application and compiling them into a single, working whole that can be reproduced and installed as a unit. With the advent of component-based development, this is no mean feat. The build may encompass dozens, if not hundreds, of discrete modules, libraries, and files. As a result, the build can take days ... if not weeks, or even months, to get it right.

In the time-box, rolling release world, builds are done no less than weekly. The only way for this to work, and work consistently, is for the code to be under tight management and control and for the build process to be strict and streamlined. Speed has a way of burning off fat, and sloppy coding practices cannot survive the friction of this new model.

Standard Standards

Many development shops have adopted, documented, and published development standards, only to find them in useless repose, stored in binders, never to be referenced again. Without constant training, consistent code inspections, and other oversight practices, standards quickly fall by the wayside. To a developer, standards are straightjackets to be worn only unwillingly.

The new millennium will not tolerate nonstandard practices for the simple reason that they will not work. Delivering increments of functionality means that each succeeding layer must fit smoothly with the others: it is like trying to build a brick wall — the bricks must be of uniform size and shape to keep it from falling over.

Not to be overly harsh, but maverick programmers will not cause the organization to step up enforcement procedures; they will cause the organization to cull them out. When running a tight train schedule, one does not coddle late passengers ... one leaves them behind.

Owning Responsibility

Users, on the other hand, must step up to the plate and own the system being developed for them. No longer can the test organization serve as a staging area for new hires or misfits, following a random, spontaneous agenda that shifts with time and turnover. It must be an elite corps of experts who bring their professionalism to bear.

Nor can users hide behind the excuse that they are not technical and must rely on development to tell them how and what to do when. Nonsense. They must take the responsibility for articulating what they need, assuring that they get it, and deciding when to release it. They pay the price to have it developed; they will pay the price if it cannot be used.

SUMMARY

While no one questions that development technology is taking quantum leaps almost every day, few question the fact that our process for applying that technology can still be found in a 1950s textbook. This anomaly is crippling our ability to move into the next millennium, and must be exposed and removed. If something quits working, it needs to be fixed ... or replaced.

Chapter 6
Back to Basics: Getting Systems Development Right

Polly Perryman Kuver

The United States is the most computer-dependent country in the world. From custom software designed and constructed for unique functions such as a global tracking system to standard software for commercial use such as word processing and spreadsheets, the development life cycle is basically the same. The approaches to the life cycle vary according to the size, scope, and nature of the system. The biggest reason for the variance in approaches comes down to funding in the four major areas in which software is developed.

Commercial

The software development practices in the commercial world vary greatly from one organization to another and really fall into two categories. The first category is the product developer. Product developers are companies like Microsoft, IBM, Hewlett Packard, and many, many smaller companies. They produce software for mass use, and their products include everything from operating systems to browsers to financial packages. The second is the in-house information technology departments of industry and service companies, such as the automotive industry, the food industry, health care, and retail.

Product Developer

Software development at product development companies is rigorously managed. For these companies, staying competitive, being on time, and keeping costs low is business survival. The formalities of the government projects give way to streamlined practices aimed at promoting productivity. Depending on the size of the company, requirement lists and specifications may resemble more of a task order than pseudo code. Version control

0-8493-1190-X/02/$0.00+$1.50
© 2002 by CRC Press LLC

may be maintained on a grease board as opposed to using a sophisticated configuration management tool. The concentration of effort is to keep the user documentation current, and the project plan includes a direction and focus for the product, ensuring that new features and capabilities keep up and surpass the competition.

In larger companies, coding standards and quality control exist and are continuously improved. In smaller companies, the coding team is compressed and the teams work closely, borrowing techniques from each other and standardizing modules on the fly. Product developers rely on government and non-computer industry organizations to buy their products and thus stay in business.

It is from the product developer that much new technology is developed and displayed to a marketplace composed of large and small businesses and personal computer users. Funding for new development and maintenance of existing products means business survival. Requirements change based on profit and loss statements, the direction of the computer industry, and development of new technology.

Documentation is put out on the Internet and made available for downloading. It primarily consists of installation guides, operations manuals, and user manuals. The quality and usability of the documentation has created a solid market for periphery books. These books are written and published outside of the computer companies that manufacture the products and are almost essential to users that want to gain product proficiency without spending hours aimlessly "playing" on the computer.

Information Technology Department

From the health care industry to large retail organizations, the only software developed is on an as-needed basis. If commercial off-the-shelf (COTS) software can be used, it will be. If COTS software can be modified for use, surround code will be written. If new software needs to be developed, a team is formed to develop it. The team leader generally sets the rules for coding and documentation that may interpret corporate guidelines much differently than the team leader on the last project.

In many cases, IT departments have created one or more and sometimes several "quick and dirty" applications with little or no documentation. These applications may have been written to accommodate an immediate, but unplanned business need, such as specific membership data needed by sales representatives that might not be available through the current application set. There may be long-term plans for resolving a mass of temporary applications quickly put into place to accommodate combined data from company mergers. Seldom is there sufficient documentation to flesh out the inner workings of the system and, due to employee turnover, there may not even be anyone that understands why it was done the way it was. Survival of the business is based on users being able to do what they have to do in order to meet the business needs of the company. Funding for IT efforts becomes a competition with primary business products and services.

The result of these methods being used by IT organizations at one company after another is a complex web of applications with undocumented interface and application modules. The problems that this causes were brought to full light when these companies had to deal with the Year 2000 remediation effort. Even getting an accurate inventory of program assets was challenging and putting a quality program in place to ensure Year 2000 confidence of continuing operations too often included as many exceptions as audit criteria.

Government

When United States government agencies decide to install a new computer system, it is most often accomplished through a joint effort between the agency and one or more contractors. When a new computer system will include new software, specifically developed for the unique needs of the agency, the development effort is governed by extensive engineering and documentation standards. This is true even when the system will include a mix of commercial off-the-shelf (COTS) packages and new code. The value of these standards is as much in the level of communication they force during development as anything else.

The development team has a road map and the agency project team has tools to assess and evaluate the software during every phase of the development. During the requirements phase, the agency's needs and wants are analyzed, and the technological methods and techniques for meeting the needs are determined and documented. There are formal presentations, weeks of scheduled reviews, negotiations, and compromise in order to stay within budget. In the end, there is a great ceremonial meeting where acceptance by the agency is given to proceed with the development of the system.

The design phase is often two-tiered. The first part of the design can be referred to as high level. It is at this level that the grand system and all of its subsystems are clearly defined. The requirements agreed to in the previous phase are clearly mapped to the system design. Decisions are made about how the system will be tested to prove it has met the requirements. Again, there are meetings, reviews, documentation, and a great ceremonial meeting to grant approval to proceed. Another milestone is marked; the low-level design begins and will be followed by other ceremonial meetings at the conclusion of each subsystem design.

ESSENTIAL CONCEPTS OF PROJECT MANAGEMENT

By now there are type A specifications, type B specifications, interface specifications, database specifications, project plans, configuration management plans, quality assurance plans, and programmer guidelines at a minimum. There are hundreds, and sometimes thousands, of pages documenting what the system will do, how it will do it, how it will be managed during development, and how it will be tested to ensure it meets the specifications. According to the standards used by the agencies, such as the FAA, the DOD, and the IRS, to name a few, all of this is supposed to occur before a single line of code is written.

During the coding phase, the system is documented in user manuals, operations manuals, and maintenance manuals. Detailed test procedures with expected results and text repeated from previous documents are put into place. Much of the text in the manuals is redundant to the specifications. It is these manuals that will survive when the system goes operational. In some agencies and for some systems, these manuals are maintained throughout the life of the system. In many, they are not. The level of funding justified and made available for development is not extended to maintaining many of the systems or their documentation once they are migrated into production.

This level of documentation may be warranted on mission-critical projects such as software for man–space travel. In most instances, it is sheer overkill and can actually impede the development effort by forcing focus on documentation deliverables while coding and testing time are diminished.

SYSTEM DEVELOPMENT — WHAT IS RIGHT

The integration of systems and the expansion of internal systems to communicate with external systems dictates that some consistency in the varying approaches needs to be established. Methodologies attempting to fill this need have sprung up everywhere. Browsing through any computer science section of Amazon.com, Borders, or Barnes & Noble will reveal book after book on the approaches that can be used. Government contractors hoping to secure work in the private sector as budgets of many agencies are cut, are coming forward declaring that they have the answers. They bring with them approaches developed for full-scale, complex efforts that are overkill for commercial systems development. The benefits of tools such as the International Standards Organization (ISO) quality standards, series 9000, and the Software Engineering Institute's Capability Maturity Model (SEI CMM) are expensive to realize if the tools are not adequately tailored. For some profit-based companies, funding for the use of these tools is nearly impossible.

Efforts are being made throughout the computer industry to find some common ground for the approach to software development. Industry leaders are standardizing interfaces to increase application portability, broadening the need for companies to know how their systems work. The point of all of this is perhaps viewed as reference material in much the same way as an encyclopedia. Use the information to get smarter and then apply the information with common sense. Keep in mind that some very smart people can be very good at telling others how to do things, but lack the ability and know-how to get the job done. People who have been in the trenches on small and large projects know and understand that there is a happy median that can and must be achieved.

Get the Basics

At a minimum, a description of each application, existing and planned, needs to be written down and maintained. Whether the application is a stand-alone database that allows queries to be made using a variety of personal computer products or code that will convert a legacy system to the latest and greatest technology, it is critical to know what is going on in development. A good description of an application will include the following information.

- Application purpose statement
- Input and output requirements
- Hardware requirements
- Software environment requirements
- Location of current version of source code or COTS installed
- Version/last modified descriptions

With this information, all else can be reconstructed on an as-needed basis.

Application Purpose Statement. The application purpose statement tells the business reason for having the software, the limitations and capabilities of the product, and the point of contact for getting questions answered about the product. This is a nontechnical statement that explains what the application is and what it does. It is written at the application component level rather than system component level. For example, a financial system will in all probability include applications for general ledger, journal processing, and accounts payable. A purpose statement is written for general ledger, journal processing, and accounts payable. They can then be bound in one document but each needs to be clearly described independently of the others because they will be maintained and upgraded individually over time.

The purpose statement needs to be text. Diagrams are nice, but are only supportive to the text because diagrams generally cannot contain all of the necessary information without becoming too complex to read.

Input and Output Requirements. It is essential to know what data is expected by the application and what data is generated by the application. When an application expects data, it is going to come from one of three sources: a file input, a program process, or a user. That information needs to be stated. If the application gets the information from a file or outside database, the file name and database tables need to be identified. When the application gets the information from a process within the program logic, the logic needs to be described. When the application gets the information from a user, valid values and ranges must be documented.

When an application generates data, it is going to either send it somewhere or keep it. If the application is sending the data somewhere, the target file name and database table need to be given. If it is going to display the data, this needs to be explained. If the application only stores the data within the application to be used for queries and reports, rules governing update rotations, archiving, and purging need to be provided.

The input/output information is best presented in a table format. The data items can be listed alphabetically, making it easy to find the data path for application maintenance and troubleshooting.

Hardware Requirements. This should be a very basic list of what equipment is needed in order for the application to run in any organization. The list should give the minimum requirements for processor capability and memory.

Software Environment Requirements. This list needs to specify any software components needed on the system in order to run the application. This includes the operating system release and version, database release and version, and any other applications the application being described needs.

Location of Current Version of Source and Object Code or COTS Installed. This piece of documentation becomes essential in maintaining the integrity in the development environment. The best way to have this information available and accurate is to use configuration management tools.

Version/Last Modified Descriptions. This piece of documentation specifically states what changes have been made to the application and when they were made. Additional information about who made the changes can be of value only if the coding organization is static. The "who did it" factor becomes meaningless in dynamic organizations.

It is best to have individual version reports for each release, rather than continuing lists of changes. This approach promotes more thorough documentation.

SYSTEMS DEVELOPMENT — IS THAT IT?

Having the basic documentation enables a company to build any additional documentation that may be planned. In the government world, it can be used to generate as much paper as the project demands. In a commercial product development world, it provides sufficient information for technical writers to generate operations and user manuals. In IT departments, it ensures that code is managed and can be upgraded, converted, and used in constructive and productive ways.

Within each organization, there needs to be a standardized format for the basic documentation. Peer and management reviews of the basic documentation should be included in the development schedule. The reviews may be conducted as formal meetings where everyone gathers in a room and goes through the documentation page by page, or as informal reviews where the document is distributed and comments are submitted to the authoring team. Procedures for maintaining and updating the electronic and hardcopy versions of the documentation must exist.

SYSTEMS DEVELOPMENT SUMMARY

Using a checklist as shown in Exhibit 1 can help to get things started. The point is that basic documentation imposes order on every development effort. Increased order allows for more thorough and consistent management of development processes. More thorough and consistent management results in more realistic schedules and staffing for future development work, whether it is new application development, legacy system conversions, maintenance work, or additional types of documentation for the marketplace.

Establishing a practice of basic documentation provides ancillary benefits in that contract employees can be brought up to speed faster and their work can be checked and managed better. New technology can be adopted into environments more readily. Short- and long-term planning and bids for funding can be developed more meaningfully and documented more completely. In all, just sticking with the basics creates a win–win situation for everyone from management, to developers, to users.

Exhibit 1. Basic Documentation Checklist

Item No.	Category	Items	Status
1.	Application purpose statement	Business reason for application Limitations and capabilities Point of contact Exaplanation of application components and what they do	
2.	Input and output requirements	Database tables used by application Files used by application Internal interfaces Sending application with file names sent External interfaces Sending system with file names sent	
3.	Hardware requirements	Processor Disk space Memory Printer name	
4.	Software requirements	Operating system Database Send to interface applications Receive from interface applications	
5.	Location of code and COTS	Name of machine Name of directory Name of files	
6.	Version descriptions	Name of application Name of each program changed Recompile complete Description of changes made for each of the programs Name of database table change Description of changes made to each table	

Chapter 7
Process Management: Integrating Project Management and Development

Chris Gane

To most software developers, the areas of project management and systems development methodologies are related only loosely. Systems development methodologies provide general information about standards and practices; project management is concerned with budgeting and reporting of project activity cost and time.

Automated tools to support project management and systems development methodologies have evolved separately. However, it has become apparent that the two areas need to be unified into a single discipline of process management that has a single underlying metamodel. This chapter provides the rationale for unifying systems development methodologies and project management and describes one type of process management metamodel as well as an approach to its automation.

Process management has much in common with business process reengineering. Organizations that have adopted process management are applying the principles of business process reengineering to application development. In this chapter, process management is defined as the unification of methodology with project management.

PROJECT MANAGEMENT: FORMAL AND INFORMAL

There has always been tension between the formal and informal aspects of project management. Formal project management is concerned with the generation and execution of plans; informal project management is concerned with the motivation and coordination of project staff.

Formal Project Management

Formal project management involves project planning as well as project control. Project planning attempts to provide answers to such questions as:

- Which tasks have to be done?
- Which tasks must be complete before others can be started?
- Which skills are needed for the tasks defined?
- Who is available when and for how much time?
- How long will the project take, given the people available (i.e., resource-driven estimating)?
- How many people are needed to get the project done by a certain date (i.e., date-driven estimating)?
- How much will the project cost?

The questions on estimating time and cost are always difficult to answer; one of the main objectives of process management is to make estimating easier and more reliable.

Project Control. Project control deals with executing the project plan and is concerned with regularly (e.g., weekly) answering the following questions:

- Where does the project stand?
- Based on this status, when will it be done now?
- What has been spent so far?
- Which assignments are critical this week?
- Who needs help?

Project control also deals with coping with such unplanned problems as

- When employees are pulled off a project, how is the work to be reassigned so that it gets done as soon as possible and as inexpensively as possible?
- A program was estimated to take 100 hours to complete; 80 hours have already been spent but the program is only halfway through. How does this affect the project deadline?

Informal Project Management

Formal project management can be automated because it makes use of such approaches as critical path analysis. Informal project management is concerned more with intuitive judgment and relationships among personnel. Informal project management tries to answer such questions as:

- How reliable are an employee's estimates?
- A group of programmers is on the critical path this week; how can they be motivated to finish faster?
- Who needs formal training in which areas, and who needs coaching?
- What is the state of the team morale? Should anything be done to improve it?

Some of these judgments can be decided with quantitative information. If the history of an employee's estimates can be accessed as well as the actual time the employee took for each assignment, this information can be used to correct estimates.

In this way, formal project management skills can support and improve informal project management, although they are no substitute for intuition and judgment. People who are proficient at formal project management may not have outstanding interpersonal skills. Similarly, good informal project managers may be impatient with the effort involved in creating plans and revising them as a project unfolds. Formal project management can be learned, and it appears that informal project management cannot — either someone simply is or is not good at it.

Organizations are thus under pressure to find talented informal project managers and to support them with aids for formal project management. Some organizations provide staff to help project managers with project planning and control; automated tools are being used increasingly, but they will be commonplace only if they are easy to use and provide obvious value to the project manager.

THREE APPROACHES TO ESTIMATING

Project managers are under a lot of pressure to produce estimates of time and cost for systems development very early in a project, typically in the first two weeks. However, estimating a development project from outline requirements and not from a physical design is like a home buyer saying, "Quote me a price for building a house, but I am not sure where I want the house located, or about the number of rooms, or whether it should be of brick or wood." It is not surprising that project estimates are as bad as they are, but that they can be made and met at all. Three approaches can be taken to estimating:

1. Using industry experience
2. Using the experience of one's own organization
3. Rolling up more or less detailed estimates of the project effort

Using Industry Experience: Function Points

Perhaps the most useful form of recorded industry experience comes in function point counts. Many people measure software efforts based on the number of lines of code. The trouble with this measure is that the same function involves many more lines in a low-level language than in a high-level language. Often, an algorithm coded in one language requires more lines to be coded in another language.

A function point count is a more stable measure of software size than lines of code, because it is based on the number of inputs, outputs, files, and other measures of complexity. The International Function Point Users Group (IFPUG) has put considerable effort into devising and maintaining standard methods for sizing software.

The Function Point Method. Briefly, one counts the files, inputs, outputs, and queries involved in an application. Each is rated as simple, average, or complex. Each rating is weighted to yield the unadjusted function point count. For example, if five files in an application are of average complexity (for which the IFPUG method specifies a weighting of 10), they add 50 function points to the total.

The whole application is rated on 14 measures of overall complexity, which include the degree of distributed processing and the proportion of transactions that involve online data entry. Each complexity measure is rated on a five-point scale (i.e., 70 is the highest score possible). The complexity rating is divided by 100 and 0.65 is added to yield a factor ranging from 0.65 to 1.35. The unadjusted function point count is multiplied by this factor to obtain the adjusted function point count.

For example, the counting and weighting of files and other items produces an unadjusted function point count of 1000. The application is of significant complexity and the rating of the 14 complexity measures gives a total of 60 points. As 60/100 + 0.65 is 1.25, the adjusted function point count would be 1250.

Measuring Productivity in Function Points. Many thousands of projects have been analyzed to build up function point databases, which can be used to compare the effort that went into each project with the number of function points created. Wide ranges of productivity exist. For example, with inexperienced staff, unstructured methods, ordinary tools, and low-level languages, productivity ranges from 0.25 to 5 function points per staff month. At the other end of the range, with experienced staff, structured methods, power tools, and high-level languages, productivity ranges from 20 to 100 function points per staff month. IS projects generally range from 3 to 50 function points per staff month, and the average is 8 function points.[1]

If a project team can achieve ten function points per staff month, then a 1250-function-point project takes 125 staff-months or ten people a little longer than a year. If productivity is 20 function points per staff month, then the work can be done in half the time.

Although function points are a reasonable sizing measure, they are not much use in estimating effort unless productivity can be estimated. To do that requires a track record of the project productivity of the staff.

The Value of Project Experience

Despite its importance in estimating, very few organizations have a database of project experience. Instead, experience on a project is in the heads of project team members and is not easy for the manager of the next project to access. Indeed, very few organizations keep reliable figures on the actual hours taken in project development. As automated process management tools become more widely used, it becomes less expensive and easier to use past project history.

A process management tool should help in answering the following questions:

- Which past projects are similar to the current one?
- What was the effort on similar projects overall and by task?
- How do the skills of the people on similar projects compare with those of the current project staff?

Finding Similar Projects. A similar project may be one that has the same tasks that were done by the same people, used the same programming language, or met other criteria. A project history database must enable the search for similar projects. This implies that all projects must be performed using a standard set of tasks, just as accounting costs must be analyzed using a standard chart of accounts. If each project manager makes up the names of the tasks on each project, how can projects be compared with one another? As discussed in the next section, a methodology should provide the enterprise with its chart of accounts.

Determining Past Effort and Skills. Once the similar projects are chosen, the manager of the new project needs to know the effort on similar projects, overall and by task, and the skills of those who worked on these projects. The manager can find this information if the time and cost spent has been recorded in a standard way and if data is reasonably complete. To quote productivity expert Capers Jones, "The historical data for projects used internally by corporations is close to worthless for economic studies. Direct user costs are essentially never tracked, unpaid overtime is seldom tracked, and carelessness in charging time to the correct set of project accounts is rampant in the MIS domain."[2]

Automated process management tools must make the recording of actual effort against standard categories inexpensive and easy for everyone putting in time on a project; then project history can become a meaningful aid to estimating.

Roll-Up of Estimates

Using experience to size a project from the top down has value because it can be done early in the project when only general knowledge about the physical design is available. Function point counting, however, is based on physical information about files, inputs, and outputs.

The most reliable method of estimating, although the most time-consuming, is to make an estimate for each piece of work jointly with the team member who is responsible for it and to combine the estimates from the bottom up. Bottom-up estimating involves answering three questions:

- What tasks have to be done?
- Who is going to do them?
- How long will they take to complete? (Detailed estimates can be imposed on or negotiated with employees.)

A project leader talented in informal project management can negotiate tight but achievable estimates as well as obtain personal commitment from the staff members. Firm commitment can only be made once the design is known at least in outline form.

Top-down estimates are made early in a project, done cheaply, and often changed. Bottom-up estimates are set, costly to produce, and established later in a project.

METHODOLOGY: WHAT IT IS AND HOW IT HELPS

Methodology, a word with multiple meanings, is often used carelessly to make some simple technique or approach sound more impressive than it is. A precise definition of the term is:

> A methodology is a generic knowledge base about tasks, techniques, deliverables, roles, tools, and tool use for carrying out some complex class of projects such as system development, plus a mechanism for adapting a generic knowledge base to each specific project.

Methodology Tasks. At minimum, a methodology is a description of tasks to be done in developing a system. The scope of a methodology might be wider than just development and cover planning, enhancement, and maintenance. Tasks can include designing the database and coding the programs. Each task typically has one or more recommended steps to be done in sequence.

Methodology Techniques. Some methodologies provide a somewhat detailed description of how to do tasks. However, these descriptions usually apply to more than one task. For example, a description of how to do a data flow diagram applies to the task of defining the process model as well as to the task of designing the transaction flow. Especially when a methodology is stored in a knowledge base on disk, it is convenient to separate the technique descriptions from the tasks and to provide a way (e.g., hypertext) to display a technique for a relevant task only when needed.

Deliverables. Each task should produce some tangible output, usually called a deliverable or work product. For example, designing a database should produce a deliverable — database design — and the methodology should specify what a database design may contain.

Roles. A methodology should also deal with the skills for each task. The most flexible way of doing this is to define roles. On a given project, one person may play several roles, or one role may be played by several people. The methodology should specify the role responsible for each task, and the other roles that may contribute to the task. Thus, for the task of designing the database, the primary role might be the DBMS specialist and the contributing role, the modeling specialist. For each role, a methodology should define the skills, experience, and background that are relevant.

Exhibit 1 shows an example of a task/deliverable description, with the names of the various roles and techniques associated with it.

Roles are an important way to involve the right businesspeople in the project in the right way. Just as one of the principles of business process reengineering is to consider how the process adds value for its ultimate customer,[3] so the definition of roles that need to be played by various members of the business community helps to ensure that the application adds value to the business.

Task Dependencies. If a methodology is to be useful for project planning, it should contain information about which tasks must be completed before other tasks can be started. For example, a methodology can stipulate that the task of designing the database is a predecessor to the task of specifying data security constraints.

Tools and Their Use. Increasingly, deliverables are produced with software tools that often run on workstations. A methodology must describe each relevant tool and enable tools to be linked to tasks so that developers know which tools are recommended for which tasks. In many cases, a methodology also lists tips, tricks, and traps that are associated with using a specific tool to do a specific task.

Exhibit 1.   A Simple Task/Deliverable Entry from the Knowledge Base

Task	Carry out Discovery Prototyping	Task-ID A0540

Purpose	If users find it difficult to describe their requirements in terms of data and logic, discovery prototyping can help clarify their needs by getting their feedback on generic prototypes. The technique prototyping gives details of three types:
	1. Discovery prototyping
	2. Behavior prototyping
	3. Production prototyping
	Discovery prototyping is used as an aid to uncover requirements when users do not relate well to modeling techniques. It may consist of screen mockups, visits to other computerized offices, and product demonstrations. The prime purpose is neither to build a system nor to determine in detail how the system will work; rather it is to determine what, exactly, are the requirements that users have.
Responsible	Development Team Member (Hypertext to Role Descriptions)
Contributors	User Team Members
Need to start	Development Project Manager Decision
Other inputs	Any available data model or data requirements
Steps in task	If the development project manager decides that this task is relevant, then:
	1. An assigned development team member develops generic screen or report layouts and exercises them with selected user team members. Development team members must emphasize that what they are seeing is only a false front with no necessary similarity to the eventual system or interface. See Technique: Prototyping (Hypertext to Technique Description)
	2. The development team member revises the generic layouts based on user feedback and exercises them iteratively with user team members until no more requirements are identified.
	3. The development team member revises the data model on the basis of the discovery prototype findings.

This Task Produces:

Deliverable	Discovery Prototype	ID 1.40.05
Contents	Screens, screen-to-screen flow diagrams, or pointers to files where actual discovery prototypes can be found.	

It is convenient to store tool usage descriptions separately from the tool description itself. For example, in addition to a description of a spreadsheet tool, the tool usage of a methodology for the task *define the users at various locations* might read, "Always list the locations down the y-axis of the spreadsheet and the types of user across the top."

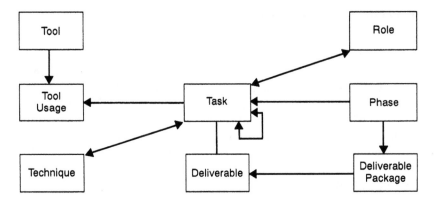

The relationships shown between these methodology objects are:

A task must result in only one deliverable.
A deliverable must be produced by only one task.

A phase may group together one or more tasks.
A task may be grouped in only one phase.

A task may be a predecessor to one or more other tasks.
A task may have as predecessor one or more other tasks.

A phase may produce one or more deliverable packages.
A deliverable package may be associated with only one phase.

A deliverable package must be made up of one or more deliverables.
A deliverable must be part of only one deliverable package.

A tool may be associated with one or more tool usages.
A tool usage must be for only one tool.

A tool usage must relate to only one task.
A task may have detailed guidance in one or more tool usages.

A task may require background knowledge in one or more techniques.
A technique may apply to one or more tasks.

A task may involve one or more roles.
A role may be involved in one or more tasks.

Exhibit 2.   Methodology Metamodel

Phases and Deliverable Packages. Tasks are usually grouped in phases, primarily for management control purposes. As development projects become more iterative, phases have less and less meaning, because the same tasks are being repeated for each iteration of the prototype or each version of the development application. It is often clearer to focus on packages of deliverables that may be grouped for management or user review. These deliverable packages may have such names as *requirements package, discovery prototype package,* and *outline design package.*

Metamodel of a Methodology

The components (i.e., objects) of a methodology and their relationships are shown in the simple metamodel of Exhibit 2. In automated methodologies these objects hold text and bit-mapped diagrams, with hypertext cross-references between them. In the future, a knowledge base will contain multimedia objects as well. Looking up a technique will involve opening a video window on a workstation, with an overview explanation of the topic, followed by a menu of more-detailed subtopics. This kind of adaptive video briefing will provide just-in-time training in the future.

Need to Customize

Obviously, no methodology of this kind is static; it needs to be an evolving knowledge base customized for the vocabulary and practice of each organization. Commercially available methodology products should be regarded as starter sets from which the evolving organizational knowledge base is to be built. Each organization needs a methodology administrator who is charged with the constant improvement of the knowledge base and adapting mechanism, as part of the continuous process improvement approach.

Need to Adapt for Each Project. The knowledge base for a methodology can become quite large; several binders on a shelf or 3 to 20 megabytes of online disk space are common. Valuable as this information is, it is often useless to the people on the project. A project manager is in the position of saying, "Out of all this good material, which parts are relevant to me and my people on this specific project, and which parts can we neglect?"

The Adapting Mechanism. A methodology must include in the description of the knowledge base a mechanism for adapting the generic knowledge base to each specific project. Pulling binders apart by hand to make a project subset of the methodology is obviously not feasible. Some methodologies offer templates for the various types of projects, which can include package installation projects and client/server projects. Even within such a template, however, projects differ markedly, and a project manager is still left with the job of adapting the template to the project at hand.

What seems to work well is to have an automated questionnaire that asks a project manager such questions about the new project as "Will the application serve multiple departments?" or "Will there be a change in communications network loading?" Once the questions have been answered, a rule-based job can be run, to extract the minimum set of tasks from the generic methodology and create a methodology that is unique to the project. The rules can have the following form:

```
IF the answer to the question "Will there be a change in
   communications network loading?" is Yes
      THEN include in the project the tasks:
      "Review the network map"
      "Do performance analysis of network loading"
```

Helping the Project Manager

With the sort of organization-generic, project-specific methodology described here, projects can be started up more quickly and, given a project history database, can be estimated and staffed more effectively. In an hour or so a project manager can answer the first six project planning questions:

1. What tasks have to be done?
2. Which of them must be complete before others can be started?
3. What skills are needed for them?
4. Who is available when, for how much time?
5. How long will it take?
6. How many people are needed?

To answer the first question, a project manager works through the questionnaire and runs the rule-based job to generate what the methodology thinks is the minimum set of tasks for this particular project. The second question is answered by the same job, which has the ability to work out project-specific dependencies from generic dependencies.

To determine these dependencies, the methodology says that task A must be done before task B, which must be done before task C, which must be done before task D. For example, if a result of the questionnaire is that tasks B and C are ruled not relevant to the project, the tool should then create the project-specific dependency that task A must be completed before task D.

To answer the third question, using the project tasks the tool can determine the subset of roles that are relevant to the project, list them for the project manager, and, given a project history database, list the people who have played each role on previous projects.

To answer the fourth question, the project manager needs access to the future schedules of the people who have the necessary skills. Of course, people are sometimes assigned to a project full time and this simplifies the scheduling job. The most effective way to answer the last two questions is to have project histories available, so that estimates can be based on actual experience.

The adaptive mechanism of a modern methodology means that, although every project is different, the same chart of accounts is used to build up the history. So, in every project that involves database design, for example, the time involved is charged to a generic task with a standard identifier and a standard name.

PROCESS MANAGEMENT

Modern adaptive methodologies support effective rapid project planning and estimating. Although each project is different, process management treats each one as an instance of a generic process rather than as a unique unrepeatable event. Given a methodology to define it, the generic process can begin to be managed, both day-to-day and at a strategic level.

Day-to-Day Process Management

Short-term process management is concerned with smoothing the work of the project team. It helps a staff member to answer such questions as:

- If I am a team member, what am I supposed to be working on?
- If I am waiting for someone to answer a question on one assignment, what should I work on while I am waiting?
- What software tool should I use? Where is that tool on the LAN?
- I am not sure how to do this piece of work; where can I get guidance?
- What is the status of each piece of my work? How long has the work taken so far?

A process management support tool combines access to the automated methodology with the management of to-do lists of people's work, flagging the status on each piece of work, and helping people capture the hours that they spend on each assignment. First thing in the morning, staff members may look at their to-do list, and pick the work that is most urgent or critical. The process management tool knows the generic task and the relevant software tool and can launch the tool if the staff member wants. At the end of each work session, staff members can record the time that they spent, and if the status of the piece of work has changed, record the new status.

Defining the Term Piece of Work. Each task in the project may imply a single piece of work or multiple pieces of work assigned to different people. The task of producing database design may be done by one person; however, developing code for version test may involve ten people each writing ten programs.

To automate process management, an assignment object is needed. This object describes a piece of work done by a single person that is part or all of a project task, which may be done using a software tool. Each assignment has a status and may involve one or more work sessions, each of which generates a time-spent record that becomes part of the project database.

Incidentally, this means that the tool can generate the person's status report and time sheet at the end of each week. Process management should make the worker's life easier too. Process management feeds project control. If up-to-date status and actual hours-to-date are captured on all the assignments in a project, the project manager can answer many of the project control questions.

Process Management Model. The process management metamodel in Exhibit 3 unifies the object methodology and project management. Exhibit 3 is, of course, a very simplified picture. Real-world implementations must deal with many other objects and relationships and resolve the many-to-many relationships shown in the models of Exhibits 2 and 3.

Once deliverable status is automated, changes in status can be used to trigger project events that send messages to the project manager and other people who need to know.[4] For example, possible status values for deliverables might include:

- In progress
- On hold
- Completed

Project events might be specified: If a high-priority deliverable has the status of "on hold" for three days, notify the project manager. In this way the project manager can receive messages that give exception reports about the ongoing status of the project, as a by-product of everyday work.

CONCLUSION

With day-to-day process management in place, building reliable project histories based on a consistent chart of accounts, project managers can start to ask the classical question common to continuous process improvement and business process reengineering: Now that the process is defined, how can it be improved?

Everyone on every project should take responsibility for giving suggestions about enhancements to the methodology administrator. The methodology itself should contain an explicit task for post-installation review, when customer satisfaction with the application is measured and methodology enhancements are sought from the project team.

Other questions related to process improvement and project management include:

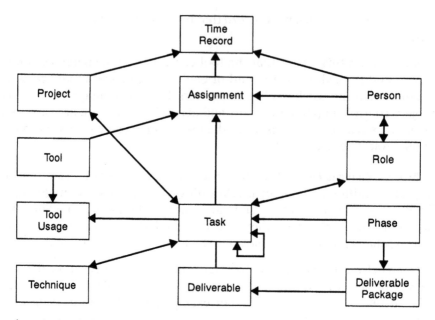

Important project management relationships include:

A project may involve one or more tasks.
A task may be part of one or more projects.

A task may be carried out via one or more assignments.
An assignment must be part of only one task.

An assignment may give rise to one or more time records.
A time record must be associated with only one assignment.

A project may have one or more time records.
A time record must be charged to only one project.

An assignment must be the responsibility of only one person.
A person may be responsible for one or more assignments.

A person may play one or more roles.
A role may be played by one or more persons.

A time record must be for only one person.
A person may set up one or more time records.

An assignment may be done with only one tool.
A tool may be used for one or more assignments.

Exhibit 3. Process Management Metamodel Combining Methodology Objects and Project Management Objects

---

- How was the time spent on the project divided among the various tasks?
- If the project is repeated, would a different amount of time be spent on such tasks as requirements definition?
- Did the time spent on every task contribute to the quality of the product? If not, should the task be changed or deleted, or should the adaptive questionnaire be changed to exclude this task in similar future projects?

- Was there anything needed for the project that was not covered in the methodology? If so, should it be added?
- How many times were the estimates of effort and delivery date revised? How could more realistic estimates have been made?

As well as these questions about the nature of the technical process, project managers should ask questions about its output:

- What measures of deliverable quality are relevant?
- What defects in deliverables were found, during development and after installation?
- How is customer satisfaction measured, other than in post-installation review?

With a defined process and metrics of success, project managers can move on to ask more profound questions about the culture and whether the process should be continuously improved or obliterated and replaced:

- Does the incentive climate focus on activity or on results?
- How are project teams and project managers rewarded for meeting user needs for timely quality applications?
- What penalties are there for people who disrupt the process, for example, users who constantly change their minds about what they want? The best methodology and process management tools may be useless if there is no incentive for anyone to deliver quality.

Process Management and Business Process Reengineering

Process management allows senior managers to contemplate business reengineering and ask, "Should there be an application development function in this organization?" Business process reengineering "doesn't mean tinkering with what already exists or making incremental changes that leave basic structures intact. ... It means asking the question: 'If I were recreating this company today, given what I know and given current technology, what would it look like.' ... It involves going back to the beginning and inventing a better way of doing work."[5]

The "better way of doing work" is, of course, a new methodology. How does management encourage the staff to work with a new methodology? By rolling it out in a process management tool. Thus, the cycle is complete — process improvement needs better estimating, better estimating needs meaningful project history, project history needs a standard chart of accounts, a standard chart of accounts must come from a methodology, a methodology needs to be automated with a process management tool, and a process management tool provides the basis for process improvement.

ESSENTIAL CONCEPTS OF PROJECT MANAGEMENT

Notes

1. C. Jones, *Applied Software Measurement,* New York: McGraw-Hill, 1991.
2. Jones, pp. 127–128.
3. M. Hammer and J. Champy, *Re-engineering the Corporation,* New York: HarperCollins, 1993.
4. K.D. Saracelli and K.F. Bandat, "Process Automation in Software Application Development," *IBM Systems Journal,* 32, no. 3, 1993.
5. Hammer and Champy, p. 31.

Bibliography

Brown, D. "Understanding and Using Function Points." *Software Engineering Strategies,* 1, no. 5, 1993.

Release 3.4. Westerville OH: International Function Point Users Group, 1992.

Chapter 8
Project Meetings: A Communication and Coordination Tool

Ulla Merz

Good coordination is an important factor in project success. In turn, coordination success is based on interpersonal networks and informed project members, as reported in the survey study "Coordination in Software Development" by Robert E. Kraut and Lynn A. Streeter.[1]

Data from that same survey of 65 software projects suggests that personal communication is important for successful coordination in software development projects. The drawbacks are the high cost of one-on-one interaction and the lack of tangible results. The same survey also found that project members do not find formal impersonal communication, such as written requirements documents, source code, and data dictionaries, very valuable.

Project meetings are an opportunity to combine the benefits from personal communication and formal impersonal communication. Meetings are a place for personal interactions. Documenting the outcome of a meeting by writing meeting minutes or updating a design document realizes the benefits of the work accomplished in the meeting.

WHAT IS WRONG WITH MEETINGS

Review the following questions and check the ones that can be answered with a "yes."

- Have you attended meetings where you did not get the information you needed?
- Have you attended meetings where the atmosphere was hostile or abusive?

0-8493-1190-X/02/$0.00+$1.50

- Have you attended meetings where most of the decisions were postponed?
- Have you attended meetings where the purposes was unclear?

In all the cases where the answer was a yes, the meeting was not an effective coordination tool.

MAKING MEETINGS A VALUABLE COMMUNICATION TOOL

What do meetings that one experienced as valuable to attend — meetings one keeps going back to — have in common? Here are some responses people gave in a survey for a project post-mortem:

- The meetings address issues of concern.
- It is important to get everyone face to face, but also limit the time spent doing so.
- Everyone gets the same information.
- Everyone is made aware of the changes.

Personally, the Sunday church meetings and the weekly toastmaster's meetings are meetings the author keeps going back to, because they seem valuable. Effective meetings have several things in common:

1. The needs of each participant are met.
2. Concerns important to the group as a whole are addressed.
3. The purpose is clear.
4. The atmosphere is comfortable.

The following sections discuss what can be done to make meetings an effective communication tool:

- Identify the purpose of the meeting
- Define the deliverables or work products of meetings
- Create the atmosphere/context for success

Define the Purpose of the Meeting

There are mainly three types of meetings:

1. Meetings for exchanging information
2. Meetings for making decisions
3. Meetings for solving problems

Examples for each are (1) the project status meeting, which has the purpose of exchanging information; (2) scope/issue meetings, which have the purpose of making decisions; and (3) design meetings, which have the purpose of producing a quality product design.

An information exchange meeting achieves its purpose if all team members get the information they need to proceed with their work. Information exchange meetings are the place to disseminate product requirement changes, raise technical issues, announce changes in the lives of project team members, and report on risks that have either increased or decreased. Information exchange meetings are great forums for team members to use each other as sounding boards for their upcoming decisions.

An important part of a decision-making meeting is to provide participants with the facts they need to make decisions. A decision-making meeting does not achieve its purpose if the decisions are postponed. The purpose is to arrive at decisions that all participants agree to and can support.

The purpose of a problem-solving meeting is not only to develop a solution, but also to formulate jointly a common problem definition. It is important that all meeting participants have a chance to make a contribution. Just as with decision-making meetings, the purpose of problem-solving meetings is to decide on a solution.

Once the purpose in general has been defined, the next step is to prepare a specific agenda. An agenda is an outline of the content for the meeting. What needs to be on the agenda depends on the task at hand. For example, the agenda for a change control board meeting will list the specific cases to be discussed. It also may contain a discussion and vote on procedural changes and an announcement of a personnel appointment. An agenda for a status meeting will list important milestones, such as the documentation freeze, the beta release, and the version of the upcoming software build.

When preparing a meeting agenda, ask questions that will help identify the topics to be addressed. For example, when preparing an agenda for a status meeting, ask the following questions:

- Which information is needed to begin work on upcoming tasks and who needs it?
- Which external information and decisions have an effect on the project?
- Which deliverables require coordination between several team members?
- Are there any concerns that were brought up?
- Which activities and tasks have been worked on?

Define the Work Products That Result from Meetings

No matter what the kind of meeting, it is necessary to record the information shared and the outcome of the meeting in meeting minutes. Without meeting minutes, all work accomplished in the meeting is lost. Having a person record the information shared, the decisions made, and the problems

Exhibit 1.   Template for Status Meeting Minutes

Who attended?

General Information:

Issues and Decisions:
  Issue

  Action Plan

  Owner

  Due Date

  Comments

Summary of accomplishments and outlook for each area

---

solved relieves other participants from keeping records themselves and allows them to participate in the meeting.

Using a template for the meeting minutes makes them fast to prepare, easy to read, and assures that nothing is forgotten. Exhibit 1 presents a template for status meeting minutes.

There are additional work products, depending on the particular purpose of a meeting. Information exchange meetings usually have a list of action items as a result.

The work products of decision-making meetings are the alternatives that have been evaluated, the decisions made, and their supporting reasons. The resulting decisions are recorded in a permanent repository, preferably accessible to all team members now and in the future.

The work product of a problem-solving meeting varies and depends on the problem. It can be a design document, a project schedule, or a budget. Just as with the meeting minutes, it is important to assign ownership to a participant who is responsible for recording the work product and for distributing it to all participants. For example, the purpose of a meeting may be to define a documentation plan consisting of templates for all internal documentation. The recorder/owner is responsible for creating the final electronic form of the templates and for sharing them with all interested parties.

Create an Atmosphere for Success

The atmosphere or context of a meeting is an important factor that allows people to share information, make decisions, and solve problems jointly. Knowing the purpose and work products of a meeting are necessary, but if meeting participants do not feel comfortable enough to share information or opinions, the meeting will not achieve its objective. People need to feel comfortable so they can focus on the task at hand. Participants need to feel and know that they can communicate openly, that their perspectives are respected, and that they can express their creativity.

HOW TO MAKE PEOPLE FEEL COMFORTABLE

Meeting participants will feel more comfortable, if:

- A meeting adheres to a common format.
- The facilitator provides guidance.
- The facilitator uses context-free questions to solicit needs and feelings.

People feel comfortable if they know what they can expect. Think of that recent Sunday church meeting. How is it different from the one before? It is the content that is different, but not the format. A common format makes people feel comfortable that they can participate and that they know how. This is also the secret formula of toastmaster's meetings. Every meeting has the same format, an invocation, a joke, two speeches, and table topics followed by evaluations. The content is what is different. One can think of the familiar format as a ritual that makes participants feel at ease.

A standard format for the different types of meetings will provide comfort, as people know what to expect and how to participate. Exhibit 2 presents formats that may serve as suggestions for particular meetings.

Even if meeting participants are familiar with the format of the meeting, they still appreciate some guidance through the meeting. Just as written overviews, summaries, and transitions are included to help a reader understand the written word better, spoken transitions, summaries and overviews help meeting participants to follow along better. By suggesting an agenda, the facilitator can provide an overview of the meeting. Articulating a transition will remind participants to move on to the next topic. The facilitator can bring closure to a discussion by summarizing the items of agreement.

Gerald Weinberg and Donald Gause in *Exploring Requirements — Quality before Design*[2] point out the importance of context-free questions in requirements gathering. There is also a place for context-free questions in meetings. The purpose of context-free questions is to clarify and define the process. Example questions are:

- How much time should be spent discussing a particular item?
- How should decisions made in meetings be documented?
- How should decisions be made?

The facilitator can use context-free questions to solicit and comment on the perceived mood, to verify a common understanding, and to inquire

Exhibit 2.   Suggested Meeting Formats

Information Exchange Meeting
• Share general information
• Follow up on decisions and action items from previous status meetings
• Summary of accomplishments
• Outlook of upcoming work and decisions in the different functional areas
• Summary of action items

Decision-Making Meetings
• Presentation of facts
• Input and comments from stakeholders
• Discussion and evaluation
• Decision making
• Summary of decisions made and postponed

Problem-Solving Meeting
• Share problem perception
• Joint problem definition
• Joint problem analysis
• Joint development of alternative solutions
• Evaluation of solution
• Decision making
• Summary of solution

whether or not the needs of individual participants are met. Example questions are:

• Did people get all the information they needed?
• Is the meeting moving too slowly?
• Does this summary express it clearly?

OPEN COMMUNICATION ALLOWS INFORMATION EXCHANGE

Making participants feel comfortable is the first step to open communication. Open communication is based on trust and trust can be earned by maintaining neutrality in all work products that result from meetings, especially the meeting minutes. For meeting minutes that means no editing, no omissions, and no additions to what was said and decided in the meeting. Open communication means not holding back information, not judging information or opinions, and includes respectful listening. Open communication is absolutely essential in status meetings, because without quality data, the wrong picture is painted.

ADVOCACY AND INQUIRY IMPROVE DECISION MAKING

When it comes to decision making, it is important to hear all sides that have a stake in the decision. Project scope meetings that discuss changes in the product requirements depend on input from all stakeholders, especially those that are not present, such as the customer. The technical architect needs to advocate the integrity of the product, technical support may represent the customer's view, and marketing may argue the position of the company compared with the competition. As much as each view needs to be communicated assertively, there also needs to be inquiry to learn more about the different perspectives. As the different views are presented, the assumptions, reasons, and facts behind them need to be questioned. A balance between advocacy and inquiry will contribute to better decisions.

CREATIVITY AND PROBLEM SOLVING

Meeting participants need to be ready to solve problems jointly. Creating a comfortable environment goes a long way toward making participants ready. It is true for training that more learning happens if people take ownership in the learning process. It is also true for meetings that participants need to have ownership in the problem to be solved. People feel ownership if they receive confirmation that their contributions are appreciated and important. The facilitator can emphasize the ownership by acknowledging each contribution.

Brainstorming is still the best-known and best-understood technique for stimulating creativity. Its ground rule is — *no judgment of the different contributions.* To make sure everyone gets a chance to contribute, the facilitator can give each person the floor by going around the room and asking each person for his or her input.

USING PROJECT MEETINGS AS SUCCESSFUL COORDINATION TOOLS

For project meetings to serve as communication and coordination tools they have to achieve the following goals:

- Inform project members
- Provide opportunities to contribute expertise and knowledge
- Achieve agreement and support for the outcome

To attain these goals this chapter has focused on three aspects of meetings:

1. A well-defined purpose
2. A tangible outcome
3. A comfortable and supportive atmosphere

All three are important for successful and effective communication. Defining the purpose of a meeting and the work products that result from it will sharpen the content. Creating the right atmosphere for the meeting helps participants to focus their attention. No matter whether the purpose of the meeting is to exchange information, make decisions, or solve a problem, people need to feel comfortable to participate.

Once the purpose of the meeting has been identified, the deliverables have been defined, and the atmosphere for getting work done in meetings has been created, one can watch for indicators that signify it is happening. One can look for tangible evidence that work is coordinated, decisions are carried out, and solutions are implemented. It will also be noticed that people are on time for meetings, that they are fully engaged during meetings, and that they ask to hold meetings to get their work done.

References

1. Robert E. Kraut and Lynn A. Streeter, "Coordination in Software Development," *Communication of the ACM,* Vol. 38, No. 3, March 1995.
2. Donald C. Gause and Gerald M. Weinberg, *Exploring Requirements — Quality before Design,* Dorset House, ISBN 0-9322633-13-7.
3. Larry L. Constantine, "Work Organization: Paradigms for Project Managment and Organization," *Communications of the ACM,* Vol. 36, No. 10, October 1993.
4. Michael Doyle and David Straus, *How to Make Meetings Work,* Jove Books, ISBN 0-515-09048-4.
5. Peter Senge et al., *The Fifth Discipline Field Book,* Currency Book, ISBN 0-385-47256-0.

Chapter 9
Managing Systems Requirements

Polly Perryman Kuver

Requirements management is composed of four major activities: capturing the requirements, organizing them, reviewing them, and controlling them. Each of these activities provides benefits to both the customer and developer in ensuring the project is moving in the right direction. All of these activities occur in conjunction with the requirement definition and analysis phase of the software development life cycle (SDLC). This includes establishing and implementing a process for maintaining control of the requirements for the remainder of the SDLC.

The working definition of each of the four activities in this section provides a starting place for understanding requirements management. Further sections of this chapter present a more detailed discussion of each of the activities.

Capturing Requirements

To take a product from concept to reality, the expertise and desires of the client are conveyed to the system analyst. The system analyst in turn must assess the information in relationship to the desired technology and then prepare a feasible customer and developer plan for product development. The feasibility plan is used as the basis for discussions. The requirements are the output product from these discussions wherein the customer and development experts expose the must have vs. the it would be nice to have items while considering the available schedule and budget.

Organizing Requirements

Organizing the requirements by project, system, and subsystem gives both the customer and the developer clear requirements that should be tracked during the development effort. Organizing the requirements in this manner supports simultaneous development work in multiple functional areas, which increases productivity and improves quality. Organizing requirements

0-8493-1190-X/02/$0.00+$1.50
© 2002 by CRC Press LLC

within these classifications additionally ensures that potential risks to the project can be identified and assigned more easily to the right people, ensuring that viable mitigation of the risks are planned. Organizing the requirements by project, system, and subsystem also helps control change, provides a better definition of what must be tested, and makes sure necessary functionality does not fall through the cracks.

Reviewing Requirements

It is important that the requirements be reviewed by the right personnel to ensure that all of the necessary items have been included and planned for development. When the requirements are organized, the selection of review groups is easier and the review will be better because the right people are assigned to evaluate and approve the requirements. It is during the review of the requirements that the customer gains significant insight as to the developer's true understanding of the properties the product must possess to ensure success in the marketplace. Skewed perceptions can be corrected at minimal cost at this point in the project.

Controlling Requirements

Once the initial set of requirements has been evaluated and approved, the course of action for moving the project to completion can be planned meaningfully. Impacts to the project plan are minimized by controlling changes to the requirements. The value in controlling changes to the requirements is that the project stays on course, thereby reducing or eliminating cost overruns and schedule delays. The other significant benefit occurs as the system is tested because everyone who has been involved in the project has been able to understand what requirements will be tested and what the product will have, do, and use. In other words, the boundaries established by the requirements can be used to measure the success of the development effort.

CAPTURING REQUIREMENTS

In March 1996, Frank McGrath addressed the problem of capturing requirements at a meeting of the Project Management Association in Tysons Corner, Virginia. In summary, McGrath pointed to the software community as being simply arrogant in starting development work without having requirements nailed. By example, he pointed to the building trades. What general contractor would start construction of a building with a requirement that states, "It will be a big building with offices inside?" What does that mean? What is the requirement for a manufacturing plant in which airplanes will be made or a skyscraper where many businesses will reside?

McGrath continued using the general contractor example, pointing to the fact that the general contractor finds out not only what type of building, but also what materials need to be used in the construction of the building. The general contractor then finds out what tolerances are needed in the materials and so on and so forth. Given some thought, it is easy to see how important clarifications are in defining requirements in the building trades. They are no less important in the software business, but all too often software developers wrongly feel that they deal in the creative zone where it is far more difficult to articulate and capture requirements effectively.

It may not be as hard as it seems. Software developers must first remember that they are capturing people's dreams, not what they need — though they may need it — not what they want — though they may want it. Software developers are capturing their dreams, their true desires. In this respect it is very personal for each person participating in the requirements definition process. They may argue over minor points and fail to communicate what is going on in their mind. A leader of the requirements definition process can overcome this by:

1. Conducting regularly scheduled meetings with a previously distributed agenda so that the right people attend and the attendees know what will be covered and what is expected of them.
2. Structuring each meeting to ensure that previously identified requirements are documented for review and analysis, allowing new requirements to be submitted and recorded for review at a future meeting and making sure that requirements that are out-of-scope for a specific project or release of a project are identified and tabled.
3. Making sure that each person at the meeting has an opportunity to speak and be heard without criticism or fear of being laughed at or made to feel dumb or stupid.
4. Spending time to make certain the information communicated as a requirement is meaningful; that is, make sure everyone understands that the big building is a tall skyscraper and not a warehouse or a manufacturing plant.

Although it may appear that a significant effort is being spent to capture and review requirements, there is a big pay-back if the requirements are identified correctly up front. The cost of correcting software for missing or incorrect requirements goes up significantly the later in the development process the error is found.

These unattractive and very costly statistics can be brought down significantly when the ambiguities common enough to everyday conversation and exaggerated by the separate areas of expertise brought to the table by the customer and the developers are eliminated. Use the helpful hints and techniques proven over time by software professionals such as Donald Gause and Gerald Weinberg, who are noted in the field of requirements definition. The result will be a negotiated understanding of the customer's desire and a certainty that everyone involved in the project is working toward completion of the same system. Start by removing ambiguities at the statement level.

Clarifying Ambiguous Requirements

Ambiguity at the statement level is tested through verbalization of visualizations. For example, if the requirement is to build a structure to protect a human against wind and rain and snow and ice is given to five people, each of the five people may have a different visualization. One might visualize a kiosk at a bus station, another a three-bedroom ranch house, and someone else a nice shiny Rolls Royce. As people at the meeting explain their visual image of what has been stated, clarification can be made, and agreement can be reached.

So, how does one visualize the following requirement statement: The user will be able to store one or more windows in a scrapbook, and how does one express that vision. The visualization here may not be as obvious, but one certainly would want to know if anyone around the conference table is getting the impression that they will be able to store windows into a scrapbook the way files can be stored in directories for indefinite periods of time. So, test the statement:

- What is the customer interpreting the statement to mean?
- What does the developer intend the capability, i.e., a brief functional description of what will be implemented to satisfy the requirement, to be?
- What are the system requirements, i.e., How many windows will be stored? How long are they required to be stored? What are the retrieval time requirements for different types of storage?

Document the negotiated understanding that is reached between the customer and the developers regarding the requirement(s) and how it (they) will be implemented.

At the word level, use synonyms and comparisons to clarify and ensure the correct interpretation of what is being said. For example, if the requirement is initially stated as:

A big clock will be displayed ...

It should be restated as:

A large clock will be displayed ...

Start by using the synonym large for the word big. Then, clarify the use of the word large again using a specific comparison, i.e., does large mean it fills the entire screen or just half of the screen? Finally, restate the requirement to spell out the specific size or range of sizes to which the customer and the developers have agreed. In this way, the understanding by both the customer and the developer are consistent. There will be no surprises when the product is presented as complete. More importantly, the incidents of on-the-spot fixes that add up so quickly at the end of a project will be reduced significantly.

Determining Scope

The value of eliminating compound requirements can be seen at all levels, from upper management to project developers and from the customer to the quality assurance team. Only after compound requirements are eliminated can the true scope of the project be assessed, change control applied, testing be correctly managed, and meaningful metrics be collected.

A simple example of a compound requirement is: The user must be able to add, delete, and modify a row. What causes this to be a compound requirement are the multiple things that the user must be able to do. In determining the scope of the work, the compound requirement will be considered as one unit of work, when in fact to provide this capability within the system it may take three separate programs to make it happen. Additionally, if any portion of a compound requirement encounters a problem during testing, the entire requirement is shown as not satisfied. This can skew test result metrics.

To rid a project of compound requirements, identify the statements within each requirement, then make each statement a standalone requirement. This action not only helps to clarify the requirement, but it also provides a more accurate view of the size and scope of the project. The other thing that eliminating compound requirements does is allow requirement dependencies to be identified and tied together in a database.

ORGANIZING REQUIREMENTS

Now that the requirements are single-statement directives, it becomes easy to classify them by type. The three major types of requirements are:

- Project requirements
- System requirements
- Subsystem requirements (also referred to as application, module, or functional requirements)

Project Requirements

Project requirements are the customer-imposed schedules, deliverables, and resources under which the project will operate. One example of a project requirement is "Each project will have an ABC company representative assigned to the production team." Another might be: "The product will be delivered not later than (NLT) July 10, 199N." Still another might be "Monthly Status Reviews will be conducted."

System Requirements

System requirements are the performance, storage, protocols, standards, and conventions that must be met by the product. These requirements guide the development effort. Being able to reference easily the requirements list for system requirements ensures that decisions made by developers always will consider the goals for the product in setting down the development direction and methods.

Subsystem Requirements

Subsystem requirements are the product-specific content, capabilities, limitations, and look and feel of the planned end product. It is advisable to classify further functional requirements into logical groups of requirements, for example, purchasing and forecasting. Still further organizations may desire to ensure that art requirements, text requirements, and action requirements are identified and then arranged together in the flow of the logical grouping selected.

By classifying requirements, three very important things are accomplished. The first of these is staff composition because it should be clear what skill sets are needed. The second is that it becomes easier to see what test scenarios need to be developed and when the test scenarios provide many (requirements) to one (test) opportunities and when multiple tests may be required to demonstrate the full capability of one requirement. This type of information helps in planning the overall testing effort because the scope of the effort can be predicted more accurately thus ensuring the machines, networks, and people needed for testing are in place when the system is ready to be tested.

The third thing classifying requirements is to simplify the change controls essential to managing requirements. The value in this is that during the course of the project should technology shift or requirements change, the total impact of the change can be assessed because all components of the change will be identified early in the process. Neither the customer nor the developer will get to the end of the project thinking all is well only to find out that something fell through the cracks. The requirements list becomes easy to reference, maintain, and use when the requirements are classified by type.

Documenting Requirements

Documenting for maximum benefits means less work later. For example, when the different types of requirements are gathered and a numbering scheme ensuring distinction between the types of requirements is used;

tracking and impact analysis is more easily performed. This distinction is important in tracking the requirements for compliance, gathering data related to the various types of requirements for analysis of performance, and quality. Being able to gather this information means developers readily and consistently can offer customers documented quality improvement on both technical and business fronts. Measurable data will become available from which determinations can be made regarding the size and scope of projects and the impact of technology issues.

Whether the classified requirements list is stored in a database, word processing tables, or a spreadsheet, it is important that it is located and formatted in such a way that it is accessible and useable to the majority of people on the team. The requirements list is a project asset and should be thought of as such. Management, the development team, and the customer have a ready tool for determining what is within the scope of the project and what is not.

REVIEWING REQUIREMENTS

When the requirements analysis has been completed and the requirements have been organized, then three types of reviews need to be conducted:

- Peer reviews
- Management reviews
- Customer reviews

Peer Review

Peer review is made up of senior-level system designers and testers, preferably those who have had little or no involvement in the definition and analysis of the requirements for this project. They bring the objectivity needed at this point to identify ambiguous requirements, nontestable requirements and potential risks, and to make recommendations for improvement in the documentation of the requirements. Using the insight gained from the peer review, the system development team should get additional information from the customer as needed to develop corrections. When the proposed corrections have been developed, a management review should be conducted.

Management Review

Management review is the formal presentation of the requirements in terms of budget, schedule, and risks for the project. Executives, senior managers, marketing and account representatives, and quality assurance specialists need to participate in this review. The review itself should be structured to ensure that the output from it results in firm commitments to the creation and implementation of the detailed project plan for meeting the requirements. If this commitment is not strong at this point, it is an indication that one or more of the requirements needs to be further assessed for feasibility within the defined scope of the project budget and schedule. This assessment must be made with the customer to achieve consensus on the requirements that will be met by the proposed system. When management has reviewed the requirements list and all modifications and adjustments have been made, a formal customer review should be scheduled and conducted.

Customer Review

Customer review should include the management review counterparts on the customer side, the customer project team, the development project team, and full quality assurance representation. The purpose of this review is to finalize the requirements list. This is accomplished by presenting the fully analyzed requirements list, presenting and explaining the differences between the requirements list and the initial wish list the customer presented, and providing the documentation that supports the information presented. The customer review should result in a requirements list that clearly states what the system will do, how it basically will operate, and what users can expect in terms of usability, ergonomics, and learning curves. At the conclusion of the customer review, all of the players who have a stake in the system development effort should be in agreement about what the project, system, and subsystem requirements are. The requirements list thus is finalized and baselined to ensure control of the requirements throughout the life of the project.

CONTROLLING REQUIREMENTS

Controlling the requirements may be the most important aspect of achieving success on a project and ensuring the full usability of the developed system. Control does not mean that there are never any changes to the original baselined requirements. It does mean that all of the stakeholders in the project are informed of and involved in a requirements control process that eliminates the single greatest threat to any system development project — requirements creeping.

Requirements creeping can and probably should be viewed as a villainous saboteur who, like a chameleon, takes on many different colors. This villain strikes out with only one purpose: get someone, anyone on the project, to make a change in the baselined requirements without assessing the impact and logical disposition of the change and informing all parties of the need for the change. To eliminate requirements creeping:

- Make certain that there are baseline requirements.
- Have a change control method in place for handling any type of modification to baselined requirements.

- Make certain that all people involved in the project, both on the publishing side and on the development side, understand the process and methods used to baseline requirements and to affect change to the baselined requirements.

The requirements list baseline is established following the customer review meeting and should be given a unique identifier at that time. It must be distributed to all participants as the only requirements list to be used as design work commences. The identifier should have provisions for indicating the version or edition or release. If an approved change is made to the requirements list, the identifier must be updated and the revised requirements list distributed to all participants.

Controlling the Change of Requirements

For example, say that as the design of the Graphical User Interface (GUI) gets underway, the designer realizes that there is no requirement for the GUI to provide transportation to the query subsystem, a function the designer thinks will be essential to the user. Using the requirements control process, the designer does not add the function (which would creep the requirements). Instead, the designer prepares an incident/problem report that notes the fact that there is not a requirement for the GUI to query transportation and notifies the keeper of the requirements list, who may be the quality assurance manager, the engineering manager, the project manager, or someone in configuration management.

The information provided by the designer is assessed for project impact and disposed of in one of the following ways:

1. The change is approved as a necessary component of the current system development effort. In this case, the schedule and budget will be assessed for impact. If the schedule must be maintained, a management decision will need to be made regarding adding a resource to do the programming, increasing hours for one or more existing programmers, or contracting out that piece of work. If the budget is already at bare bones and the schedule must be met, then the increased hours most likely will be included in the nonpaid exempt employee overtime category, but management must realize that they are increasing the project risk.

2. The change is approved as a modification to the current system to be implemented in the first software release subsequent to the initial delivery of the system. A work-around may or may not need to be developed for the initial implementation. The point is to make sure that there is agreement with the customer as to who is going to develop the work-around should it be needed. The other critical point to be made here is that the change control records and the process for using

them must be implemented so that items such as this do not fall through the cracks as development for the next release gets underway.

3. The change is approved as a potential future enhancement to the current system without a specific schedule for implementation. Similar to the change approved as a modification, the change control records must be precise to ensure that the decision specific to this change is not lost. Because this change will not become part of the next release, it will go back to wish list status and be carried through the entire requirements process. The reason for this is to make certain that the development of this enhancement is scheduled for work and delivery within the context of all other existing work.

4. The change is rejected. This closes out the incident report. No work is scheduled now or for the future. There may be many reasons for this type of a response. Whatever the reason, the rejection action and the reason for rejection should be recorded within the change control process. A record of all closed changes is maintained to ensure accurate project history and to provide the rationale on why the change was rejected.

Whenever any software is released to the customer, the release should follow a defined release management process that includes the specific identification of all of the components that are included in the software release as well as the components that are assumed to be present (i.e., system software). This identification also should include the specific incident/problem reports that were corrected by the release and any work-arounds that were developed for the known problems that exist in the software.

Section 2
Critical Factors for Project Quality

Chapter 10
Using Project Management to Become ISO 9000 Certified

Ralph L. Kliem

The information systems (IS) community has always had a concern about quality. The pressure for delivering systems of high quality has never been greater. Time-to-market of products is accelerating; customers want the product faster and better. Offshore programming and outsourcing agreements threaten to produce systems not only cheaper but better. Software solutions can arise that can make the existing state-of-the-art obsolete virtually overnight.

The IS community is also going through rigorous self-analysis. The Software Engineering Institute's (SEI) Capability Maturity Model (CMM) is raising questions about the way IS shops build and deliver quality system.

Self-analysis is being forced from somewhere distant and is growing in popularity. The pressure is for IS organizations to seriously consider becoming ISO 9000 certified. As companies, in general, and computing, in particular, become more global in nature, the IS community will increasingly face pressure to comply with the ISO 9000 series.

Project management plays an important role for becoming ISO 9000 certified. According to a study of ISO 9000 certified firms in Colorado, project management would have made their certification easier and more efficient. The Colorado firms cited teamwork and project management as the two most important lessons learned; the former is really project management, too. The firms also emphasized the need for training, greater appreciation of time required, and better project management. Arguably, the first and second items are project management-related, too.[1]

BASICS OF ISO 9000

The ISO 9000 series, developed by the International Organization for Standardization (ISO), are standards that provide a framework for developing quality systems. Currently, five standards exist:

Standard	Subject
9000	Guidelines on using standards
9001	Design, manufacture, install, and service of systems
9002	Production and installation
9003	Final inspection and testing
9004	Quality management

In 1991, the ISO developed ISO 9000-3 for software development. It identifies quality controls (QC) for developing, supplying, and maintaining software; focuses on conforming to requirements throughout the life cycle of software; calls for defining, documenting, and communicating policies and objectives on quality; and requires reviews, inspections, defined responsibilities, version control, and other QC-related disciplines being in place. These QC disciplines and others should be documented in a quality plan.

Putting such QC disciplines in place is, however, not enough. The standards require the companies to be certified, too, via a registrar who audits for compliance with the standards. If it passes the review, the firm becomes ISO 9000 certified, subject to periodic recertifications.

The ISO 9000 series is gaining recognition in the IS community. Firms like Sybase and Hewlett–Packard have already embraced ISO certification.

PROJECT MANAGEMENT AND ISO 9000

A business endeavor must meet three criteria to be a project. It must have a fixed duration, require performing a sequence of tasks, and produce something once the tasks are complete.

Becoming ISO certified satisfies all three criterions. Becoming certified typically takes up to one-and-a-half years: a series of tasks must occur (e.g., conducting pre-audits) and "deliverables" (e.g., quality control policy) and a final product (e.g., ISO 9000 certification) are produced.

Being classified a project is an academic exercise. What is really important is that the ISO project completes successfully. Project management is the way to obtain that result.

Project management is the systematic application of concepts, techniques, and tools to plan, organize, control, and lead a project. Plan, organize, control, and lead are the four basic functions of project management. Planning is deciding in advance what the project will achieve, determining the steps to execute, and identifying when to start and stop. Organizing is orchestrating resources cost-effectively to execute the project plan. Controlling is assessing how well the project manager uses the plans and organization to meet project goals and objectives. Leading is influencing people to achieve the goals and objectives of the project.

PLANNING

Planning consists of seven basic elements:

1. Statement of work (SOW)
2. Work breakdown structure (WBS)
3. Estimating
4. Scheduling
5. Resource allocation
6. Budgeting
7. Risk control

Statement of Work

The SOW is a contract between the person performing the tasks and the internal or external customer of the product. From an ISO 9000 perspective, the customer is frequently an internal one (such as the manager of an IS department) and the people performing the tasks (e.g., ISO 9000 implementation team members).

The SOW describes the project scope, major responsibilities, deliverables and final product description, constraints, and signatures. Below is an outline of an SOW with corresponding examples:

I. Goal
  A. Obtain ISO 9000 certification of all IS development processes
II. Objectives
  A. Complete ISO certification by August 28
  B. Document 100 percent of the software development processes
III. Product/Service Description and Deliverables
  A. Develop and publish quality manual
  B. Document all as-is and to-be processes prior to certification
  C. Train entire IS development staff on new processes
IV. Constraints
  A. Training cannot exceed 40 hours per person
  B. Third party registration cannot exceed $50,000
V. Responsibilities
  A. Implementation team
  B. Executive steering committee

CRITICAL FACTORS FOR PROJECT QUALITY

Work Breakdown Structure

The WBS is a top-down, hierarchical list of the deliverables and the steps to produce them. The purpose is to identify the major deliverables and the final product and list the tasks to build them. An effective WBS has a level of granularity that makes estimating and tracking of tasks meaningful, usually requiring less than two weeks of effort. The WBS is based upon the content in the SOW and the input from the people who perform the work. Once complete, the project manager does estimating, develops schedules, and allocates resources. See Exhibit 1 for an example of a WBS.

Estimating

With a good draft of the WBS, the project manager estimates the effort required to complete each of the lower level items in the work breakdown structure. Often, estimating is highly subjective, reflecting extreme optimism or pessimism. Rarely do estimates emerge realistic. To overcome the effects of extreme optimism or pessimism, a formula — called the three-point estimate technique — exists to compensate for the tendency towards exaggeration. For each low level item, the project manager looks at three variables: most optimistic, most pessimistic, and most likely. The most pessimistic is the time required to complete a task under the worst conditions. The most optimistic is the time under the best conditions. The most likely is the time under "typical" or "normal" conditions. Next, the variables are plugged into a formula:

$$\text{Expected Time} = \frac{\text{Most Pessimistic} + 4\,(\text{Most Likely}) + \text{Most Optimistic}}{6}$$

$$\text{Example:} \quad \frac{120 \text{ hours} + 4\,(80 \text{ hours}) + 60}{6} = 83.33 \text{ hours}$$

After estimating, the project manager translates the figures into flow, or work, days to develop schedules. The time is typically divided into units of eight hours.

Scheduling

With the SOW, WBS, and estimates complete, the project manager can draft an integrated, or network, schedule for the project. The integrated schedule is based upon the logical relationship among lower level tasks in the WBS and the time estimates; the result is a calculated set of dates for each task. These dates are: early start date, early finish date, late start date, and late finish date. Early start date is the earliest time that a task can start and early finish is the earliest time to finish; late start is the latest that a task can finish and late start is the latest time to finish. These dates become significant because they determine not only the flexibility in starting and completing

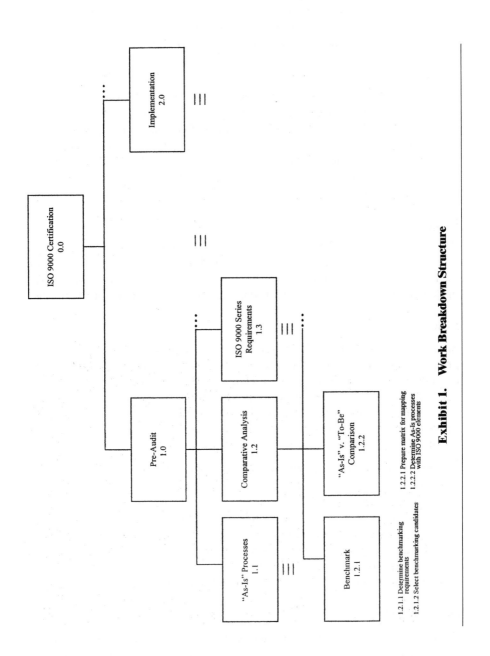

Exhibit 1.   Work Breakdown Structure

tasks but also the critical path. It is the path in the network diagram that is the longest and has the tasks that cannot slide. Sliding these tasks will jeopardize the project completion date. "Float" is the degree that a task can slide past its completion date; tasks on this path have the least float. Exhibit 2 is part of a network diagram for an ISO 9000 project.

Resource Allocation

The initial draft of the network diagram is sufficient, but it is unusable until resources are applied against it. The project manager looks at the available resources and allocates to each task. This allocation is mainly manpower-based for an ISO 9000 project; the project manager assigns people according to their education, knowledge, and experience. The project manager may, in turn, adjust estimates, schedule logic, or dates to reflect the expertise level of those people assigned to a task.

Budgeting

Calculating costs is relatively easy upon completion of resource allocation. The project manager, using the project database, calculates the direct and overhead costs for each task and the grand total for the entire project. The project manager then has a realistic estimate of the entire cost for the project.

Risk

All projects, even ISO 9000 projects, are not without risks. As with other projects, these risks, or vulnerabilities, can lay waste to the best plans. The project manager who performs a risk assessment can determine where some of the vulnerabilities may occur and adjust the estimates, schedules, and resource allocations accordingly. Doing a risk assessment enables the project manager to effectively control the project. Some common risks facing an ISO 9000 project include:

- Failing to agree upon what is an acceptable level of defects
- Failing to follow a standardized audit process
- Failing to receive ISO 9000 certification
- Lacking "buy-in" from key project participants
- Lacking senior management support or commitment
- Not agreeing upon a measurement criteria
- Not identifying a process owner
- Using an ill-defined criterion for benchmarking

ORGANIZING

Having good plans in place are necessary but have little use if no infrastructure exists to support them. A project manager can put an infrastructure in place by instituting one or more of these elements: team organization, responsibility matrix, project manual, meetings, and software.

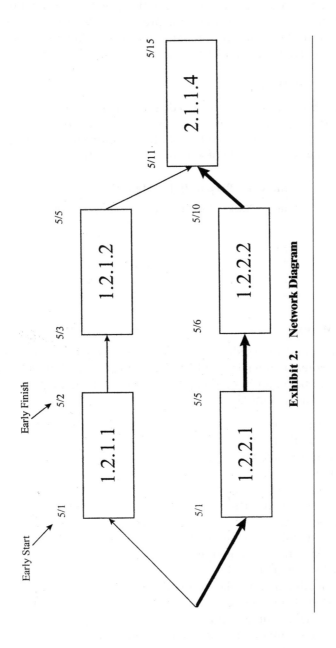

Exhibit 2.   Network Diagram

Team Organization

Assembling a group of people is not enough to form a project team. Structure is necessary so that the synergy of the group is meaningfully captured and directed. An effective way to capture that synergy is to organize the team into relationships that reflect clear reporting and authorities and reflect that arrangement, as shown in an organization chart (Exhibit 3).

Responsibility Matrix

The work breakdown structure and resource allocation provide the basis for developing a matrix showing responsibilities for tasks. The project manager decides whether to distribute the entire matrix or selected portions. Below is an example of a responsibility matrix:

Exhibit 4. Responsibility Matrix

Name → Task	Banks	Valdez	Rogers	Franks
1.2.1.1	X		Lead	X
1.2.1.2		X	X	
1.2.2.1		Lead	X	
1.2.2.2	X	Lead	X	

Project Manual

Ideally, team members should have the necessary information to do their work. A project manual is an effective way to provide that information. The manual can be either in hard copy or electronic form. Here is an outline of a typical project manual:

   I. Introduction
       A. About this manual
       B. How to keep it current
  II. Plan
       A. Statement of work
       B. Responsibilities
       C. Schedules
 III. Documentation standards
       A. Narrative documentation
       B. Flowcharting
  IV. Procedures and policy statements
   V. ISO 9000 guidelines
  VI. Internal documentation
 VII. Service support functions and responsibilities
VIII. Documentation
       A. Reports
       B. Forms

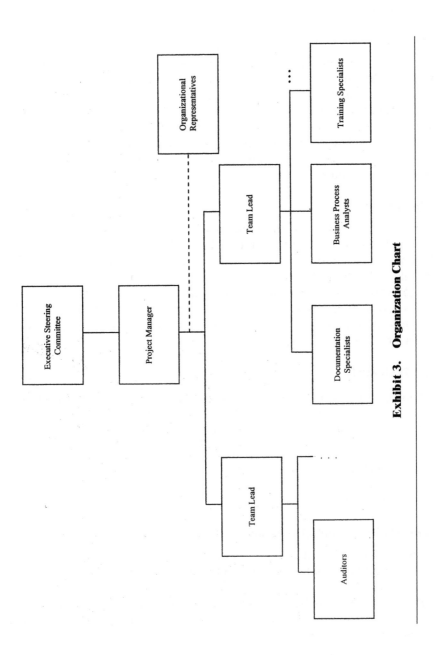

Exhibit 3. Organization Chart

Meetings

In a project environment, the project manager conducts three basic meetings: checkpoint review, status review, and staff. The checkpoint review meeting is held after the occurrence of an important event, such as the completion of a major milestone in the schedule. The focus of this meeting is to learn what has and has not gone well and decide whether to proceed. The status review meeting is held regularly, i.e., weekly. Its purpose is to assess schedule status, cost, and quality. The staff meeting, to communicate and share information, is held regularly.

Software

The larger the project the more important is the role of software. Because the number of tasks and their interrelationships become more complex, the compilation and analysis of data require speed and reliability. Some popular, reliable project management packages include *Microsoft Project* and *Primavera Project Planner.* Using software requires, however, a caveat. The software does not manage a project — the project manager does. The software is only a tool, like the project manual or schedule, to attain desired results.

CONTROLLING

A plan lays the basis for good project management but does not guarantee success. A project manager must still ensure that the plan is being followed — that he is controlling the project. Controlling involves these four elements:

1. Status collection and assessment
2. Tracking and monitoring
3. Contingency planning
4. Replanning

Status Collection and Assessment

To determine how well a project is progressing requires collecting useful data about its overall performance. In other words, status collection. Collecting data is, however, not enough. The project manager must also assess performance vis à vis the plan. In other words, status assessment. Status collection and assessment work together to help the project manager track and monitor project performance.

Because ISO 9000 projects last one to one-and-a-half years, on average, a tendency exists to give status collection and assessment a lower priority than "doing the work." Relegating status collection and assessment to such a level can lead to an illusion of optimism and, subsequently, to grave oversights that require a rush to successfully complete the project. It is best to set a regular time for collection and assessment to constantly review performance.

Tracking and Monitoring

To assess project performance, the project manager looks at the past and into the future. Looking at the past, or tracking, gives the project manager an understanding of where the project is currently and uncovers any problems or oversights. Looking into the future, or monitoring, gives the project manager an understanding of where the project will be in the future based on previous performance to date. Together, tracking and monitoring enable the project manager to "get a bearing" on the project and steer it in the right direction.

Tracking and monitoring play a key role in certification, especially if time-to-market is essential. If tracking and monitoring reveal a negative condition, the project manager can quickly determine if and what action is necessary to improve project performance.

Contingency Planning

As mentioned earlier, the project manager performs a risk assessment. Not only is the risk assessment necessary for estimating and scheduling, it is also important to respond appropriately to circumstances not directly incorporated in the project plan. Contingency planning enables the project manager to respond to an expected circumstance that had a low likelihood of occurrence (e.g., failure to implement certain quality control processes).

Replanning

Occasionally, circumstances arise on a project that were not anticipated and renders the plan obsolete. Replanning then becomes necessary. But replanning is not free. It slows the momentum of the project, reduces production, increases costs, and adds anxiety to team members. It is important, therefore, that the project manager determine the impact of replanning before taking such a drastic action.

LEADING

Although listed as the fourth function of project management, it is by no means the least important. Arguably, it could be the most important for it is the only function that occurs simultaneously with the other functions.

CRITICAL FACTORS FOR PROJECT QUALITY

Leading a project requires:

- Providing vision
- Communicating
- Maintaining direction
- Motivating
- Being supportive
- Building a team atmosphere

Providing Vision

The project manager leads by giving team members a sense of purpose and direction. To some extent, the project manager does so by developing an SOW and a schedule. The project manager must also continuously "paint" that vision in the minds of the project participants.

This is no small task for a project manager of an ISO 9000 project. Because of the length of the project and the nebulous nature of "certification," people have a difficult time keeping the vision clearly in the forefront. The project manager must assume the responsibility for keeping that vision ever present in everyone's mind.

Communicating

People on the project team must be continually kept abreast about their own work, in particular, and about the project, in general. The project manager plays the central role to keep communications ongoing. To some extent, the project manager does that by holding meetings, distributing the project manual, and publishing responsibility matrices.

Communicating for ISO 9000 projects is not, however, as easy as it might seem. The number of participants can be large and their backgrounds diverse, especially as the size of the organization to be certified increases. The project manager must then be able to communicate the same messages to different audiences.

Maintaining Direction

Plans serve absolutely no function unless people follow them. The project manager leads by following up on whether the project occurs according to plan. However, the project manager also ensures that all activities focus on achieving the goals and objectives of the project. The project manager does that largely by holding status review meetings, collecting information about status, and taking necessary corrective actions.

ISO 9000 projects can easily succumb to scope creep, that is, expanding the boundaries of what a project must accomplish. Because QC processes can span multiple functions and organizations, the scope is easily expanded. The project manager must constantly perform "stewardship" to ensure that the project does not go beyond its original intent.

Motivating

First and foremost, the project manager motivates people. Motivation is difficult because the project manager frequently lacks direct control over people. For example, if many team members work in a matrix environment, the project manager lacks control. In addition, the project manager often deals with individuals and groups with greater "rank" or authority. Motivation best occurs if all the key players participate in planning, organizing, and controlling the project.

Being Supportive

The project manager facilitates by removing obstacles that hinder achieving goals and objectives. These obstacles might be something as tangible as acquiring better software or as ambiguous as political interference in the performance of specific tasks. In other words, the project manager leads by establishing an atmosphere where people can perform at their best by building an infrastructure to execute the plan.

Building a Team Atmosphere

Finally, the project manager leads by ensuring that all the people work together. On an ISO 9000 project, the number of participants can be large, especially if an entire organization seeks certification. The project team, sponsor, and customer must work together to have a successful project. To a large extent, the project manager leads in this regard by ensuring all the major participants are involved in planning and controlling the project.

POOR MILEAGE?

ISO 9000 certification is becoming popular throughout the world, in general, and the IS community, in particular, is starting to give it the same attention as it did with the SEI CMM. Ironically, many IS organizations strive for quality in an unqualitative way. They pursue certification like a poorly tuned engine; very little mileage is gained per the amount of gas consumed. The IS organization may reach its destination but at a price that far exceeds the value of the results attained. Project management is the tune-up that many ISO 9000 projects need to improve the mileage.

Note

1. *Quality Progress,* October 1995, pp. 71–72.

Chapter 11
SEI CMM or ISO 9000: Which Is Right for Your Organization?

Polly Perryman Kuver

There are two methodologies that organizations are using to declare their commitment to quality. These methodologies are ISO 9000 and SEI CMM. While these methodologies may not be thought of as tools, they each possess the characteristics of tools. That is, they are used to construct, maintain, and refine the essential elements of quality for products produced in an environment. Both the ISO 9000 Standards and the SEI CMM provide separate and distinct sets of guidelines for attaining and measuring quality. As such, each of them in their own way has caused the redefinition of quality.

No longer is quality considered an illusive term in the software community, promised by many, delivered by few. Quality is no longer just about testing software. Both the ISO 9000 Standards and the SEI CMM set forth guidelines that force the establishment of processes and procedures that extend well beyond testing and even beyond the MIS, IT, IS, and data processing organizations.

Each of these sets of guidelines, while developed independently of each other, is designed to resolve specific problems for the developers and customers. Both sets of guidelines are based on the premise that if an organization has good business procedures that can be reviewed, assessed, and graded, then the organization can be determined to produce quality products. The question it raises is: Do process and procedures, even when adhered to, really ensure quality? The answer is, unrefutably, no.

Managing quality goes beyond the institutionalization of processes. While a good quality management program will have defined and repeatable processes, what must really be defined are the quality goals as they pertain to a company's specific business. That means that before quality processes are defined, the company will have performed the analysis necessary

0-8493-1190-X/02/$0.00+$1.50
© 2002 by CRC Press LLC

to determine what the characteristics and attributes of quality are for their products, their customers, and their environment.

The success of the quality program will lie in the clear definition of productivity and quality goals, a solid explanation of the value in achieving the goals, and both formal and informal communication about all the aspects of the goals. The approach for any quality program must be commitment, consistency, and willingness to continuously improve.

To really have an active and successful quality management program, the culture of the company must be aware of the investment that will be required and the benefits of the program to them. This is accomplished by defining and measuring quality in products and people as well as processes. All of this has to be done considering the environment in which the company operates and the nature of the competition. The inherent danger in using ISO Standards and the CMM lies in producing the procedures and the paperwork that allow certification or rating to be granted without providing the education and integrating the processes into the corporate culture to ensure real quality.

Unfortunately, as consumers demand more proof of quality, organizations feel pressure to achieve the ISO 9000 certification or SEI CMM rating in order to make the company look good. More and more organizations are trying to determine how to make either or both of these quality management structures work for them. Questions are being raised, such as: What CMM level does one need to achieve in order to become ISO certified? Why does one have to choose between them?

There are even people dedicated to drawing the parallels between these two sets of guidelines. There are, however, some inherent dangers in traveling down that path. The danger is not because the two sets of guidelines are incompatible. Quite the contrary; there are parallel points between them. The problem is that they are two separate and distinct things. One is a standard that requires compliance and provides for certified proof of quality. The other is a model that can be evaluated and validated to show capability to produce quality.

Thus, it may be assumed to be correct to use CMM to achieve ISO 9000 certification! Wrong! It is not that this is an impossible task, but there are two problems that surface when this approach is attempted. First, both the ISO Standards and the CMM have unique and distinct vocabularies that are used in the program and the certification/evaluation processes. Second, the certification/evaluation processes are conducted differently. Thus, when on the CMM train, one does not automatically end up at the ISO 9000 station.

Since the costs associated with implementing either of these methodologies can be formidable, it is important to understand both methodologies and to determine, in advance, which structure best fits the needs of the organization. Then, one can build or improve on the internal quality management program from there.

ISO 9000 STANDARDS

The International Standards Organization (ISO) was created as an economic undertaking to ensure that agreements between countries have a solid value base. The primary objective of ISO, as stated in its statutes, is to promote the development of standards and related materials to facilitate the exchange of goods and services between countries and to develop cooperation within the intellectual, scientific, and economic communities. To this end, the ISO structure supports technical advisory groups and technical committees for the standardization of goods and services in 172 areas ranging from steel, tractors and machinery for agriculture and forestry, to cinematography, air quality, and biological evaluation of medical devices. The technical committees are structured into subcommittees to ensure focus on specific areas within their major field. Work is performed by working groups defined within the subcommittees and approved by the ISO general assembly.

Included within the family of technical committees, their designated subcommittees, and approved working groups are two committees more pertinent to software development and system integration than others. These technical committees are: Technical Committee 176 (TC176), and Quality Management and Quality Assurance and Joint Technical Committee 1 (JTC1), Information Technology. The implications of work performed by TC176 has had a steadily increasing impact in the software world during the past 5 to 7 years.

Within the JTC1, Subcommittee 7 (SC7) was established to address standardization of software engineering. It was in 1982 that A. Neuman, from the National Institute of Standards and Technology (NIST), petitioned ISO to change the United States membership status from observer to principal member. As a result, the number of U.S. member companies and individual technical experts participating in ISO work grew substantially. With that growth came an increase in the scope of influence on newly developed standards and the revisions of existing ISO Information Technology (IT) standards. This influence has been greatest in JTC1/SC7, which has undertaken the development of Software Engineering and System Documentation standards worldwide.

As a principal member, the United States has become a major player in JTC1/SC7. Many of the U.S. Department of Defense Standards and Military

Specifications have been introduced into global working groups as a starting point for revamping old standards and developing new standards. Software development and system documentation standards approved by the Institute of Electronic and Electrical Engineers (IEEE) have also been introduced.

Similarly, the Canadians, the British, the Germans, the Australians, and other member countries have brought their country's existing standards to the table. These existing standards are discussed, revised, and rewritten at the working group level until the international membership reaches a consensus. Only then is the work submitted to the entire subcommittee for a vote. An affirmative vote places the standard on the ISO calendar for action.

Because JTC1/SC7 and TC176 are working together to ensure that the standards for quality management adequately address software quality needs, software developers and system integrators need to take the ISO Software Engineering Standards into consideration when electing to focus their energies on achieving ISO 9000 certification.

The set of guidelines that have become known as ISO 9000 were established through the International Standards Organization. ISO 9000 is actually a series of standards. The ISO 9000 series comes complete with a certification process that conveys recognition of quality achievement for a specific ISO 9000 standard, as determined by a registered external auditing team. For instance, a company may be ISO 9001 (Model for Quality Assurance in Design/Development, Production, Installation, and Servicing) certified, ISO 9002 (Model for Quality Assurance in Production and Installation) certified, or ISO 9003 (Model for Quality Assurance in Final Inspection and Test) certified, depending on the type of product being produced. There is no such thing as a blanket ISO 9000 certification.

At first, the ISO 9000 series appeared to focus only on manufactured goods and services and many people felt this series of quality management standards would never impact the software community. Software companies have tried to convince themselves of the insignificance of ISO 9000 in the software development community. Some of the arguments that have been heard included statements that this set of standards were too loose and too vague to be able to ensure quality of developed software. This, of course, was a matter of interpretation that may have initially had some degree of truth to it. Taking this under advisement, Technical Committee (TC) 176, which was initially chartered to standardize quality management by the International Standards Organization headquarters in Geneva, Switzerland, undertook the tremendous effort of updating the ISO 9000 Standards. Some of the issues were successfully resolved in the revisions; others still beg to be addressed. Nevertheless, the argument that ISO 9000 standards are not useful in software development companies has faded away.

Another argument, used primarily in the United States, was that this standard was not going to have an effect on U.S. companies. Its popularity and usefulness in Europe and Pacific Rim companies made sense, but U.S. companies felt that they were beyond compliance. Wrong! It was not long before companies whose tentacles reach out beyond the shores of the United States began to seek ISO 9000 certification in order to maintain their competitive option in their overseas operations. The ripple effect of this led to the creation of ISO certified companies within the United States from whom quality systems, services, and products could be bought. National companies now had to reassess their own positions based on the implications of these standards on their market.

SEI CMM

The development of the Software Capability Maturity Model (CMM) was undertaken at Carnegie Mellon's Software Engineering Institute (SEI) beginning in 1986 under the sponsorship of the U.S. Department of Defense. Work on the CMM continues today; it is a living document that espouses the principles of continuous process improvement for users and applies them in maintaining the model. The goal in undertaking the development of this model was to help organizations improve their software development process.

The CMM was initially created as a tool that could be used by the Department of Defense to evaluate and measure the quality of contractors bidding to develop complex software-based systems for them. The CMM carries with it an evaluation process that defines the corporate qualification boundaries in the following five prescribed levels of software process maturity:

1. *Initial.* The software process is characterized as ad hoc and occasionally even chaotic.
2. *Repeatable.* Basic project management processes are established to track cost, schedule, and functional capabilities. The necessary process discipline is in place to repeat earlier successes on projects with similar applications.
3. *Defined.* The software process for both management and engineering activities is documented, standardized, and integrated into a corporatewide software process. All projects use a documented and approved version of the organization's process for developing and maintaining software. This level includes all characteristics defined for level 2.
4. *Managed.* Detailed measures of the software process and product quality are collected. Both the software process and products are quantitatively understood and controlled using detailed measures. This level includes all characteristics defined for level 3.

5. *Optimizing.* Continuous process improvement is enabled by quantitative feedback from the process and from testing innovative ideas and technologies. This level includes all characteristics defined for level 4.

These levels provide guidance for measuring the degree of quality of processes used within an organization for software development efforts. The entire premise of SEI CMM is directed under the principles of total quality management and continuous process improvement. As such, the model itself and related evaluation activities are under constant improvement status at the SEI.

Organizations demonstrate that they meet the goals for each level by producing evidence of work processes performed within key process areas (KPAs) of the individual projects and within the company. KPAs can be thought of as functional areas or offices, such as quality assurance, configuration management, or the office of system design and development. It is within the KPAs that specific guidelines, in the form of questions, are provided. When questions within each KPA at a given level can be answered in the positive, the answers validated with some form of physical output, and the personnel who produced the output can explain how the output is produced, how it is used, and what happens to it after it is produced, ratings are awarded.

The formal CMM evaluation process is conducted by auditors from outside the organization who want confirmed levels of capability in order to conduct business with the federal government. The audits are performed by people trained in assessing software development efforts that are based on the criteria spelled out in the model. Specific pieces of information, referred to as evidence, are validated for all functional areas of a project. The assessment training is provided by the SEI, which is associated with Carnegie Mellon University, in Pittsburgh, Pennsylvania.

Representatives from the SEI are actively promoting the concepts and methods presented in the CMM, both nationally and internationally. What was originally developed as a tool for the Department of Defense is now being used by other federal government agencies and is beginning to reach into the commercial marketplace as well.

PARALLEL POINTS BETWEEN ISO 9000 AND SEI CMM

The strongest areas in which a parallel effort may be drawn between ISO 9000-3, 9001, and CMM appear to be: peer reviews, software product engineering, software configuration management, software quality assurance, and requirements management. Practices that are more strongly addressed by the ISO quality standards than by CMM include: process change management, technology change management, defect prevention, quantitative process management, integrated software management, organization process definition, and organization process focus. It is important to note that both the ISO standards and the CMM address many additional areas wherein the relationship may be moderate to weak.

An international organization dedicated to the quality assessment process has undertaken an initiative called Software Process Improvement and Capability dEtermination (SPICE). This international organization is committed to the development of a standard for software process assessment or through the implementation of some other means in order to support companies doing business across borders.

DOES ISO 9000 CERTIFICATION OR SEI CMM RATING CONSTITUTE QUALITY MANAGEMENT?

An important element to keep in mind is that both ISO standards and SEI CMM are tools that an organization can use to achieve a true quality program. If either of the methodologies has been institutionalized and developed until a formal certification or rating has been achieved, the organization has been recognized by external sources as having a viable quality management program at the time of the audit. However, as previously stated, maintaining a quality management program goes beyond the institutionalization of processes. Because a good quality management program will have defined and repeatable processes, what must really be defined are the quality goals as they pertain to a company's specific business.

Since this is not a static environment, a company must continue to perform necessary analyses to determine what characteristics and attributes of quality are right for its products and customers as the business environment continues to evolve. This means that the quality management program must sustain activity in all areas affected by ongoing and new development projects. Personnel at all levels should be encouraged to contribute and participate in the analysis and evaluation. The culture of the company must continue to be aware of the investment and the benefits of the program to them. The quality management program should undergo continuous improvement by updating the goals as well as the processes used to achieve the goals as the environment changes. In this way, a company is assured of having a successful, ongoing quality management program.

The inherent danger in relying on tools to accomplish this, rather than culture and commitment, lies in producing the procedures and the paperwork that allow ISO certification or CMM rating to be granted without providing the education and integrating the processes into the corporate culture to ensure real quality. It is possible that neither of these methodologies is the right tool for a particular organization to follow to develop a quality management program, especially if industry standard practices and the customer base does not require the formal certification of the organization's quality by an external agency.

Chapter 12

An Almost Perfect Software Project: Using SEI Core Measurements

J.W.E. Greene

Is it possible to successfully plan and manage software development with minimal data? The Carnegie Mellon Software Engineering Institute (SEI) recommends that four core measures be made on software developments, namely, software size, time, effort, and defects.[1] Thus, the interesting question becomes whether or not software development can be done with these core measures.

The only way to prove the practicality and the benefits is to use the core measures and show the results. The background to the development set out here involves the purchasing department of a telecommunications operator (telco), which insists that all development proposals be quantified using the core measures.[2]

First, the telco checks if the proposal plan is realistic. This plan data allows a quantified baseline contract to be agreed upon. The supplier is then contractually required to provide progress data at least every month. The progress data is used to evaluate and report progress. The goal is to ensure that delivery of the full function is on time and within budget, and that the software is delivered with high reliability.

Naturally, suppliers are motivated to get the telco's business, and hence to supply the data on the plans and progress. The core data allows the telco to quantitatively assess each supplier proposal. These measures complement the SEI's Capability Maturity Model (CMM) Maturity Levels,[3] which are also used to by the telco to assess the qualitative factors in the supplier's development process.

In the development described here, it was the first time the supplier had been requested to provide the plan data using the core measures. In particular, the requirement to estimate the expected size range of software was completely new.

It is worth noting a recent report dealing with software purchasing to understand why purchasers of software development should be motivated to use the core measures.[4] This report is a highly critical evaluation of the software purchasing competence of the U.S. Federal Aviation Administration (FAA). The report sets out how the FAA is exposed commercially if it does not get and use core data.

THE PERFECT PROJECT PLAN DATA

Before the contract is awarded, the supplier is required to estimate the size range of the software to be developed. The size range is expressed in logical input statements (LIS; i.e., what is to be written by the team), and estimated as the minimum, most likely, and maximum values.[5] This takes into account the uncertainties in the requirement specification by estimating the size range of each software module. The supplier did this based on the 18 modules identified for development. The result is shown in Exhibit 1.

The proposed development staffing plan for 13 months is provided and shown in Exhibit 2.

Using the Basic Measures to Evaluate the Plan

The core plan data of size, time, and effort allows comparison against industry reference measures available for different application types.[6] In this case, the comparison is made against telecommunication (telecom) developments, and the plan can be confirmed as realistic and within the bounds of known industry values.

In the project, the basic data consists of the expected size at 32,000 LIS, the development time of 13 months, and the total effort planned at 87 person-months.

Exhibit 3 shows the main build (MB) plan (black square) compared against the telecom industry trend lines derived from a database of similar developments. The core planning data shown is also used to calculate the process productivity of the development team assumed by the supplier. In this case, the process productivity value is determined at 12.5. This is consistent with the expected industry average telecom development value of around 12.[6]

Thus, the "health check" on the plan shows that it is in line with expected industry values. The plan now forms the baseline to track and report development progress.

Exhibit 1. Module Size Range Estimate Data

Complete for all Modules		SIZE ESTIMATE IN LOGICAL INPUT STATEMENTS (LIS) All Modified and New Modules Estimated Size Range Modified + New LIS		
	Module ID	Least	Most Likely	Most
1	MOD 1	2000	2500	4000
2	MOD 2	2000	3000	6000
3	MOD 3	2800	3000	4000
4	MOD 4	1000	1200	1500
5	MOD 5	2000	3000	4000
6	MOD 6	2000	2000	3000
7	MOD 7	800	1000	1200
8	MOD 8	2000	3000	6000
9	MOD 9	1500	2000	2500
10	MOD 10	1000	2000	3000
11	MOD 11	500	1000	1500
12	MOD 12	2500	3000	4000
13	MOD 13	500	1000	1500
14	MOD 14	300	500	800
15	MOD 15	500	1000	1500
16	MOD 16	500	1000	1500
17	MOD 17	500	1000	1500
18	MOD 18	500	1000	2000
TOTAL		**22900**	**32200**	**49500**

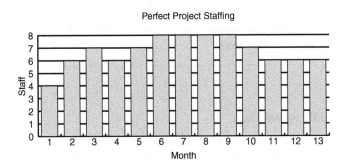

Perfect Project Staffing

Exhibit 2. The Software Main Build (MB) Time and Effort

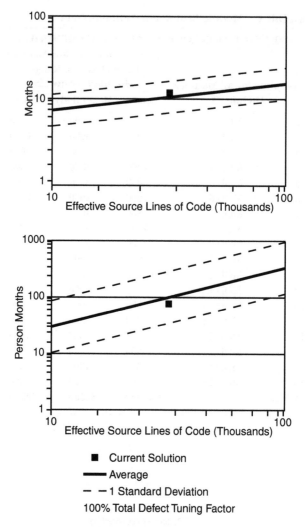

Exhibit 3. Comparing the Planned Size, Time, and Effort Against Industry Reference Measures

Contractual Progress Data

Mandatory contract progress data is returned every two weeks, and is used to track progress and identify if there is any risk of slippage. The progress data is used to perform variance analysis (a form of statistical control) against the baseline plan.

Exhibit 4.   Variance Analysis and Forecast to Complete

	Plan	Actual/Forecast	Difference
Elapsed months	13.93	13.93	0.00
Aggregate staff	2.00	2.78	0.78
Total cumulative effort (person-months)	96.08	101.47	5.39
Total cumulative cost (thousands of Netherlands Guilders)	2802.00	2959.00	157.00
Size (thousands of effective source lines of code)	35.39	35.38	–0.01
Total defect rate	3.00	5.00	2.00
Total cumulative normal defects	209.00	187.00	–22.00
Total mean time to defect (days)	7.22	4.77	–2.45
Productivity index	12.00	11.60	–0.40
MBI	2.20	2.10	–0.10

The progress data consists of:

- Staffing: how many people are allocated to the project
- Key milestones passed: for example, program design complete, all code complete
- Program module status: if it is in design, code, unit test, integration, or validation
- Program module size when the code is complete
- Total code currently under configuration control
- Software defects broken down into critical, severe, moderate, and cosmetic
- Number of planned and completed integration and validation tests

This progress data is essential for the management of software development. Without this basic data, the development is out of control.

Tracking, Reporting, and Forecasting Completion

At each reporting period, the progress data is used to determine the status of the project against the baseline plan. Advanced statistical control techniques use the data to determine if there is significant variance against the plan. If significant variance is found, then weighting algorithms enable the new completion date to be forecast, as well as forecasting the outstanding data to complete. This can include code production, defects, and tests.[6]

Exhibit 4 shows the situation in the development project after nine months.

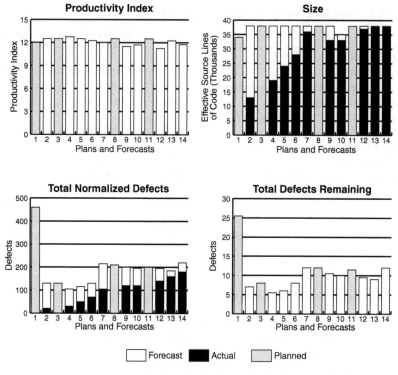

Exhibit 5. Logged Plans, Actual Data, and Forecasts

Defect behavior is of particular interest because it is following the expected theoretical curve with occasional excursions. These rate variations are smoothed out in the accompanying cumulative curve. The corresponding mean time to defect (MTTD) is indicating high reliability at delivery.

KEEPING THE AUDIT TRAIL

The system used to track the telco development allows all plans and forecasts to be logged. At the end of the project, there is a complete history in terms of plans, progress at a given date, and the corresponding forecast.

This capability is shown in Exhibit 5 where the gray lines are plans, while the black parts of lines are actual progress data with the outstanding forecast shown as white. Each entry represents a plan or forecast logged at a specific date.

Controlling Requirement Changes

At month 10 in the development, a change request was raised. Using the size baseline (this is confirmed by the actual code produced), it is practical to evaluate the impact of such a request. To do this, the total size is increased by the size estimated for the change request. The new size is used to produce a forecast of the new delivery date, as well as the additional staffing needed. The results showed that an unacceptable delay would result; thus, it was decided to postpone the change to the next release.

FINAL TESTS AND ACCEPTANCE

Once the code is complete, then the main activity in development is to execute the integration and validation tests. These tests detect the remaining software defects and characterize almost all software projects

Post-Implementation Review: Keeping and Using the History

Using the basic data described here provides visibility and control during development. In addition, it means that a complete history is available when the project completes. This is invaluable in understanding how the project performed, and to add to a growing database of (in this case) supplier performance.

Notes are also kept throughout development. These are used to investigate the history in the development, and to learn lessons for future projects.

CONCLUSIONS: THE (ALMOST) PERFECT PROJECT

In the case being discussed, all went according to plan until the final validation tests performed in the last two weeks. At this point, there was concrete evidence that high reliability would be achieved and delivery from the supplier would be on time with all the functionality required.

The final validation tests of this complex telecommunications software development included testing the interfaces to network equipment and systems. Unfortunately, the telco had not assembled one essential set of interface equipment required to perform the final validation tests. The result was that completion slipped by six weeks. This was, however, due to the telco — not to the supplier.

In all fairness, the telco did comment that the project had been among the best in its experience. The supplier had kept to the schedule and the budget, had delivered all the contracted functionality, and had achieved high reliability.

Applying the same six criteria to assess the telco's purchasing competence gives the following results:

- *Telco corporate memory:* Suppliers' plans are kept and compared with industry reference measures. Over time, detailed measures are built regarding suppliers, as their developments complete. These measures are also used to check new plans from the same suppliers.
- *Telco sizing and reuse:* Each supplier is formally required to estimate software size, including uncertainty and reuse. This size data is used to assess the plan and to quantify the risk. The size data forms part of the contract baseline, and is used to track progress in each software module and control requirement changes.
- *Telco extrapolation using actual performance:* The core progress data is used to determine progress against the contract baseline. Variance analysis determines if progress is within agreed-upon limits. If it is outside the limits, then new extrapolations are made of the outstanding time, effort, cost, defects, and actual process productivity.
- *Telco audit trails:* The initial baseline plan is recorded, together with potential alternatives. All progress data, new forecasts, and the agreed-upon contractor plan and size revisions are logged.
- *Telco integrity within dictated limits:* Each supplier proposal is evaluated against acquisition constraints of time, effort, cost, reliability, and risk. Development progress is reviewed continuously to confirm that it is within the contract limits.
- *Telco data collection and performance feedback:* The development history is captured using the core measures, including the initial proposal, contract baseline, progress data, forecasts, and revised plans. This history is used to continuously update the data repository of supplier performance, and highlight those that provide value for money.

Thus, one can see that the telco motivates suppliers to get and use the SEI core measures to their mutual advantage. This parallels the U.S. Department of Defense's motivation in applying maturity assessments to suppliers.

The telco is concerned with getting commercial benefits from exploiting the SEI core measures. There are real bottom-line benefits to using the core measures, as illustrated here.

It is a pleasant change to describe a real development success. Indeed, use of the SEI core measures facilitates success. All too often, software case studies are based on disasters, many of which could have been avoided by actively using the SEI core measures.

Notes

1. Carleton, A.D., Park, R.E., and Goethert, W.B., "The SEI core measures," *The Journal of the Quality Assurance Institute,* July 1994.
2. Kempff, G.W., "Managing Software Acquisition," *Managing System Development,* July 1998.
3. Humphrey, W.S., "Three Dimensions of Process Improvement. Part 1: Process Maturity," *CROSSTALK The Journal of Defense Software Engineering,* February 1998.
4. GAO Report to the Secretary of Transportation: Air Traffic Control GAO/AIMD-97-20.
5. Greene, J.W.E., "Sizing and Controlling Incremental Development," *Managing System Development,* November 1996.
6. Putnam, L.H., *Measures for Excellence: Reliable Software, On Time, Within Budget,* Prentice-Hall, 1992.

For further information on the practices described here, refer to Lawrence H. Putnam and Ware Myers, *Industrial Strength Software: Effective Management Using Measurement,* IEEE Computer Society Press, Los Alamitos, CA, 1997.

Chapter 13

Does Your Project Risk Management System Do the Job?

Richard B. Lanza

When a project is approved, business owners are making a conscious investment in time — and therefore, money — toward the development of the project's deliverables. Because all these owners are not project managers, it must be ensured that they understand and have promptly quantified the risks affecting the project. Normally, this should be done by the project manager, but many times, depending on the size of the project or the human resources available, anyone on the project team may step in to assess and measure risk. This chapter addresses risk management, regardless of the resource enacting the process. Although the principles discussed in this chapter could be applied to various types of projects (e.g., bridge construction, railway expansion) this chapter focuses mainly on software development projects.

GENERAL DEFINITIONS

In order to begin understanding project risk assessment, it is necessary to start from a common understanding of the following definitions.

What Is Project Management?

The generally accepted definition is presented by the Project Management Institute in its Project Management Body of Knowledge (PMBOK) as the "application of knowledge, skills, tools, and techniques to project activities in order to meet or exceed stakeholder expectations from a project."

The project lifecycle can be generally broken into three categories as follows:

0-8493-1190-X/02/$0.00+$1.50
© 2002 by CRC Press LLC

1. *Definition* — the earliest part of the project, in which the purpose and requirements are clarified.
2. *Planning* — the second part of the project, in whcih responsibility is assigned and work is scheduled.
3. *Implementation* — the final phase in which deliverables are produced to meet the project objectives.

What Is Risk Management?

One of the most beneficial tools for ensuring a successful project is risk management. The PMBOK defines risk management as "processes concerned with identifying, analyzing, and responding to project risk."

Risks can be categorized as follows:

- *Known risks* — risks whose existence and effect are known (e.g., knowing you could get a $100 ticket for driving your car past the inspection date)
- *Unknown known* — risks whose existence is known whose effect is not (e.g., driving away from an officer of the law who is trying to enforce the late inspection sticker)
- *Unknown unknowns* — risks of which there is no awareness at the present time of their existence and effect (e.g., not remembering to inspect your car and driving it past the inspection date)

How Is Risk Management Implemented?

Risk management follows a pattern that can be explained using various terms but can be quickly outlined in the following four steps:

1. *Identify.* Risks are identified but not judged as to their scope, magnitude, or urgency.
2. *Assess.* Risks are evaluated and prioritized based on their size and urgency.
3. *Respond.* All risks have a corresponding response that ranges from full acceptance of risk to prevention procedures.
4. *Document.* The identification, assessment, and response is documented to display the decision making process used in the project and to assist in knowledge sharing on future projects.

Note that risk management is normally initiated in the planning stages of a project (after the project has been properly defined) and continues routinely throughout the implementation of the project.

What Are the Common Ways to Respond to Risk?

There are three standard ways to deal with risk:

1. *Prevention* — eliminating the cause before it is an issue
2. *Mitigation* — completing tasks to lessen the risk such as implementing a new strategy or purchasing insurance so that the risk of loss is shared with outside investors
3. *Acceptance* — noting the risk and accepting any consequences it may entail

Therefore, action plans could avoid the risk completely, reduce the risk, transfer the risk (insurance), or recognize the risk and take a chance. The key determinant as to whether to take a more stringent approach (e.g., prevention) is dependent on the cost benefit relationship surrounding that risk.

Using the risk categories above in *"What is risk management?,"* the following corresponds a response for each known/unknown risk category:

- *Known risks.* If the effect of the risk is large, chart a new strategy to prevent the risk or, if the risk effect is small, mitigate or accept the risk.
- *Unknown/known risks.* First, estimate the effect of the risk and, depending on the projected risk magnitude, use the strategies explained for "known risks."
- *Unknown/unknowns risks.* As much as the likelihood and magnitude of this risk cannot be predicted, it is wise to add a contingency estimate to the project — for example, adding 10 percent of cost to a financial plan for "contingency allowances" without knowing exactly where this reserve will be applied.

COMMON RISK MANAGEMENT MISTAKES

Now that many of the definitions have been established, focus is now directed on the most common oversights in implementing a risk management system.

Most projects follow the principle of "if it ain't broke, don't fix it." As a result, small issues early in a project later become major problems. Risk management quickly transforms itself into crisis management, leading to missed deadlines or over-budget situations. These "crisis" situations generally follow a pattern in which the environment was not initially set for risk management to flourish. If only the benefits of a properly functioning risk management system were seen by business owners, they would begin to understand its necessity in any project, which leads to the number-one mistake.

Mistake 1 — The Benefits of Risk Management Are Not Presented to Business Owners

Business owners want results and many times do not want to be told of the multitude of issues affecting the completion of their project. They just want the project done, regardless of how a project team gets it done. Business owners tend to stay in a passive role when they should be actively operating in the project. Like a homeowner who is having a house built, a business owner needs to see the work site at set intervals throughout the build process, or the investment may fizzle away.

It is recommended that a meeting be called in the early stages of the project to present the concept of risk management and to explain the benefits of this process. Below is a list of key benefits of risk management listed in priority order:

- *An early warning system of issues that need to be resolved.* Risks can be identified either before the project begins or during the course of the project. Once identified, they need to be prioritized, not only as to the effect they may have on the project but also to what level they need to be presented to management for resolution. A properly functioning risk management system can provide a daily assessment of the top ten risks affecting a project for immediate resolution. If the risks are not assessed routinely, the environment is set to allow these risks to fester. In this environment, a small issue can become much larger if not a damning problem down the road.
- *All known risks are identified.* Being able to sleep well at night is tough enough these days without having to think about all the unknown risks on a project. Through a properly designed risk management system, all probable and potential issues are likely identified. Reacting to this knowledge is key, but in order to act, a risk and the corresponding resolution must first be identified.
- *More information is made available during the course of project for better decision making.* By identifying all of the problems and projected solutions associated with a project, a deeper understanding of the project's feasibility can be obtained. Especially early on, this information is invaluable and can provide more confidence to business owners and the project team that the project can be achieved on time and within budget. Further, risk management normally leads to improved communication among the project's stakeholders, which can lead to improved team management and spirit. For example, a highly challenging project leads people to bond together in order to get the job done, just as passengers on a sinking ship need to stick together in order to save themselves. Finally, this information promotes a learning process for future periods during which risks (and their resolutions) can be reviewed as raw material when similar future projects are underway.

Mistake 2 — Not Providing Adequate Time for Risk Assessment

There is no getting around the fact that risk management provides a layer of management and additional time to the project, which leads to a layer of resources — or does it? It could also be argued that by completing a proper thinking phase up front, there is an application of the rule "Measure twice, cut once." This phase should not be underestimated inasmuch as many projects tend to work under the principle of "Get it done by a certain date, regardless of the quality of the end product" rather than "Do it right the first time." In many projects, there never seems to be enough time to do it right the first time but always enough time to do it right the second time. This mistake can be avoided by getting the agreement from business owners that the cost in time to implement risk management is fully outweighed by the benefits.

Mistake 3 — Not Assessing the Most Common Risks in Projects

There are risks that are common to all projects, regardless of the industry, based on various studies and research of past project performance. Three groups of common risks are now reviewed and then summarized to arrive at a final list of common project risks.

One such group of common risks was created by NASA, which sponsored a study of 650 projects occurring during 1960 and 1970 to identify key factors that led to unsuccessful projects. The major findings were as follows:

- Poorly defined objective
- Wrong project manager
- Lack of management support
- Inadequately defined tasks
- Ineffective use of the PM process
- Reluctance to end projects

Another study as to why teams fail, completed by the Hay Group and reported in September 1997 in *USA Today,* reported the following five factors in team failure:

1. Goals unclear
2. Changing objectives
3. Lack of accountability
4. Lack of management support
5. Ineffective leadership

Now that some failure symptoms have been identified for projects at large, the reasons why IT projects fail should also be reviewed. *Rapid Development*, a book by Steve McConnell, who spent many years working with Bill Gates at Microsoft, presents several reasons (discussed in the following paragraphs) why IT projects fail. For each reason, some methods of prevention have been prescribed.

Scope Control. Scope in a project can be defined as the range of functionality the end system will provide to the user. Scope is determined by the IT system requirements which, if poorly obtained, can lead to many problems down the road. It must be noted that a scope change of one half could lead to a two-thirds decrease in the project effort. Therefore, the project manager must strive to identify the minimum requirements of the system so as to ensure that minimum level is obtained *before* adding "bells and whistles" to the system. These additional requirements that are added to the system are otherwise known as gold-plating and have detrimental effect on the project because once they are announced to be completed, the project could be viewed as a failure if they are not delivered. This is true even if the minimum requirements of the system are met. There are many techniques for increasing the chance of obtaining a complete and accurate set of requirements while also understanding which requirements are the most critical to the final system.

Prototyping. Talking about system functionality is well and good, but actually seeing the end product can provide a wealth of new knowledge. Many times, the true requirements of the system are not known until a prototype is completed. A prototype could be drawn on a piece of construction paper and have no computerized functionality behind the facade. Regardless, this tool should be used on all IT projects prior to the actual design and development of the system to ensure that a common goal is understood before major work hours are expended.

Joint Application Development. Otherwise known as JAD sessions, this occurs when a cross-functional group of all system end users (and business owners) are gathered to review the business reasons for the functional requirements of the final system (what and how the system will perform). Before a JAD session is held, a working document is completed that summarizes the business reasons and functional requirements, based on interviews with key project stakeholders. This list is then reviewed, discussed, and debated by the JAD participants while a scribe documents the discussions. The goal at the end of the JAD session is to walk away with a final set of business reasons and functional requirements that everyone agrees with (given compromises among the JAD participants). The JAD session, from a deliverable standpoint, achieves the main goal of defining requirements, but it also has some added benefits:

- Increases "buy in" from project stakeholders prior to development
- Removes responsibility from the project team to define system requirements (and gives it to end users/business owners)
- Increases the quality of the product by arriving at a complete and accurate set of requirements
- Improves project estimates by exposing any items within scope prior to the project plan creation (allowing time for proper estimation)

Overly Optimistic Schedules. In today's fast-paced environment, where time is recorded in Web years (which may amount to only a few weeks or months), development speed exacerbates any identified risk. For example, because of the need to meet a predefined project deadline, if a project team rushes the system testing phase, a system may ship with unknown bugs. In this case, the short-term goal of a deadline is reached but the long-term goal of customer satisfaction and company brand image is compromised. In the majority of cases, a predefined date leads to an optimistic schedule. For example, when Microsoft Word was being developed for the first time, it was promised in six months from its initial inception, but took well over three years to finally produce. In this case, a seasoned project manager would submit the three-year plan while the "yes-man" project manager would still be showing a six month plan well into the second year!

Poor Team Dynamic and Programmer Heroics. At the start of the millennium, the need for project managers and more specifically, technology project managers, has outstripped the supply, and this gap will only continue in the future. Employees are getting large signing bonuses, stock options, and many other benefits that are making it increasingly difficult to hire and maintain top talent. Some key traits of a solid human resource management system are as follows, in that the project team:

- Is provided challenging assignments
- Meets with a career counselor periodically to discussion long term career progression
- Receives generous acknowledgement of successes (other than more work)
- Is appropriately matched to the resource requirements of the project
- Has a backup for key tasks (for knowledge transfer and to act as a contingency if the initial person leaves the organization)
- Does not work under an overly optimistic schedule, leading to "burnout"

With regards to "burn-out" the project team should be on the lookout for team member heroics when a person is expected to complete a task that would normally require months or extensive additional assistance in a shorter timeframe. These situations may be self-inflicted or imposed by a project manager and may not only burnout the person completing the task (leading, many times, to that person's departure) but also may jeopardize the entire project.

Picking the Wrong Technology or Vendor. Business is sometimes seen as a cold, impersonal activity as reflected in the old saying, "Nothing personal — it's just business." Nothing could be further from the truth as human nature does not allow us to easily separate the personal from impersonal. This leads to decisions being made not from the standpoint of

Exhibit 1.   Common Project Risks

Top Risk	Quick Response Description
• Unclear or changing goals	• Complete prototype and JAD sessions to ensure proper requirements are gathered
• Lack of management support	• Ensure business owners understand they must be active rather than passive participants to guarantee project success
• Overly optimistic schedules	• Review schedules for preset deadlines (without regard to reality) and suggest more appropriate timelines be applied for key tasks
• Inappropriate project team/team dynamic	• Assign proper resources for the task based on the job responsibilities and ensure employee satisfaction through improved human resource practices
• Selecting the wrong vendor/technology	• Complete quantitative decision analysis for all major vendor or technology decisions

quantitative analysis but because "the vendor rubbed me the right way." Many vendors have surmised that you do not need the best product or service — just great advertising and salespeople. Therefore, project teams should be wary of decisions that are based solely on personal judgment rather than on a quantitative decision analysis using a generally accepted method (e.g., Kepner Tregoe). A due diligence process should have been completed for all major vendor and technology decisions, and for the short list of key vendors, a reference check should be performed and documented.

One example of a technology decision gone sour was a company (that will remain nameless) that believed it could settle its Y2K troubles by selecting a package that would, in one weekend, fix the Y2K problem. The cost of the product was high, but it would save months if not years of development and testing — well worth the cost. It was even based on a principle that made sense to even those who were not technology savvy. Months went by, and no Y2K work was completed because a solution was always available — or was it? Once the millenium was near, the product's capabilities were further analyzed and, more importantly, existing customer were surveyed. It was determined through these interviews that the product did in fact do its work in a weekend. But, it then took numerous other months to reprogram many of the existing programs to understand the change in the system. Without a detailed analysis, these facts may not have been uncovered until the last hour, leading to tragedy.

Summary of Common Risks to be Assessed in Projects. From the three lists (and the author's experience) of common project risks, a correlation can be seen, which leads to the top five risks affecting project success (see Exhibit 1). These risks should be reviewed on all projects to ensure they are being appropriately addressed.

Exhibit 2.   Critical Risk Information

Risk Management Step	Information
Identify	Risk description
Identify	Identified by
Identify	Identified when
Assess	Quantify Impact (funds allocated, project work hours, or project duration)
Assess	Quantify likelihood (e.g., likely = 85 percent, Probable = 60 percent, and Possible = 25 percent)
Assess	Calculate loss (impact * likelihood)
Assess	Quantify urgency (related to the need for timely action)
Respond	Proposed solution (could be prevention, mitigation, or acceptance strategy)
Respond	Person(s) assigned to complete solution
Respond	Date of expected resolution
Respond	Work hours expected to resolve risk
Respond	Approver that ensures the resolution properly met the risk
Respond	Contingency plan (plan to enact if proposed solution does not materialize)
Respond	Trigger event (event for which it is determined that contingency plan needs to be enacted)

Mistake 4 — Not Identifying and Assessing Risks in a Standardized Fashion

As presented previously, there are four steps to implementing a risk management system: identify, assess, respond, and document.

Tracking System. One popular method of tracking risks is to begin by having project team members submit their issues in a common centralized database. Although this may sound difficult to establish, one such database could be a simple Excel spreadsheet with various columns for the required information. Exhibit 2 contains sample fields that could be maintained in the database.

Monitoring. Once the risks have been identified, they should be monitored weekly (possibly even daily in critical times). The desired result of such analysis is to attempt to ensure 100 percent visibility into the project. One benchmark to follow is to ensure that the top three risks are analyzed on a weekly basis (even better if the top ten risks are analyzed). To assist the monitoring process, it is helpful to segregate risks between those that relate to the project (which should mainly be reviewed by the project team with some oversight by business owners) and those to which only the business owners can respond.

REVIEW ASSESSMENT AND CONCLUSION

Given the top four mistakes that are made in maintaining a risk management system, the following questions can be arrived at, asked of the project team, and documented as to the responses to them. In addition to asking the questions, a walk-through should be performed to *observe* key risk management components. The major questions are as follows:

- Have the benefits of risk management been properly communicated to business owners?
- Has adequate time been provided for a risk assessment phase of the project?
- Has a specific individual been assigned to ensure that project risk management is completed?
- Has project scope been finalized *and documented* through either a prototype or a JAD session?
- Have project schedules been reviewed by an independent party for symptoms of schedule optimism (e.g., preset deadlines)?
- Based on the tasks at hand in the project, have the appropriate personnel been assigned, both at the project manager level and at the project task level?
- Have employee satisfaction techniques been employed, such as career counseling and acknowledgement programs?
- Have major vendor and technology decisions been based on a quantitative, documented decision analysis?
- Does a risk management tracking system exist?
- If yes, does the system contain all of the critical risk tracking elements (see the table of key elements in Exhibit 2)?
- Are risks segregated into those that can be resolved by the project team and those by the business owners?
- How often are risks and their proposed solutions monitored?

Chapter 14

Evolution of a High-Quality Development Process in an Existing Software Project

Susan Phillips Dawson

The adoption of a high-quality software development process is a daunting task, even for people trained in the methods with a funded and supported project on which to apply the principles. It is especially difficult in an environment where the culture does not support disciplined software development, where most people have not been educated in the methods, and the project has been perpetuated for many years in an *ad hoc* environment. Even with the advent of total quality management, few business managers understand the application of quality principles to software.

Applying continuous improvement in software development is extremely difficult, but it is also paramount to the ongoing success of a heterogeneous, mission-critical project. This chapter describes the evolution of a disciplined process in a large, ongoing, mission-critical development project at Motorola Austin.

QUALITY INITIATIVE

The Paperless Integrated Manufacturing System (PIMS) is a project that arose from real and urgent needs in Motorola final manufacturing. Semiconductor final-manufacturing sites exhibit many problems indicative of a lack of integrated systems support. Five years ago, there were few automated systems to support manufacturing — a single Tandem computer at each site provided simple inventory tracking, and a variety of small, homegrown data collection systems were available. The systems that existed were not integrated between factories or even within factories. High-quality production information was unavailable or, at best, held in isolated islands of automation within the factory.

Over and above the systems problems are severe logistics and coordination difficulties. Products from just one of the Motorola Austin divisions can be produced in any of ten assembly sites and six final test sites around the world. This leads to coordination problems (often the product owner is thousands of miles from the producer), as well as problems stemming from language and cultural differences.

All these difficulties led to multiple environments where paper has prevailed. Even today, 87 separate paper documents must be completed to have a product assembled in the Malaysia factory. This paperwork is time-consuming, difficult to track, often inaccurate, and wasteful.

The factories understood these problems only too well; unfortunately, there were few resources to help fix them. The traditional line of support — the IS organization — was focused on legacy system maintenance and on solutions for accounting and financial needs. Consequently, in 1989, the Austin Final Manufacturing Group (FMG) Computer Integrated Manufacturing (CIM) organization agreed to initiate a paperless shop order system, contracting Sterling Information Group as the primary project developer to Motorola.

The factory system needs were defined as:

- Online access to factory information and data collection on the manufacturing process
- A means to input the necessary data easily through interfaces usable by all operators in all factories
- Current tracking and history of all production lots through the manufacturing process (e.g., where and how they were processed, lot splits, combines, bonuses)
- Ease of querying and reporting of all production data
- Online shop order creation and maintenance to control the process specification and the data collection
- All these functions available in a general-purpose manner to support multiple, diverse factories throughout the world

This undertaking would form the central nervous system of a 24-hour-a-day, 7-day-a-week production facility — a true mission-critical system.

SOFTWARE QUALITY PROCESS: THE EARLY DAYS

When the development of PIMS began, few of the people involved with the project had formal computer science training. Most were manufacturing personnel or engineers who could help define production needs but did not yet recognize the need for a software development process specification analogous to a production process specification.

The corporate quality improvement effort at Motorola had been well under way for years, but was only rarely being applied to such soft activities as administrative functions, personnel management, and software. This meant that there were few if any accepted models for developing high-quality software systems. The Motorola Six Sigma Quality program — a statistical approach defining quality goals of fewer than 3.4 introduced errors per million opportunities — was being applied to software in only a few remote areas within Motorola.

Manufacturing improvement efforts undertaken at the time required massive amounts of production data to support measured Six Sigma improvements. Ironically, the subsequent drive for data often caused information systems to be developed rapidly and with little or no control, so that several poor-quality information systems were a legacy of production quality improvement efforts.

Because the full requirements of PIMS were not well understood by the factory users or the developers, the early process life cycle used was essentially a spiral model: the goal was to place some capability out onto the manufacturing floor, exercise it, find the problems, and determine the real requirements, and then reiterate to build on each release. Methods were applied informally (e.g., the "back of the napkin" approach). The development model in use meant that design occurred simultaneously with editing the code. This approach resulted in fast product turnaround and an increased understanding of user needs early in the project, but it also meant that little of the process was documented and plenty of mistakes made their way to the users.

The project was managed essentially on a contract basis — there was little description of specific requirements for product releases, so programmers worked as time and materials were available and the project continued as long as management was satisfied with the progress. Releases occurred often and were not well controlled; access to programs was controlled even less.

In early 1990, Motorola began asking local software contractors to conform to sector and corporate requirements for higher-quality software development. Because PIMS was of a magnitude and importance that it could have significant impact on Motorola manufacturing, requirements were specifically placed on that project. Unfortunately, few experts from IS were available to help guide process improvements. An initial process plan was developed by Sterling and the FMG, which helped to lead the evolution from an informal, *ad hoc* environment to a more formal process.

147

About the same time, an initial, informal Software Engineering Institute (SEI) assessment had been made of the FMG CIM Development Group that was overseeing the PIMS project. This assessment indicated many deficiencies in the development processes used both internally and in contracted work. The internal recognition of the need for significant software process improvement was strong, especially for large projects such as PIMS. By then, the factory was depending on the complex PIMS system, which was more than 100,000 lines of code in Tandem COBOL and SQL. (It is now about 250,000 lines excluding libraries.) Quality was critical.

EVOLUTION OF THE PROCESS

Once the need for higher software development quality was ackowledged internally, improvements to the process were made in several areas. Following is a brief overview of the status of many of the improvements that have been made.

Project Management

Project Planning. Besides the strategic (one to five year) planning that takes place, specific release planning is continuously performed for PIMS according to business and manufacturing needs. A balance is maintained between enhancements that help current and future users and features affecting ongoing product support, such as data archiving. All these needs are weighted against budget and time constraints. Preliminary estimates of budget and schedule for a release are made, then updated as functional analyses are performed. Bull's-eye charts showing schedule and budget variation are used to track progress to the release estimates (Exhibit 1) throughout the course of a version.

Managing the Life Cycle. As the process grew more formal, it became apparent that a new life cycle model was appropriate. Rather than a spiral model, the more formal modified waterfall life cycle for each release was adopted (see Exhibit 2). In the PIMS modified waterfall life cycle, a number of enhancements are targeted for each version release. Each enhancement undergoes a detailed functional analysis that includes a current system analysis, functional requirements, design options, recommendations, and a work plan. Only after this analysis has been completed is an estimate of implementation work given for that enhancement or group of enhancements; a well-documented design is then performed. Ongoing meetings of the design team, as well as design review with users, support staff, and other developers, ensure that the final sign-offs are usually a formality. After coding, the software undergoes three tiers of testing to ensure system reliability, functional correctness, and performance.

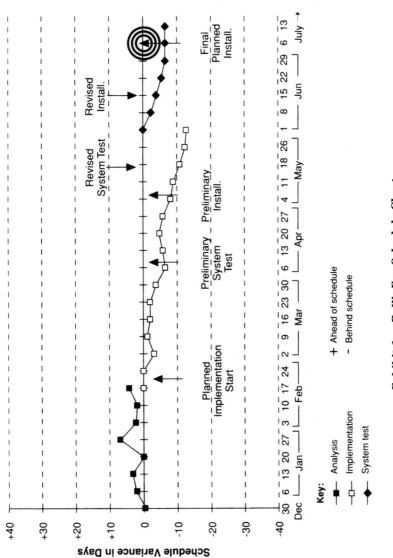

Exhibit 1.   Bull's-Eye Schedule Chart

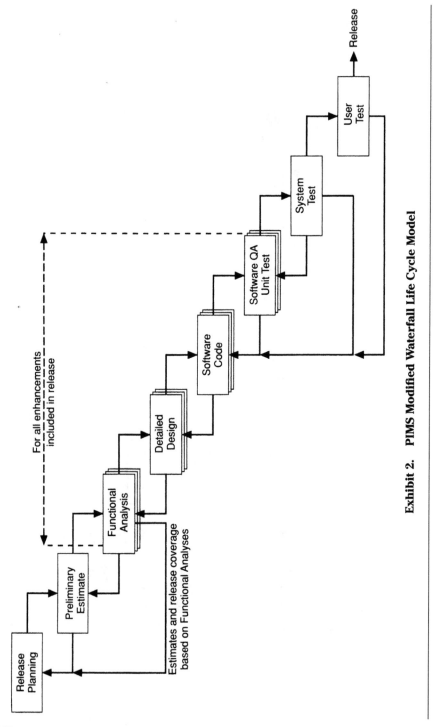

Exhibit 2.   PIMS Modified Waterfall Life Cycle Model

Because of the increased complexity and size of the PIMS project and the larger project team involved, a modified organizational structure was necessary to effectively handle all the project responsibilities and variables. A more effective, cross-functional development team structure was put into place. Detailed resource tracking charts were used to help allocate programmer/analyst resources, as well as overall resource balancing and budgeting. The Motorola project manager remains responsible for long-term strategy, overall budget and planning, business and project coordination issues, leading improvements in the development process, and coordinating efforts with the Motorola implementation team.

Configuration Management

The complexity of the project and the product also demanded much more formal program configuration management than was necessary when only a few people were working on a few thousand lines of code. However, there was no configuration management system or tool available on the Motorola Tandem system. Therefore, the PIMS team created both a process and an integrated tool to support configuration management and change tracking.

The PIMS program management system provides for work request tracking, security, and change management. All work requests (e.g., proposed enhancements and defect reports) are tracked through an automated system. All program files are secured to prevent unauthorized modifications. When work is to be performed, a program is signed out using a work request reference number, and only the person who signed out the program is allowed to work on it. After modifications are made and the program passes unit quality assurance (QA), it is signed back with the previous version saved. Sign-out and sign-back procedures update work request status, and every PIMS program maintains a complete change history.

Structured Requirements Analysis and Design

Much more discipline has been adopted in the analysis and design of enhancements since the early days of the project. Design options are iterated and reviewed in early project phases, and complete documentation is maintained. Design — and design reviews — are viewed as a process rather than an event. Because reviewers attend design meetings throughout the creation of a design, they can understand subtleties often impossible to catch in one or two review sessions. Data flow diagrams, data structure diagrams, and program structure charts are used to capture and communicate analysis and design ideas. Entity–relationship diagrams of the overall relational table structure are maintained. All these are used for formal design reviews with support staff and key users before sign-offs are obtained.

Development Tools

The Tandem development environment is an extremely difficult one in which to create a large, complex system because there are no integrated computer-aided software engineering tools and few development support tools available. Most of the standard development support tools available in other environment either do not exist or are not available in the Motorola Tandem environment. To increase the quality and productivity of the process, unique and custom approaches have had to be developed. For example, the PIMS team developed the Tandem online tracking database in SQL to track bug reports and enhancement requests that drive both project metrics and future development. In addition, the automated configuration management tools described earlier were developed internally.

Testing and Acceptance Criteria

All programming work goes through a three-tier testing process. First, a software QA test of each new or modified program unit is performed by a PIMS developer other than the author. These tests are based on unit test plans that are documented for use on future releases. When all enhancements for a given release are completed, system integration testing is performed to exercise interfaces between all programs and to verify the integrity of overall database designs. Finally, user testing based on predefined functional test plans is completed to ensure functional and regressional integrity. Before any version is released to production, it is installed on a separate Tandem test pathway (i.e., a nonproduction mirrored system partition) for verification in a realistic environment. Metrics on testing are collected throughout the system and user testing tasks. Bug-detection rates help determine testing progression and provide insight into how clean the releases are (Exhibit 3).

Metrics

After the process had evolved to a fairly stable level, metrics were needed for better understanding of the process itself and the improvements being attempted. An automated database for metrics data collection has been developed. It includes problem report entry screens for key problem variables, as well as status tracking of open problems. The severity of each bug is ranked, and separate trends are maintained for what are ranked the major and medium problems versus the minor ones. The product quality metrics currently tracked (Exhibits 4 through 8) are as follows:

- *Released software quality:* The total released number of defects per 1,000 assembly-equivalent lines of code (by release version).
- *Customer-found defects:* The total customer-found number of defects per 1,000 assembly-equivalent lines of code (by release). This and the released software quality metric target the Motorola corporate goal of a Six Sigma quality level.

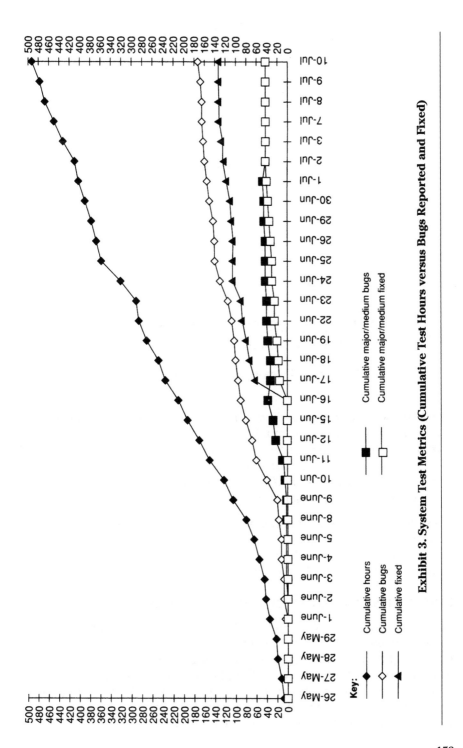

Exhibit 3. System Test Metrics (Cumulative Test Hours versus Bugs Reported and Fixed)

153

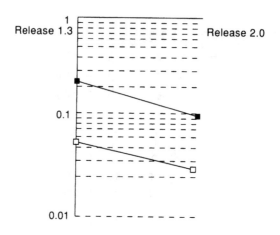

Note:
4 sigma = 6.21
5 sigma = 0.23
6 sigma = 0.0034

Key:
—■— Total released defects per 1,000 assembly-equivalent lines of code (KAELOC)
—□— Total major/medium released defects per KAELOC

Exhibit 4. Released Software Quality Metric

- *Post-release problem report activity:* The number of newly opened and total open problems by month.
- *Post-release problem report aging:* The mean age of open problems and the mean age of closed problems per month.
- *Cost-to-fix post-release problems:* The total billed cost spent fixing previously released problems each month.

These metrics give Motorola the best view into items critical to both end users and project managers. The project team plans to expand metrics collection and tracking as it determines other measures that would indicate software quality and project success.

PERCEPTIONS AND ROLES OF THE PROJECT PLAYERS

All the individuals involved in the PIMS project have had some effect on, and have been affected by, the changing development process. As in all far-reaching quality initiatives, changes affecting people are much harder than those relating to technology. All the players, especially managers, must perceive value in their role in process improvement or they will not accept and adapt to the change. This is especially true when each player's job is evolving along with the evolution of the process.

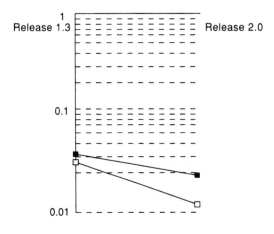

Note:
4 sigma = 6.21
5 sigma = 0.23
6 sigma = 0.0034

Key:
—■— Customer-found defects per 1,000 assembly-equivalent lines of code (KAELOC)
—□— Customer-found major/medium defects per KAELOC

Exhibit 5.   Customer-Found Defects Metric

Developers

The original manufacturing and contracted development group had little experience in formal methods. Most of the developers were at first reluctant to adopt a disciplined development approach because of the change to their jobs and because of the bureaucracy they associated with documenting and formalizing the methods. One person who felt inhibited by the process left the project. Overall, the developers recognize how the process improvements have helped, and most of them state that they would not consider undertaking the project without the formal process.

Support Personnel

The PIMS project support personnel consists of those Motorola employees who maintain online shop orders on the PIMS system, work with PIMS relational databases for custom and *ad hoc* reporting of production data, and provide implementation support for the factory operations. These individuals have had to take a much more active role because of the enhanced development process. Their input to requirements definitions must be strict and

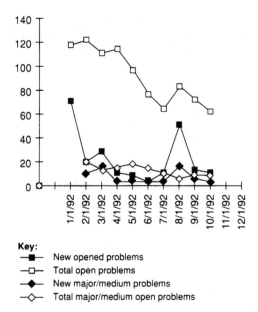

Key:
- ■— New opened problems
- □— Total open problems
- ◆— New major/medium problems
- ◇— Total major/medium open problems

Exhibit 6.   Post-Release Problem Report Activity

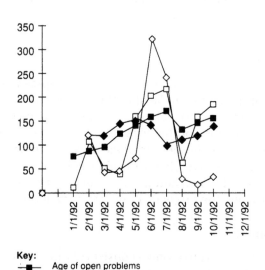

Key:
- ■— Age of open problems
- □— Age of closed problems
- ◆— Age of major/medium open problems
- ◇— Age of major/medium closed problems

Exhibit 7.   Post-Release Problem Report Aging

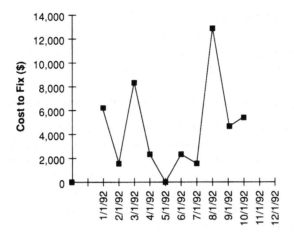

Exhibit 8.   Cost to Fix Post-Release Problems

well investigated. They perform the primary role in the now-formalized user testing. In addition, they provide disciplined tracking of problem and enhancement reports through the PIMS online database.

Managers

The PIMS team is fortunate because the manufacturing managers support-ing the project actively promote a culture of continuous process improve-ment. Like many others, however, these managers have much to learn about software engineering and the systems development process. Every presentation of the PIMS project now contains reports on process improve-ment efforts and metrics to help shape the expectations of managers and other customers.

One interesting outcome of the formal methods is that the managers are sometimes bound by the process as much as others — they no longer have the ability to request quick enhancements to be done on the fly. Managers must support the process the same as all the other players for it to be successful.

Users

In general, the end users are not aware of all the process improvements that have taken place; however, they do see clean releases. One release two years ago had dozens of medium to major bugs, and it took weeks for the system to be fully installed and running. The most recent PIMS release had only a handful of minor customer-found bugs. PIMS was running smoothly five minutes after the expected system downtime was over.

Software Quality Assurance Personnel

Much as in an effective manufacturing area, the quality of the process is everyone's responsibility, not the purview of a specific quality expert. Consequently, there are no software QA personnel.

BENEFITS AND COSTS OF CONTINUOUS PROCESS IMPROVEMENTS

There are many costs and benefits from process improvement. The metrics being tracked are expected to shed more light on the quantifiable effects of the process improvement efforts. Currently, the project team believes the benefits of the improvement efforts outweigh the costs. This is all the more significant because the improvements were made in an existing, ongoing project — not one in which the team could start with a clean slate. Among the benefits credited to the project:

- A higher-quality software is produced, one that is more robust and solves user problems without creating new ones.
- Less rework is required, so there is lower long-term product cost and shorter cycle time to a useful product.
- More accurate project estimates are produced.
- There are fewer fires to fight. Unforeseen emergencies for management to deal with are now less than one third of what they were two years ago.
- There are much cleaner releases with far fewer problems seen by the users. This in turn improves the credibility of the developers.
- The process forces developers to take into account more general needs and to find more flexible solutions.
- A common process, and the common knowledge base for the project, improves the project continuity, enhances communications, and makes the product more supportable.

There are also associated costs, among them:

- Less responsiveness to enhancement requests: Every enhancement must go through the entire life cycle to a controlled release.
- Increased cost of initial development.
- Changed job descriptions: Everyone is responsible for the process, and not just hacking out code. This change in job descriptions has been a difficult and frustrating change for some.

FUTURE IMPROVEMENTS

Although significant advances have beeen made in the PIMS development project, systematic improvement is a continuous process. Improvements that are planned for the near future include:

- The collection and tracking of more metrics, and the better use of metrics to help the team identify areas for improvement
- The use of testing metrics to predict more effectively the time and effort necessary to achieve clean, yet efficient releases
- Fully automating the integrated problem tracking and configuration management support system
- Applying Delphi estimation techniques to achieve more accurate estimations for major enhancements
- Involving the team in a formal SEI assessment to identify areas of highest leverage for improvement
- Transferring the improvement lessons from PIMS to other projects, both in Motorola and in other Sterling projects

CONCLUSION

Without a doubt, PIMS is a higher-quality system than it was a few years ago. It forms the central nervous system of a number of factories and consists of hundreds of thousands of lines of code; yet recent major installations have been almost trouble free. Ongoing maintenance costs are one quarter of what they once were, and key metrics indicate that the project is close to a Six Sigma quality deployment effort. This success can be directly attributed to improvements in PIMS software development.

One of the major lessons learned is that the techniques and philosophies of continuous quality improvement are as important and as applicable to software development as they are in more traditional functions like manufacturing. Other beneficial lessons drawn from the PIMS experience can be applied to the continuous improvement program in general:

- *Systematic improvement requires dedicated support from developers and managers.* It has taken many years of coordinated effort to achieve the improvements Motorola has made in the PIMS project, and the team is still far from satisfied. IS managers hoping for instant measurable improvement will almost certainly be disappointed.
- *It is harder to change culture — people's thoughts and habits — than it is to change technology.* The PIMS project team wrote its own defect-tracking tools in a few weeks, but convincing people to use the tools consistently to track their own errors was far more time-consuming.
- *A formal development process pays for itself in improved quality and efficiency.* It is always painful to spend the time up-front to do the analysis and design thoroughly, but doing it right the first time is less costly than redoing work at coding, or even worse, after the product is released.
- *Metrics are the key to measuring, understanding, and controlling the development process.* No gut feeling is worth the measurement of a 100 percent defect improvement rate.

- *Any project can benefit from formal management of the basic development process.* These lessons have been transferred to other projects, large and small, old and new, thus proving that the techniques are valuable in all types of systems.

Chapter 15
Incorporating Six Sigma Concepts into Systems Analysis

Christine B. Tayntor

Six Sigma. Cynics may claim that it is nothing more than the program *du jour*, just another in a string of management fads, and that it will soon be supplanted by a different promise of improved productivity. Companies that have embraced Six Sigma's concepts say otherwise.

At its most fundamental, Six Sigma is a measurement of defects. A company that has reached the Six Sigma level will have only 3.4 defects per million opportunities. In other words, it will have virtually defect-free operations. For those companies, Six Sigma is more than measurement. It is a way of doing business that reduces costs by focusing on customer requirements, by making decisions based on facts, and by improving processes. All of these result in reduced defects.

Some companies, particularly those in the service industry, shy away from Six Sigma because they view it as a program for engineers — one with too much rigidity. Although emphasis has been placed on the statistical analysis tools that assist in the identification of opportunities for improvement, the value of Six Sigma is far more than statistical analysis, just as the program itself is more than a measurement of defects.

While becoming a Six Sigma company may mean a cultural change that some corporations are unwilling to undergo, it is not an all-or-nothing proposition. The basic five-phase model that many Six Sigma companies have adopted can benefit information technology (IT) organizations, even without the detailed measurements that are part of statistical analysis. Following the basic tenets of Six Sigma processes will help ensure that IT fully understands the problem, chooses the right solution to the problem, and implements that solution on time, using a schedule that customers have approved. The result is reduced rework, which translates into lower costs and higher customer satisfaction — two primary goals of most IT departments.

0-8493-1190-X/02/$0.00+$1.50
© 2002 by CRC Press LLC

Exhibit 1.   The Five-Phase DMAIC Model

Phase	Objectives
Define	Identify the problem and the customers; define and prioritize the customers' requirements.
Measure	Confirm and quantify the problem; identify and measure the various steps in the current process; revise or clarify the problem statement, if necessary.
Analyze	Determine the root cause of the problem.
Improve	Develop and implement the solution.
Control	Measure the improvements and ensure that they continue.

THE FIVE-PHASE MODEL

IT organizations are accustomed to projects being broken into phases, typically those defined by a system development lifecycle (SDLC) model. Six Sigma initiatives are frequently described as using a DMAIC model, where DMAIC is an acronym for the five phases of a process improvement model. The phases and their primary objectives are listed in Exhibit 1.

While these may appear to be similar to a traditional SDLC, there are some important differences. The following example illustrates the use of the DMAIC model and Six Sigma processes in IT systems analysis.

THE PROBLEM

It was the beginning of March and the CIO of the XYZ Corporation was returning to his office after lunch when the Vice-President of Marketing happened to see him in the hallway and began berating him. "That payroll/HR system you put in a couple years ago stinks. When I moved, I changed banks. Although my assistant filled out all the paperwork, it has been months, and I still do not have my pay deposited in the right account or my deposit slips sent to the new address. What a mess!" The VP of Marketing was clearly angry as she continued, "All I hear is that there are backlogs in keypunch and some quality problems. This can't continue! Why don't you get one of those fancy imaging systems that I read about a while ago and eliminate all that keypunch effort? I'll bet that would reduce costs and improve quality."

The CIO nodded at the irate executive, "This sounds like an ideal process improvement project. I'll charter a team. Will you serve as the executive sponsor?" And so the project began.

The CIO had taken the first critical step to the project's success: obtaining a sponsor. Whether called an executive sponsor or a champion, each project needs someone at a high enough level in the organization to obtain appropriate funding and other resources, and to break down barriers if problems should arise. Choosing a champion like the VP of Marketing, who has a vested interest in the project's outcome, helps improve its chances of success.

THE DEFINITION PHASE

The objective of the first three phases of the DMAIC model (define, measure, and analyze) is to fully understand the problem and the underlying process, as well as the customers' requirements, before beginning to implement a solution. Although this extensive analysis effort without even a prototype system as a deliverable may seem unnecessary to organizations more used to the "you start coding; I will find out what they want" or the "ready, fire, aim" approaches to systems development, the success of Six Sigma companies attests to the value of careful planning and fact-based decisions.

The steps typically included in the definition phase are:

1. Define the problem.
2. Form a team.
3. Develop a project charter.
4. Develop a project plan.
5. Identify customers.
6. Identify and prioritize customer requirements.

Based on his conversation with the executive, the CIO drafted the following problem statement: "We need to implement an optical scanning front end to eliminate keypunch input to the payroll/HR system. The new system will reduce costs and improve quality." The CIO then convened a team consisting of a project leader and systems analyst from his organization, the manager of the department that had already implemented an imaging system, the marketing VP's assistant, and the manager of the keypunch effort.

When the team met for the first time, it began the process of developing a project charter. The purpose of this document is to ensure that everyone working on the project shares common expectations. Charters should include the following elements:

- Problem statement
- Goal statement, including measurable targets
- Target completion date
- List of team members and the percentage of time they are expected to devote to the project
- Resource constraints (e.g., budget)

Exhibit 2. Using SMART Guidelines for Defining Requirements

When defining customer requirements, the team should ensure that they are as detailed as possible. One way to determine whether requirements are sufficiently detailed is to apply the SMART criteria.

Specific	Requirements should be specific. For example, rather than saying "Keypunch errors must be resolved," a specific requirement would be "Keypunch errors must be resolved to the customer's satisfaction within three hours of their being reported to the help desk."
Measurable	The performance must be quantifiable. In the example shown above, "to the customer's satisfaction" could be made more measurable by stating "to the customer's satisfaction as measured by an average score of no less than 4 on a scale of 5; such measurement to be taken during follow-up telephone interviews."
Attainable	The requirement needs to be both realistic and attainable. If it greatly exceeds industry standards, it may not be attainable.
Relevant	The requirement should have relevance to the success of the program. For example, a requirement to respond to problems is less relevant than one to resolve them because customer satisfaction is predicated on successful resolution, not simply by answering the phone.
Timebound	When quantified, requirements should be measured during a specific time period. To expand the first example, "98 percent of all problems reported must be resolved within three hours of their being reported to the help desk; the remaining 2 percent must be resolved within eight hours. Reports will be produced no later than the fifth day of the month, showing daily, weekly, and monthly volumes and resolution percentages for the previous calendar month."

Problem and Goal Statements

As part of this process, the team reviewed the initial problem statement and found that, rather than being a problem statement, it was a goal statement. Unfortunately, it was not even a very good goal statement because it did not meet the SMART criteria. That is, it was not Specific, Measurable, Attainable, Relevant, and Timebound. An example of the SMART criteria, which are also used to define customer requirements, is shown in Exhibit 2.

Further review showed that the initial problem/goal statement presented a solution before definition, measurement, and analysis had been performed. Rather than succumb to the "if the only tool one has is a hammer, all problems appear to be nails" syndrome, the team resolved to propose a solution only when it had completed the analysis phase. When the team explained its logic to the marketing VP, although she had proposed the imaging system as a solution, she admitted that her desire was to have the problem fixed. If there was a better or cheaper answer, she would be happy. She confirmed that the team was empowered to find the best solution.

The revised problem statement became: "15 percent of all requests for updates to the payroll/HR system are not processed the same day that they are received. An additional 5 percent of all updates have at least one error in keying and must be resubmitted, resulting in processing delays of at least two days, rework costs of $10,000 per year, and reimbursement of bounced check fees of $5000 per year. Customer satisfaction has dropped from 4 to 2.5 on a scale of 1 to 5." It is important to note that this statement quantifies the problem and its consequences.

The team then drafted the goal statement, outlining what it planned to accomplish. "Ensure that 99 percent of all updates to the payroll/HR system are processed the same day they are received, with an error rate not to exceed 2 percent; and improve customer satisfaction to 4 by the end of the calendar year." Although the marketing VP wanted 100 percent completion and zero defects, and asked that the project be completed by the end of the second quarter, the team applied the "attainability" criterion when it wrote its goals and refused to doom its project to failure by having unrealistic expectations.

By making both the problem and the goal statements extremely specific, the team and anyone reviewing the project will have a clear understanding of why the team was chartered and what it intended to accomplish. Clarity and common goals are key tenets of Six Sigma.

Developing the project plan, which is the next step in the definition phase, is frequently the easiest for IT staff because Six Sigma plans are no different from the project plans that IT professionals are used to creating. Like all project plans, the one the team developed included milestones, deliverables, and dependencies. To provide a clear linkage back to the process model, the team used the five phases of DMAIC as summary tasks, and broke down individual steps within them. This use of shared terminology helped non-IT staff understand the project plan.

Customers and Their Requirements

The final steps in the definition phase are to identify customers, their requirements, and the relative priority of those requirements. The objectives of these steps are to ensure that the project is addressing the right problem and to align project deliverables with customer expectations.

When identifying customers, the team realized that there were two different groups. The ultimate customer was the employee whose records were to be changed (e.g., the VP of Marketing). Although it was critical to satisfy those customers, it was equally important to address the needs of intermediate customers such as the vice-president's assistant, who actually filled out the forms. Both use the services delivered by the payroll/HR system and the keypunch department. While their requirements are similar, the team discovered some important differences in their perspectives.

Similar to the creation of a project plan, identifying customer requirements is a task with which most IT departments are comfortable. Virtually every IT project has as one of its preliminary tasks the definition of requirements. Within Six Sigma organizations, however, this process includes additional steps that may not be part of the traditional requirements definition phase.

Obtaining customer requirements can be accomplished in a number of ways, including interviews, surveys, and reviews of complaint logs. The XYZ team chose interviews because it had a limited number of customers, could afford the time, and believed it would get more information by encouraging open-ended answers rather than asking customers to choose from a menu of predefined responses.

When the team conducted its requirements definition, it discovered that in addition to the processing time and accuracy requirements it had expected, customers identified other requirements, notably the time required for them to complete the input form and the desire for confirmation of system updates. Similarly, while they were interviewing customers, the team members learned that many were frustrated by the need to enter what seemed like arcane system codes, such as a "1" for "full-time employee" or "9" for "retired." Although these codes and their translations were listed on the input form, their use frustrated the customer. This discovery of new requirements is common and is one of the primary reasons for the requirements definition step.

Where the XYZ team's process initially differed from standard requirements definition was the application of SMART criteria to ensure that the requirements were specific. This was a fairly rigid process that resulted in each requirement being carefully scrutinized and rewritten to ensure that all possible ambiguities were removed. As shown on Exhibit 3, rather than phrasing the first requirement as "Requesting the change must be easy," the team worked with the customers to clarify "easy."

When the team had completed the definition of requirements, it asked the customers to give each requirement an importance ranking. The customers understood that this ranking would be used in subsequent steps to ensure that the proposed solution addressed the most critical problems. As shown in Exhibit 3, the team established an importance ranking scale of 1 to 10 but used only four values: 1, 4, 7, and 10. The reason for this was to simplify customer decision making and to make final rankings more definitive.

Exhibit 3.   Sample Customer Requirements

Customer: **VP of Marketing**
Output: **Updated Payroll/HR Records**

Requirement	Importance (1, 4, 7, 10)[a]
Completing input form requires no more than one minute	1
Completing input form does not require the customer to use any system codes	4
Updates are applied to system the day form is completed	7
Updates are correct the first time	10
Customer receives confirmation that updates have been applied within eight working hours of the system update	7

Customer: **Assistant to VP of Marketing**
Output: **Updated Payroll/HR Records**

Requirement	Importance (1, 4, 7, 10)[a]
Completing input form requires no more than one minute	10
Completing input form does not require the customer to use any system codes	7
Updates are applied to system the day form is completed	4
Updates are correct the first time	7
Customer receives confirmation that updates have been applied within eight working hours of the system update	4

[a] Importance scale: 1 = Unimportant; 4 = Moderately important; 7 = Very important; 10 = Mandatory.

THE MEASUREMENT PHASE

As noted above, the purpose of the measurement phase is to validate and quantify the problem statement by identifying and measuring the various steps in the current process. The XYZ team began by constructing a SIPOC chart. SIPOC is another Six Sigma acronym, this one for Supplier, Input, Process, Output, and Customer. Its purpose is to provide a high-level understanding of the problem and process. For this project, the SIPOC elements were as shown in Exhibit 4.

When the team completed its SIPOC, it noted that the supplier and the customer were, in many cases, the same. Although this is not typical for most processes, it was a key point for this project and was instrumental in determining the proposed solution.

Once the team had developed a SIPOC chart, it expanded the "process" section into a separate process map. As shown in Exhibit 5, the process

Exhibit 4. SIPOC Elements

Category	
Supplier	Employee needing HR/payroll records updated; assistant to employee
Input	HR/payroll system update form
Process	Keying of data; system update
Output	Updated records
Customer	Employee needing HR/payroll records updated

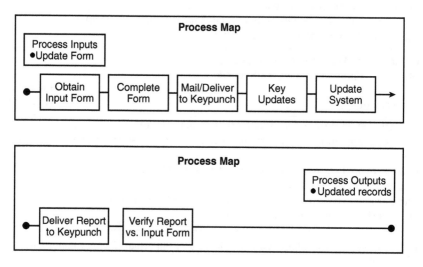

Exhibit 5.   Current Process Map

map outlines the primary steps in the current process. The team confirmed these steps with customers and measured the elapsed time between steps. Because there were a number of "hand-off" steps, including the mailing of forms to keypunch, the elapsed time from first obtaining the form to updating the records could be as long as one week. The team knew it could — and would — improve that.

THE ANALYSIS PHASE

With measurement complete, the team began to analyze the data it had gathered. In doing so, it determined that the root cause of the problem was the inherent design of the process with its hand-offs. Although the fact that keypunch was measured by the number of transactions it processed rather than by the number of transactions it processed accurately was identified as a secondary problem, the team believed that resolving that problem

Process Map

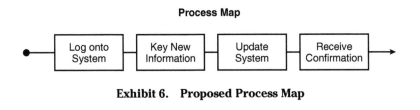

Exhibit 6.   Proposed Process Map

would result in only a marginal improvement in customer satisfaction and reduced processing time. The primary opportunity for improvement was in streamlining the process.

TIME FOR IMPROVEMENT

The team then moved into the improvement phase, where it brainstormed a number of solutions. The first solution to be considered was the imaging front end that the VP of Marketing had proposed. Although the team recognized that an imaging front end would address the first portion of its goal statement (ensuring that 99 percent of all updates are processed the same day they are received), it did not believe that this solution would improve customer satisfaction or accuracy.

Ultimately, the team determined that an intranet-based employee self-service approach would have the greatest chance of satisfying customer requirements. The team based its recommendation on the following facts:

- The supplier of input and the customer were frequently the same person.
- Virtually everyone in the company had easy access to a workstation and was computer literate.
- Employees were already accessing the intranet to obtain the blank input forms.
- Keying data would take most employees less time than completing and mailing a paper form.
- Employees had a vested interest in data accuracy and would be less likely to make errors than keypunch.

The next step was to validate the proposed solution. This process consisted of two major steps: developing a revised process map (Exhibit 6) and ranking the proposed process improvements' effect on customer requirements.

The team constructed a process improvement ranking spreadsheet to provide an objective, clearly quantified measurement of the effect each step would have (Exhibit 7). The team's first action was to take the requirements customers had identified *without the importance ranking they had*

Exhibit 7. Process Improvement Ranking

| | | Improvement Steps and Effects | | | | | | |
| | | Replace keypunch with online front end | | Use pull down menus for all coded fields | | Provide online confirmation of changes | | |
Customer/Requirement	Importance Ranking	Effect	Impact on Req.	Effect	Impact on Req.	Effect	Impact on Req.	Total Impact
VP Marketing								
Input requires no more than one minute	1	10	10	7	7	1	1	18
No system codes required	4	1	4	10	40	1	4	48
Updates applied the day form is completed	7	10	70	1	7	1	7	84
Updates are correct the first time	10	10	100	7	70	1	10	180
Confirmation of updates within eight hours of the system update	7	1	7	1	7	10	70	84
Degree of satisfaction from implementing improvement			191		131		92	414
Assistant to VP Marketing								
Input requires no more than one minute	10	10	100	7	70	1	10	180
No system codes required	7	1	7	10	70	1	7	84
Updates applied the day form is completed	4	10	40	1	4	1	4	48
Updates are correct the first time	7	10	70	7	49	1	7	126
Confirmation of updates within eight hours of the system update	4	1	4	1	4	10	40	48
Degree of satisfaction from implementing improvement			221		197		68	486
Average Ranking								
Input requires no more than one minute	5.5	10	55	7	38.5	1	5.5	99
No system codes required	5.5	1	5.5	10	55	1	5.5	66
Updates applied the day form is completed	5.5	10	55	1	5.5	1	5.5	66
Updates are correct the first time	8.5	10	85	7	59.5	1	8.5	153
Confirmation of updates within eight hours of the system update	5.5	1	5.5	1	5.5	10	55	66
Degree of satisfaction from implementing improvement			206		164		80	450

assigned and determine how well each proposed improvement would satisfy that requirement. To create clear distinctions, the team used the same 1, 4, 7, 10 scale that customers had used for their importance ranking. As shown in Exhibit 7, an online front end would have a high impact on the requirement to enter data in less than one minute, but would not significantly affect the requirement to eliminate system codes.

Although the ultimate goal of the process improvement ranking is to consider both the customers' ranking of each requirement's importance from Exhibit 3 and the degree to which each revised process step will satisfy that requirement (its effect) to determine the total impact that implementing a specific step will have on customer satisfaction, the team realized that to be as objective as possible it should not see customer importance rankings when it developed its own effect ratings. It was only when those were completed that the team retrieved the customer rankings and entered them into the chart.

The spreadsheet multiplies the importance ranking by the effect weighting to calculate which steps will have the greatest impact on each individual requirement. The column totals show the overall effect that each process step will have on customer requirements and provide an objective method of prioritizing the steps. Although the XYZ team had funding to implement all three recommendations, if it had been necessary to reduce functionality, this ranking would have shown them the impact on customer requirements of eliminating individual steps.

A separate ranking was prepared for each customer and the results were compared. As would be expected, because the customers had assigned different importance rankings to each requirement, the results of the improvement ranking varied. To determine an overall ranking, the team averaged the results of all the customer rankings. This average was used to determine the priority of process improvements.

Once the team had developed its proposed solution, validated it with customers, and received the champion's approval to proceed, it was ready to begin implementing the solution. This step did not vary significantly from normal IT system development.

THE FINAL PHASE: CONTROL

When the new system was implemented, although the majority of its work was completed, the team knew that the final phase — control — was the one that would ensure that its work achieved the desired benefits. As part of the control phase, the team implemented a formal customer survey process to capture customer satisfaction metrics. It produced a monthly scorecard showing the number of transactions processed using the new system, the rework rate, and the customer satisfaction statistics. When it was clear that the project goals were being met, the team renamed the final phase of DMAIC "celebrate."

CONCLUSION

Even companies that do not plan to use all the concepts of Six Sigma can benefit from the structure and methodology that many Six Sigma tools bring to the systems analysis and development process. A high degree of focus on customers, combined with careful measurement of requirements, and the effects that proposed changes will have on those requirements can reduce rework and improve customer satisfaction.

Chapter 16
Solving the Software Quality Management Problem

James L. Mater

In its capacity as an independent software testing lab, QualityLogic, Inc. has worked with the information systems groups of both small and large companies, and with software and systems companies. This work provides a unique opportunity to observe the struggles that organizations go through in attempting to solve their software product quality and quality management problems. This article presents resulting observations and thinking about the basic quality management problem, as well as a new solution for the industry.

Profit and loss (P&L) managers,[1] referred to here as business managers, do not clearly understand or value software quality management. Software companies and projects fail to deliver quality products because they do not treat quality management as a strategic, critical aspect of the product development process that is equal to requirements, design, and code development.

The basic problem is that software quality management is not properly "owned" within organizations. Instead, because it has historically been relegated to a software quality assurance function, it is considered technical, thus, few business managers would ever consider directly "owning" it.

In traditional industrial businesses, product quality management, quality assurance, and quality control are treated as major corporate functions, reporting to the business manager. However, few software organizations have yet adopted this approach. Indeed, the software business is such a recent "discipline" that the issue of product quality management[2] remains a mystery, especially to business managers without software training or experience.

0-8493-1190-X/02/$0.00+$1.50
© 2002 by CRC Press LLC

The software quality issue — which ensures the quality of software products delivered to customers — is not a technical one. It is achieved through a combination of good customer understanding (developed into requirements) and good product development processes.

There are many excellent software development processes and techniques that are both proven and available. The software industry knows how to build high-quality, reliable products that meet the feature, cost, and schedule needs of customers; and that are easily maintained and upgraded. It is a myth that the industry needs better processes or tools to solve the quality problem, which skirts the real issue of business manager responsibility.

Unfortunately, the industry typically does not have that combination of discipline and organizational structure required for consistently delivering successful products; that is, a well-defined, well-executed quality management function. Responsibility for this must start at the business management level. The quality problem will remain unsolved until these managers think long and hard about the quality requirements for their products, until they have clearly communicated their conclusions, until they actively monitor product quality, and until they are willing to act on that information to enforce their policies.

SOFTWARE QUALITY POLICY

Business managers have two critical responsibilities relative to software quality. First, they must set and communicate clear policy, empowering their people to carry out that policy. Second, they must ensure that these policies are implemented. This entails monitoring quality on an ongoing basis and taking action as needed to keep the organization on track.

Business managers must give serious thought to software quality policy, answering the following questions:

- Is the organization's policy to be first to market with the right features at the right price — and fix reliability issues later?
- Is it to have the most reliable product available in its class?
- Is it to aim at the low end of the market, which will accept poorer quality at a lower price?
- Are there critical safety or customer issues that demand perfection, in terms of 100 percent reliability? (This is the case, for example, for medical instruments, defense systems, and avionics components.)
- Is the company committed to a zero-defect policy?

The task of determining policy cannot be delegated. Only the business manager can set this policy, because all others in the organization will let the policy be influenced by their (individual) quality goals and the design/implementation of the software.

Thus, the policy should carry the weight of the business manager, reflecting serious consideration and commitment. It should have lasting value, and be unambiguous to those implementing policy.

There really is value in thinking about and articulating such a policy. Quality problems in the software industry are caused by the lack of clear direction from the business manager and the will to enforce such policy.

Business managers can only hold their teams accountable for meeting quality standards if these are stated. A decision to ship a product can only be made when there are clear criteria for making such a decision. A development team can only be disciplined for causing exorbitant support headaches when team members are told that minimizing support costs is a critical issue at the time of software design. A product manager can only set quality goals for a product when the standard corporate policy is consistent from day to day and product to product.

The right policy must be set and articulated before it can be enforced. A business manager who does not step up to this issue is negligent in leading his organization.

MONITORING AND ENFORCING QUALITY POLICY

Once a quality policy is put in place, the second major issue is monitoring product quality to ensure that the policy is carried out. This means that business managers must establish a good quality management function that provides their organizations with good information about the quality of the products under development, and enforces their quality policies. The policies and their enforcement have failed if the business manager only finds out that customers are dissatisfied *after* a product has shipped.

The proactive business manager must determine if the products in development will be delivered on time, on budget, and with the quality required to succeed in the market. Uncommon managers, who have put in place the right organization and people with the right direction, need merely ask for the information, and it will be available in some form, providing an accurate view of the quality of products in development.

Unfortunately, for most organizations and business managers, this is an unrealized dream. While there may be a test team in place to measure product quality, it is probably buried in the development organization, wherein inexperienced staff report to an inexperienced test manager. Here, the right information seldom reaches the right people in time. Rather than an independent function, quality management is a lower-level quality control function, performed by the test team, which has minimal understanding of corporate quality policy and issues.

What the organization needs is a quality management team that:

- Is independent of the development team
- Is empowered with the authority of the business manager
- Is working with the product on a day-to-day basis
- Has the skills to thoroughly evaluate the product against explicit or implicit criteria, and can ferret out the evaluation criteria[3] from whatever internal sources are available — or raise a flag if adequate product requirements do not exist
- Can professionally[4] provide documented information to both the development team and the business manager
- Clearly understands the manager's business problem and is helping to solve this above all else
- Operates very efficiently and effectively

Unfortunately, it is difficult — if not impossible — for a business organization to put this definition in place internally.

MANAGING THE QUALITY FUNCTION

Product quality management is the executive function that owns the process for delivering products of the quality required by the marketplace. The function starts with good product requirements, moves to a development process that is designed to deliver predictable results based on the requirements, and ends with a quality control process (testing), which validates that the product indeed meets the defined requirements.

The development process must include explicit quality assurance steps to succeed. However, most company executives concentrate on requirements and other aspects of development, treating quality assurance activities as an afterthought.

Few organizations have a designated quality management function, although some have a software test department. Others have a quality assurance department that they refer to as "software QA," but it is really a software test group. Invariably, and despite protests to the contrary, this "software QA" department is often the weak link in the chain. Companies manifest the symptoms of this weakness in various ways:

- *The software quality assurance function itself is typically a "hot potato," which no senior manager wants to own.* The function is moved around from engineering to manufacturing to operations and back to engineering. It seesaws between a centralized and decentralized function every couple of years.

Two companies that QualityLogic recently interviewed dissolved the central QA function, redeploying the engineers to the product teams and causing a great deal of disruption. Both organizations came to the conclusion that the central function was not working well after two to three years of effort to make it an effective business tool. In another case, the vice president who had been "given" QA was all too happy to hand it off to an outside company.

- *There is discontinuity in the management of the QA function itself.* It is difficult to find and keep a good manager in software testing or software QA. Instead, managers often move out of the function. If they are really good, they are often hired away for more money; if they are ineffective, they are often fired. In any case, it is rare to find stable management of the software QA or test function.

- *There is no encouragement; it is rare that highly respected developers move to software QA.* In fact, the opposite is true. Many companies are proud of the fact that they can use software QA as an entry point and training ground for development. The most attractive career path available to the QA engineer is to move to development. For example, one of QualityLogic's major customers has a terrible time keeping good test leads. Hired right out of college, they have been screened for good development skills and are moved into development as soon as they become effective test leads. While this works well for the development organization, it continually leaves software QA with an inexperienced staff.

- *There is a constant turnover in QA staff.* The consequence is that the QA organization never matures to the same level of skill and professionalism as development teams. Companies are often proud to have a stable QA organization for one or two years. This is in sharp contrast to the stability and maturity of the development team, which has typically been the same for five years or more. Thus, the company should recognize that the QA team is not even close to adequate for the task.

- *The use of developers as testers.* A major QualityLogic customer recently needed help with a critical project. Its division management had just fired all of the QA engineers in an attempt to "fix" the quality problem. The company's ISO 9000 model stated that developers should actually do all of the quality assurance and final acceptance testing themselves — but this group just did not have the bandwidth to do so.

Although developers should indeed "own" the quality of their work, and should conduct such quality assurance activities as unit testing and peer reviews, they should not be the final product testers. Developers are seldom motivated or particularly competent as final product testers. In addition, the lost-opportunity cost of pulling them off of development work is staggering, when analyzed.

- *The development engineers successfully lay the blame for quality/schedule/feature problems on software QA.* The weak link is a test or QA team that is unable to effectively advocate its own position; the team gets dumped on over and over again.

  One major company is currently debating how to fix this very problem. The organization has an excellent QA team that does system test, but it works under the vice president of engineering. Because it is part of engineering, the QA team relieves the development teams from passing all the entry criteria before a product's acceptance for system test. Of course, QA is then blamed when the ship date slips.

  While this situation is very typical, it is also easily solvable. The business manager must determine clear accountability for both development and QA functions, and establish a quality management function to enforce policy.

- *The QA team is unable to communicate product quality information to decision-makers — primarily the business manager.* The team might lack the experience to decide when information is critical to the business manager. Alternatively, the team's information may be filtered through the current owner, usually a vice president of development or engineering. As a result, the information serves the VP, but not the business manager.

- *Ship dates are frequently delayed, and the delays come as surprises (at first)—to everyone except the developers and testers.* The testers did not try to make the information available to the business manager, or were unsuccessful in doing so.

- *Product design or features are routinely changed, causing schedule slips and expensive rework and retest, before release.* Management accepts major design or feature changes because the basic process discipline was not controlled from a quality perspective. No one enforced the early steps of requirements verification or design review, and the impact on quality control activities was ignored in the decision process. This happens more often when there is an inadequate quality management function in place.

These problems all result because the business manager is not adequately investing in quality management. Nor is he or she willing to insist on accountability by the development group. In many cases, the definition of "adequate" is not understood, and quality management is underfunded. Because quality in software is treated like an engineering function that no one really wants to own, it is no wonder that software QA people are also inadequately treated.

Thus, software test and QA engineering jobs are entry-level positions used as a training ground for development. Because the best people are routinely migrated to development, this perpetuates the weakness in quality organizations. An organization will have difficulty maturing when all of its members are entry level and intent on moving to development.

Furthermore, software test and QA engineers are treated as second-class citizens. They are not considered as good as developers because of a bias that suggests: "those not good enough to code, test," or "those who can, write code; those who can't, test."

In addition, software test and QA engineers are poorly paid relative to development engineers, and there is little or no career path for the former. Therefore, test and QA engineers do not have nearly the same opportunity as developers to rise in grade and pay.

This inequity extends to budget decisions, which also favor development over QA. If, for example, both QA and development ask for tool sets for their functions, and the company cannot afford both, development usually wins. Finally, management is willing to let QA suffer if development slips its schedule.

All of these problems and indicators stem from the business manager's lack of clear understanding and valuing of software quality functions. This set of problems may be seen as cultural and management challenges facing the business manager.

SUCCESSFUL SOFTWARE QUALITY MANAGEMENT

Solving this problem set is simple: business managers must clearly understand the quality requirements of their products, be willing to make appropriate strategic decisions about them, and then put in place a quality management function. In the past, this has meant funding an independent software quality management group that does not report to engineering, and insists on disciplined behavior during the whole process. The group is typically used as a measurement and control mechanism.

Traditionally, an executive-level vice president, director, or manager of quality probably reported directly to the business manager. This provided adequate budget, experience, and power to enforce quality disciplines, and act as a gate for product release cycles. Currently, quality is often approached by integrating the quality functions into development teams via senior quality people, and establishing a clear, appropriate process for control of quality during development. While this can improve the organization's ability to develop high-quality products on time and within budget, it does not provide an objective, independent view of product quality to the business manager.

Alternatively, strong business managers can require that the quality function (usually just a test group) report to them directly. They can hire a vice president of quality to work directly for them, and manage the test function. They can ensure that the development vice president also views product quality management as important and sees the need for an independent quality function.

In the end, the business manager must spend a significant amount of effort and dollars to develop a strong QA organization. Three years ago, for example, one CEO of a leading software company placed QA directly under him. Unfortunately, the QA manager was not strong enough, and a major release was shipped with significant problems. Only then did the CEO finally understand the caliber of manager required, and it took another few months to find that person. Now the company is in the rebuilding phase, and the jury is still out on the success of this approach. It is actually unusual that a business manager would make these decisions. Instead, most continue to struggle with this problem but never really solve it.

For business managers to succeed in the software business, both internal and external quality management functions require the following characteristics:

- The business manager's clear definition and enforcement of a quality policy
- Authority directly from the business manager, and independence, at least within the organization
- Team stability and maturity as evidenced by pay, promotional opportunities, and team tenure comparable to development; an understanding of the business of developing successful software products; and earned respect from the whole organization
- Ongoing investment in generic software testing and QA skills
- Ongoing investment in tools and process improvement for the QA and test functions
- An incentive structure that reinforces both effectiveness and efficiency in the QA and testing functions

If a company spends its resources in meeting these requirements, it can and will maintain a powerful quality assurance function equal to the other elements required for product success. However, these investments are often difficult for organizations to justify, and they require sustained interest by the business manager. A viable alternative is to outsource some or all of software quality management, software quality assurance, or quality control to a third-party specialist in this area.

Outsourcing some or all aspects of the software quality management function is an emerging approach to the quality problem that has evolved naturally. This solution recognizes that the quality function must be done well, but it need not be a strategic internal competency. Quality management, quality assurance, and test comprise a discipline, complete with a generic methodology, process, and tools. Companies must determine whether it is a strategically good investment for them to outsource, or to develop and maintain this functional expertise themselves — which is an expensive proposition.

THE EVOLUTION OF SOFTWARE QUALITY MANAGEMENT

The business aspects of software quality are evolving, along with hardware platforms, software languages, software development tools, and the process of defining and building software products. There are at least five distinct models for organizing the software quality management function:

1. Developers do their own QA.
2. Test or QA engineers are integrated within the development teams.
3. A separate QA group belongs to the engineering manager or VP.
4. A separate QA group belongs to a VP other than the engineering VP.
5. A separate QA organization reports directly to the senior business manager (or a VP of quality who then reports to him or her).

The variety of specific solutions is not surprising, because the industry is still struggling to figure out this problem. Like the software business in general, each company seems intent on inventing its own model for software quality management. Because all the models are based on a do-it-yourself approach, they are subject to the problems identified earlier. Outsourcing software QA activities is an emerging model that offers the business manager a viable option to solving product quality and quality management problems.

Historically, QA outsourcing consisted of low-cost, fast-turnaround supplements to internal testing efforts. Several outsourcing companies thrived by providing compatibility testing of software against various hardware platforms and components.

Typically, client software companies would be running late on development and lack the in-house resources or equipment for fast-turnaround compatibility testing. So they turned to software QA outsourcing, contracting with independent test labs for specific test projects. And while this offered independence and objectivity, it aimed at solving a QA manager's staffing shortfall, rather than a business manager's basic quality management problem.

This early model of outsourcing testing is rapidly evolving as major companies try to improve their quality processes. The use of outsourcing is not only accelerating, but changing, as is illustrated by an outsourcing relationship with a leading PC manufacturer.

In 1995, the PC manufacturer started systematically investigating testing laboratories, which it then used on small, noncritical projects that were not adequately staffed internally. There were reviews after each early project that tested localized software versions. The reviews identified how to improve the testing and communications processes on the next project. Thus, over time, the manufacturer developed trained, trusted people available to the its test organization for overflow work. The organization also planned to outsource some portion of the work and develop a set of trusted, long-term vendors.

By 1997, the manufacturer had decided not to grow its internal testing resources at the rate necessary to deal with an exploding workload. Instead, it formed an internal group whose sole function was management of software test outsourcing activities. A key strategy was to encourage the best vendors to open local labs to improve focus and communications.

In early 1998, QualityLogic, Inc. opened a dedicated lab as a joint venture with another company near the manufacturer's facilities. This lab marked a watershed for the test outsourcing industry in two critical ways. First, it was the first instance of a local software testing lab dedicated to working with a single customer at that customer's[5] invitation. Second, the lab was entirely staffed by local people, many of whom the manufacturer had employed as software QA engineers. The new lab manager, who formerly headed the manufacturer's test center, brought with him a number of senior software test engineers.

A further evolution is already in process, whereby companies are completely outsourcing some or all aspects of the software quality management function. For example, several organizations have engaged QualityLogic to build and manage their entire software quality function. The vendor hires the company's existing staff or new staff members, as required, who then become an integral part of the client organization.

The team works on the client site, reporting directly to the business manager or through a designated representative. The vendor's QA manager is responsible to the business manager for ensuring product and process quality within the defined budget. In fact, the vendor's QA manager is also the client's business manager for the specific software QA activity involved.

In all cases, the vendor has a direct company-to-company business relationship with the business manager. In other words, the vendor is solving the business manager's problem at the same time as it solves the engineering organization's quality control problems.

This model opens the door for the outsourced QA organization to be an influential participant in the client's internal development process and tool improvement initiatives. The vendor not only conducts the actual testing activities, but also provides the clients with quality assurance services. The activities include implementing both a defect tracking and a configuration management process (and tools), as well as planning and implementing other process improvement actions.

THE FUTURE OF SOFTWARE QUALITY MANAGEMENT

In determining the future management of the software quality function, early successes indicate that the next logical development is outsourcing the entire QA function, or some appropriate portion thereof. This outsourcing model can directly address the critical cultural and management problems identified in this article. It can also provide improved quality and cost savings for the software company served.

These advantages result from the unique characteristics of the outsourced QA team. First, many of the cultural problems are solved, because the personnel belong to a company whose primary focus is software QA. In such an organization, the software QA engineer is a "first-class" citizen, with all of the status and advantages the term implies. There is a well-defined career path, with the associated training and financial rewards. Stability and maturity can develop because the QA engineers are motivated to stay with the organization and develop as first-rate professionals.

Second, the QA team is set up as a profit-and-loss center with its own competent P&L or business manager (who is the vendor's QA manager). Therefore, the team has a profit motive for doing a better and more efficient job of providing the customer with software QA services.

Although top-notch internal QA teams are often dedicated and self-sacrificing, it is extremely difficult for a company to financially reward them when they do a great job. QA is not a typical career path to senior management positions, and QA salary levels are generally capped below those of development. Even when a company offers a bonus plan or stock options, such rewards are only indirectly tied to the actual effectiveness and efficiency of the QA team.

By contrast, when a QA team is set up as its own P&L center, it has a very tangible financial motivation for finding the most efficient ways to be most effective at its tasks. While an internal QA manager has little incentive to terminate a "temp" when the project is complete, a P&L manager with a bonus tied to financial results does have this incentive. When equipment is no longer required to perform a testing task, the internal QA group typically keeps it for some undefined future use. A P&L manager cannot afford to keep unproductive equipment as an expense. Most importantly, a profit-motivated group with an experienced management team will find creative ways to increase effectiveness, making the customer happy, and improve the efficiency of the activities — that is, decrease costs.

Dozens of QA organizations waste thousands of dollars and hours of time attempting to automate testing — only to fail. Not only did the team lack the experience required to succeed, but there was no serious enough consequence for failure. Neither factor operates in an outsourced QA team. The costs of failure are reflected in the team's paychecks, and the relationship with their single customer is placed at significant risk. A broken promise to automate testing can cause serious mistrust, ending in potential disaster for both the client company and the outsourced QA team.

The third critical factor is the direct relationship between the outsourced QA team and the business manager of their "parent" company (i.e., the customer that the QA team came from). This alone solves both critical problems of software business managers. The very act of making the QA team independent and directly responsible to the business manager (instead of an engineering or other vice-president) places strategic emphasis on software QA. In addition, the business manager has an effective mechanism for monitoring the quality of products under development, in order to take decisive actions.

Through its direct relationship with the business manager, the QA team can also influence the overall software development process. The relationship offers power to "push back" development managers and teams who are shortcutting their own processes. This cannot happen effectively when QA reports to the same vice-president as development.

The QA team can also suggest improvements to the development process that will enhance product quality and increase effectiveness. For example, programming hooks can be added to support test automation, or the product architecture standards can be improved to enhance testability and maintenance.

Finally, outsourcing software QA can result in lowered overall costs for the client company. These take the form of improved quality and lower costs for customer support, of interim fixes and releases, and of better customer retention. In addition, because a profit-oriented QA team is more cost conscious than an internal team, the software QA organization's cost savings can be passed along to the client. Finally, in the new model of full QA function outsourcing, costs can be lowered even more, as there is more emphasis on process improvement for the entire development cycle.

Notes

1. The term P&L manager refers to the executive ultimately responsible for both the revenue and expenses for the product organization. In larger companies, this is likely to be a division general manager or president. In smaller companies, it is likely to be the CEO or president. In this article "business manager" will be substituted for "P&L manager" in most cases, as the former term is more commonly used.

2. Product quality management consists of the quality management function (ensuring that good quality policies are in place and enforced), the quality assurance function (developing and implementing practices and processes that ensure that quality products are produced), and the quality control function (actual testing of products to ensure conformance to customer requirements).
3. Most organizations call these criteria "requirements." These are the specifications that the organization believes a product must meet in order to satisfy a customer need.
4. Professionally means that the team provides information in a form, at a time, and in a way that is perceived as non-threatening, objective, and valuable. There is no appearance of a hidden bias or agenda. In short, the test team is respected and listened to by all parties. This is not usually the case with test teams.
5. While a number of companies have contracted to put dedicated software test teams on a customer's site, these companies have typically not been dedicated software testing companies, nor have they put dedicated labs in place without specific long-term contracts.

Section 3
Managing Business Relationships

Chapter 17
Prescriptions for Managing IT Priority Pressure

Tom Rose

Ideas for better managing IT priority pressure become clear when the demands placed on IT professionals are viewed through the lens of the project management discipline. What is meant by the project management discipline is not the complex set of methods and tools that are generally associated with project management, but rather the resourceful and disciplined management of few key attributes of IT projects. Looking at IT work in this way focuses attention on the set of critical power and influence issues that lie at the heart of implementing successful IT-based performance improvement. This chapter contends that those IT professionals who effectively manage this aspect of IT projects better manage priority pressure. The goals of this chapter are to outline the project management perspective and enumerate a few key prescriptions for effectively addressing the power and influence challenges of IT projects.

THE NEW IT PERFORMANCE ENVIRONMENT AND THE PROJECT MANAGEMENT PERSPECTIVE

The project management-based perspective of IT work reveals that throughout the project life cycle of design, development, implementation, and maintenance, IT professionals face the challenge of managing dynamic tensions that exist between a few critical project factors. Better management of priority pressure begins with an understanding of these project factors and their relationship.

The Power of Three

As project managers, IT professionals must produce deliverables that satisfy three task factors. Deliverables must (1) meet certain quality standards, (2) be installed within a specified period of time, and (3) be completed within a specific budget. From the project management perspective, the principal task of IT professionals is helping users fit their aspirations for information technology-enhanced performance improvement with the realities of time and resource constraints.

To keep these interdependencies in mind and in the minds of users, one IT organization uses the slogan "Good, Fast, and Cheap: Pick Two." "If you want fast and cheap, then you cannot have good." "You can have good and cheap, but then you cannot have it fast," and so on. A key implication of the project management perspective is that IT professionals today more carefully manage the interdependencies between quality, time, and cost.

While engaged in this task today, IT professionals are being asked to more evenly divide their attention between each of the task factors. Historically, IT professionals have been perceived to focus more on quality (as they, not the user, defined it) to the near exclusion of time and cost considerations. The legacy of such practice was user complaints that work products were off target, late, and over budget. The specter of outsourcing that haunts IT managers today is, in part, due to the unfortunate legacy of these complaints.

Better managing the relationships between quality, time, and cost occurs when IT professionals successfully address a couple of key project planning and project tracking and control challenges. In the project planning phase, when requirements and specifications are being established, disagreements among users about performance improvement priorities or user anxiety about making costly decisions (e.g., large financial investments in IT; significant changes in business processes) are common and can make it difficult to establish commitments about quality, time, and cost. Directly engaging these difficulties (e.g., implementing a group priority-setting session to resolve user manager disagreements, working with the user management team to build a common vision of how requirements will be implemented, influencing users to adopt a more gradual and incremental approach to innovation) is necessary to resolving them. Proceeding without such clarity creates problems later in project life cycle.

Later in the project life cycle, changes in the project environment frequently occur and invalidate initial commitments about quality, time, or cost. User requirements shift; tasks exceed their estimated completion times; budgets are slashed. When project tracking and controlling practices detect changes, trade-offs between quality, time, and cost must be negotiated. Deliverables may have to be scaled back to address budgetary constraints. Timelines may have to be extended to allow for the development of increases in desired functionality. Budgets may have to be increased to complete project deliverables more quickly, and so on. Assertively engaging

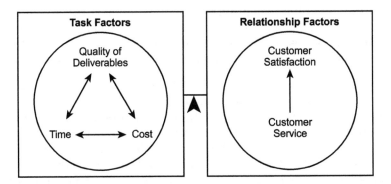

Exhibit 1.   Maintaining the Balance: The Project Management Framework

users in problem solving about such tradeoffs is another important aspect of better managing the project task factors.

To maintain the proper relationship between quality, time, and cost, tough choices are often required. What makes these choices difficult is that one is not often selecting between a clearly good and bad choice. Rather, the choices are often between good and good.[1]

A Question of Balance

As IT budgets have soared and user demands for optimal ROI have increased, managing quality, time, and cost must be accomplished with recognition of a fourth critical project factor — customer satisfaction. User complaints about a lack of responsiveness, the inability of IT professionals to engage users about their IT needs in "user-friendly" terms, a lack of reliability about time lines along with related service sins have all produced a heightened awareness of customer satisfaction and the means used to secure it in many IT organizations.[2]

To address the greater importance of customer satisfaction, the quality, time, and cost framework introduced earlier has been expanded. Exhibit 1 displays this expanded view of IT project management.

The implication of this framework is that IT professionals must balance alignment among the task factors (i.e., quality, time, and cost) with the press of the relationship factors (i.e., customer service and customer satisfaction). If IT professionals allow the balance to tip too much in the favor of task factors, too little emphasis is given to the relationship factors. Project managers may successfully complete the tasks on their project plans but create off-target work products and frustrated customers.

On the other hand, if the balance is allowed to tip too much in favor of the relationship factor, the opportunity to deliver timely and cost effective work products is lost. Creating a service balance is the second major theme underlying changes in the IT field. When the balance is achieved and maintained, IT professionals come to be respected as business partners by users because they build useful work products for satisfied customers.

Viewing IT work through the lens of this project management framework emphasizes the importance of balancing four critical project factors: quality, time, cost, and customer satisfaction during project planning and later in the project life cycle. To achieve and maintain this balance, IT professionals must directly engage in the power and influence dynamics of implementing organizational innovation. Productively managing these dynamics helps preserve the balance between the project factors and enhances the IT professional's ability to manage priority pressure. Five prescriptions for achieving this are as follows:

1. Sell good ideas by emphasizing benefits that the user or customer perceives as valuable.
2. Build a common vision of project outcomes and how people will work together to achieve them.
3. Generate commitment to ideas or implementation plans by getting users to modify them in the direction of personal and business interests.
4. Engage conflicts directly and resolve them efficiently and effectively.
5. Assertively enforce standards of IT excellence.

Each of these ideas is developed in the following sections.

PRESCRIPTIONS AND "HOW-TO" SUGGESTIONS

Sell Good Ideas by Emphasizing Benefits that the User Perceives as Valuable

The starting point for an IT project is selling senior management within the user group and within the IT function on the idea. Consequently, the efficiency with which ideas are sold is one important means of managing priority pressure. The power of persuasion depends largely on whether the rationale used to support an idea resonates with the decision-maker's interests. To sell ideas more efficiently, the rationale for an idea must reflect the user's priorities. In short, reasoning should always outline "what is in it for them."

When selling ideas, IT professionals sometimes get stuck on technical issues, specifications, and justifications. Although technical details are critical, as facts, they have limited power to influence users and senior IT management. As a result, one of the main priority management prescriptions is that IT professionals need to develop sufficient business expertise to engage users in terms that they will find compelling. IT professionals who add this expertise to their technical competence have the greatest organizational impact. Many IT organizations are experimenting with the role of user or client relationship manager to help establish client sensitivity within IT organization.

Selling ideas effectively also means having good ideas. Good ideas are designed with knowledge of the practical time and resource constraints within which they will be implemented. Not all business problems require state-of-the-art solutions. Sometimes, small is beautiful. Making incremental enhancements over time can moderate the negative influence of organizational politics, limit risk, and create success experiences. A track record of successful enhancements can build momentum for bigger, more ambitious projects.

Having a good idea is not sufficient, however. Good ideas are often not met with enthusiasm. How the IT professional responds to the objections raised by others as the idea is being sold affects one's eventual success. Arthur Schopenhauer, the nineteenth-century philosopher said that ideas go "through three distinct phases: ridicule, opposition, and finally enthusiastic acceptance." Advancing ideas through these phases means (1) increasing perceived need for the idea, (2) modifying the idea itself to increase personal and organizational benefits to key stakeholders, (3) reducing costs, both personal and organizational, and (4) decreasing perceived risks. By adjusting good ideas iteratively based on feedback from stakeholders, IT professionals can efficiently win a critical mass of support for IT projects from key stakeholders.

Sustaining Focus and Maintaining Motivation with Common Vision

Once an idea for IT-based performance improvement has been sold to senior user management, effective IT professionals work with those who must live with and use a solution to build a common vision of the performance improvement and how people will work together to achieve it. This is vital because many IT projects are difficult and complex undertakings. Costly technology is required. The multiple factors that influence business problems must be analyzed. Difficult design choices must be made. Complex implementation and maintenance problems must be solved throughout the life cycle of the project. A healthy dose of common vision during the early phases of a project helps guide and motivate both the IT professional and the user through these challenges in later project phases. Rarely does a critical mass of support for an IT solution exist at the outset; it must be constructed from conflicting interests and motives that exist within the user community.

Common vision has two main parts. Common vision describes the outcomes the project is pursuing. It also contains the infrastructure of agreements people develop to guide how they will work together to accomplish the project outcomes. Each is now dealt in turn.

Common Vision as a Description of Project Outcomes. Common vision is different from a statement of work, although it should inform it as an expression of mission and purpose. In common vision, greater emphasis is placed on the contribution the deliverable will make to the efficiency, effectiveness, or quality of the user's group (otherwise known as requirements) and less on the features of the deliverable itself (otherwise known as specifications). In a large consulting firm, for example, one might install text-based groupware to help members of the firm in locations across the country identify and retrieve the best parts of proposals used by members throughout the firm. This is a general description of the deliverable. The requirement in this situation may be to dramatically increase the efficiency of the sales process by reducing by half the time its takes to prepare high quality proposals. Clear description of how business results will be different and how users who will be working with the installed technology will be performing differently to achieve those results is a key part of common vision.

One difficulty in developing shared commitments about outcomes is that significant points of difference can exist among users about the requirements. Field sales groups and headquarters sales management within a single sales unit can and will have different and conflicting priorities. Quality control and production units within a manufacturing operation may also have conflicting and competing priorities. Finding common ground in these circumstances requires imagination and insight as competing interests are easier to see than common ones. This insight because easier to achieve when one takes time to understand in detail the needs and concerns of various constituencies within the user community.

In the circumstance of high conflict within the user group, it can be helpful to bring user groups together and employ a group conflict management or negotiation process to find a way to address conflicting priorities. IT professionals who pursue this option often find outside experts to facilitate such a session.

If a common vision of requirements is not achieved with users early in a the project, one of important consequences is that downstream project costs are high. Typically, maintenance of an installed IT solution is the last step in the project lifecycle. Unfortunately, 82 percent of costs incurred in the maintenance phase are attributable to problems created in the initial phase of a project — the establishing-requirements phase. Communication problems between the user and IT professionals result in poor specification of requirements. The consequences of proceeding without clarity about requirements is dramatically high system maintenance costs.[3]

Common Vision as a Description of How People Will Work Together. In addition to creating a picture of the targeted performance improvement, common vision also contains agreements about how people will work together on an IT project. Agreements about customer service practices such as responsiveness, decision making, and mutual accountabilities are key issues for which agreements are ideally made. Working through such issues can be experienced as tedious or irrelevant by IT professionals and by users on a project team who are anxious to get to the real work. "Who needs this warm and fuzzy stuff!" is a familiar refrain. The response, of course, is that the project does. Failing to take the time to build the infrastructure of agreements that are the basis of high-performance teams can mean serious derailments later on. When timelines get critical and stress and pressure mounts, tough decisions are required. Teams that are missing a strong infrastructure struggle or fail at such key moments.

An IT group within a major consumer products company now conducts visioning sessions as a preliminary step in all major projects. In these sessions, a vision of the performance improvement is developed, requirements are detailed, and deliverables are clarified. Agreements are also hammered out about how the IT team and the user team will work together. Particular attention is devoted to how parties will notify each other about the need to make adjustments in the project plan and how these adjustments will be approved and implemented.

How to Build Common Vision. Activities which are used to create common vision foster dialogue up and down the user chain of command and within the IT project team about needs, priorities, and requirements as well as the infrastructure of agreements about how people will work together to complete the project. Effective visioning procedures feature detailed meeting outlines and specification of the concrete deliverables that will be created by the common-vision effort. This structure allays user concerns that people will be asked to participate in a directionless "group grope" that will produce general goal statements that specify nothing of real value beyond an understanding that the participants are "all in this together." Without a solid foundation of shared commitments, visioning devolves into "blue sky" statements about future project deliverables that have little real chance of influencing project outcomes.

The logic of common vision is easy for most to grasp but difficult to operationalize into concrete action steps. A sample template of the steps one can take to build common vision is provided in Exhibit 2.

When difficult long-term IT-based performance improvement is the mandate, building common vision early in a project's life cycle about requirements and how users and IT professionals will work together can

Exhibit 2. Generating Common Vision

1. Steps for Generating Outcomes
   a. Participants generate personal visions of project outcomes.
   b. Individual responses are summarized and distributed to team members.
   c. Team members meet to identify priority themes.
   d. Team members identify and resolve conflict that may exist in priority themes.
   e. Agreements are summarized and adopted by the team.
2. Customer Service Agreements: How will people work together to achieve the outcomes.
   a. Team members identify potential service commitments. At a minimum this should include defining the standards of responsiveness, determining how communication channels will be maintained, identifying the procedures which will be used to keep the project on track through the project lifecycle, specifying how adjustments in project plans will be made, outlining how conflicts will be resolved.
   b. Team selects priority commitments.
   c. Team identifies project practices and behaviors that will hold the IT group and the user to intentions established in B.
   d. Team identifies procedures and develops a schedule for (i) monitoring priority practices and behaviors and (ii) formulating corrective action.

decrease the priority pressure IT professionals face later in the project's lifecycle.

Build Commitment to Ideas or Implementation Plans through User Participation

Once common vision has been established, successful IT project plans regularly solicit the participation of those who must use applications on a daily and ongoing basis to refine the application and the strategy that will be used to install it. This commitment to participation has several benefits. With greater involvement, user knowledge of the factors that influence timelines and milestones increases, IT-user communication is enhanced and expensive missteps can be avoided and efficiency improved. Participation has a second benefit. It has been consistently demonstrated that involvement with project design enhances commitment to implementation. Giving the user community the opportunity to experiment with prototypes, recommend upgrades, and influence implementation plans early on and often increases the likelihood that the installed system will be well received and ultimately used.

Putting participation into practice presents the IT professional with a few challenges. For participation to work, users must trust the process, view their input as voluntary, experience the process of participating as rewarding, and see their ideas significantly affecting work products.[4] IT professionals may have to intervene to insure these conditions will exist before asking for user participation. This means influencing user management. For user managers to support participation, IT professionals must illustrate that the benefits of participation exceed the risks to productivity created by having their people devote time to project work.

Engage Conflicts Directly and Resolve Conflicts Efficiently and Effectively

Once project plans are underway, change happens. Requirements shift, the client does not meet its obligations in the project plan, and budgets can be reduced. Changes within the IT group can also occur. Tasks may exceed initial estimates. Key programmers leave to join other firms. Differences in opinion among IT professionals about the best approach can erupt into conflicts that push projects off track.

When this happens, IT professionals must assertively engage key stakeholders (e.g., users, user management, IT management) in problem solving about the trade-offs that must be made in quality, time, cost, and perhaps even customer service agreements. Assertiveness is critical because users (and admittedly IT management on occasion) would prefer to avoid making necessary but difficult decisions about trade-offs between quality, time, and cost. Interestingly, resolving such conflicts may be best viewed as a typical and not unusual part of what IT project managers do. In survey research of professional project managers, it was discovered that they report spending an average of 12 hours per week resolving conflicts.[5]

When engaged in problem solving about trade-offs, stakeholders sometimes become frustrated and retaliate by challenging the competence or creativity of the IT project manager. IT professionals sometimes respond to such challenges by retreating from their legitimate interests. In a misguided effort to please, some over-commit to all three factors although significant changes in the project environment necessitate adjustments. The result is priority overload, stressed-out IT personnel, a loss of credibility and influence, suboptimal IT work products, or missed timelines.

Assertively championing one's basic interests, exploring alternatives with affected parties even when they are not enthusiastic to do so, and collaborating to construct win-win agreements is the better response. Unfortunately, many people drawn to information technology (like many drawn to other technical disciplines) have a personal aversion to conflict. Consequently, for some IT professionals, enhanced negotiation skills is necessary.

Faithfully applying project management disciplines can limit the amount and scope of project conflicts that IT professionals have to manage. Conducting risk assessments early in the project life cycle to identify factors that might threaten project deliverables is one such discipline. If a risk is detected early (e.g., weak user management consensus on requirements) and focused problem solving occurs about what contingencies are necessary to address it (e.g., identifying a resource that can be used to do team conflict resolution with user managers), project disruptions caused by the risk can be effectively contained.

Providing regular user management updates is a second project management discipline. When updates work most effectively, not only is progress reported, but threats to project deliverables are reviewed and user management support of efforts to limit or resolve those threats is secured.

For some complex projects, more substantial organizational conflict management mechanisms are required. On large IT initiatives, the relative priority of the needs of different user groups can change over time. Because IT resources are often relatively fixed, reallocating resources to respond to a increased urgency for one user often means reneging on commitments made to other users. To address shifting priorities between users, some IT groups convene regular, periodic meetings of steering committees or users councils. When such mechanisms work well, users collectively learn about urgent priority changes, explore alternative responses to these situations, and finally make mutual decisions about priority changes and IT resource reallocation. In these settings, IT professionals facilitate the preparation of information that enables these groups to make sound decisions. By promoting quality dialogue between users, IT professionals enhance organizational problem solving.

Assertively Championing Standards of IT Excellence

In certain circumstances the primary task of the IT professional is to ensure compliance with organizational standards concerning how IT technology is used. In other words, IT professionals are sometimes asked to give greater emphasis to their role as enforcers of senior management IT policy and less to their role as internal consultants. Occasionally, it is necessary for IT professionals to use the full measure of the positional power vested in their role by the organization and prescribe specific actions that users must take to be in compliance with corporate IT standards.

Although such standards help optimize the efficiency management of IT resources, on occasion, they can be inconvenient for some user managers. When users fail to comply with important standards, tough but skillful enforcement is required. Consider the following case as an illustration. An IT manager was working with a user manager who disagreed with corporate IT policy and began contacting IT suppliers directly to acquire the technology he desired. In response, the IT manager approached the user manager with the goal of assessing the particular difficulties the officially sanctioned technology was creating for the manager and offering assistance in working through such problems. The user manager responded by complaining that the IT professionals were being unresponsive and resisted attempts to assess his particular objections to the approved technology options. Further, the user manager began manipulating the IT professionals against themselves to secure the technology he wanted.

The project manager's response was to talk with the manager directly about the policy violation and IT's role as enforcers of this policy. The IT manager also offered his support in helping the user manager escalate the issue to senior policy makers. The IT professional said that he would advocate an exception to corporate policy as well as minimize the negative consequences the user manager feared the approved technology would create for his group if the exception was not granted. As this approach was more firm and direct than the user manager had experienced from other IT professionals, the IT manager wisely briefed his management before undertaking his plan.

In this case, the IT professional applied the positional power invested in his role by the corporation to enforce established IT policy and practices. Using the positional power invested in one's role is another underutilized means of managing IT priority pressure.

SUMMARY

The starting point for effectively managing priority pressure is to view IT work from the perspective of project management. In particular, this means recognizing that IT professionals must engage end users in the decision making about how the balance between quality, time, cost, and customer satisfaction is preserved. When IT professionals adopt this perspective, they embrace the practical politics of implementing innovation. This requires both courage and competence from the member of IT organizations. Effective human resource management practices can ensure that both traits are being selected for and systematically groomed. By encouraging the expression of courage and competence, IT professionals can become masters of, and not victims of, priority pressure. The investment organizations make in IT and the effectiveness of the professionals who are stewards of its appropriate application depend on this mastery.

Notes

1. This idea is borrowed from Quinn, R. (1999). *Managing Deep Change.* San Fransisco, CA: Jossey-Bass.
2. Longenecker, C. O., Simonetti, J.L., and Mulias, M. (1996). "Survival Skills for the IT Professional." Information Systems Management, Spring, 26- 31.
3. McLeod, G. and Smith, D. (1996). *Managing Information Technology Projects.* Cambridge, MA: Course Technology.
4. Hunton, J. E. and Beeler, J. D. (1997). "Effects of User Participation in Systems Development: A Longitudinal Field Experiment." *MIS Quarterly,* December, 359–369.
5. Kerzner, H. (1995). *Project Management: A Systems Approach to Planning, Scheduling, and Controlling.* New York: NY: Van Nostrand Reinhold.

Chapter 18
Business and IT: Developing Strategic Alliances

Andy Roquet

Every day, headlines across the country announce new partnerships between companies. In the current economic business cycle, strong companies are partnering with other strong companies where objectives are congruent, and each can bring value to the other. These partnerships come in the form of mergers, acquisitions, and strategic alliances. Strategic alliances are different in that both companies must be involved in making decisions and implementing the alliance because both have a vested interest going forward. Typically in strategic alliances, the parts of each business that overlap must be "cleaned up," sold, or discontinued, and new linkages must be established between the companies. In the context of this chapter, strategic alliances entail the maintenance by each partnering company of its own management, identity, and ownership; and bringing mutual benefits to the table in terms of product, market, or other strategic advantages. In other words, this is a symbiotic relationship.

In today's fast-paced business environment, where decisions are made quickly, strategic alliances are often put together and approved expediently. There are a number of valid business reasons for this, including confidentiality, timeliness, and competitive advantage. Unfortunately, however, information technology (IT) is traditionally brought in only after the deal is signed, and must then catch up, learning enough about the deal and the line of business to support the transition.

Inevitably, while IT is trying to get up to speed, the alliance is progressing into initial production mode. Playing catch-up may create technology-related issues during the alliance, whereby organizations implement short-term tactical solutions that require rework and increased costs over the long term. A better solution is to involve IT from the start of negotiations, so it can start adding value by helping to lay out the transition and establish new linkages.

ROLE OF IT IN STRATEGIC ALLIANCES

Strategic alliances are initiated in a number of ways, but those implementing the alliance (that is, IT) seldom play a part in the initial deal-making process. Too often, the business areas negotiate and sign the deal, with little or no IT involvement. Alternatively, the business areas might seek IT involvement in a fragmented manner based on specific questions.

Admittedly, a decentralized IT organization makes it difficult to pinpoint the correct person to contact on a particular issue. Also, while organizations might discuss the relevant requirements of the strategic alliance with those specifically involved, such as application development support, they often leave important linkages out of the discussion, such as telecommunications, data sharing, or call-routing topics.

Even if the organization has centralized IT support, the business area might still only feed parts of the strategy to IT, instead of taking the time to fully engage IT in the potential alliance discussions. Additionally, because IT is critical to existing business operations, the individual business units might be reluctant to use IT resources for such exploratory activities. For their part, IT organizations are often reluctant to make time available for such discussions, unless they are confident that concrete activities will result.

Of course, if an organization is creating a new business unit from an alliance, the business processes *should* be set up first, and the supporting IT infrastructure developed secondarily. However, these realities lead to a fragmented approach in setting up an alliance, and produce inefficiencies and weak links in the union between the companies.

The Issues

There are many problems when IT is not involved from the outset of negotiations through finalization. When IT does not understand the entire strategy, it cannot provide the most effective, right-sized solutions. For example, if the alliance is already proven, and needs to be set for a long-term relationship, IT should invest considerable time so things are done correctly from the beginning. However, if the alliance is merely to be tested before the requirements are known, IT should invest less time, and the technology processes should be set up more quickly.

On the one hand, the two IT departments involved in the alliance will have technological differences. Even if both organizations use the same basic technology, and have similar business applications, both must make changes in order to build a working environment. Because smoothing out the technological differences between the IT installations will take time and patience, IT representatives should be brought into the process as early as is practical.

In addition, it will require time to resolve the cultural differences between the two organizations, so they can reach a common ground. Therefore, the sooner IT from both sides can start planning and working together, the better it will be for everyone involved. Dealing with production problems at the same time as blending the cultural and technical aspects will only make an already tension-filled process worse. Involvement and input will be rushed to meet immediate requirements; and compromises will be made, requiring later IT rework.

Because IT staff members are generally analytical and critical thinkers, they tend to point out problems, instead of seeing new-found "challenges" and providing solutions. If IT is brought in early, it can raise issues and bring solutions at the same time. As a result, the business area will more likely realize the value of IT involvement, and start to include IT more naturally. If, however, the proper business/IT relationships are not established from the start, the two areas will have difficulties working together.

Unforeseen costs will also arise when IT costs for the alliance are not researched and accounted for in the financial transaction. The cost of software has increased in the last 10 to 15 years as vendors realized the value that software adds to business productivity. In addition, vendors continue to enhance and create product functions and features leading to upgrades. There are also more productivity tools available, which have become necessary in day-to-day business. And the many platforms that software is designed to run on also contribute to the continued rise in costs.

Third-party processing provides one real example of how software licensing can delay or add significantly to the cost of an alliance. Thus, after the deal is executed, the original company might continue to run the application on its mainframe to benefit the new company, thereby creating a third-party processing arrangement. Because software contracts often do not address third-party processing, there will be additional fees.

In addition, each software contract must be systematically inventoried and negotiated to ensure that application software packages are properly run and maintained. This also requires the IT departments to begin working together as soon as possible, and developing plans for the transition. Once developed, the plans must be communicated to everyone who will be involved in the changed environment.

The organizations can thus save money by fully understanding what will be required on both sides. In addition, appropriate planning and communication can mitigate the high frustration levels resulting from the changes.

Since IT staffing is critical to the success of an alliance, the organizations must pay special attention to retaining the necessary IT staff, particularly in light of the current IT market. The organizations should focus on those staff members who support the current systems, who work on the business transition, and who build the new linkages. The organizations might negotiate "stay" bonuses for existing staff, hire contracting firms to continue to run the applications, or combine the two strategies.

If organizations can retain their staff, training will generally not be required to keep the systems operational. However, additional skills may be required at appropriate intervals for transitioning the business and building new linkages, including specific languages, tools, or platforms.

The Business/IT Relationship

The lack of a good relationship between the business and IT areas often figures prominently in the problems that arise when IT is left out of alliance negotiations. In the past, the data processing (DP) staff members were the only employees who knew anything about computers. The DP operation often featured a mainframe hidden in a basement corner. The computer performed batch operations, with viewing capabilities only during the day.

By contrast, today's PC/Internet environment allows significant, individual processing capabilities. Over time, the business community has also become far more knowledgeable about technology. In addition, some successful IT staff have moved to the business side of the organization, bringing their IT knowledge. As business users' computer knowledge increases, they feel less need to involve IT early on in the alliance process.

At the same time, however, the IT environment is becoming far more complex. The environment of mainframes and dumb terminals has changed to one of fully networked PCs, servers, and mainframes across LANs and WANs. Systems are no longer developed in flat file formats; developers now use relational and object databases with new languages. So the business areas cannot keep pace with IT changes. For their part, IT staff members easily get caught up in the newest toys and latest technology, implementing solutions for the sake of using new technology, rather than meeting business needs.

The "expense factor" also contributes to the ineffective business/IT relationship. Here, because the business areas view IT as an expense that is constantly increasing, they try to avoid dealing with it until absolutely necessary. Because IT is often critical to company-set priorities, resources are too tight to designate time up front. However, up-front time is necessary in alliances, just as investing time up front in system development helps save time on back-end rework and retesting.

If IT spends time developing and fostering a positive value-added relationship with the business area, the business will naturally include IT sooner. In addition, it helps if a good business/IT relationship is developed before the two must interact in the stressful, time-sensitive manner that an alliance requires.

Understanding the Alliance

Because there are so many possible alliance options, IT should review and evaluate the specific alliance in question. When the organization first determines its business direction, IT should assess and understand top management's corporate prioritization for the alliance, as well as the financial aspects. While ideas are easy to develop, a successful alliance requires full corporate backing. For example, success is more likely if the CEOs have met and signed the deal, rather than vice-presidents' authorization in one line of business. In addition, public relations must communicate to the marketplace about the alliance.

IT should also consider the other company, determining if it has experience with alliances or is subject to any special or sensitive issues. Different alliances have contracts with different requirements and success factors. Although work on the contract might be time-consuming and take attention from current work, knowing the terms of the agreement will be invaluable later on.

Due diligence work is typically required before a deal is signed. Companies look favorably on IT managers who offer to complete the IT due diligence section. In addition, IT managers might thereby meet counterparts with whom they will work during the alliance project. Examples of due diligence areas include the company background, terminology, competitors, types and volumes of data to share, timeliness of communications, and data definitions. Some industries have common file sharing formats and data definitions that can quickly bridge the data definition knowledge gap.

The due diligence process also involves clearly identifying the methods of data transfer, communication, and security between the alliance partners. It is important for the data to move smoothly, and that it be protected at all times. IT should not make assumptions about the communications hardware and software in the other organization. Furthermore, the organizations want to prepare beforehand, rather than straightening out incompatibilities while trying to process the data. The latter will not only cause frustration on both sides of the transactions, but can become critical if the difficulties involve the alliance's customers.

The organization's financial investment in the alliance project can reveal the criticality of the alliance. The importance can be gauged by comparing the project budget to the corporate budget, or the revenue projections to the corporate total.

In general, larger alliances can support more investment in infrastructure up front to set up the alliance. Smaller alliances must move quickly to prove themselves, in order to justify additional investment in infrastructure. Even in developing a shorter-term solution, however, it will still benefit IT to build a solution that can be built upon, rather than thrown away or replaced.

CORPORATE CULTURE

All companies have their own corporate culture, which can be as diverse as two multinational companies or as similar as two mutual insurance companies. No matter how similar or different the alliant entities appear to be, it is critical to assess the cultures of both. Easy factors to understand and compare include general work hours and time zones, experiences with cross-site teams, and teleconference etiquette for newer team members. More difficult, critical items include:

- How the internal IT shops operate
- How the other company's business and IT units get along
- How work is prioritized
- How priority conflicts get resolved

The relationship between the human resources (HR) and IT areas could seriously affect an alliance project. Because IT staff is critical to many alliances, it is important for the organizations to retain the current knowledgeable staff, who understand the systems and can create transition processing. If IT staff members do not find it valuable to remain, they might leave at the first opportunity. Therefore, organizations should develop "stay" bonus packages, which will likely be different for IT than those of other staff members. It is important to have an HR area that understands the IT environment and can help in developing these packages.

The two IT cultures will likely have different organizational structures and processes. For example, large companies operate very differently than smaller companies in decision-making abilities and the formality of communications. Other factors that IT should consider include: whether there are formal project management or systems development methodologies, the standard desktop configuration and software available to share information, and how voice and e-mail are used internally and over the Internet.

Vendor relationships within each of the IT organizations will also affect alliance efforts. Larger companies usually have more influence in vendor negotiations, whereas smaller companies must often accept the pricing as presented.

In addition to potential third-party factors, different releases of the same software can cause incompatibilities that must be resolved. It is critical to analyze software package-by-package to make sure the packages are compatible where necessary, and to develop a vendor negotiation strategy.

Companies also have different products and vendors fulfilling the same functionality. Again, it is critical to walk through each situation, identifying the necessary course of action. Sometimes, different packages can communicate with other similar packages and no additional action is needed.

Early on in an alliance process, often before the contract is signed, the IT front-line staff members must start working together to define the detailed requirements. Each company has its own cultural way of working through issues. For example, some cultures tightly control communications and decision delegation, while others let staff members make decisions and be accountable for them. It is important to identify processes and lead people in order to quickly address any conflict. If the respective IT and business areas do not get along, the alliance will be more challenging.

A company's culture is developed over time, and is often held sacred — for both old companies and new start-ups. Assessing and understanding an alliant company's cultures up front can help IT understand how it operates and quickly work through issues.

DEVELOPING AN IT ALLIANCE STRATEGY

When IT is supporting a strategic alliance, it must take the time to plan. The time spent up front will be well worth it, ensuring that all parties are clear on the needs and desired results. A thorough project management methodology is critical to success and to compress the overall timeline. In particular, IT should:

- *Understand the business area's strategy and objectives for the alliance:* This includes reading the strategic alliance contract, charter, and other documentation. It is also important to meet with the project manager, and potentially the sponsor, to start building the relationship and to discuss the critical success factors. Once the overall objectives are understood, they should not change going forward. It is important to stay on top of changes in lesser objectives.
- *Understand the other company's objectives in the alliance:* If the objectives of the two companies are congruent, both will work toward a common goal. If the objectives are not complementary, conflict may arise. Although the overall objectives may be the same, there may be legitimate but different subobjectives. It is important to take the time

to understand and agree upon all the objectives, clarifying and resolving all issues.

- *Get to know the other company's IT area, culture, and processes:* Understanding how the other company operates will be important in working through issues that arise. Up-front knowledge of the other company's decision-makers, as well as its processes for setting priorities and change management, will speed conflict resolution.
- *Develop a project plan in conjunction with the business areas:* With the overall plan established, the IT portion must be detailed. Both business and IT representatives should develop and walk through the IT plan, for understanding and clarification. It is key to define the roles and responsibilities for each company, as well as for the business and IT players. The project manager must be informed if the implementation timelines change from the initial to the detailed plan.
- *Execute and monitor the plan, making changes as necessary:* Once the project plan is initially established, it must be tracked. To do so, the steering committee and front-line team should hold regular meetings, documenting and communicating the content of the meetings, as well as decisions to be made. When changes are identified, a formal change management process is necessary to communicate the effects to all interested parties.
- *Follow up with lessons learned:* This process can be undertaken during the project at appropriate phases, or, as is typical, after the project is over. The facilitated session is an open discussion to document the project's positive aspects and potential improvements. This is where the organization learns and grows by clearing the air and setting expectations for improvements going forward.
- *Create a checklist for future alliances:* Since the organization will be entering into more alliances, it can learn from its experiences by developing a checklist of the necessary steps, illustrating what worked well, as well as the pitfalls to avoid. This checklist can be used as a starting point for the next alliance, although there will be changes, additions, or items that may not apply going forward.

The Detailed Plan

The most difficult part of the process is to develop the detailed plan, possibly because there might be a gap between the business's initial expectations of the alliance and what can really get accomplished at a detailed level. The project plan includes scope, timeline, and resources. While project managers cannot dictate all three, they should be able to determine at least one. Of course, even if the scope and timeline are set, IT cannot always accomplish the objectives by adding more resources to the project. No matter how many resources are available, some processes cannot be completed more quickly.

Scope. The project plan's scope should be as complete as possible. Here, a number of issues will be raised, and solving them quickly will be a key success factor. An issues log with origination date and required answer date is a necessity.

In an alliance, one company will typically have an unsuccessful line of business that is a strength of the other company. It is necessary to decide what to do with the potentially competing line of business: continue it, convert it, or sell it. This determination usually differs from establishing new linkages between the different IT resource efforts.

However, it is also critical to define new linkages between the companies in terms of systems integration and data sharing. Examples include marketing and financial information, revenue, and financial compensation. Detailed discussions are necessary for data definitions and mapping.

The size of the alliance effort depends on related experiences and expectations on the part of both companies. Companies with previous alliance experience are more likely to reuse programs, interfaces, and file generation. Companies with little or no such experience will require more time, effort, and communication.

Identification of all the hardware, software, and staff costs involved will help expedite the transition. For example, an alliance will close more quickly if software licensing costs continue to run transition systems on the selling company's infrastructure as a third-party administrative function.

In addition, both organizations should include enough travel budget and time to develop proper face-to-face relationships. IT should also build solid relationships with the vendors involved to ensure a smooth transition for packaged applications. Success depends on having a strategy for contacting vendors. For example, if one alliance company has a better working relationship with various vendors, it should be leveraged.

Planning should be included for all phases of the effort. These include requirements development, systems development, testing (of IT, the business area, systems, performance tuning, etc.), conversion, and implementation.

Unforeseen costs will arise. If the contract wording specifies that all costs are shared equally, all profits might also be shared equally.

The business's general, high-level scope must be compared to the detailed scope as defined above. This checkpoint raises new issues that must be validated regarding if they are in or out of the initial project scope. This determination might require cost-benefit information.

Timeline. A timeline is typically established during the contract discussions. It might be a vague statement targeting the end of the third quarter, or it could be based on a company year-end.

IT should understand the exact commitments in terms of the business deliverables and logic, in order to gauge the flexibility for changes. When IT understands the business logic behind the timeline, the only options for change may be to reduce the scope or increase the costs.

Once the timeline is agreed to, there must be communication of status at established milestone checkpoints. Contingency plans must be developed in case the timeline cannot be met.

Costs. The business area usually has a cost in mind for the alliance that has been approved in the project plan. Once the detailed IT costs are validated, they must be immediately communicated to the business area, to determine disparity between the initial and detail plans. All costs must be included, from hardware and software to staff time. The latter requires an assessment of the necessary skill sets, and some hard dollars may be needed for contracting.

The costs should be itemized and attached to specific scope items and deliverables so that the business area can analyze the costs and benefits of scope decisions. In some cases, IT and the business can work together to reduce specific requirement costs by scaling back or making slight changes that dramatically reduce the timeline and cost. No matter what the final figure, the plan should include some level of contingency funding to ensure sufficient money to complete the project.

IT SUPPORT AND DIRECTION

While the above activities are IT responsibilities, IT can also help the business area by:

- *Defining the alliance's critical success factors:* IT can identify specific items to be measured and communicated regarding the alliance's success, including conversion ratios, revenue, expenses, and quality factors. It is much easier to design systems to meet these needs up front, rather than redesigning them later.
- *Working with the business area to map out key processes:* IT can draw a diagram of all the processes to show what is happening and when, so people can clearly understand what must take place in the alliance efforts. If there are gaps, it is easier to find them early on. Understanding the timing is key for daily, weekly, monthly, quarterly, and yearly exchanges. Mapping will also highlight differences in the companies' reporting schedules; for example, use of calendar year versus the corporate year-end.

It is important to map key business, financial, and systems processes, including critical dataflows and timing. Mapping business processes requires showing how the current processes work now and how the new processes will flow in the future. Changes to business processes might target phone call routing, procedural changes, and technological changes based on different systems used.

Financial processes will be mapped in different degrees of detail. For example, high-level financial reporting can be shown by summary numbers from a paper report, while detailed reporting is necessary to pay compensation based on transactions.

Systems flows are important in showing different physical implementations of technology. Also, when an IT organization is switching to the new environment, it should not remove the old technology infrastructure too soon, in case there are transition issues.

- *Defining gaps in data definitions:* In new alliances, where there is no existing business to transition, this step may not be important because each company will bring its own definitions to the table. Gaps in data definitions become more important when there is a transition of business from one company to another and detailed data mapping is required. The first step is to define data requirements for each system; for example, to illustrate what each field or file layout represents. Key business and IT staff must be assigned to work through the issues.
- *Developing comprehensive plans to address the gaps:* It is important to bring alternatives and solutions to the table because IT has invaluable experience and knowledge. When IT understands the overall alliance objectives, it can strengthen its relationship with the business area by offering recommendations in solving business problems.

HOW TO AVOID COMMON PITFALLS

IT should build a positive relationship with the business area first. This cannot be emphasized enough because the alliance project will face obstacles and stressful times, and a good business/IT working relationship will greatly enhance the resolution process.

The companies' business and IT areas should also spend time face-to-face and one-on-one. Not only is it important for IT to develop a good working relationship with its business area, but also with its strategic alliance peers. After the initial relationships are established, telephone calls and videoconferences are good tools to continue them. However, there must still be periodic face-to-face contact.

IT should understand the business and remain plugged in. Things change hourly during and after negotiations. Keeping up to date with the business can happen through formal status meetings or through informal talks with the project lead and sponsors.

The business area should direct and lead the negotiations. While it is the responsibility of IT is to benefit the business, there are other ways to provide necessary input to the business area.

IT should not publicly point out all the problems and pitfalls between the companies. Although IT staff members can be analytical and often correct in their assessments, they should remember to bring solutions to the effort. Options to overcome issues should be communicated to the business area.

IT should avoid having too many leaders. Instead, a point person from each company should be identified to direct the IT effort, which will help others understand their roles.

IT should also make sure both sides understand the other's definitions of key data elements. In addition, IT should stay in tune with software and hardware versions and releases for both companies during the alliance effort. Versioning control is important in eliminating rework later on. Finally, IT should prioritize work and have a steering committee to elevate any issues when necessary.

CONCLUSION

In an alliance effort, IT can add value by partnering with the business area to become involved as early as possible in negotiations. A successful alliance will be more likely if IT takes the time to carefully plan up front, and then communicate broadly as soon as possible in the alliance effort. IT should also pay attention to the subtle cultural differences within and between the two organizations. Related problems are likely to arise and must be managed or they will create difficulty as the project moves forward.

Strategic alliances are here to stay and will continue to occur, both horizontally and vertically. It is critical for IT to change the business area's perception of the function from that of a necessary evil and expense, to one of a partnership that can add significant value. IT can be valuable in helping the alliance get started and implemented faster, and with a higher degree of quality. This translates into a strategic advantage for the company.

Chapter 19
Managing the Change to Self-Directed Teams: Myths and Miseries

Jeanette R. Newman

In the information age, manufactured products have become commodities. Global expansion in particular has allowed companies to clone products faster and at less cost with more regularity than ever before. Because the need for product differentiation becomes increasingly important when products are commodities, organizations are competing to bring the most innovative product to market in the shortest possible time and with the strongest customer service.

The ability of organizations to adapt to these marketplace changes is closely tied to the search for infrastructures that strengthen the organization and maximize its human potential. One such structure is the self-directed work team.

The process of developing a high-performance self-directed team profoundly influences the membership of an organization, management, and the organization itself. Innovation, creativity, collaboration, ownership, and employee satisfaction or even passion about work are some of the positive outcomes of the team-based organization that increase effectiveness and efficiency and help ensure market recognition and differentiation.

The movement to self-directed work teams and more interactive and innovative organizations is not an event or a program implemented through a basic and clear-cut plan. It is a profound and basic transformation in the way organizations relate, interact, and respond to each other and their customers. Although its path is unclear at times and the final possibilities uncertain, what is clear is that the transformation emphasizes relationships, processes, and learning. This chapter is designed to support

0-8493-1190-X/02/$0.00+$1.50

IS managers who have recently made the decision to implement self-directed teams and those who have already achieved varying degrees of progress with the team structure. This chapter focuses on recognizing and managing the myths and the miseries associated with the organizational transformation to teams.

ESTABLISHING THE CONTEXT FOR TEAMS

Significant learning must occur before an organization embarks on the transformation to teams. A framework and link (i.e., context) need to be established between the current organizational state and the reason for having the conversation about the desired state. The context thus provides the basis for the conversations that are necessary for building a strong foundation for change.

The important context regarding teams concerns definitions of terms that are frequently interchanged in organizations. Clarifying the following definitions is the first step toward group unity:

- *Groups:* Two or more people who work together toward a common goal, individually, with little interdependency.
- *Self-directed or self-managed teams:* Groups that have learned over time to take on higher levels of responsibility for their work with higher incidence of interdependency.

Each of these definitions contains degrees of variation across a spectrum ranging from limited intrateam interaction and dependency to highly integrated, highly dependent interaction among team members. This concept is illustrated in the graph in Exhibit 1, which depicts the type of team opportunities existing in an organization based on the duration a group is to work together to meet an objective and interdependency of the work being performed.

The graph does not provide a linear or absolute view. It is intended to generate thoughts and guide related dialogues about teams and to help develop a spectrum of opportunity that more closely resembles a particular organization. There is no right or wrong place to be on the graph, no better or worse arrangement of groupings. The important point is for an organization to have the conversation about the range of possibilities and how teams could fit into the organizational structure. Even in the lowest quadrant of opportunity, an organization can achieve benefits of the team structure by polishing relationships and communication skills.

MYTHS OF SELF-DIRECTED TEAMS

Myths are described as fiction, parables, stories, tradition, and, most appropriately, legends. According to the *American College Dictionary*, legends are

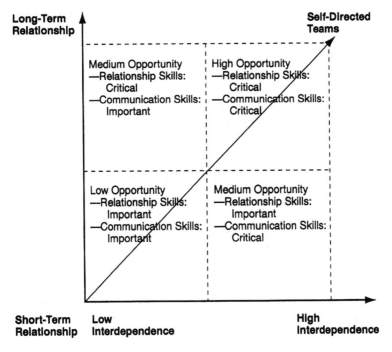

Exhibit 1.   The Spectrum of Opportunity

"nonhistorical or unverifiable stories handed down by tradition from earlier times and popularly accepted as historical [factual]." In other words, the legend is considered fact until disproved.

This same definition is at work in organizations. Organizational myths or legends are the truth for the people in the organization, who make decisions based on a combination of these myths and facts. Because myths lead to additional myths and subsequently to miseries, IS managers should recognize and prepare for them. Five myths appear most frequently in organizations implementing the team structure.

Myth One: Managers Know How to Do This

The first myth regarding teams is that managers know how to implement and build teams; they have all the right answers, the most profound vision, the best competencies, and the grandest insight into the workings of the institution or organization. For the most part, the people of the organization expect the managers to make the right decisions, delegate effectively, and know what they are doing. The managers, in turn, also believe in this myth and its related expectations, which tend to reinforce the traditional hierarchy and one-way communication of information, knowledge, and experience.

Expecting that implementation of teams cannot be too difficult because it falls under the rubric of managerial experience, the managers begin to implement teams with the best form of leadership they know: to direct, delegate, and control. Once the teams begin their journey, however, the managers intellectualize that the role of the manager needs to change. This leads to the next myth.

Myth Two: If Left Alone, Teams Will Naturally Develop

Much of the literature on team-based organizations suggests that a manager's role needs to change. These articles go on to describe the manager's role at a macrolevel, as a coach with minimal involvement in the team's day-to-day operations. Managers usually interpret this material to mean: do not meddle or interfere in the natural group development of the teams; stay out of the team's way; take a distant position in relationship to the team; and focus more intensely on other challenges, such as global, architectural, and strategic issues. All of these actions are intended to give the teams the space they need to develop into fully functioning self-directed teams.

At the same time, managers still exhibit some of the tendencies associated with myth one; they become involved with great zeal when there is a problem, providing direction and leadership as in the past to save the day, but they retreat to their offices or conference room when the incident is over to handle their global tasks. In the initial phases of team development, this management at arm's length with associated spurts of crisis intervention is not the most effective method for implementing teams. A more effective approach to the relationship between managers and teams throughout the team process is depicted in Exhibit 2.

The first stages of team implementation require far more managerial involvement than managers realize. It is in the final stages that the transfer begins to take place and the team vision is realized. Organizations try to implement the vision — the final stages — without living through the natural growth steps. Several different methodologies explain the various stages that groups experience in their development. IS managers should familiarize themselves with the natural development expectations of this living entity called groups and recognize that management functions continue to be a part of the ongoing health of the team, even in the final growth stages. The third myth addresses the interesting related inference that managers will no longer be in the picture in the final stages of team development.

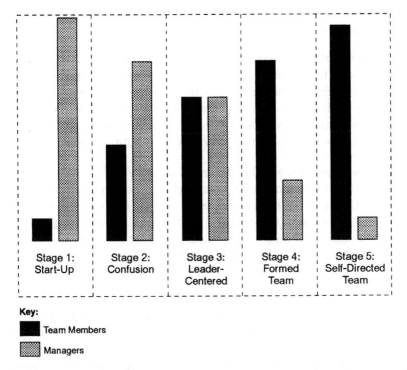

Key:

■ Team Members

▓ Managers

Exhibit 2. The Transfer of Authority (From J.D. Osborn et al., *Self Directed Teams: The New American Challenge,* Homewood, IL: Business One Irwin, 1990, p. 62.)

Myth Three: Teams or Hierarchy — An Either/Or Choice

Several questions and comments are frequently heard in organizations regarding the interaction between the hierarchical and the team-based organizations. These comments generally concern the respective roles of managers, team leaders, and team members.

Role of Managers. Two questions are generally asked about the role of managers:

1. What are the managers going to be doing now that the teams are doing all of their work?
2. Does the manager still conduct performance reviews?

These questions result from the popular inference that self-directed teams eliminate, flatten, squash, and render obsolete the organizational hierarchy. The expectation that there will be fewer managers and fewer layers of hierarchy is not always realized. Some companies look to the team-based structure to assist them in adapting to significant downturns in their industry sector. Other companies are making the structural change because it is the right thing to do to remain competitive and progressive.

In either situation, the traditional hierarchy remains a core structure for the foreseeable future for most corporations. American business systems, education systems, community systems, government systems, and family systems are all largely based on hierarchial structures. When the relationships between members of both the hierarchy and teams are flexible and adaptable, team-based organizations maximize both systems.

Role of the Team Leader. The hierarchy dilemma raises the related quandary regarding the team leader. One organization, for example, changed the title of this function from team leader to team facilitator to team representative, even though the essence of the role did not change. The title "leader" implies that the balance of the group assumes the role of followers. Yet the followers ask why they should follow the leader when the leader does not conduct their performance review and has nothing to do with their merit rewards or other forms of recognition.

The title "team leader" and the inferred role work against the good intentions and essence of the original function, which is the role of focus person, meeting moderator, synthesizer of group decisions or indecisions, and communicator of information between the team and the outside world of customers, management, other teams, and other organizations. This role can rotate throughout the team and should do so more frequently than quarterly. It is also important to allow the team to decide the process for the group leader or representative as well as the clarification of the role for this person.

The function of leadership needs to be accomplished by the team but not necessarily by a single individual or by the team representative. Sometimes the term *self-directed* in regard to the leader or team members carries more meaning and empowerment than is originally intended, which leads to the next myth.

Myth Four: Self-Directed Means Autonomous

The outcome of this myth can be surprising. For example, the members of one team in pursuit of fulfilling their newly acquired responsibilities decided they would no longer provide support to a business application that was a maintenance and support nightmare. The team informed its customer to upgrade, rewrite, or purchase other software to handle this business application. On hearing of the team's action, the application manager quickly clarified the intent of team empowerment and reestablished customer relations.

To this team, the term self-directed was misinterpreted as meaning self-government or autonomy. As teams struggle at times with their roles and the depth and breadth of their responsibilities, such misinterpretation provides a ready source of discontent and an easy answer to difficulty. This leads to another myth about the homogeneity of the team function and roles of its membership.

Myth Five: Teams Are Most Successful in Homogeneous Work

Many IS managers think that successful teams have more homogeneous work than teams within their own organizations. Despite the fact that there are obviously successful, high-performance nonhomogeneous teams, such as emergency room teams, this myth tends to provide a rationalization for nonhomogeneous groups that are struggling with their responsibilities. Holding onto this myth stifles group growth and contributes to frustration, disappointment, and lack of confidence.

Taken together, the five myths associated with self-directed teams cause teams and their members to feel a sense of frustration, low self-confidence, disappointment, and confusion. The following sections speak to the miseries that result either directly or indirectly from the myths associated with the change to self-directed teams and provide some tips on their management.

TEAM MISERIES AND MISERY MANAGEMENT

Miseries are a natural part of change and movement from a place of relative comfort to somewhere unknown. As a well-known adage of unknown origin says, "Some people prefer the certainty of misery to the misery of uncertainty." Because miseries can keep people from moving from where they are to their desired target, they have to managed. Some miseries can even be avoided.

Misery One: Teams Are for Every Organization

Organizations looking for ways to increase efficiency and effectiveness risk the tendency to force-fit the latest structural concept, like self-directed teams, into their organizations. Definite dangers exist with this line of thinking. Teams are not for every situation in an organization, department, or function. It is possible to have one area that is suitable for team implementation and the balance of the organization more suitable for remaining in the traditional hierarchical structure. Trying to implement teams in an organization or function where they are unsuitable is like trying to pound a square peg into a round hole.

Misery Management. Because organizations require a receptive culture for successful implementation of teams, the key to the management of this

Exploitive-Authoritarian	Benevolent-Authoritative
• Dogmatic • Manipulative rewards • Top-down communications	• Parental approach to management.
Consultative • Management listens to employees but reserves right to decide. • Some reliance on intrinsic rewards; most based on extrinsic (i.e., monetary) rewards.	**Participative** • Leadership based on influence. • Intrinsic rewards predominate. • Two-way communication.

Exhibit 3. Organizational Types (From R. Likert, *New Patterns of Management* and *The Human Organization,* New York: McGraw-Hill, 1961 and 1967, respectively.)

misery centers on assessment of the culture of the organization and its receptivity to the team concept. If an organization does not appear receptive, the champion of the team idea needs to spend time influencing and preparing the organization for the team structure.

The spectrum of opportunity depicted in Exhibit 1 provides a starting point for the assessment of organizational culture. A valuable exercise for IS managers would be to plot the groups or functions within an organization in the appropriate quadrants. An enlightening conversation is sure to ensue if managerial staff and a cross section of employees are asked to do the same. The learning potential is great regardless of whether the groups surprisingly plot the organization the same or, better yet, plot the organization differently.

As Exhibit 3 illustrates, the works of Rensis Likert on organizational types are also helpful in assessing organizational receptivity to teams. The four quadrants also represent four different styles of decision making that corporations or individuals assume to varying degrees during the course of their work. Even the most participative of leaders or organizations balances the use of the exploitative-authoritarian style and other styles at certain times. In the case of self-directed teams, for example, a vice president who announces that an organization will move toward teams is working from the top left exploitive-authoritarian quadrant. The same person then moves into the participative quadrant to involve the other employees in the development and implementation of the directive.

The first step IS managers should therefore take in assessing organizational readiness for the team structure is to consider and then compare the predominant management style of the larger organization in relation to their own personal style as well as to the style of the IS department or division. If the two styles widely differ, then the managers need to work on influencing the relationship between the two groups to gain organizational support for the transformation to self-directed teams. When the two groups share borders, there is less work to be done in preparing for the transformation.

Misery Two: Team Killers

Team killers are those actions or observations that despite the admirable intentions of managers immediately stop the progress of a team in its tracks or suppress the growth process. The following sections describe some of the ways in which team killers play out in an organization.

Codependent Behavior. Imagine a team meeting at which the IS manager asks a question regarding potential solutions or innovative ways of handling an opportunity currently challenging the organization. The silence in the room is soon broken, but not by a member of the group. Instead, the manager begins to answer the question. Like most managers, this manager mainly wants to contribute, share knowledge, and discuss ideas with the members of the group. Managers, however, are only own part of this team killer. The group membership contributes to the problem by deferring to the manager and waiting for direction.

The process of team building requires patience on the part of managers, because organizational members may have been functioning for several years in a dependent relationship. It will take deliberate new methods and time to make the change to a truly open environment.

Lack of Management Support. Managers who distance themselves from teams to allow for the natural growth of the group sever the informal, day-to-day conversations of the previous organizational relationship. Team members may infer that the manager does not care what the teams are doing or if they are successful. In addition, because the teams are more distant from what is happening in the organization, they end up feeling somewhat abandoned and isolated. IS managers must maintain informal avenues of communication as a source of information exchange and a demonstration of their interest and stake in the team development process.

Say "Team" and Act Autocratic. "Your actions are so loud, I can't hear what you are saying." Research has proved that people learn far more from what they see than from what they hear or read. Significant misery is experienced when an IS manager speaks about and even intellectualizes the movement of the IS organization to the team-based structure but does not follow through with appropriate actions.

Although it is certainly difficult for managers to move from previous autocratic tendencies and styles of management that have served them well in their careers to a more participative style, this pattern of behavior can damage the self-esteem of the team and lessen its energy for making decisions and continuing the effort toward successful implementation. Members of the IS organization begin to doubt the honesty and sincerity of the team-based structure as they find themselves in a situation that does not differ greatly from what they had known before teams were implemented.

Misery Management. Although these managerial actions can stop team progress immediately, there is tremendous opportunity for learning in each of them. The IS manager's challenge is to remain open and somewhat vulnerable to learning while challenging the team to participate in a successful conversation on inferences and actions. One strategy is for the manager to schedule specific times, whether at the end of each team meeting or at another time, for free-flowing discussion of open-ended questions.

Because team members are also responsible for building the team relationship and moving closer to the vision, they need to learn to be more comfortable voicing respectful critiques of specific situations. In addition, team members need to be willing to participate in the deliberate effort necessary for the successful implementation of the team-based organization.

As dialogues continue, the group may realize that there is a need for increased decision-making and problem-solving effectiveness. Remember, the managers and the teams do not know, intuitively, how to achieve this. It is the responsibility of the entire membership of the organization to push the edges of the envelope to experience its own empowerment. Managers are responsible for coaching and mentoring increased empowerment of the the team and for supporting its success.

Misery Three: Misalignment of Support Structures

Implementation of the team-based structure in an IS department or division may be the best structure for the function. However, if the balance of the organization is not making the move at this time or ever, potential misery is possible.

Relationship to the Balance of the Organization. Teams are encouraged to work directly with internal customers and external suppliers to provide quality and innovative services. The internal customers and external suppliers, however, may be accustomed to working and establishing a relationship with organizational management. This situation can cause great misery if not well supported by the IS manager.

Misery Management. IS managers are responsible for building and sustaining the position that teams are the first line of assistance for all aspects of day-to-day operations and service provision. This can be accomplished through discussions with customers and suppliers about the new structure and its meaning for relationships and respective roles. The transition to smooth team interaction with customers and suppliers is not effectively handled in a single conversation, however, but rather through consistent and repetitive messages from managers delivered both proactively and reactively. The effectiveness of the transition and the minimization of this misery depends on the managers' ability to stand by the structure change and the teams while maintaining strategic and long-term relationships with the supplier and customer communities.

Alignment of Rewards. Another important facet of misery three is misalignment of the reward structure with the new team-based organization. Managers have professed the importance of teamwork and that the team will be evaluated and rewarded based on both team accomplishments and individual achievements. When managers do not follow through on their commitment and rate people as individual performers without mention of the performance of the team, the pain begins. The misery only intensifies if other managers are awarding performance in very different ways. Misery management in this case begins with the manager's ensuring that performance evaluations and various reward systems are congruent with the team-based structure.

Blending with Highly Individual Contributors. Every IS organization has its prima donnas — people who are extremely talented in their particular area of technical expertise and who know their value to the organization. Generally, these individuals are pleasant while working with others but prefer to work with other highly technical people or alone. They also like to move ahead without the formality and baggage associated with work relationships and bureaucracy.

Because these individuals see little benefit from the team concept, they may escape the team training and relationship-building sessions. Other members in the IS organization may wonder why these highly technical people are treated differently. If the expectations of the organization regarding these individualists are not well managed, the perceived lack of fairness and inequity may cause resentment.

Misery Management. Organizational managers need to take a united position on the purpose of the team structure and how various functions and individuals contribute to successful implementation of the teams. Although placing highly technical people on teams may not seem to make the best immediate use of their time or skills, IS managers who consider future required competencies will see the benefit of improved relationship and communication skills for all technical staff. Managers should assess and clearly communicate the different development needs of individual contributors to team development and the team structure.

Misery Four: Personal Fitness

In today's world, personal physical fitness and healthful lifestyles receive a great deal of attention. A career has an element of personal fitness too. In this context, personal fitness is the match of the gifts and contributions of an individual with the receptiveness of the corporate culture and the opportunity to maximize these gifts. There are times when the larger organization recognizes the gifts of an employee and seeks to develop this opportunity. More frequently, however, people in organizations become stuck in a situation, position, or occupation that is not a good match for them.

Lack of work fitness results in misery for both the person and the organization at some point. Waning or apathetic performance on the part of the employee affects productivity (i.e., organizational strength), especially as actions and contributions become more routine and less innovative over time. The organization is forced to bring in people capable of the higher levels of performance and competency. The original members of the organization are passed by for promotions and more-challenging opportunities.

Misery Management. Managing personal satisfaction and minimizing personal work miseries necessitates that an individual take charge of satisfaction. This can be accomplished in several ways.

Personal Preference. It is important for IS managers and professionals to understand their personal preferences for work and to recognize the types of activities, events, or projects they gravitate toward or away from. In addition, some individuals feel more comfortable with one type of organizational environment than another. As employees of an organization that is moving from an autocratic environment to one of higher levels of participation, IS managers may need to assess their personal preferences in the work environment as well as to ensure that there is a proper fit between the two. Knowing one's personal work and organizational preferences and using self-observation to confirm initial thoughts or ideas help ensure personal fitness in the work environment.

Continuous Development. The larger organization usually provides the initial training and education on the reasons for the change to a team-based structure, the context associated with the change, and the intended direction. This initial introduction and context is only the beginning or the foundation upon which to base continuous learning and to build competencies. The larger organization does not necessarily know what a manager's shortcomings are. It is the responsibility of IS managers to implement methods to identify the developmental needs of the IS organization and its teams and to promote a learning organization. Ongoing learning needs to be planned fully and deliberately.

Performance Tuning through Reflection and Coaching. IS managers should take the time to reflect on their style and competencies. At the same time, they need to remember myth one — managers know how to do this — as well as to learn from the experience of athletes, who continue to use coaches throughout their careers.

Few managers use the coaching technique, and even fewer women remotely consider its use. A coach serves to guide a person through self-reflection activities and other exercises that provide objective perspectives about current competencies and the desired state. Some people use a mentor for this purpose, but most mentor relationships are established to provide encouragement and advice and do not reach the level of a coaching relationship.

RECOMMENDED COURSE OF ACTION

Recognizing the myths associated with self-directed teams and managing their related miseries are important first steps along the road to successful self-directed teams. Awareness and acknowledgment that miseries are a natural part of the growing cycle of living structures — like organizations — provide some grounding for the normal feelings of discomfort and excitement associated with significant change and the transformations yet to come. Through deliberate, respectful, and thoughtful management, IS managers can minimize or eliminate some of the miseries that accompany the transformation to teams.

Bibliography

Block, P. Stewardship: *Choosing Service over Self-Interest.* San Francisco: Berrett-Koehler Publishers, 1993.

Kline, P. and Saunders, B. *The Ten Steps to a Learning Organization.* Arlington VA: Great Ocean Publishers, 1993.

Melrose, K. *Making the Grass Greener on Your Side: A CEO's Journey to Leading by Serving.* San Francisco: Berrett-Koehler Publishers, 1995.

Nadler, D.A. et al. *Discontinuous Change: Leading Organizational Transformation.* San Francisco: Jossey-Bass, 1995.

Shipka, B. "Softstuff Application: Developing Work Teams in Technical Organizations." In *Community Building: Renewing Spirit & Learning in Business,* ed. K. Gozdz, pp. 95–102. San Francisco: New Leaders Press, 1995.

Chapter 20
Improving IS Performance: The Role of the Value Chain

Warren Harkness

It is crucial for IS managers to understand current implementation problems in order to focus their systems development efforts on winners. Time and effort spent on resolving implementation problems prevents organizations from applying that energy to critical new system applications. The goal is to free up resources, reduce wasteful activities, and dramatically improve business performance. The results mirror those sought in all aspects of business performance: faster cycle times and increased customer satisfaction.

This chapter is designed to help IS executives understand performance improvement within the information systems domain. It is critical to the success of an enterprise that its ability to *meet or exceed the needs of the customer* is driven by an ability to do so for the right expenditure of effort and resources, thereby *meeting or exceeding the needs of the enterprise.* For IS groups to demonstrate "effectiveness," they must address in the affirmative the following two questions:

1. Are the installed information systems capable of the level of performance required by the business processes?
2. If so, are the installed information systems currently performing at that level of performance?

If the answer to either of these questions is no, then the correct response is to evaluate the systems portfolio and analyze which systems need to be enhanced or replaced.

0-8493-1190-X/02/$0.00+$1.50
© 2002 by CRC Press LLC

Exhibit 1. Process Management Strengths and Weaknesses

Strengths	Weaknesses
Focuses on long-term systematic understanding of problem-solving within process framework	Takes a long time to see significant results
Builds a deep organizational learning of process	Difficult to sustain the effort over a long period of time

For IS groups to demonstrate "efficiency," they must address in the affirmative the following two questions:

- Can the projects currently underway be delivered on time, within budget, and to the client's requirements?
- Can the process by which the systems projects are delivered be improved to better meet client needs, reduce delivery costs, or meet the delivery schedule?

If the answer to either of these questions is no, then the correct response is to launch a directed systems delivery process improvement effort.

PROCESS IMPROVEMENT APPROACHES

There are a number of approaches for improving the IS process. Organizations need to understand which approaches would best meet their goals within schedule and resource constraints. Approaches range from ad hoc and just-in-time methods to TQM approaches and structured intervention. This chapter focuses on a process management approach to IS improvement.

Process Management Approach

A process management approach to focused improvement is characterized by creating a capability throughout the IS organization (see Exhibit 1). Initiating a successful change effort requires:

- Understanding the current business processes within IS
- Selecting key processes to be improved
- Developing process metrics
- Managing processes long-term using process owners who report key metrics

In the short term, the management group of an organization can select the key processes to be improved and then launch improvement efforts. In the long term, the process owners have the responsibility to put in place process metrics, assess the current processes using these metrics, and launch improvement teams based on the gaps between targeted performance levels and actual performance levels. The process management approach is often a logical evolution from the TQM approach, which tends to focus on empowering teams continually to fix problems.

Process Mapping

The process management approach is based on a continual understanding, refining, and uncovering of the linked activities that form the process layers of an organization. This approach uses process mapping to provide straightforward assessments of how organizations get things done. A modified process-mapping technique is applied to minimize the problems associated with traditional process-mapping techniques.

Process-mapping exercises often fail. In an effort to document the detail of the process steps, the individual or team doing the documenting gets lost in the overwhelming detail of the process steps. The resulting process maps look like detailed logic flowcharts, with dozens or even hundreds of activity steps. Unable to comprehend or keep in mind the details of the processes, those doing the documenting often fail to grasp the essence of the overall process. The key to effectively executing process mapping is managing and displaying the levels of detail. At the highest level, a set of enterprise processes are described and then decomposed to lower levels of detail.

A detailed examination of the major steps for successful process mapping is provided next.

Eight Major Steps for Successful Process Mapping

1. Identify major processes.
2. Determine key process for focus.
3. Understand existing key process at lower level of detail.
4. Choose area for focus (quality, cost, or delivery).
5. Find bottlenecks, waste, and defects in existing process.
6. Eliminate delays, waste, and defects.
7. Document the new process.
8. Deploy to organization.

Identify Major Processes. The high-level process chart shown in Exhibit 2 is from a nonprofit enterprise. It depicts key business and support processes necessary for the organization to be managed effectively. To create this Business Process diagram, the group performed the following steps:

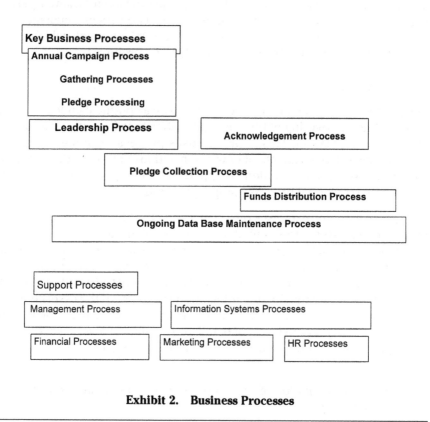

Exhibit 2. Business Processes

1. They brainstormed the processes in the enterprise.
2. They grouped similar processes.
3. They titled process groups by creating a higher level name.
4. They divided the titled groups into those that were considered to be key business processes and those that were considered support to the key processes.

Determine Key Process for Focus. This high-level process map is used to prioritize and choose the area for focus and improvement. Ideally, metrics have been created for each process block (e.g., cycle time or quality level expected). The metrics provide actual data and the ability to set and track target levels. The data collected drives the determination of which processes to focus on, by providing a means for selecting the largest gaps between target and actual. Without metrics and actual data, management groups typically choose improvement targets based on qualitative data or by discussion and consensus.

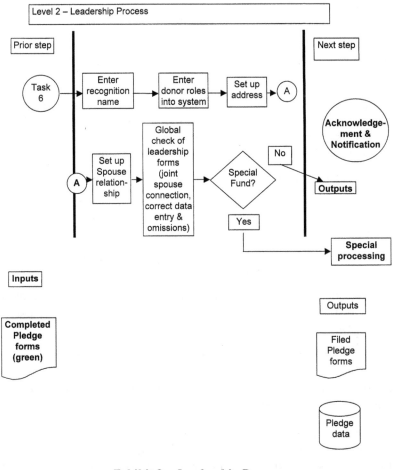

Exhibit 3.   Leadership Process

Understand Existing Key Process at Lower Level of Detail. If, for example, the management group selects the Leadership Process to focus on, the task now becomes drilling down into the next level of detail for this process. There is now a reason to really understand this process, so one can map the process as shown in the diagram in Exhibit 3, moving to a greater level of detail.

The documentation of the process should describe the major steps in no more than seven to ten blocks on a single page. When more than ten blocks are created, combine some of the blocks and create a higher level block that replaces the three to four blocks that are detailed at a lower level.

For example, for the following steps:

1. Receive pledge forms
2. Sort pledge forms into different methods of payment
3. Summarize totals by method

this could be described as one block called "consolidate by method of payment."

Choose Area for Focus (QCD). Once the lowest level of detail process map has been drawn for the existing process, then metrics are created for the process at hand and data is collected to depict actual performance versus target level. Quality, cost, and delivery are typically major categories.

Suppose that for the Leadership Process, the key metrics are:

- **Quality:** accuracy of completed pledge forms (measured by percentage of forms without errors in key fields such as name, address, total pledge amount, etc.)

  The target is 95 percent accuracy and the actual is currently 45 percent to 65 percent.

- **Delivery:** Cycle time of Leadership Process (measured by elapsed time from when pledge forms enter process to when pledge data is in database)

  The target is less than 24 hours and the actual is currently 14 to 36 hours.

There are now two explicit areas from which to choose: decreasing defects (increasing accuracy) or decreasing cycle time — or, perhaps, even both.

Find Bottleneck, Waste, and Defects in Existing Process. If the team chooses to focus on one area (e.g., decreasing defects), then barriers inherent in the existing process are explored. The cross-functional team "walks the process" in the detail process maps. As the processes are reviewed in ever-increasing detail, the people on the team gain a greater understanding of how the process currently works and begin to suggest improvements in the way the process should work in the future. A blend of experience and insight is offered by open discussion.

For example, a team member might say, "You mean you don't do anything with the green copy we have been sending to you?" Process changes can be suggested and discussed with managers and employees throughout the enterprise to test the concept of proposed changes.

Document New Process. The new process is usually built upon the design of the existing process, replacing major blocks with new ones, dropping redundant steps, consolidating multiple overlapping tasks, and streamlining the process. It is also possible to redesign the total workflow if changing the total process can make significant improvements. The new process maps with detailed steps and metrics become the basis for the new work process.

Deploy to Organization. One of the biggest challenges the improvement effort faces is successful deployment of a revised process. If possible, existing methods of training and change management should be utilized if the organization has such methods in place. If there is an existing training mechanism, use it for training employees on the new process tasks.

The deployment package can consist of:

- Detailed procedures
- Training courses
- Handbooks and manuals
- Computer-aided instruction

SUMMARY

This approach to process management in IS organizations is based on decomposing processes into subcomponents in order to make the whole more understandable and manageable. The process works equally well whether one is installing new application systems, managing IT projects, or selecting the IT portfolio. After deciding on the focus (decreasing the project cost overruns, decreasing the schedule slips, or increasing customer satisfaction with delivered applications), key processes are defined at a detail level and barriers to improvement are identified. The barriers are removed and a new or revised process is defined. Finally, an implementation plan for the newly revised process is created and deployed.

This approach has a number of benefits, including:

- It results in an increasing clarity of work actually being performed in the organization; people refer to, monitor, and improve the process.
- It diffuses personal attacks in the organization. It changes the focus from people and personalities to processes and task steps.
- It establishes clear direction. The management group can select a process to focus on for the current period. The approach does require some managing group or person to select a focus (quality, cost, delivery, or multiples). This sets the expectation for what is to be fixed and the level of change required, both of which are often unspoken or unknown.

Chapter 21

The Myths and Realities of IT Steering Committees

Ken Doughty

The ITSC performs a critical function in supporting the implementation of the corporate information technology strategic plan (ITSP). Further, the committee ensures that it minimizes the risks associated with implementing the IT strategies and receives a return on its investment.

Too often organizations do not monitor the activities and decisions of their IS department. Rather, they rely on the IS department to provide the IT solutions because executive management does not understand technology.

However, this attitude must change; otherwise, the organization may find that decisions made in isolation by the IS department may cause the organization to waste valuable resources (both human and financial) in implementing technologically superior solutions, and not business solutions. When this occurs, the organization receives a poor return on its investment in IT.

It is critical from the outset that the ITSC be empowered to monitor and control the IT investment of the organization.

ISACA has recognized the need for organizations to have an ITSC. The Control Objectives for Information and Related Technology (COBiT) PO4 — Define the Information Technology Organization and Relationships Control Objective states:

The organization's senior management should appoint a planning or steering committee to oversee the information services function and its activities. Committee membership should include representatives from senior management, user management, and the information services function. The committee should regularly meet and report to senior management.

0-8493-1190-X/02/$0.00+$1.50
© 2002 by CRC Press LLC

However, IS auditors do *not* review this critical organizational control process. If this control were part of the system development life cycle, it would be reviewed. Because it is outside of the IT department and is seen as an extension of executive management, it is not reviewed. Because of the impact it may have on the success of the organizational investment in IT, it is essential that the IS auditor audits the role and the effectiveness of the ITSC of the organization.

CONDUCTING THE AUDIT

Audit Objectives

1. To determine that the responsibilities and duties of the IT Steering Committee are documented and communicated throughout the organization
2. To determine the effectiveness of the IT Steering Committee in monitoring and controlling the activities of IT within the organization
3. To determine that the members of the ITSC understand the responsibilities and duties of their positions and are suitably qualified to undertake the role

Audit Scope

The scope of the audit encompasses an evaluation of the effectiveness of the ITSC (see Exhibit 1).

Control Risks

During the audit of the effectiveness of the ITSC, the following control risks may be encountered:

- No ITSC charter
- The ITSC charter is not communicated
- The ITSC charter does not provide a "watchdog" role over the implementation and investment in information technology
- The lack of management skills by the ITSC members to understand the impact of noncompliance with the approved IT strategic plan
- Poor understanding by the ITSC members of their role and responsibilities
- Inappropriate membership by organizational manager(s) (political forum)
- No key performance indicators (KPIs) to measure the effectiveness of the committee
- Lack of empowerment for the ITSC to take action (where appropriate)
- ITSC requirements are not communicated to line management and the IS department

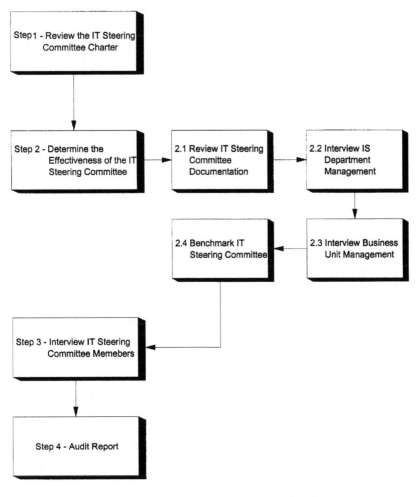

Exhibit 1.   IT Steering Committee Audit

- No monitoring processes on IT investment within the organization
- No reporting by the ITSC to executive management

STEP 1 — REVIEW THE IT STEERING COMMITTEE CHARTER

The IS auditor is to obtain a copy of the ITSC charter. In reviewing the charter the IS auditor is to determine that:

- The role of the ITSC has been defined and its responsibilities clearly specified (this should be supported by position descriptions for its members). Where there are position descriptions, the IS auditor is to review the descriptions to determine if they are appropriate.

237

- The charter of the ITSC is aligned with the corporate strategic objectives of the organization including the IT objectives.
- The ITSC has provided for the continuous review of the ITSP to ensure compliance with the corporate plan and overall corporate requirements and that the plan is kept current by revision.
- The ITSC has the authority to review (and approve/reject) all proposals for IS development over a specified amount (e.g., over $10,000) from user/managers. The ITSC is to prescribe the required format of the IT proposals, e.g., business case format, including a cost/benefit analysis with a rate of return — internal rate of return (IRR) or net present value (NPV). However, in some circumstances proposals may not be justified on a rate of return basis, but on a community or customer benefit.
- The ITSC has the authority to manage the IS project portfolio, setting priorities for the development of the business information systems development, allocating the necessary resources, and monitoring the progress of each project against objectives and budgets.
- The ITSC requires postimplementation reviews to be undertaken that are independent of the IS department and requires that the findings and recommendations of the review are presented to the committee with a response from the IS department.
- The ITSC oversees and directs the activities of any subcommittee including project steering committees.

In essence, the role of the ITSC is that of a corporate watchdog. The watchdog role will ensure that the IS department does not lose focus in providing the organization with cost-effective IT products and/or services and meets its commitment to assist the organization in achieving its strategic objectives.

Too often the IS department becomes involved in "technical issues" rather than in implementing a "business" solution(s) to meet the requirements of the organization.

STEP 2 — DETERMINE THE EFFECTIVENESS OF THE IT STEERING COMMITTEE

For this step there are a number of audit procedures to be performed. The effectiveness of the ITSC will be measured by the following.

2.1 ITSC Documentation

This audit procedure requires the IS auditor to review the minutes/reports and associated supporting documents of the ITSC. By reviewing the documentation, the IS auditor can determine if the ITSC has carried out its role and responsibilities not only in accordance with the charter, but also in accordance with any processes that have been established.

Sample selections of the documentation, e.g., minutes/reports, business case(s) are to be reviewed. However, the sample size will be dependent upon

- The elapsed time since the establishment of the ITSC and the audit being undertaken
- The frequency of ITSC meetings
- The format, quality, and quantity of the documentation
- Availability of the documents

The contents of the documents are to be reviewed. The details are required to be checked against supporting documentation, e.g., ITSP, corporate plan, business unit action plans, project plans, budgets, etc. For example, any variances or exceptions to the ITSP are to be referred to the ITSC chairperson for clarification.

It is important that all variances or exceptions are investigated as it may be an indicator that the ITSC has either not understood its role and responsibilities or that the supporting processes have internal-control weaknesses.

2.2 Interview IS Department Management

This audit procedure requires the IS auditor to interview the IS department's management. The objective of this procedure is to identify what processes are used to monitor, measure, and report on performance of IS function's performance. ITSC is required to provide the IS department with its reporting requirements of IT activities (including resource utilization, project status, etc.).

During the interviews, the IS auditor is to determine if the IS department's management is given the opportunity to raise issues with the ITSC, particularly if the issues may impact the process or success of implementing the IT Strategic Plan.

Often the IS department management feels that the ITSC is an imposition on its activities, because it believes that it is in the best position to determine what the organization should have in regard to IT.

If the IS department is raising issues that are not being addressed by the ITSC, it may be indicator (i.e., KPI) of the effectiveness of the committee. However, the IS auditor must be aware of any attempt by the IS department to influence unduly the opinion of the effectiveness of the ITSC without supporting and compelling evidence. Any issues raised should be followed up, provided there is sufficient evidence to justify the effort.

2.3 Interview Business Unit Managers

From the information gathered in Section 2.1 the IS auditor is to select a sample of IS projects (accepted or rejected by the ITSC) and interview the responsible project sponsors, i.e., business unit managers.

During the interviews and an examination of any documentation provided by the project sponsors, the IS auditor is to identify:

- Deviations from the processes implemented by the ITSC with regard to

  Requirements in preparing a business case
  Submission and presentation of the business case
  Project monitoring and reporting
- Communications from the committee with regard to changes in project implementation status, i.e., priorities, resource allocation, and objectives, etc., which is important as it may have an impact on the business unit achieving its strategic business objectives approved by the corporate executives
- Reasons for the rejection of business case(s)

The interviews should also be an opportunity for the business managers to express any opinion on the effectiveness of the ITSC in fulfilling its role as per the charter.

The interviews may provide sufficient evidence which would support audit recommendations to change

- The charter
- Membership of the ITSC
- ITSC processes

2.4 Benchmarking

The fourth audit procedure requires the IS auditor to benchmark the ITSC against similar organizations or appropriate international standards or recognized industry best practices.

The benchmark exercise is undertaken to provide compelling evidence that the structure, role, responsibilities, and supporting processes of the ITSC are sound.

To benchmark the ITSC, the IS auditor will be required to contact a number of similar organizations to obtain the necessary information. For example,

- ITSC charter
- Member position descriptions
- Number of members
- Composition
- Reporting structure

- Processes
- Copies of "edited" minutes/reports (where possible)

From this information, the IS auditor can benchmark the organization ITSC. The benchmarking exercise will provide evidence if the shape of the organization ITSC is appropriate.

STEP 3 — INTERVIEW IT STEERING COMMITTEE MEMBERS

The IS auditor is to interview members of the ITSC to determine if the members fully understand their duties and responsibilities in monitoring and providing a supervisory role of the IT activities within the organization.

During the interviews, the IS auditor is to ascertain that

- The committee members have the relevant experience, skills, and available time to undertake this critical role.
- The committee is "balanced" to ensure that there is no "bias" by the committee members or any one member.
- The chairperson has the delegated authority of the chief executive officer of the organization to take appropriate action on his or her behalf.
- Resources have been allocated by the organization to support the functions or processes of the committee.
- The charter is supported by processes to increase awareness, understanding, and the IT skills of the ITSC members.
- There are processes (i.e., policies and procedures) to support the operations and decisions of the ITSC.
- The committee has prepared, documented, and communicated
  Guidelines and procedures for the preparation and submission of business cases to the committee,
  Reporting requirements, i.e., format, contents (e.g., actual results against planned deliverables), and timing of reports,
  ITSC meetings, i.e., format, structure, and timing.
- Key performance indicators (i.e., KPIs) have been determined to measure the effectiveness of the committee.
- Processes (i.e., procedures) for reviewing submissions, reports, and presentations to the committee have been formalized and agreed upon by the committee members.
- The IS department management is given every opportunity to explain variances or exceptions.
- Decisions and action taken by the ITSC are documented and communicated to all stakeholders.
- Minutes and supporting documentation of the ITSC meetings are prepared and distributed to all interested parties.

Ideally, the committee is to include a member who is independent of any line function who will provide the chairperson of the committee with an impartial view.

The IS auditor is to verify, where appropriate, information provided by the ITSC members to ensure it is complete and accurate and to document its findings.

STEP 4 — AUDIT REPORT

After performing the audit of the ITSC, the IS auditor is to prepare an audit report detailing his or her findings and audit recommendations. The IS auditor has to be aware of the organizational "politics" when preparing the draft findings and recommendations. In particular, the ITSC chairperson may have significant "political" power within the organization.

Therefore, from the outset, the IS auditor must "sell" the contents of the audit report and ensure that all findings and recommendations are discussed with all the stakeholders. The findings must be supported by documentary evidence (where appropriate) to ensure acceptance of the recommendations by the ITSC and executive management. Any errors of fact will detract from the objective of providing executive management with a detailed analysis of the effectiveness of the ITSC.

The audit report must provide sufficient detail to allow management to take specific action to address the issues found during the audit.

SUMMARY

Today, organizations are highly dependent upon their IT to assist the organization in achieving its corporate objectives. Executive management, therefore, requires the IS auditor to deliver an independent appraisal of the effectiveness of the ITSC in monitoring and supervising the investment in IT.

The effectiveness of the ITSC is of strategic importance to the overall success of the organization in achieving not only its IT strategic objectives, but also in gaining a competitive advantage from its investment in IT.

The IS auditor must convey to executive management the importance of having an effective ITSC and its value to the board of directors of the organization in the discharge of its fiduciary duties. There is overwhelming evidence to support the assertion that the failure of the ITSC of an organization to monitor and supervise IT investment decisions and operations has been the one of the main contributors to the failure of an organization in failing to achieve its corporate strategic objectives.

APPENDIX

INFORMATION TECHNOLOGY STEERING COMMITTEE CHARTER

Where it is the policy of the organization to have a committee to monitor and control the implementation of information management–related policies and procedures, an Information Technology Steering Committee (ITSC) has the delegated authority to implement information management related policies and procedures throughout the organization.

Role of ITSC Committee

The overall responsibility of the committee is the monitoring and enforcement of information management–related policies and procedures, which are conveyed through various forms, e.g., corporate plan, corporate policies, executive directives, etc.

Specifically the role of the committee is to:

- Review on a continuous basis the information technology strategic plan (ITSP) to ensure compliance with the corporate plan and overall corporate requirements
- Initiate and oversee information systems and technology development plans and major business projects
- Consider all proposals for information systems development from user/managers and approve their adoption or otherwise in terms of cost, resource requirements, net benefit, organizational impact, and technology impact.
- Manage the information systems project portfolio, setting priorities for the development of the business information systems development, allocating the necessary resources, and monitoring the progress of each project against objectives and budget
- Oversee the conduct of postimplementation reviews to assess whether or not projected benefits are achieved
- Monitor and control "end-user computing" or any *ad hoc* information systems or technology development that is unplanned, has the potential to create excessive computer demand, duplicates effort, or does not create a "shared" business or corporate resource
- Oversee and direct the activities of any subcommittee including project steering committees
- Ensure that the ITSP is maintained up-to-date and that all changes are approved before being implemented
- Determine policy on subjects such as research and development, user charging, and data custodianship

Chapter 22

Achieving Enterprise Culture Change Through a Project Management Program

Layne C. Bradley
Ginger H. Eby

Project management is one of the most difficult and challenging disciplines in any field, particularly IT. Statistics that have been gathered over many years support that statement. For example, according to the Gartner Group Symposium IT Expo '97, "30 percent of all software projects fail outright. Of the successful projects, 70 percent are completed over budget or schedule."

Clearly, effective project management is a difficult goal to achieve. It is critical to the successful implementation of information systems. Delivering systems on schedule and within budget has long been the major target of project management. Many organizations collect and analyze these budget and schedule metrics in an effort to improve them. Many of these same organizations have defined service level agreements that the IT organization must meet. In commercial contracts between IT providers and companies, failure to meet project management targets can result in significant financial penalties.

Few IT professionals would argue against the concept that effective project management is mandatory. How to make it effective is the subject of much debate. There have been, and continue to be, many project management methodologies. All of them attempt to define a controlled process that leads to consistent successes in systems delivery. The degree of success, however, is not usually rooted in the process itself. Rather, it is controlled to a substantial degree by the attitudes and culture of the people who must use it. Therefore, implementing a truly successful project management program is more of a culture change effort rather than merely installing the latest project management methodology. In fact, unless there is a culture change, the chances of the methodology being successfully used on an ongoing basis is minimal.

In the following sections, the authors describe a major culture change effort that was successfully accomplished using a project management program as the vehicle.

CASE STUDY BACKGROUND

The enterprise in this case study was part of a multi-billion dollar international manufacturing corporation, with a significant investment in IT. The enterprise prided itself on its innovative use of technology, and the internal IT organization had been recognized for excellence in influential industry publications.

Several factors within the customer organization contributed to the need for an effective project management process. The enterprise had experienced major business change, including a significant downturn in business, followed by a divestiture of the business unit and a merger of the parent company with another major manufacturing corporation. During this time, IT funding had been significantly reduced and then restored. As the business unit pursued new opportunities, systems with current technology were required to address the market more effectively.

The IT organization was mature and centralized, and had been outsourced five years previously to a major IT services firm. A proprietary waterfall methodology developed by the customer was used throughout the 1980s, but the rigor with which it was employed had diminished with enterprise downturns (and related funding lapses) in the late 1980s and early 1990s. A clause in the original outsourcing contract required the IT provider to use the customer proprietary approach unless authorized to do otherwise, because that methodology had been successfully applied in the past.

While the enterprise and technology were changing, the proprietary methodology was not being updated or adapted to the changing environment. Methods were not available to address client/server implementations, expanded project teaming situations, software package implementations, or deployment of projects in multiple small releases as needed to address rapidly changing business conditions. The environment provided an excellent opportunity to introduce a new methodology that would better fit the business needs.

THE BUSINESS NEED

Customer Drivers

Over a period of three to five years, the customer organization progressed from demanding that the IT service provider remain static in delivering services (as had been done successfully prior to the outsourcing), to demanding innovative IT solutions and approaches from the provider. The enterprise was finding that its own customers demanded innovation, speed, and predictability in their products, and this demand had to be met by the IT service provider to enable the business to respond quickly to its own market demands.

With the change in business direction, the IT work evolved from maintenance and small enhancement tasks to more new development and major modification projects. During this time, the customer noted that some projects were run successfully, while others failed. Often, significant investments were made in projects that eventually were determined not to be viable, or that took much longer and cost a great deal more than originally planned.

The planning and tracking for a project depended on the assigned project manager. Those with more experience or more exposure to industry-accepted project management approaches tended to do more documentation, planning, and tracking — and tended to be more successful. Others struggled to hit target budgets and schedules, or failed outright. Even those who were successful used different methods and work products to achieve the goals of the project. Both methods and results were unpredictable from the customer's perspective.

IT Service Provider Objectives

At the same time, the service provider was undertaking efforts to standardize project management tools and techniques across its own sites. Significant workforce flexibility could be achieved by using common processes at all work sites. Consistently defined work breakdown structures and deliverables would enable employees to step into a project at any location or in any work group within a location, and immediately understand the project status and expected results.

The provider was winning new work, but suffering along with the rest of the industry in resourcing that new work. Experienced project managers were among the critical resources sought at almost every new outsourcing account. A program to define project management in a step-by-step manner, and to deliver training and tools to enable the successful rollout of the program, was considered a key objective. This program could then complement existing programs to identify and assess project managers for further career development.

Need for Predictability

Industry studies have shown that the deployment of standard processes in project management across an enterprise will result in improved consistency of results. Budgets and schedules will be closer to reality. Over time, budgets and schedules will actually be reduced as a result of the improved consistency.

By implementing a consistent and repeatable approach to project management, both the customer and the provider saw that they could achieve increased productivity, better ability to quickly move employees to the projects where they were most needed, and greater predictability of the cost and duration of each project. It was in the interest of both parties to pursue a standard project management methodology.

APPROACH

A Three-Pronged Approach

Based on past experience, the methodology team determined that three components would be needed in the deployment plan:

- Standard processes and procedures, defined at a detailed level
- Tools to enable productivity in following the standards
- Training that integrated the tools with the processes

Delivering any one piece without the others would not be successful.

A comprehensive set of techniques that could be used as a framework for the methodology was already available in the service provider's proprietary methodology. What was needed was a very specific implementation of those techniques that incorporated the tools to support the process and delivery through a training class to all expected practitioners.

Standard Processes and Procedures

Definition of detailed, step-by-step procedures is by nature difficult and time-consuming. In this case, the complexity of the procedures, combined with their interrelationships, made the task especially daunting. The methodology team was composed of experienced project managers who also had the skills to document the process. They worked both independently and as a group to write, review, integrate, and test the processes through a case study to ensure that they could be implemented in the customer environment.

The enterprise consisted of multiple functional areas, each of which operated differently and interacted with the service provider in different ways. A methodology was needed that would produce consistent results despite the differences in the ways requirements were received, and the differences in size and nature of the projects.

The processes had to be designed in such a way as to make them applicable to projects of all sizes. Any effort that was not solely intended to correct a malfunction was considered a project for the purpose of following the methodology. For that reason, the process had to be flexible in allowing a project manager (with the help of a trained methodologist) to select those steps that were pertinent to the project and avoid unnecessary steps. However, the tailoring of the path through the methodology had to be a result of conscious review and decision, rather than automatic elimination of requirements. Even small projects might be high risk or mission critical, requiring a fuller implementation of the methodology.

Tools to Support the New Process

Previous attempts at introducing new processes had failed when the implementation proved too difficult or time-consuming for the staff. While they might agree with the conceptual need to plan and document, when these tasks became overwhelming, they were tempted to move on to the more exciting challenges of technology. Often, the customer encouraged them to cut corners as well, wanting to move quickly into visible, deliverable code. This approach turned out to be shortsighted when the code delivered did not meet the customer's real requirements, or the maintainability of the resulting system was diminished by loss of the original developer and lack of documentation for the unfortunate employee required to pick up support.

The methodology team determined that it was critical to ensure that easy-to-use tools were available to help the staff resist the urge to short-circuit the methodology. The team relied on a central repository, referred to as a toolkit, that contained an online textual version of the methodology. This generic toolkit was tailored to include the forms, templates, and examples that project leaders and team members would need to efficiently and consistently produce the required deliverables.

Training in How to Apply the Process

Finally, a training class was needed. Before launching into the specific subject matter, the students needed some introductory information to help them understand the need for project management, and, in particular, rigorous project planning. Examples of projects that failed when project planning was not done or was done haphazardly were given. The business drivers for both the customer and the service provider were covered in some detail. Once they understood why the subject was important to them, the employees were ready to learn the new methods.

The students needed to become familiar with the detailed procedures and to be confident in how to find the procedure they needed and apply it to the task. They also needed to understand the components of the toolkit and how it would assist them in following the methodology. To achieve these goals, hands-on lab sessions were incorporated into the training. These labs were intended to ensure that what was being discussed in the lectures could be applied once the student went back to the job.

The course material was constructed and reviewed by the team, followed by a pilot class delivered to the management of the target audience project personnel. Piloting with management gave needed feedback on the content and duration of the course, and also assisted in getting buy-in from management to support the process when it was deployed.

The students in each class offered feedback and suggestions for improvement. Where possible, these suggestions were incorporated. All suggestions were carefully reviewed and considered, and the conclusion of each class included a management review of refinements in work and planned. This review also addressed all the concerns raised during that class, whether the suggestion was in work, planned, or neither. In this way, the students were able to see that their concerns were being considered by management, even if every single concern could not be accommodated.

What was originally planned to be training for a small pool of 10 to 15 project managers grew into a training initiative that covered over 200 project personnel. As the project managers attended training, they recommended that their team members attend as well. Personnel with responsibility for very small, one-person projects saw the methodology as an opportunity to practice proven techniques that could lead them to greater responsibilities in the future.

Those trained were, for the most part, enthusiastic about embracing the new methods. By obtaining the knowledge and tools to do effective project planning, they became more confident that they could develop a plan and commit to a realistic schedule and budget to meet their customers' needs. The new approach also made them feel more professional — more capable of seeing the broad perspective associated with planning a project. Much like the general contractor building a house, they could understand how all the subtasks fit together, rather than seeing the much narrower view of a subcontractor.

CRITICAL SUCCESS FACTORS

Mutual Goals

The primary purpose of this chapter has been to discuss how to go about effecting a culture change using a project management program as the tool to do so. For any such program to succeed, it must be based on clear, specific goals. Since culture is primarily a behavioral issue, to change the culture, one must change behavior.

Changing behavior is an extremely difficult endeavor. This is particularly true when the culture has been entrenched for an extended period of time. Of course, changing a culture does not necessarily imply that the existing culture is bad. Culture provides a framework for the effective operation of any enterprise. This statement is certainly true for most enterprises.

In the case being discussed, the culture had been in place for such a long period of time that an "entitlement" mentality had begun to develop. The same group had supported the same customer, the same way, using the same procedures such that it had begun to take the customer for granted — or at least that was the perception of the customer. Real or not, perception becomes reality.

For a culture change to take place in this kind of environment, it is necessary that both the customer and the IT organization have mutually agreed-to goals. In this case, the management of both parties wanted change.

For both the customer and the IT organization, predictability of results was an overriding goal. Due to the inconsistency of project management procedures and processes being used, it was very difficult to do effective budgeting and scheduling. Often, the success factor seemed to be primarily the skill of the individual project manager involved, rather than any well-defined process that was used on a regular basis.

One of the primary reasons that both parties were so interested in change was that their respective businesses had changed. The competitive environments for both had increased dramatically. Business costs had risen significantly; thus, profit margins were coming under increased scrutiny. Consistent, predictable results for IT projects were critical.

The customer's major goal was to have a project management methodology that was standard, effective, and used across all IT projects and groups to achieve consistent project success. The IT organization's primary goal was to develop a new culture that was based on a strong sense of urgency, the use of standard processes, accountability, and a focus on successful business results, such as consistently achieving budget and schedule targets, as well as technical excellence.

Discussions between the management of the customer and the IT organization revealed a commonality of goals and a desire to work together to achieve them. Thus, the foundation for a successful culture change effort was put in place.

Sponsorship

Once the goals for a culture change effort have been put in place, the next most critical task is to clearly identify the sponsors for the program. It must be clear that the appropriate levels of management of both parties are strongly behind the effort and actively involved in making it happen. Memos, e-mails, and statements of support are not sufficient. Active participation is the only approach that identifies to employees that the management team intends for the change to take place and is personally involved in making it happen.

In this case, the head of the IT organization where the project personnel reported made a personal appearance at each class. This person was able to reinforce the importance of the new approach (and indirectly the new culture) by showing enough personal interest and advocacy to take time to address each group of students.

In addition, the new management team was given direction that their group's compliance with the new approach would be used as a measure of their success. While they were given freedom to give input for improvement to the defined processes and training, expectations were clearly set for following the methodology once it was in place.

Reward and recognition played a part in the sponsorship effort as well. When customer ratings improved, and the new methodology was cited as the driver for that improved perception, several forms of recognition were used to reward both the methodology team that defined and deployed the process and the project teams who implemented it.

Employee Buy-in

The third, and perhaps most important, critical success factor in a culture change effort is employee buy-in. When these types of programs are attempted, this factor is the one that most often determines success or failure. Goals are necessary, as is sponsorship. Without the support of those who will actually use and implement the program, however, its chances of succeeding are minimal.

In this particular case, there were a number of actions taken in order to help ensure success. The first of these was the recruiting of a new management team. Senior managers with a wide range of experience in different companies and cultures were conscripted. Each was hired with the knowledge that a major effort to change the existing culture was going to be put in motion and they would be held responsible for implementing it.

Knowing they would be accountable for implementing the program was certainly important in ensuring success. More importantly, however, they were given the opportunity to help develop the program. When the training class was being developed, the management team was the pilot class. Their comments, criticisms, and suggestions for improvement were incorporated into the class in order for them to achieve a sense of ownership; thus, they felt that they were owners of the process.

The first class was taught to a select group of existing project managers. The intent was to gain their acceptance of the program and have them become the "thought leaders" for the effort. Additionally, they were given the opportunity to discuss how the processes and related training should be changed. Using their input, the team made modifications as needed.

Gaining support and acceptance of the new management team and allowing the employees to have a voice in the development and implementation of the overall program created employee buy-in. Consequently, the new approach became "business as usual." As new employees joined the group, additional training classes were scheduled to assimilate them as quickly as possible into the organization and culture.

CONCLUSION

The major premise of this chapter is that culture change in large, well-established enterprises is often needed and very difficult to accomplish. Combine that situation with the need for effective project management, and managers have a very difficult task. In the case presented by the authors, the enterprise recognized the need for a major culture change to reflect the changing business environment, and a corresponding need for a much more disciplined project management approach than what was being used. The enterprise combined these two needs into a year-long program that involved the development and implementation of a project management approach that was used as the driver to effect a major culture change. The most noteworthy measure of the success of this effort is that customer ratings of the IT organization went from barely adequate to excellent, and have been maintained over an extended period of time.

Chapter 23
Developing Applications with the User in Mind

Edward G. Cale, Jr.
Jerome Kanter
Donna B. Stoddard

The corporate scenario described in this chapter is an example of a common problem in the development of management support systems: in both systems design and implementation, too little attention is given to the needs and perspectives of the end user. Inadequate attention to ease of use in system design and lack of appropriate training and conversion preparedness affect applications aimed at salespeople, production people, administrators, middle managers, and senior management. These shortcomings can be observed in companies across all types of industries.

ROLLING OUT A NEW SYSTEM — ONE CORPORATE SCENARIO

A major investment company developed a new system that allows its portfolio analysts to obtain detailed analysis of the performance of a particular portfolio with comparisons to relevant industry benchmarks. The new system is a significant improvement over the current approach, and the company feels that it will provide a major competitive edge in acquiring and maintaining new customers. The rollout of the new system was planned for the beginning of the year, and more than 200 portfolio analysts in 20 locations throughout the world were to be involved.

Six months after the rollout, the company returned to the old system. Portfolio analysts found the new system difficult to use, leading to serious delays in sending statements to customers. Consequently, the company decided to postpone the conversion until problems could be resolved. The systems developers claimed the problems resulted from a lack of understanding on the part of the analysts, whereas the portfolio analysts said the new system was too complicated and prone to errors. Part-time portfolio analysts in particular, who represent a significant portion of intended users, complained that the system was extremely difficult to use, and that what little training was provided was geared toward full-time employees.

Delays and Added Costs

Management estimates that system implementation will be delayed for nine months to a year. Some systems changes are envisioned, but the major difference planned in the future rollout is the formulation and delivery of a training program that first will be tested with a small but representative group of portfolio analysts and then extended to the entire staff before declaring the system ready to be used by all.

The cost of additional system tuning and training is significant: it includes the redesign work to make the system more usable, the training design and delivery time on the part of the training group, the time the portfolio analyst group will spend in training, and the cost of hiring temporary help that may be required during the training period. Furthermore, although no specific monetary value has been assigned to it, the delay in obtaining a competitive portfolio analysis program could threaten the competitive position of the company. However, there is no question in the minds of developers that the benefits of the new system (i.e., increased level of business and the ability of the analysts to handle more accounts) will still more than justify the added training and conversion costs.

Although this scenario is only one example, it is typical of a real problem that is common in the development of management support systems — in both system design and system implementation, too little attention is given to the needs and perspectives of the end user.

For a good fit between an application and its intended users, designers must either create the system to fit the end user or develop a training and support program to make the end user fit the application. Attacking the problem both in design and in implementation ensures the highest probability of success. This chapter describes strategies that help companies ensure a good fit between an application and its intended users.

DESIGNING SYSTEMS TO FIT THE END USER

Three major factors affect the fit between an application and an end user:

1. The relative advantage of the application to the end user vis-á-vis whatever systems they were using previously
2. The relative technical complexity of the application compared to the end user's level of experience or comfort
3. The relative compatibility of the application with other day-to-day activities of the end user

Relative Advantage

Relative advantage addresses the questions, What is in it for the end users? Why should they use the new application? Will it allow them to better service clients and collect larger commissions?

Most users hope that an application will make their lives easier and help them to do their jobs better so that they will be justly rewarded. Users do not want to interact with applications that will isolate them from their fellow workers or allow management to better oversee and micromanage their daily activities.

Although developers usually do not consciously create applications that negatively impact users, sometimes it is necessary to develop applications that can, for example, increase the ability of management to monitor and control the employee. If this type of system must be developed, this fact must be dealt with both in system design and implementation. To reach a solution or compromise, there must be a close working relationship between system designers and intended users.

If a system must be developed that has negative ramifications for the users, one possible solution is to have the end user directly share in the benefits that fall to the organization as a whole (i.e., through bonuses or a similar reward). During training and implementation, trainers need to try to make the end users understand and identify with the overall gains to the organization.

Relative Technical Complexity

The relative technical complexity of an application refers to the level of technical sophistication that proper use of the application assumes in the end user. Whereas an airline reservation representative who is used to working with multiscreened systems with cryptic symbol input and output might find a new application with a similar interface easy to learn, the high school student working at McDonald's probably would not.

As with relative advantage, to ensure system success, there must be a clear vision of the technical experience and educational sophistication of the intended users. Again, if a system must be built that stretches the technical abilities of the end user, this discrepancy must be addressed during training and implementation.

Relative Compatibility

The relative compatibility of an application refers to its fit with the end user's other frequently used applications. For example, the new application may not define customer and product information in the same way that other applications do, which would require some retraining. The new system should fit with the way the end user is accustomed to viewing the world, rather than require the end user to keep two "sets of books." If the new systems do not mesh easily with other systems and procedures with which the end user is familiar, this is a strong indicator of the need for substantial training.

The best-case development scenario would result in systems that have a high relative advantage for the end user, that are not complex compared with the end user's capabilities, and that fit with the other activities, perspectives, and systems of the end user. To do so, it is critical for the system designers to be able to see the application from the perspective of the end user. The important point to realize is that ease of use is defined differently by systems developers who are experts and accustomed to dealing with complexity and by intermittent users who want to spend as little time as possible handling systems problems.

Users Are All Different. Complicating the issue of understanding the end-user perspective is the fact that there is never a single, monolithic end user. End users possess differing levels of expertise, patience, and dedication. Some will spend most of their day inputting and inquiring directly into the system. Others will be intermittent users.

Also, some systems cross corporate boundaries, involving either suppliers or customers. Therefore, the range of expertise extends from experts to intermittent users, and includes individuals directly under the control of the organization and others who are not. Some of the latter users can often be the most important to business success. If its systems are too difficult to use, a company may face the loss of valued customers.

The requirement to understand the end-user perspective in all its complexity is a strong argument for embedding systems analysts within end-user organizations, where they can get to know and identify more closely with the end users. It is also an argument for using a prototyping approach to systems design whenever possible to obtain user feedback as often as possible. Highly structured applications (i.e., transaction processing systems) should prototype the user interface. Where applications are less structured (i.e., decision support systems or executive support systems), designers would want to prototype both the user interface and as many aspects of system functionality as possible.

USABILITY LABS

One interesting approach to better understanding the end-user perspective was developed by an insurance company that set up a usability lab. Although the company emphasizes a user-centric design approach, it wanted to do more to ensure system acceptance and use by the end-user community. Thus, after systems are developed, the lab is used to test the applications for usability with typical users prior to system release.

The various classes of users are identified and scheduled for lab sessions. The lab is equipped with movie projectors to record body language and facial expressions as well as to time the various operations. The videotapes are carefully reviewed by those responsible for the eventual system rollout to learn what they can about difficulties and training issues. If the lab experience indicates that changes are required, they are made and the results tested again.

Multiple Data Interfaces

An interesting offshoot of the usability lab is the concept of providing more than one user interface to an application. Historically, systems designers have focused on a single interface to be used by all users regardless of their positions within the company, their degree of computer literacy, or their frequency of use. One size does not fit all, however.

Although it is generally true that 80 percent of the usage is accomplished by 20 percent of the users, the intermittent users may be quite significant to the overall success of the application. Also, intermittent users may be very influential within their organizations.

A simple example is the experience a well-positioned professor had when trying to use the college library's new search tool. The professor needed only one book, for which he knew the name and author. However, he still had to:

1. Log onto the school network
2. Get to the school home page
3. Click on the library navigator
4. Click on the library catalog
5. Click on local library
6. Click on search the catalog
7. Type in the title of the book
8. Click on search
9. Click on view

The professor was frustrated by the amount of time it took him, as a seasoned user, to access the information he needed. He suggested that IS place an icon on every faculty and student desktop that gets them to step 6 or 7 in one click, or the setup of a few stations in the library that are set to stay on step 6 or 7.

The system that was developed was suitable for first-time users, but not for frequent users. Having multiple interfaces can prove a valuable feature for many systems, particularly when the user base is heterogeneous.

DEVELOPING TRAINING AND SUPPORT PROGRAMS

Whether or not systems are designed to fit the end user, training and support programs can be an effective way to create a fit between a new system and its users. When developing training and support programs, it is important to consider the relative advantage, complexity, and compatibility of the system. Other factors that should be considered include the type of user (intermittent versus power user), the user's cognitive style, and the user's position in the organization.

Marketing a New System to the User

When implementing a system that does not provide direct advantage to the end user, but is important to the larger organization, a well-orchestrated training program can be one way to market the new system.

For example, a consumer products organization recently implemented a sales force automation system that greatly reduced the lead time to move orders on the books to the factory. When implementing the system, they found it was difficult to get the sales representatives to attend scheduled training classes. Given their compensation plans, salespeople preferred to spend time with customers, not in classes. The IS organization discovered that the most effective way to reach the sales force was to attend its regularly scheduled sales meeting. Training for the new applications was delivered in one to two hour modules during the sales meeting.

Training Users with Fewer Technical Skills

There are several effective ways to implement an application that exceeds the technical sophistication of end users. First, a training program could be developed that upgrades the skills of the end users, concentrating on the shortcomings between their existing skills and those required by the application. As a second option, a more technically sophisticated employee who is specifically seeking out those skills required by the new system might be hired. A third option, which has been successful in a number of companies, has been to develop user teams consisting of one or more sophisticated users and one or more less-experienced people.

Improving the Fit of New Applications

In cases where the new application is not particularly compatible with other applications that end users employ or activities that they routinely conduct, consideration must be given to redesign of the other applications and activities to improve fit. Where this is not possible, an aggressive training program, possibly linked to the evaluation and incentive program, would be useful.

USER DIFFERENCES

Beyond targeting a training program at addressing areas where the fit between the application and potential end users is poor, designers must also realize that people learn in different ways, and that no one generic training program is likely to succeed with the total population. Users may differ because of the frequency with which they interact with the application. Users of the same systems may also represent different levels of authority in the organization.

User Intelligences

One school of thought says that people have different types of "intelligences," with different parts of the brain controlling different abilities. For example, some people learn better from pictures than from words. Thus, the most effective training program would take into consideration the different learning approaches of the end-user population.

The theory of multiple intelligences, developed by Harvard psychologist Howard Gardner, is recognized by corporate America and is being used by companies, including General Motors, Saturn Corp., and the Los Alamos National Laboratory in New Mexico. Gardner suggested there are seven intelligences — linguistic, musical, logical-mathematical, spatial, bodily kinesthetic, interpersonal, and intrapersonal. Gardner's work can be used to develop computer-learning techniques. Individuals with high logical-mathematical or musical intelligence do best with programmed instruction; those with high linguistic intelligence do best with written documentation; those with high spatial intelligence prefer to start with the big picture and a fast overview; and those with bodily kinesthetic intelligence prefer a hands-on, do-it-yourself, trial-and-error approach. Although this is an oversimplification and it is apparent that most people have more than one kind of intelligence, it should be obvious that, to be as effective as possible, a training program will take into consideration the preferred learning styles of the end users.

Motivating Users to Learn

Another factor in developing an educational program is timing. The frenetic wall-to-wall meeting style and activity load in businesses today make it difficult to pique the interest of people if there is not a pressing reason for learning. Thus, it is important to schedule the training when there is motivation for learning, for example, when the new system will be rolled out. The just-in-time element is a needed motivator to capture the attention of those involved.

The use of inside versus outside trainers depends on the in-house capabilities. If available, insiders who are familiar with the company and its culture can probably do the job better. However, it may be better to go outside than to stretch the capabilities of the inside staff.

Designing Content

Content is a vital factor in the effectiveness of training. For the most part, a discussion aimed at the basic level of how to interact with a new system should begin with and include a description of the total system — why it was designed and implemented, the major objectives, the connection with other systems, and overriding elements of the system.

For example, a large bank has recognized that its employees have differing training styles and training needs. If executives need to use systems, which in this organization is infrequent, a trainer is dispatched to deliver training one-on-one. Although traditional classroom training is still offered, the bank has migrated toward multimedia training where a computer is coupled with video and audio. The bank has found multimedia training to be effective because of the richness of the media and because it allows people to try out the system and make mistakes. Another advantage of the computer-based multimedia training is that it allows people to complete the training when they need it, not on a schedule.

THE COSTS OF IGNORING USABILITY AND TRAINING ISSUES

The investment firm scenario provides an example of the types of problems that can emerge when the end-user perspective is ignored; however, there have been a number of studies identifying the high costs associated with end-user difficulty with new systems. One study in particular by Nolan, Norton & Company reported by *CIO* magazine examined the costs of end-user computing over a six-month period. The study involved ten major companies in a variety of industry settings, including Ford Motor Company, Cigna Corp., and Xerox Corp. The study found that the measured cost per workstation ran from $2,000 to $6,500 per year, which included the cost of PC and LAN hardware, software, peripherals, dedicated central IS personnel, and technology and personnel support of the host or server environment. It was emphasized that these were the measured costs.

The startling conclusion of their study was that the so-called unmeasured costs, which consisted of "peer-support costs," averaged two and one-half times the measured costs, or from $5,000 to $15,000 per year. Peer-support costs comprise the time value of non-IS personnel who render guidance and assistance to their peers in the use of applications.

Lack of application fit with the end user and lack of proper training programs are the main culprits of the peer-support phenomenon. As the use of systems continues to extend to a broader and more diverse population of end users, these hidden peer-support costs, as well as the costs of outright implementation failures, will continue to grow.

CONCLUSION

This chapter opened with a description of a company that had considerable difficulty rolling out an important new system to its portfolio analysts. The cause of the problem was lack of consideration for the classes of users. Also, training prior to the rollout was not emphasized to the degree that it should have been.

Three factors that affect the fit of the application and the end user include the relative advantage, technical complexity, and compatibility of the system from the end user's perspective. Systems developers often neglect to consider these elements properly. They have become more important over time as information technology has evolved from central control to the democratization of computing, putting users in direct contact with both input and output.

Furthermore, the advent of business process reengineering and client/server computing has created additional users out of those who formerly handed off computer contact to others. The use of systems prototyping and gaining early user feedback are critical to successful system rollout. Also, the development of a usability lab can be an effective tool to assess user reaction before systems roll out. Multiple interfaces to handle different classes of users are also helpful.

Organizations should preplan training programs to be implemented before new systems are rolled out. Training should emphasize flexibility of timing and approach, and should be carefully tailored to the intended audience. People learn differently depending on their individual cognitive styles. One size does not fit all; yet in many cases this truth is not heeded because of timing or cost considerations. The stakes are high when the hidden costs of a user workstation exceed the known costs — a situation greatly influenced by lack of proper attention to the usability of systems and effective training programs.

Section 4
Effectively Managing Outsourced Projects

Chapter 24
A Practical Guide to Staff Augmentation and Outsourcing

Christine B. Tayntor

Almost from the inception of information technology (IT), back in the dark ages when the function was called data processing, the use of contract staff has been a fact of life for many companies. These outside "consultants," as they are sometimes called, have consistently provided a variety of services, augmenting permanent staff. In the early days, contracting was the only method an IT manager had of obtaining additional manpower or specialized services. Over the past decade, however, a new word has entered the IT lexicon. "Outsourcing" has become a popular method of obtaining IT services.

Although there are similarities between the use of contractors and outsourcing firms, the two types of services have fundamental differences. This chapter defines the services, differentiates between them, and suggests the functions where each is most appropriately used.

DEFINING STAFF AUGMENTATION AND OUTSOURCING

Whether called contractors, consultants, or rent-a-body firms, the primary function of these IT service providers is to supplement existing IT staff. They are typically engaged when the IT department is unable to obtain or retain permanent staff, or when it needs specialized skills for a short period. As may be surmised from the term "staff augmentation," contractors function as members of the department, taking their day-to-day direction from IT managers. Except for the fact that their paychecks come from a different company, and that their assignments can be terminated on short notice without cause, contractors are virtually indistinguishable from other members of the IT department.

0-8493-1190-X/02/$0.00+$1.50
© 2002 by CRC Press LLC

Although some companies have exclusive agreements with one service provider, it is more common for a single IT department to use contractors from a number of firms. The reason for the use of several firms is the IT manager's desire to find the individual whose skills most closely match the department's needs. That is because the key component in staff augmentation, as in permanent staffing, is the individual person. Success or failure tends to be measured at the task level, and is dependent on specific staff. Because of this focus, when it contracts for staff augmentation, IT faces many of the same risks that it does with its own staff. Contractors may not perform as expected, or they may quit before a project is complete.

Contractor agreements are frequently informal, and, while engagements may be long-term, many are of short duration. From a contractual perspective, staff augmentation can be viewed as the dating stage of a relationship.

If staff augmentation is dating, outsourcing is marriage. It is legally binding, is typically monogamous, has long commitments, and — in most cases — divorce clauses. In contrast to staff augmentation, outsourcing focuses on services rather than individuals, and success is measured at the engagement level.

Some IT departments use a manufacturing analogy to describe outsourcing, explaining that they have chosen to "buy" a service rather than "make" it in-house. They argue that this is similar to the situation where a plant might choose to buy a standard part rather than make it itself. The analogy is valid; the risks and rewards of outsourcing IT services are similar to those of buying parts. Just as a manufacturer may sacrifice the ability to customize a part for its use, but gains speed or cost savings by buying it, IT outsourcing involves similar trade-offs in flexibility against cost and speed.

Outsourcing differs from staff augmentation in several fundamental ways. When an IT department outsources, it turns over day-to-day responsibility for specific services to a supplier. Although overall accountability for the success of the relationship remains with IT, detailed management and direction is provided by the outsourcer, and measurement is not of individual tasks, but rather of compliance with service level agreements (SLAs).

By design, outsourcing distances IT from the service provider. Work may be done on-site, but it is frequently performed remotely, further reducing IT's involvement with the service. Because outsourcing creates a distance between the IT department and the service it formerly provided, and because agreements are typically long term with penalties for early termination, companies do not undertake it lightly. It is normal to spend months going through a formal request for proposal (RFP) and selection process

Exhibit 1. Staff Augmentation versus Outsourcing Matrix

Characteristic	Staff Augmentation	Outsourcing
Formality of contract	Frequently low (or none at all)	Normally formal
Length of engagement	Typically short	Long (normally 2 to 5 years)
Time to engage/disengage	Short (days)	Long (months)
Number of suppliers	Many	One or two
Management of staff	IT department	Supplier
Location of staff	Normally within the IT department	Can be either on- or off-site
Measurement of success	Individual project tasks	Service level agreement
Key to success	Individual contractor	Entire service provider company
Pricing	Time and materials	Fixed fee
Right to hire supplier's staff	Occasionally	Infrequently
Co-employment concerns	Possible	No
Flexibility	High	Low
Overall program	Tactical	Strategic

before actually beginning an outsourcing engagement. Exhibit 1 provides a summary of the differences between staff augmentation and outsourcing.

STAFF AUGMENTATION CONSIDERATIONS

When would an IT department use staff augmentation? Although the answers vary, most staff augmentation projects fall into one of the following categories.

1. *The department is unable to hire or retain sufficient staff to meet its normal workloads.* The booming economy of the late 1990s created a shortage of qualified technical staff in many parts of the United States. For companies that were installing large software suites such as SAP and PeopleSoft, the situation was exacerbated by the demand for IT staff with this specialized expertise. Other companies have a perennial problem retaining qualified staff for a variety of reasons, ranging from compensation policies to corporate culture. In these cases, contractors are brought in to fill the gaps. They can be viewed as temporary staff, used until permanent employees are hired.

2. *IT needs additional staff for a specific project.* During large system development projects, IT may need more designers, coders, and testers than it has on its staff. Rather than hiring permanent staff when there is no long-term need, IT organizations can use contractors to fill the gaps. Similarly, many companies used outside service

providers to assist with their Y2K remediation. Unlike the first case, which had an indefinite term, this use of staff augmentation is for a specific period.

3. *The department seeks staffing level flexibility.* Some companies and industries have a history of boom-and-bust staffing. As economic conditions change, major projects are cut and staff levels are reduced. To avoid having to periodically lay off employees, some companies keep only a core staff, and use contractors during the boom times. Although they pay more on a daily basis for contract staff, they avoid the expense and pain of severing employees.

4. *IT needs specialized skills or knowledge.* During a period of rapid technological change such as the current "E-biz craze," IT may want to initiate projects using new technology. In most cases, it will not have existing staff with the needed skills. While it could contract with an outside firm to do the development, an alternative approach is to rent the expertise in the form of contractors who will work with in-house staff, providing on-the-job training and knowledge transfer. A primary advantage of this approach is the fact that short-term staff augmentation results in a permanent upgrading of in-house skills.

5. *The company wants to retain day-to-day control of all staff.* Some corporate cultures are not compatible with the transfer of responsibility and task level accountability that outsourcing demands. For these companies, staff augmentation can fill the gaps in staffing levels and expertise, without requiring a cultural shift.

The primary advantage to staff augmentation is the flexibility it gives the IT department. Because of the short-term and ad hoc nature of hiring contractors, IT can move quickly, bringing on additional staff for specific projects and removing them as soon as the work is complete. Flexibility extends to the actual hiring decisions. Although many companies have a list of preferred suppliers, the IT manager normally has a choice of several vendors, and can choose the firm whose employees most closely meet the manager's requirements.

While staff augmentation may solve many problems, it also raises several concerns. The first is cost. It seems intuitive that, because a service provider seeks to make a profit while most IT departments need only charge out their expenses, contract help would cost more than in-house staff. When hourly or daily rates are compared to the salary and benefits costs of employees, contractors do appear to be more expensive. For short-term projects, this may not be the case. As shown on Exhibit 2, a true cost comparison includes more than salary and benefits.

The situation is different on long-term assignments. When used for extended periods, contractors normally cost more than permanent staff. In

Exhibit 2. Evaluating Costs of Staff Augmentation versus In-house Staff

1. Add:
   — Salary
   — Benefits (life and health insurance, pension, etc.)
   — Training (course fees and travel)
   To determine annual cost.

2. Subtract:
   — Vacation
   — Holidays
   — Training time
   — Illness
   From 2080 (40 hours per week times 52 weeks) to determine the number of working hours in a year.

3. Divide the annual cost by the number of working hours to determine the hourly rate.

4. Add:
   — Recruiting costs
   — Severance and other termination costs
   To determine the one-time employment costs.

5. Determine the length of the assignment in hours.

6. Divide the one-time costs by the assignment length to determine the hiring/firing surcharge.

7. Add the surcharge to the hourly rate.

An example:

Assume an annual salary of $60,000, a benefits cost of 30 percent, and annual training costs of $2000. The employee receives 10 days vacation, 12 holidays, 5 days of training, and 5 sick days.

His hourly cost, without considering recruitment and severance, is $43.86. If a typical contractor's hourly rate were between $60 and $80, it would appear that the company was paying a substantial premium for the flexibility involved in staff augmentation.

However, if the employee was hired for a six-month engagement (1040 hours), with recruiting costs of $20,000 and termination costs of $10,000, the hourly surcharge would be $28.85, making the total cost $72.71.

this case, although there is no economic justification, the IT department may decide that staff augmentation is preferable to hiring permanent staff because of the flexibility it provides.

The second concern, which is also related to long-term use of contractors, is co-employment. In several high-profile lawsuits, contractors successfully argued that they were entitled to employee benefits because they functioned essentially as employees. As a result, companies have become wary of what is termed co-employment. To avoid this, some have started to limit the length of time a contractor can work for them, in some cases to terms as short as six months. Although this does not impact limited-length assignments such as the provision of specialized skills at a critical phase of a project, the use of contractors for semi-permanent staff augmentation becomes difficult. This is particularly true when the assignments have a steep learning curve, as can be the case with support of company-specific applications. It is at this point that some IT departments first consider outsourcing.

OUTSOURCING CONSIDERATIONS

Even when an outsourcer's staff works on the client company's premises, IT is not vulnerable to claims of co-employment. This is because of the fundamental difference between staff augmentation and outsourcing. In outsourcing, the company contracts for a service, not a person. It is the outsourcer's responsibility to determine how many people will be required to perform the service, and what technical background they must have. The company normally does not interview them, and it does not direct the staff. In short, IT specifies what is to be done, not how to do it.

Although some companies believe that the primary benefit of outsourcing is to avoid the co-employment issues associated with lengthy staff augmentation engagements, there are other reasons why an IT department would outsource one or more of its functions, including:

- *The work is not a core competency.* For example, a manufacturing company may decide that its core business is manufacturing widgets rather than distributing them, and may therefore outsource the warehousing and distribution components of its business. Similarly, an IT department may decide that some functions are not part of its core competency, and may choose to transfer responsibility for them to a service provider. An example of a non-core competency is support of legacy applications while implementing a new system or integrated suite that will replace them. In this case, IT may have decided that its core business is being a systems integrator rather than an application support function.
- *The skill is a commodity.* Some functions, such as mainframe operations, help desk services, and telecommunications support have become commodities. The work provided does not vary substantially from industry to industry, or even from company to company. Because of the standardization and economies of scale, various suppliers have established

themselves as experts in these functions, and can perform them at least as well and often cheaper than the IT department.

- *IT has a major skills gap, with no short-term plan to close it.* As noted above, an IT department may use staff augmentation as a way to obtain specific expertise, and transfer that to existing staff. This approach is desirable when the skill is one the department seeks, such as an emerging technology. If, on the other hand, the department has difficulty retaining experts for key systems, such as SAP or PeopleSoft, it may choose to turn responsibility for the entire system over to an outsourcer rather than struggle to keep the department fully staffed.

There are a number of advantages that an IT department may derive by outsourcing one or more functions. The most important among these are:

- Departmental resources previously involved in the function are freed to participate on other projects, including higher priority or value-added work.
- Costs are fixed and may be less than the department was previously paying.
- Risk, especially the risk of losing key employees, is transferred to a company whose primary business is recruiting and retaining technical staff. Because outsourcers' contracts require adherence to specific SLAs, they have a high incentive to provide cross-training that will reduce dependence on a single individual.

An added advantage for some companies is that an outsourcing contract can specify that the supplier offer employment to staff whose jobs are being transferred to the outsourcer. If IT has decided to divest itself of non-core competency functions, it may not have other assignments for the staff currently performing the work. Transferring employees to the outsourcer provides continued employment for the staff, and reduced risk to both the company and the outsourcer.

Although favored by some IT managers, outsourcing raises concerns for others. The fear cited by most critics is that the IT department will lose control over its business. This is a valid concern. The simple fact is, when a function is outsourced, IT transfers responsibility for day-to-day operation to the supplier. IT has indeed given up the ability to direct the work at a detailed level. Instead, it relies on the supplier to provide that daily management, and to ensure that service level agreements are met. If an IT manager is not comfortable with relinquishing task-level control, or if the corporate culture does not support such a change, outsourcing should not be considered.

The second concern is reduced flexibility. Because outsourcing is normally a long-term engagement, bound by contractual terms, it is not designed for day-to-day changes in the scope of work. Instead, it is predicated on the fact that a finite scope of work has been transferred to the service provider, and that the vendor will be held accountable for clearly defined service levels. Although good outsourcing contracts provide for periodic adjustment of service level agreements, they do not lend themselves to frequent changes. If the workload is volatile, outsourcing may be an inappropriate solution.

USE OF STAFF AUGMENTATION AND OUTSOURCING FOR SPECIFIC FUNCTIONS

Although virtually any IT function could benefit from either staff augmentation or outsourcing under specific circumstances, certain functions are more obvious choices for one type of service provider than the other.

Data Center Operations

If asked to define classic IT outsourcing, many managers would respond with "data center operations." This has traditionally been the first function that most IT organizations consider outsourcing, and it is in many respects ideally suited to outsourcing, because the work is typically not a core competency and the skill is a commodity. It is also one with documented successes and proven cost savings, both of which encourage other companies to consider it.

The reasons why data center outsourcing is often successful at reducing costs include:

- *Tasks are clearly defined and repetitive.* In most cases, the company has well-established procedures for the operation. This simplifies the outsourcer's transition time and reduces the impact on end customers.
- *The workload is not volatile and changes in the nature of the work are infrequent.* This consistency makes negotiating a contract simpler because there is less need to provide for exceptions. Costs can be clearly identified. A steady-state workload also provides the outsourcer with the incentive to invest in long-term cost-saving changes, a portion of which can be passed through to the company.
- *The work is not company specific and requires no special knowledge of the company's business.* The generic nature of the function means that there are many potential suppliers, and the company can contract with the lowest-cost provider.
- *Existing costs are normally well-documented.* Because many companies have formal chargeback systems for data center costs, potential savings from using a service provider are readily determined.

The primary concerns associated with data center outsourcing are:

- *The company may lose control of decisions*, such as a change from one mid-range computer supplier to another, or an upgrade to a new version of the operating system, which would have an impact on its staff. A carefully worded contract can reduce this risk by reserving the right to these decisions to the company, or requiring its concurrence before a change can be made.
- *Flexibility of shifting from one platform to another may be reduced by a long-term contract.* If a company anticipates a major change in its computing strategy, such as moving from mainframe systems to client/server or Web-based applications, it may not want to outsource data center operations until the change is in place.

While staff augmentation can alleviate temporary shortages of operations staff, it is not used as often as outsourcing because it does not provide the cost savings most IT managers seek from the use of a data center service provider.

Telecommunications Services

The support of a company's wide area data and voice networks is similar to data center operations in that procedures and costs are often clearly defined, the work is a commodity, and there several vendors that can provide the service. This is a second function where outsourcing can be used to reduce costs.

Local Area Network and Desktop Computing Support

Installation and support of LANs and PCs is a function where both staff augmentation and outsourcing can be used successfully, depending on a company's maturity level and objectives. If the IT department has little in-house expertise and wants to develop it, staff augmentation is an effective way to bring in experts who will train existing staff. Similarly, if IT has not developed formal procedures or standardized its methods, it may want to hire a contractor with specialized skills to develop those procedures. Even if the long-term plan is to outsource the function, it is desirable to establish procedures prior to outsourcing. In general, a company whose function is not yet mature should consider staff augmentation rather than outsourcing. Similarly, to increase the odds of successful outsourcing, IT should seek to first stabilize and standardize its function, and then outsource.

For some companies, outsourcing of LAN and PC support has been a less than successful venture. The reasons for the disappointment include:

- *Immature processes or lack of standardization.* As noted above, outsourcing contracts are managed by service level agreements (SLAs). If there are no existing SLAs, it is difficult to specify with any precision the work that the outsourcer will be required to perform. This means that measuring success will become subjective, increasing the possibility for dissention between the company and its service provider. In addition, if the processes are not clearly defined, the service provider may have difficulty pricing the engagement.

- *Incomplete due diligence.* This is a corollary to immature processes. If the vendor does not completely analyze the company's existing function, it may make inaccurate assumptions about the required staffing level or the current customer satisfaction. This can lead to faulty pricing and another opportunity for disputes. Incomplete due diligence occurs most often when the company seeks to compress the time to develop a contract, and when suppliers overestimate their knowledge of the company's function.

- *Unrealistic expectations.* A company may outsource a function, hoping that the service provider will resolve all outstanding problems, improve customer satisfaction, and reduce costs. While all of these are possible, it is unlikely that all of them can be achieved in the short term. A more realistic approach, particularly when processes are immature, would be to hire a vendor to implement formal procedures and stabilize the environment as phase one. Phase two, under a separate contract, could include cost reductions and improved customer satisfaction as its goals. Although the same vendor could be used for both phases, this is not mandatory. Some outsourcing firms that would be well-suited for phase two may not have the expertise needed for phase one.

- *Loss-leader pricing.* Occasionally, a service provider will price an engagement at or below cost as a way of getting the business. From the supplier's view, the loss-leader approach is justified by the anticipation of being awarded additional business in the future. Although loss-leaders occur in both staff augmentation and outsourcing engagements, the long-term nature of outsourcing contracts makes them particularly dangerous. Unless the additional work is guaranteed, it is possible that the vendor's expected profit margins will not be met. This typically results in the vendor reducing staffing levels or substituting less experienced staff to generate a profit. Customer satisfaction rarely rises after such actions.

The concerns associated with outsourcing of LAN and PC support include those shown for data center operations. In addition, pricing may not be accurate if the processes are immature. To improve the likelihood of success, full outsourcing of LAN and PC support should be initiated only after formal procedures have been developed and implemented. Staff augmentation can provide an effective method of developing and implementing such procedures.

Legacy Application Support

With the move to large integrated software suites, some companies have chosen to outsource support of their legacy applications. Like data center operations, the rationale includes the fact that support of these "sunset systems" is not a core competency.

A company might choose to outsource legacy systems if any of the following are true:

1. *It wants its internal IT staff to focus on other work,* such as the implementation of a new packaged system or the development of Web-enabled applications. Most IT managers will attest to the fact that it is difficult for staff to meet project deadlines when they are also responsible for maintaining production systems, because production problems are a higher priority than new work. Although it is possible to minimize permanent staff involvement by using staff augmentation, concerns about co-employment and the desire to eliminate the day-to-day management of these employees makes outsourcing a more appropriate choice.

2. *The company wants to ensure that the old systems are shut down when the new ones are installed.* Many companies have a poor history of retiring old systems, even after the new ones have been in operation for several months. To achieve the cost savings projected for the new system, it is often vital that duplicate systems be eliminated. When a company pays an outside company to support the systems, costs are more visible and easier to eliminate.

3. *It fears the flight of key employees* who are supporting the legacy systems. In a tight job market, employees who fear that their jobs may be eliminated when a system is retired, or who prefer system development to maintenance, will leave. By transferring responsibility to a service provider with expertise in system support and a large staff, the company has reduced its risk.

The primary concerns associated with outsourcing of legacy systems are:

1. *The vendor may not have staff with the needed technical expertise.* This is particularly true for very old systems, which may have been written in arcane languages on now obsolete equipment.

2. *The learning curve for the vendor's staff may be steep,* because many legacy systems were either developed in-house or are highly customized versions of packaged software. In these cases, the vendor would have to train staff, rather than having people with the needed expertise ready to deploy on the engagement.

3. *Costs may be higher than the current internal costs.* This is often true in short engagements, or when the company has been operating with a lean staff. Outsourcers typically achieve rapid cost savings on

commodity functions, which legacy systems are not. Otherwise, they depend on engagements of three to five years for cost efficiencies.

Packaged System Implementation

Some companies have chosen to outsource the implementation of packaged software, frequently to the vendor who developed the software, or to a niche service provider that specializes in the system. Unfortunately, however, the approach can be a dangerous one, and should be undertaken only after a careful consideration of the risks.

The reasons a company would outsource packaged software installation include:

- The vendor is the expert.
- Because the vendor is the expert, it can implement its software cheaper than IT can.
- The vendor's implementation will be faster than IT's.

While these circumstances can be true, they do not address the primary concerns:

- If no internal staff is involved, there is no knowledge transfer, and the company will be dependent on the vendor for ongoing support. Even if the vendor's support is cost-effective, the absence of internal expertise makes a future "divorce" more difficult.
- Without internal involvement, the vendor may install a "vanilla" version of the software that fails to meet the customers' unique needs. Business knowledge is key to successful system implementation; and, while the vendor may have industry expertise, internal staff know the idiosyncrasies of their company and its customers best.

To minimize long-term risks, IT should consider using staff augmentation for system implementation. The company can hire the vendor's experts on a time and materials basis, requiring them to work with internal staff to transfer knowledge. Alternatively, it can contract for specific portions of the work to be done by the vendor at a fixed price. Such a fixed-price contract can be considered a form of outsourcing. In this case, it is important that at least one member of the internal staff be involved in the project. If that is not possible, perhaps because work is being done off-shore, a formal transition should take place once the work is completed.

New System Development

System development is similar to packaged system implementation in that a company increases its risks by outsourcing the entire project, even if it plans to have the vendor provide ongoing support of the system. To ensure that the company retains internal knowledge of the system, it may want to use a combination of staff augmentation and selective outsourcing as outlined above for packaged system implementation. In this scenario, IT would typically retain responsibility for all strategic decisions. Working with its customers, it would define the requirements of the new system. It might outsource portions of the development, including the writing of detailed specifications, coding, and unit testing, while retaining overall project schedule responsibility.

CONCLUSION

Staff augmentation and outsourcing are valuable tools for the IT manager. Although the services provided may seem similar, there are fundamental differences between them, and they are most effective when used on specific functions. While outsourcing can reduce costs and free internal staff to work on higher-priority projects, it should be used only when work is clearly defined and when the company is willing to relinquish day-to-day control. For other projects, staff augmentation is a less risky although often more costly approach.

Chapter 25
The Essentials for Successful IT Outsourcing

Ralph L. Kliem
Irwin S. Ludin

Information technology (IT) outsourcing is the use of a third party to provide services rather than using those in-house. It has become a growth industry and will continue to grow. Today, it has become commonplace for firms to outsource at least some aspect of their IT services. Some of the more popular services are:

- Application development
- Data center
- Desktop/personal computers
- Network (e.g., LANs, WANs)
- Support services/help desk
- Training

The above list is by no means exhaustive and can, in fact, include many services that are not IT in nature. However, this chapter will guide organizations through the pitfalls that often plague IT outsourcing activities, like:

- Cumbersome transition into and out of an outsourcing relationship
- Incomplete or vague contracts
- Lack of an infrastructure for supporting an outsourcing relationship
- Negotiating a contract with an unsuitable vendor
- Poor communications with vendors

SUCCESS TIP #1: DETERMINE THE BUSINESS CASE FOR OR AGAINST OUTSOURCING

Many firms do not thoroughly analyze the need for IT outsourcing. Instead, they seek outsourcing because it provides immediate gain, only

0-8493-1190-X/02/$0.00+$1.50
© 2002 by CRC Press LLC

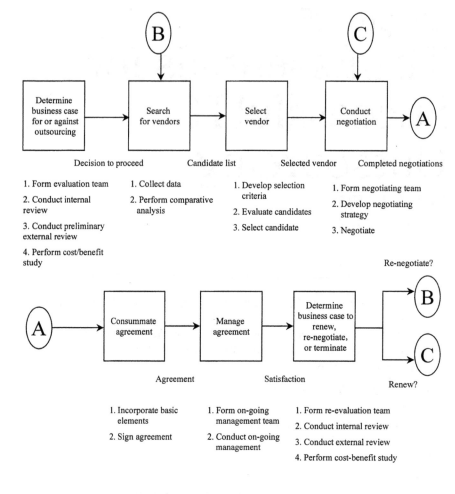

Exhibit 1.   IT Outsourcing Process

to later realize that it delivered long-term loss. As a result, some firms lock themselves into massive, long-term contracts only to find that such an arrangement is a liability rather than an asset (e.g., delivery of no longer necessary services at above market prices). A good business case, looking at different pricing alternatives (e.g., fixed or cost plus), and varying payback periods (e.g., three, five, or ten years) can help determine whether outsourcing will achieve savings (e.g., five to 20 percent), desirable levels of quality, and other objectives. Outsourcing should not occur, however, if the service is mission critical, can be done more effectively in-house, cannot provide a savings of five percent or more, or fear exists over losing controls (see Exhibit 1). When forming the evaluation team, the organization should be sure to:

- Determine the required knowledge and skills (e.g., accounting, technical, or business management)
- Designate a project manager
- Determine the objectives of the team
- Define each member's roles and responsibilities

When conducting the initial review, the organization should be sure to:

- Define the objectives and scope of the review
- Conduct an inventory of all assets (e.g., software, hardware, or data)
- Determine which services are mission critical; which are important but not critical; and which are nonessential
- Determine existing capabilities for providing current services
- Determine core competencies
- Determine the internal service requirements
- Define the requirements of internal customers

When conducting the preliminary external review, the organization should be sure to:

- Define the objectives and scope of the review
- Develop criteria for selecting which vendors to look at
- Determine the research approach (e.g., interview or literature review)
- Determine the core competencies of the firms

When performing the cost/benefit analysis, the organization should be sure to:

- Account for the time value of money
- Determine a payback period
- Determine the type of outsourcing agreement (e.g., co-sourcing, out-tasking)
- Calculate different pricing options (cost plus, fixed price, time and materials)
- List assumptions and constraints
- Develop alternatives
- Make a recommendation

SUCCESS TIP #2: SEARCH FOR VENDORS

It is very important to develop criteria for selecting vendors. The criteria should include overall reputation, market share and growth, responsiveness, expertise, flexibility in the types of outsourcing agreements, price, experience, size, and history.

It is important to ensure that the evaluation team has accepted the criteria and the selected vendors. This acceptance reduces resistance to the criteria and encourages buy-in from the team for the vendors that are selected.

When collecting information, the organization should be sure to:

- Determine the criteria for looking at a group of vendors
- Select the vendors
- Determine the sources of information and their reliability
- Determine exactly which information is needed (e.g., financial or market value)
- Follow a consistent approach to avoid "corrupting" information

When compiling information, the organization should be sure to:

- Organize the information in a readable, comprehensible manner (e.g., matrix, three-ring binder)
- Not omit any important information

SUCCESS TIP #3: SELECT THE VENDOR

Selecting the vendor should be an objective process. Unfortunately, objectivity becomes sacrificed because "exemptions" are made to the criteria when applied to a specific vendor. Bias is introduced into the process and, not surprisingly, the results are also biased. Worse, it becomes difficult to obtain buy-in from team members and senior management. Whatever the criteria being used, however, the primary criterion is whether the vendor can provide services that will help achieve the goals identified during the determination of the business case. When developing the selection criteria, the organization should be sure to:

- Create a specific, meaningful criterion
- Use criteria that minimize bias and retain objectivity
- Receive consensus from the members of the evaluation team

When evaluating candidates, organizations should be sure to:

- Apply the criteria consistently to all vendors
- Follow a methodical, logical process

When selecting the candidate, organizations should be sure to:

- Receive input from members of the evaluation team
- Reevaluate the selection to ensure objectivity and consistency
- Communicate the results to all interested parties, including, for example, senior management and evaluation team members

SUCCESS TIP #4: CONDUCT NEGOTIATION

Effective negotiation requires extensive preparation before the event. It requires knowing as much as possible about the vendor, such as its history with other clients; the vendor's market size and growth; its financial condition; its management stability; and its reputation. It also requires that the selecting firm knowing something about itself, including its strengths and weaknesses, short- and long-term goals, and technological capabilities. Such information about the firm and the vendor enables development of a negotiation strategy that has win–win results.

During negotiation, it is important that all team members support the strategy. It is also important that one person be the primary negotiator. If the vendor senses the opposite, then the negotiation may not have the desired results.

While negotiating, it is also important to recognize trends in IT outsourcing, including:

- Keeping the duration for contracts within two to three years
- Reserving the right to review and perhaps even approve subcontractors
- Focusing on a specific, narrow set of services
- Describing circumstances for renegotiation and termination
- Requiring technology transfer
- Describing minimum service levels
- Providing for penalties, damages, and incentives
- Listing reporting requirements
- Providing governance procedures

When forming the negotiating team, the organization should be sure to:

- Determine the required knowledge and skills (e.g., legal, technical, business management)
- Designate a project manager
- Determine whom to select from the evaluation team

When developing a negotiation strategy, the organization should be sure to:

- Determine the overall goals to achieve
- Develop an in-depth knowledge and understanding of the vendor's style, goals, and history
- Come prepared with facts and data to support the case
- Conduct a worst/best case scenario analysis

When negotiating, the organization should be sure to:

- Have a primary negotiator
- Seek a win–win solution
- Have the consensus of all members of the negotiation team

SUCCESS TIP #5: CONSUMMATE THE AGREEMENT

The contract is signed when the negotiation is concluded. There should be support by the entire team and senior management before it is signed. This commitment is important to ensure subsequent compliance with the contract, and to communicate to internal staff the willpower to make the outsourcing relationship work.

Prior to signing the contract, it is important to ensure that it covers some basic contractual elements. Failure to address the basic elements listed below could contractually obligate the firm in a manner that fails to protect its best interests (e.g., desirable quality of services at a competitive price).

When drafting the agreement, the organization should make sure it has incorporated at least the following basic elements:

- Conditions for renegotiation and termination
- Governance
- Intellectual property rights
- Length of the contract
- Penalties, damages, and incentives
- Pricing
- Reporting
- Services to provide and their levels
- Subcontractor management
- Technology transfer

Before signing the agreement, the organization should:

- Ensure that all clauses, phrases, and terms are clearly defined
- Ensure that there are no outstanding issues
- Obtain senior management's support
- Obtain consensus of the negotiating team

SUCCESS TIP #6: MANAGE THE AGREEMENT

Signing the agreement is not the end; it is the start of a new beginning. The relationship with the vendor must be managed to ensure the delivery of the desired quality of services for the money being spent.

For effective management, one person should be assigned responsibility for each contract. This person ensures the existence of ongoing communications, effective controls, and performance monitoring. The skills for managing a contract are less legal and technical and more account management in nature. The person should not only know contract management and have an understanding of the technology, but also possess good communications and relationship-building skills.

In addition to having the right person is having an infrastructure in place to manage the agreement. This infrastructure should include change management, scheduling activities, communication and information sharing, performance monitoring, and problem management.

When the organization forms the ongoing management team, it should be sure to:

- Determine the required knowledge and skills (e.g., account management, contract management, business management, or scheduling)
- Designate a business manager for the contract
- Define each member's roles and responsibilities

When conducting ongoing management of the contract, the organization should be sure to:

- Provide for continual communications with the vendors
- Provide the means for ongoing oversight of the services being provided
- Select software or develop a system for tracking and evaluating service delivery
- Determine the data and metrics for tracking and evaluating service delivery
- Perform a risk assessment to determine which controls should be and are in place
- Set up an infrastructure for evaluating changes that are potentially outside the scope of the contract
- Set up an infrastructure for problem management

SUCCESS TIP #7: DETERMINE THE BUSINESS CASE TO RENEW, RENEGOTIATE, OR TERMINATE

Once the IT outsourcing agreement is up for reconsideration, there are three options: renew, renegotiate, or terminate. *Renewal* accepts the terms of the existing contract. It often occurs if the customer feels the delivery of services is satisfactory or better. *Renegotiation* often occurs over dissatisfaction with the contents of the contract (e.g., it is too long in duration, or it is too costly). Increasingly, many firms are renegotiating because the technology is changing the needs for a service (e.g., movement from a mainframe-centric environment to a client/server one) or the pricing for services is not market driven. *Termination* occurs because the service is no longer necessary, is unsatisfactory, or costs too much. Terminations occur much less often than renegotiations.

Whether renewing, renegotiating, or terminating, it is important for the organization to conduct as comprehensive a study as when making the initial business case for or against outsourcing. It should use objective criteria, and make evaluations using data collected during the course of the initial contract. The data may come from metrics and documentation of past service delivery. If renegotiating or terminating, the organization should make sure the team and senior management support the decision, and understand the rights described in the contract to take such action.

When forming a reevaluation team, the organization should be sure to:

- Define each member's roles and responsibilities
- Designate a project manager
- Determine the objectives of the team (e.g., renegotiate or terminate the contract)
- Determine the required knowledge and skills (e.g., accounting, technical, legal, or business management)

When conducting the internal review, the organization should be sure to:

- Define the scope and objectives of the review
- Determine if capabilities exist for moving currently outsourced services in-house
- Determine the requirements of internal customers
- Determine which services are and are not currently being outsourced
- Determine which services are mission critical, which are important but not critical, and which are nonessential
- Document the quality of the past delivery of services
- Evaluate the current delivery of services, using the metrics that were collected

When conducting the external review, the organization should be sure to:

- Define the scope and objectives of the review
- Determine the research approach (e.g., market analysis or benchmarking)
- Develop criteria to determine what vendors look at

When performing the cost/benefit analysis, the organization should be sure to:

- Account for the time value of money
- Calculate the different pricing options, such as cost plus, fixed price, or time and materials
- Determine the payback period
- Determine the desired type of outsourcing agreement (e.g., co-sourcing or outtasking)
- Develop alternatives
- List assumptions and constraints
- Make a recommendation

THE DESIRED RESULTS

While IT outsourcing can be beneficial, it can also devastate a company. For that reason alone, management must see to it that all the necessary actions have been taken to ensure that the former occurs. In too many cases, firms are realizing that the outsourcing of their IT services could have been done better, or never should have occurred in the first place. As a result, everyone is frustrated and angry, and there are costs that no one ever thought would accrue. Fortunately, if the above actions are executed, such results need not happen.

Chapter 26
The Management Service Provider Option

Janet Butler

Conventional wisdom warns companies against outsourcing their core competencies and, at one time, management fell into this category. Now, however, especially with the rise of E-business, organizations require exceptional management to survive. Because this is not always available in-house, management service providers (MSP) are springing up to fill the need.

MSPs are an emerging type of vendor that lets customers outsource various aspects of information technology (IT) management. If an MSP can guarantee that an organization's network or applications will remain up and running, and downtime will be nearly or completely eliminated, an organization should seriously consider this option.

MSPs appeal, in particular, to small and mid-sized companies, as well as E-businesses, as an alternative to the expense of building their own management systems. While these businesses might require 24×7 availability, they do not have the resources to ensure this uptime by doing their own management. However, an MSP can do so, notifying the customer of potential problems or slowdowns.

In fact, some analysts predict that 50 to 70 percent of organizations will use a service provider to assist in building or hosting their E-commerce applications. In-house management costs are steep, and include management platforms and point products; management integration tools such as a central console; and staff to install, configure, test, and maintain systems. Businesses must also gauge the cost of downtime.

The cost savings attributed to MSPs can be substantial. Companies save not only the hefty price of the software itself, but the cost of internally hosting management software, which is estimated at three to nine times the cost of the software, plus ongoing staff costs.

Still, in turning to MSPs, IT managers give up some control and visibility into their infrastructure. Also, because the services might lack the functionality of traditional management platforms, flexibility is an issue; it becomes difficult to add new technologies and systems to the IT infrastructure. Therefore, if IT is critical to the organization, such as in the financial services and telecommunications industries, companies might want to retain management control.

According to one analyst, there are approximately 70 vendors in the management service provider category. These include Manage.com, Luminate.net, NetSolve, Envive Corp., StrataSource, and SiteLine. By the end of 2000, MSPs generated more than $90 million in revenue, and analysts predict $4 billion by 2005.

Major management solution providers are also beginning to offer MSP services, including Computer Associates and Hewlett-Packard; the latter has a new HP OpenView service provider unit. Some vendors such as TriActive are changing their marketing message from application service provider (ASP) to MSP. And other management software vendors, such as BMC, are forging alliances with MSPs, and buying companies with point products.

MSP BENEFITS

MSP drivers include the shortage of skilled professionals, the increasing complexity of network and systems management, the rapid evolution of technology, and the need to monitor on a 24×7×365 basis. An MSP offers organizations a subscription-based external service to manage their infrastructure resources or applications. The MSP vendor provides tool implementation and external tool hosting, or hosting within the customer environment. MSPs predominantly target E-business applications and small to mid-sized companies.

In addition to cost advantages, MSPs offer these organizations rapid time to value, due to quick implementation; an ongoing relationship, to ensure subscription renewal; supplementation of staff resources with additional expertise; and an outside perspective. Because the MSP hosts the solution, the organization can be up and running quickly. This fast implementation contrasts sharply with the long implementation times required for an organization to host a solution in-house.

The MSP model also supplements the IT staff in new technology areas — specifically, in E-commerce application management. By doing the repetitive work, MSPs free the IT staff to focus on higher-level, value-added programs.

One analyst group recently estimated that the demand for IT professionals exceeds the supply by 30 percent. The labor shortage is particularly acute in network and systems management, which people have not been trained for, and which does not represent a growth path.

Frameworks have failed to solve the labor shortage problem. Enterprise management tools from the likes of Compuware, Tivoli, and Computer Associates are too expensive, too difficult to implement, and require too many people. So the management solution becomes a management problem in and of itself, whereby enterprise software is partially implemented, it becomes shelfware, or its use is not widespread across all environments. When its champions leave the company, the tools are seldom used.

By contrast, the MSP allows people to manage via the Internet on a subscription basis, so a $100,000 to $150,000 up-front cost is not required. Not only is there a low cost of entry, but payment on a monthly basis means the work comes out of the services budget, rather than that of capital acquisition. Therefore, organizations do not get caught up in budget/approval cycles, where different price points require different authorizations. The monthly basis keeps the sale lower in the organization, helping both vendors and users.

In addition, the MSP bears the initial and continuing costs of investing in hardware and software infrastructure, while the customer company simply pays a monthly fee. There is also relatively low risk to companies that choose an MSP solution. If the provider is not meeting its needs, the organization can cancel the subscription and go elsewhere.

SOURCING APPROACHES

In managing their IT environments, organizations have traditionally focused on enterprise tools, purchasing them via perpetual license, and taking advantage of volume discounts. The tools range from point products to comprehensive management frameworks, providing the entire range of systems management functionality. In addition, organizations often augment their tool purchases with vendor-supplied implementation services.

The MSP offers an alternative model that takes different forms. For example, the MSP might sell directly to enterprises, or it might package its offerings with another service provider, such as an application service provider (ASP) or Internet service provider (ISP).

Some organizations have turned to the "legacy MSP." Here, the management service provider functions as a layer between the complexity of an enterprise management framework and the user. The MSP takes traditional enterprise software, installs it, and runs it for the organization, with both the customer and MSP operating the software. Characteristically, there is dedicated hardware for each customer.

For example, MSPs such as TriActive might run the Tivoli environment for a user, wrapping their technical expertise around it. In this hosted model for enterprise software, the customer gets the benefit of the framework, while being shielded from its complexity, and attains faster implementation of the software, and lower up-front costs than with a software-based approach.

However, there is a higher cost of entry than with other types of MSPs. While users pay on a monthly basis, they must commit to the cost over a longer period of time. In addition, users are still limited by the inherent disadvantages of frameworks, including the software's functionality, complex deployment, and scalability. After all, these are classic client/server products that have been extended to the Internet and tend to focus on such processes as network node management and software distribution, rather than offering service level agreements, application management, or performance management.

The turnkey MSP, which might be considered a variant or subset of the legacy MSP, is a service whereby the MSP installs products on the client site and remotely manages the infrastructure. Such MSPs will manage entire systems, an entire application, or an entire management process, such as the help desk. The turnkey MSP is subscription based and process focused, although enabled by tools — which generally come from traditional software vendors.

When these MSPs provide a holistic end-to-end systems strategy, they might be considered to be "Tivoli in MSP format." However, while the MSPs are now selling Tivoli capabilities, they could change vendor, because they all work with numerous vendors. The product partner of the moment is unknown to the end user, who just gets the required management reports or service delivery.

Turnkey MSPs that offer a complete enterprise system management solution include SilverBack, TriActive, Totality, and InteQ. For its part, StrataSource manages an entire application. While such providers get much of their technology from traditional vendors, such as Micromuse, BMC, and Computer Associates, the MSPs add value through their technology and processes.

While the software is often installed at the client site, the MSP vendor is responsible for implementation, maintenance, and ongoing use. In most cases, the MSP staff is located off-site, with secure connections to customer hardware.

Small and medium-sized enterprises with 50 to 300 servers are best suited to turnkey MSPs. Larger organizations would find them too costly because they have greater scalability and customization requirements, which bring high failure potential. However, for small and mid-sized businesses, turnkey MSPs will likely expand their offerings to include Internet-enabling infrastructure functions such as load balancing, cache management, and content distribution.

For its part, the Internet MSP is a subscription service of three, six, or nine months, whereby companies pay a monthly service fee for the management of a specific aspect of systems or applications, such as Internet monitoring or content delivery. This is what most people refer to when talking about a management service provider. Designed to manage and run over the Internet, these quick-to-install MSPs provide high functionality, although they are not appropriate for all functions. As their name implies, Internet MSPs primarily focus on managing Internet-based applications. They offer such functions as monitoring, storage, security, end-user self-help, and marketing.

These MSPs tend to sell to two camps. The first, classical example, is that of mature companies that understand what they do not know, as well as what it takes to run an IT organization, including hardware, and a network infrastructure. Here, MSPs are dealing with technical folks. The second customer camp consists of dot.coms, which are small, or do not realize they cannot do it themselves. In this case, business rather than technical people are generally involved.

Internet MSPs usually offer a service that is based on point tools that target a single management concern. Internet MSPs use brand-new technology and applications that were built to exploit the Internet. They target E-business applications, and require little or no technology to be deployed internally. Because customers need not buy and install large frameworks or applications, Internet MSPs offer a low barrier to entry, and low cost.

Internet MSPs offer specific services. For example, Keynote, Freshwater, Luminate, and Mercury Interactive provide infrastructure monitoring and testing. They can generally view application performance from outside, simulating the users' perspective. Internet MSPs also provide security testing, software maintenance, and external storage networks for storing and managing data.

As for the disadvantages, Internet MSPs are "very niche"; that is, all the functionality is not there yet. While they provide application and server management, they do not offer software distribution or help-desk functions, although broader functionality is expected in the future. In addition, use of a framework limits the number of vendors with which a company must work. Because the MSP space is new, companies might have to deal with more vendors, for example, to attain network performance functions in addition to infrastructure monitoring.

Some analysts anticipate the development of "integration MSPs," which will allow ISPs and ASPs to share real-time infrastructure events and alarms with their customers. If, as some believe, data gathering is becoming a commodity, MSPs must differentiate themselves from competitors. To do so, MSP vendors such as Ganymede, Luminate, and Manage.com are giving away a tool or service to gain customers. The free tools monitor an element or process, allowing IT departments to try them out. The MSPs hope that these organizations will then become customers and start using their other services, such as data integration.

Another approach to MSPs is that offered by service providers, which add management tools to their contracted service offerings. Operating on a subscription basis, these providers focus on performance monitoring, and delivering to service level agreements. However, flexibility is an issue because they only offer a few standard configurations.

As ISPs and ASPs become commodities, they must distinguish themselves from the competition. To do so, some are looking at offering customers services that are similar to MSPs, whereby the ISP acts as middleman. Other ISPs have acquired MSPs because of their management value; for example, Exodus Communications acquired Service Metrics to provide response time management. In general, analysts anticipate MSP consolidation, with ISPs and ASPs acting as the primary consolidators.

Partnerships are becoming common, for example, those between Keynote and Digex, and between Keynote and UUNet. ASPs are also partnering with tool vendors and MSPs to provide management services similar to those of ISPs; for example, PeopleSoft with Qwest, and Corio with Marimba. From their side, organizations must gauge whether these management services are sufficient, or if they should be supplemented.

A NEW BUSINESS MODEL: SERVICE VERSUS PRODUCT

At present, software vendors still generate the majority of Web site management products, which have comprehensive capabilities that provide testing, internal performance benchmarking, and site monitoring management tools. However, those considering an investment in an enterprise management system should consider the new business model in town. While vendors have traditionally productized enterprise management, the market for network, systems, and Web site management can now be segmented into service and software.

Luminate, for example, initially sold enterprise management as a product, but is now trying to reposition it as a service. As it moves from a pure enterprise application software provider to a service provider, it is managing applications and the Internet infrastructure. The MSP offers a series of services that let IT managers monitor the health of their E-business infrastructures, using a small downloadable tool and a subscription to Luminate.net.

The MSP is giving away a sizable piece of its offering by letting customers download its Mamba performance monitoring tool for free. The MSP expects that buyers will then plug into more advanced tools online for a monthly fee.

Mamba's package of Web server software and Java servlets tests events, performance, and availability. It can automatically discover network assets and do real-time testing — without a major deployment and without installing agents. Thousands of copies of Mamba for SAP R/3 have already been downloaded. Luminate also offers Mamba for Windows NT and Mamba for Oracle databases. Prices range from $50 per server per month for the Windows version, to $350 per server per month for R/3, to $500 per server per month for Oracle.

To motivate Mamba users to become paying customers, Luminate provides small software bundles called "energizers," by which the software communicates with Luminate.net. When customers plug into the Luminate.net site, they obtain expanded views of the data that Mamba collects, including graphical reports of performance over weeks or months. They also receive daily e-mail hotlists, which indicate trouble spots in the enterprise.

Via Luminate.net, subscribers can drill down into specific reporting areas, and access a library of help and support files. The service allows customers to monitor effectively, and retain important data, which would otherwise be very time-consuming and difficult to do.

For its part, major MSP Keynote has an approach that sells only services — not software. And NetSolve offers management services that focus specifically on network performance and availability, rather than application behavior. As for the main enterprise management vendors, they will either buy management service companies, or provide a management service with their own tools, as an offshoot of their services organization, thereby productizing it. However, this is not their strong suit.

MOVING TOWARD STANDARDS

There are already so many MSPs that they cannot all survive; so there will be consolidation. Companies have the need to manage all elements; monitoring their response time, and all protocols to and from them. Correlating all this presents a problem, and the solution is not available as a holistic tool. Therefore, organizations need an integration point, such as a performance repository or response time event console. While this is not holistic, the information is integratable, and Micromuse, for one, can serve as an integration point.

In addition, Extended Markup Language (XML) will enable data-sharing among multi-vendors. To this end, the Distributed Management Task Force, Inc. (DMTF) provides a Web-based Enterprise Management (WBEM) roadmap to give customers the ability to manage all their systems, regardless of instrumentation type, through the use of a common standard.

On October 19, 1998, the DMTF announced the first version of its XML Encoding Specification, to encode the Common Information Model (CIM) schema in XML. The specification defines XML elements, which can be used to represent CIM classes and instances. It will enable companies to leverage Web technologies to manage enterprise systems. Thus, XML lets industry groups worldwide rapidly define and implement standards for interoperability across diverse computing environments and technologies. WBEM was initiated by BMC, Cisco, Compaq, Intel, and Microsoft, but was later incorporated into the DMTF.

THE MSP FUTURE

Organizations have an increasingly complex, expanding infrastructure to manage. Even if the corporate infrastructure is manageable, the E-business environment presents new management challenges. In the recent past, efficient management provided E-businesses with a competitive advantage. Today, however, availability is no longer an option. If sites are not as or more available than the competition, organizations are no longer in business. So companies realize that management and availability have gone from being a competitive advantage to a mission-critical necessity.

The MSP premise used for the Web has helped the infrastructure management business. In the past, most organizations saw systems and applications management as a blackbox. Companies knew they needed it, but did not understand the bottom-line focus. Now they understand the business significance of management.

MSPs represent a growth market. Analysts predict that every Global 2000 company will have an MSP by the end of 2001. They also anticipate that MSPs will represent a multibillion dollar market in the next few years, reaching the $4 to $5 billion range.

The Self-integration Imperative

However, because systems, applications, and Web management represent a niche market, companies will likely use a combination of MSPs, rather than working with a single company. For example, while they might use

BMC for performance monitoring, they would still subscribe to Keynote for Web management. In choosing MSP vendors, companies should prepare to do self-integration in three to four years, identifying and covering all their systems management needs. For example, they should determine what access to tools they need for internal process integration, so they can deal with alarms internally.

Problem Resolution

Most MSPs today find potential problems and notify the customer company, which then fixes the problems. Very few of today's MSPs actually fix the problems they uncover. Some analysts believe MSPs are therefore missing a key component. If the company has neither the time nor money to invest in monitoring business-critical networks or applications to ensure they are all up and running, it might not have the means to fix mission-critical problems.

Partnering with an E-support provider could shore up this gap, whereby MSPs form solid partnerships with such E-support companies as Motive Communications and Support.com. MSPs would thereby gain competitive advantage and a stronger customer relationship. E-support providers would gain entrée into a new business market — and customers could fix problems in a timely manner, thereby keeping their business running. In addition to E-support providers, newer MSPs are emerging, which offer both problem identification and problem resolution; one such is SiteLite.

Market Shakeout

Given the market need for MSPs, the future will undoubtedly see a lot more vendors, venture capital, and functionality. In fact, some analysts predict an explosion of new MSP entrants, followed by a shakeout and a lowering of prices as vendors commoditize — thus providing capabilities for dollars.

Because the MSP is an unproven model, some vendors will go under. They will find the cost of tool ownership and the number of failures high. In addition, customers can easily change MSP allegiance, because there is a low switching cost — especially when compared with traditional software and services.

Furthermore, when customers pay a service fee, they simply get a service level agreement (SLA) as a commitment. For example, while an MSP might specify 100 percent availability, speed is not mentioned, so the vendor is only policing SLAs.

Some MSPs offer free service during the time of an outage. However, an ISP can lose $100,000 an hour every eight hours it is down, while a power company could lose $1.5 million. In such cases, the free $1000 service provides no equity.

This will have to change so that MSPs add more management capabilities and monitoring tools and shore up their service levels, backing it up by a rock-solid environment. Because this will cost more to do, it will kill some vendors. However, a number of large ones will remain.

Differentiating Offerings

Not only will MSPs have to deploy a pretty comprehensive network, but every ISP will have to offer management services. In addition, as ASPs move into the Web site management space, both ASPs and MSPs will potentially offer services ranging from Web speed monitoring to commercial transaction tracking and usage analysis. When software vendors and service providers compete for the same customers, services and products will converge, and MSPs will bundle their services with the appropriate software products.

MSPs are already acquiring such products. For example, Keynote Systems recently acquired Velogic, a provider of load testing simulation services. Keynote already offers E-commerce customers quality-of-service reporting on performance criteria such as downloading speeds, and the demand for this service is high. Velogic expands Keynote's services so the two are strategically complementary. Companies can now test their Web sites before going live, measure real-time performance after the site is up and running, and subsequently perform diagnostic maintenance.

Of Control and Value

Organizations moving to MSPs give up some control, so companies are just starting to trust them. It helps that MSPs sometimes provide a free tool for organizations to try out. Still, IT cannot give up control completely because people know they will be fired if the E-business site goes down.

While management platforms provide an all-encompassing solution for all operations, MSPs tend to be based on point products; offering help desk, performance management functions, and the like for people to use on a day-to-day basis. Thus, MSPs are generally niche players, largely providing a departmental rather than an enterprisewide solution.

MSPs' unique value is in providing functions that are difficult for an organization to do on its own, such as building enough storage space or performing security intrusion testing. And, although innovations are coming, companies using MSPs are already seeing value today.

Chapter 27
Managing the Risk of Outsourcing Agreements

Ralph L. Kliem

Outsourcing offers several advantages, which include enabling existing staff to concentrate on core competencies, focusing on achieving key strategic objectives, lowering or stabilizing overhead costs, obtaining cost competitiveness over the competition, providing flexibility in responding to market conditions, and reducing investments in high technology. There are also several disadvantages to outsourcing agreements, which include becoming dependent on an outside supplier for services, failing to realize the purported cost savings from outsourcing, locking into a negative relationship, losing control over critical functions, and lowering the morale of permanent employees.

Executive management is increasingly recognizing that sometimes the disadvantages of outsourcing outweigh the advantages, even after an agreement has been signed. Many companies are canceling their outsourcing agreements, renegotiating agreements, or deciding to hire their own staff to provide in-house services once again.

There are all sorts of reasons for having second thoughts, including arrogance or uncooperative behavior of the vendor, competitive advantage in the market no longer exists, costs of the services are too high, quality of the services are inadequate, and types of services are unnecessary.

Unfortunately, many companies could have avoided having second thoughts about their outsourcing agreements if they took one effective action: perform a meaningful risk assessment.

RISK MANAGEMENT 101

Risk is the occurrence of an event that has some consequences. A vulnerability or exposure is a weakness that enables a risk to have an impact.

0-8493-1190-X/02/$0.00+$1.50
© 2002 by CRC Press LLC

Controls are measures that mitigate the impact of an event or stop it from having an effect. The probability of a risk is its likelihood of occurrence (e.g., a 60 percent chance of happening). The impact of a risk is its degree of influence (e.g., minor, major) on the execution of a process, project, or system.

The basic idea is to have controls in place that minimize the negative consequences of a "bad" outsourcing agreement, known as risk management.

Risk management consists of three closely related actions:

• Risk identification
• Risk analysis
• Risk control

Risk identification is identifying risks that confront a system or project. Risk analysis is analyzing data collected about risks, including their impact and probability of occurrence. Risk control is identifying and verifying the existence of measures to lessen or prevent the impact of a risk.

Risk management for outsourcing agreements offers several advantages. It enables identifying potential problems with agreements. It enables developing appropriate responses to those problems. Finally, it helps to better identify mission-critical functions to retain and others to outsource.

Despite the advantages of risk management, there several reasons why it is not done. One, it is viewed as an administrative burden. Two, the understanding and skills for conducting risk management are not readily available. Finally, the information required to do risk management is not available.

There are several keys to effective risk management. Risk management is best performed as early as possible, preferably before signing an agreement. It requires identifying and clarifying assumptions and addressing key issues early. It requires having the right people involved with the outsourcing agreement, such as subject matter experts knowledgeable about key issues.

One final caveat. Risk management is not a one-time occurrence. It must be done continuously. The reason is that risk management involves taking a snapshot in time and using it to anticipate what might happen in the future. The conditions of an environment, however, may be extremely dynamic and may challenge the validity of assumptions incorporated when managing risk. Hence, it is wise to continuously revalidate risk management before, during, and after negotiating an outsourcing agreement.

RISK IDENTIFICATION

There are many potential risks confronting outsourcing agreements. These risks can fall into one of three categories: legal, operational, and financial.

Legal risks involve litigious issues, prior to, and after negotiating an agreement, such as:

- Including unclear clauses in the agreement
- Locking into an unrealistic long-term contract
- Not having the right to renegotiate contract
- Omitting the issue of subcontractor management

Operational risks involve ongoing management of an agreement, such as:

- Becoming too dependent on a vendor for mission-critical services
- Inability to determine the quality of the services being delivered
- Not having accurate or meaningful reporting requirements
- Select a vendor having a short life expectancy
- Unable to assess the level of services provided by a vendor
- Vendor failure to provide an adequate level of services

Financial risks involve the costs of negotiating, maintaining, and concluding agreements, such as:

- Not receiving sufficient sums for penalties and damages
- Paying large sums to terminate agreements
- Paying noncompetitive fees for services

These categories of risks are not mutually exclusive; they overlap. However, the categories help to identify the risks, determine their relative importance to one another, and recognize the adequacy of any controls that do exist.

The risks also vary, depending on the phase in the life cycle of an outsourcing agreement. There are essentially seven phases to an outsourcing agreement: (1) determine the business case for or against outsourcing; (2) search for vendors; (3) select a vendor; (4) conduct negotiations; (5) consummate an agreement; (6) manage the agreement; and (7) determine the business case to decide whether to renew, renegotiate, or terminate a contract. Exhibit 1 lists some of the risks that could exist for each phase.

RISK ANALYSIS

After identifying the risks, the next action is to determine their relative importance to one another and their respective probability of occurrence. The ranking of importance depends largely on the goals and objectives that the agreement must achieve.

Exhibit 1.   A Sample of the Risks in Each Phase

Phase	Risk
Determine the business case for or against outsourcing	Using incorrect data
Search for vendors	Using a limited selection list
Select a vendor	Entering biases into the selection
Conduct negotiations	Not having the right people participate in the negotiations
Consummate an agreement	"Caving in" to an unfair agreement
Manage the agreement	Providing minimal expertise to oversee the agreement
Determine the business case to renew, renegotiate, or terminate the contract	Ceasing a relationship in a manner that could incur high legal costs

There are three basic approaches for analyzing risks: quantitative, qualitative, and a combination of the two.

Quantitative risk analysis uses mathematical calculations to determine each risk's relative importance to another and their respective probabilities of occurrence. The Monte Carlo simulation technique is an example.

Qualitative risk analysis relies less on mathematical calculations and more on judgment to determine each risk's relative importance to another and their respective probabilities of occurrence. Heuristics, or rules of thumb, are an example.

A combination of the two uses both quantitative and qualitative considerations to determine a risk's relative importance to another and their probabilities of occurrence. The precedence diagramming method, which uses an ordinal approach to determine priorities according to some criterion, is an example.

Whether using quantitative, qualitative, or a combination of the techniques, the results of the analysis should look like Exhibit 2.

RISK CONTROL

There are three categories of controls: preventive, detective, and corrective. Preventive controls mitigate or stop a threat from exploiting the vulnerabilities of a project. Detective controls disclose the occurrence of an event and preclude similar exploitation in the future. Corrective controls require addressing the impact of a threat and then establishing controls to preclude any future impacts.

With analysis complete, the next action is to identify controls that should exist to prevent, detect, or correct the impact of risks. This step

Exhibit 2. Analysis Result

Risk	Probability of Occurrence	Impact
Unable to assess the level of services provided by a vendor	High	Major
Locking into an unrealistic long-term contract	Low	Major
Select a vendor that has a short life expectancy	Medium	Major
Paying large sums to terminate agreements	High	Minor

requires looking at a number of factors in the business environment that an outsourcing agreement will be applied to, factors like agreement options (e.g., co-sourcing, outtasking), core competencies, and information technology assets, market conditions, and mission-critical systems.

There are many preventive, detective, and corrective controls to apply during all phases of outsourcing agreements (see Exhibit 3).

After identifying the controls that should exist, the next action is to verify their existence for prevention, detection, or correction. To determine the controls that exist requires extensive time and effort. This information is often acquired through interviews, literature reviews, and having a thorough knowledge of a subject. The result is an identification of controls that do exist and ones lacking or needing improvement.

Having a good idea of the type and nature of the risks confronting an outsourcing agreement, the next step is to strengthen or add controls. That means deciding whether to accept, avoid, adopt, or transfer risk. To *accept* a risk means letting it occur and taking no action. An example is to lock into a long-term agreement regardless of conditions. To *avoid* a risk is taking action in order to not confront a risk. An example is to selectively outsource noncritical services. To *adopt* means living with a risk and dealing with it by "working around it." An example is a willingness to assume services when the vendor fails to perform. To *transfer* means shifting a risk over to someone or something else. An example is subcontracting.

TOOLS

The "burden" of risk management can lighten with the availability of the right software tool. A good number of tools now operate on the microcomputer and support risk identification, analysis, and reporting or a combination. Choosing the right tool is important and, therefore, should have a number of features. At a minimum, it should be user-friendly, interact with other application packages, and generate meaningful reports. One of the more popular packages is Monte Carlo for Primavera™.

Exhibit 3.   The Result of Analysis

Preventive Controls	Detective Controls	Corrective Controls
Provide ongoing oversight during the execution of the agreement	Establish minimum levels of performance in an agreement	Re-negotiating because of changing market conditions
Have the right to approve or disapprove of subcontractors	Maintain ongoing communications with the vendor	Identify conditions for discontinuing a contract

CONCLUSION

Risk management plays an important role in living with a workable, realistic outsourcing agreement. Unfortunately, risk assessment takes "back seat" before, during, and after negotiating an agreement. As a result, many firms are now renegotiating and canceling agreements. Some examples include large and small firms canceling long-term, costly agreements with highly reputable vendors. The key is to use risk assessment both as a negotiation tool and a means for entering into an agreement that provides positive results.

Chapter 28
Hiring and Managing Consultants

John P. Murray

Managing outside consultants requires a specific set of skills. Among those skills are the abilities to select the right people, to clearly identify and explain the assignment, and to maintain appropriate management discipline during the length of the assignment. IT managers must recognize the need to deal with several circumstances. Consultants have to be managed so that their leaving will not create difficulties. Once consultants complete the assignment, they should be able to move on.

IT managers and consultants should work together to provide a level of value beyond the basics of the project. For example, simply completing a project may not be enough; there will be a requirement for documentation so someone in the organization can continue to manage the project. Training staff members who take over a project prior to the consultant's leaving is another example of added value.

An additional concern is selecting consultants to carry out a project. Different consulting organizations offer different sets of skills and services. Finding a consulting organization is not difficult, but it can be a challenge to find the appropriate organization that can produce professional results. Working with consultants is expensive, and it is important to make the right choice with the first choice. IT managers who thoroughly understand how to hire and manage consultants benefit the most from using consultants.

WAYS OF MANAGING CONSULTANTS

Because IT managers are ultimately responsible for the success or failure of a project, they must thoroughly document a project's history in case the project fails. When the heat rises because of a failed IT project, facts can sometimes get lost in the scramble to place blame. Consultants have experience in dealing with projects in difficulty and they can be adroit in defending themselves. Also, consultants probably have a better set of sales skills

0-8493-1190-X/02/$0.00+$1.50
© 2002 by CRC Press LLC

than many IT managers and can use those selling skills to bolster their position in the event of difficulty.

Whether or not a project is in difficulty, an astute IT manager is careful to gather and document facts about consultants' work. Gather this information as soon as consultants arrive and continue to do so throughout the life of the project.

Too often, the introduction of a consulting firm to a project is viewed as a panacea. Often, an IT organization abdicates *de facto* management of the project to consultants because the consultants have the required skill, the experience, and the personnel to accomplish the project. Also, many IT managers mistake the high expense of hiring consultants as an assurance of success.

Ultimately, an IT organization cannot pass off a project's success or failure to consultants. Managing consultants is no different than any other IT management issue and, to be successful, it must be done well. Managing the relationship among consultants, members of the IT department, and business customers adds another level of complexity to the already complex issue of managing an IT department. A part of initial project planning is allocating resources for managing consultants.

REASONS FOR HIRING CONSULTANTS

Requiring the assistance of consultants can be due to a number of circumstances. Sometimes, as in the case of Y2K projects, consultants are needed because they possess a certain level of skill and experience to carry out specific work. Assignments of that type are referred to in the consulting industry as staff supplementation. Managing supplemental staff is the most straightforward. Usually, such consultants work under the direct control of a manager, and assignments are closely monitored. Most staff supplementation assignments are completed satisfactorily. Any problems that may arise can be easily handled because the scope of the consulting assignment is limited, and the IT manager responsible for the effort thoroughly understands the project.

When an IT project grows in size and complexity, IT management often has to decide whether or not the department has the necessary resources and experience. When the answer is no, bringing in consultants is the answer. IT projects need not be large or complex to require the assistance of consultants. In smaller projects, an IT department may not have the required staff or skill. In such a case, bringing in a consulting firm is a sound business decision.

When an organization decides to adopt new technology, it must weigh the risk associated with that technology and how long it will be until the technology yields benefits. Both risks can be reduced by hiring consultants experienced with a particular new technology. Because consultants are involved in a variety of assignments for different clients, they often become familiar with the new technology as soon as it is introduced and thereby provide sound assistance.

When considering a consulting firm for implementing new technology, move carefully. It is easy for an unscrupulous consultant to quickly gain superficial knowledge of a given technology. Such consultants banter about new terms associated with an emerging technology to deceive potential customers. IT managers must see beyond a consultant's marketing approach in order to clearly determine the level of skill and experience the consultant has with the new technology.

Another word of caution: some consultants work well with the technology but lack skill in dealing with people and documenting assignments. When selecting a consultant in new areas of technology, find someone who not only can deal with the technology, but can also provide training and documentation. The goal is not only to move to a new technology, it is also to be certain that the IT organization can manage the new technology once a consultant leaves.

IT management sometimes decides to turn an entire project over to a consulting organization because of resource or skill constraints. Sometimes, giving an entire project over to consultants is done reluctantly. Sometimes, particularly in projects seen as high risk or otherwise undesirable, IT management willingly hands over an assignment to consultants.

Often, consultants are given full responsibility for legacy systems because IT organizations would rather not manage these systems, which poses processing and management challenges. Handing over legacy systems to consultants cannot be seen as a final solution to legacy-related problems. IT management must oversee them. If, in handing the work over to consultants, an IT department has not remained aware of changes made in legacy applications or in operational procedures, unfortunate surprises may arise.

If an IT function is poorly managed or is perceived to be poorly managed by senior management, consultants may be hired to manage the IT department. In such circumstances, members of the IT department are not going to be in a position to exercise control over the consultants. As such, consultants are in charge, often in spite of pronouncements from senior management that such is not the case. Dealing with this type of situation is beyond the scope of this chapter, but it is worth noting.

RESPONSIBILITIES OF THE IT CUSTOMER

If the consulting assignment is to be successful, IT managers (i.e., customers) must understand what has to be done to ensure success. The first consideration has to be that the customer, despite any understanding with the consulting firm to the contrary, is the "owner" of the system and, as a result, has to accept final responsibility for the success or failure of the project. The work of the consultants, good or bad, affects the business of the organization to a greater extent than it affects the consultants. If the project fails, the organization is harmed. Consultants will also be harmed, but they will also move on to the next project. A salient question here has to be, "Who has the most to lose if things do not go well?" The answer is: the customer.

Because customers have the most to lose in a relationship with a consulting organization, they must understand the ramifications of dealing with consultants and be prepared to manage the relationship to their benefit. They must understand how to manage a consulting relationship. The following points help to make clear issues in selecting and managing IT consultants:

- The customer must have a very clear understanding of the work to be done. As consulting organizations are considered for the assignment, the customer must be willing to devote whatever time and effort will be required to make certain the consultants understand the deliverables they will be expected to produce. Those deliverables have to be committed to writing and the document signed by all parties.
- A search should be conducted in order to identify several consulting organizations that have the capability to do the required work. It may be that the organization has a relationship with a consulting organization, and as a result, that firm is in a favorable position; but it is always a good practice to request several bids for any work to be contracted.
- Formal proposals should be solicited from each of the consulting organizations that have an interest in the project. Those proposals should respond to the customer's set of project criteria. Part of this criteria is the set of project deliverables. Customers should develop a baseline from which all responses can be judged.
- If there is a need, the customer should hire someone to assist in developing the criteria required to prepare the proposals for the consultants. If help is required in preparing the proposal, the work should be done by a disinterested third party, who will not be involved in bidding for the project.
- The customer must be aware of, and resist, the tendency to be swayed by well-done marketing campaigns. Being able to market services well should not be taken as assurance that the same level of competency will carry over into the technical work.

- Resumes of individual consultants proposed for the project should be reviewed. The IT customer should also ask to meet with each person proposed for the project to make certain that he or she will be a good fit for the project and IT organization.
  - Establish an agreement with the consulting firm such that those candidates the customer has selected for the project are the ones who show up on the project. It does occur that people are switched. Usually, that new person is not of the same caliber as the person who was originally presented. This may cost extra, but is often worth the added expense.
- Carefully review references supplied by consulting firms. In checking those references, try to find out the names of other organizations for whom a consulting company has done work. Obviously, the consulting firm is going to provide the names of satisfied customers. A little extra digging can sometimes turn up important pieces of information. When negative information is uncovered, a customer can ask the consulting firm for answers.
- The customer should inquire about the existence of a quality assurance function within the consulting organization. Consulting organizations concerned about quality review proposals to make certain they stand a reasonable chance of successfully completing assignments. If there are doubts, such consulting firms will work with a customer to overcome any problems.
- Consulting organizations often offer a standard contract. Such an agreement may not be adequate for a customer, who should insist on adjustments. In any event, the contract must be reviewed by a customer's legal department before it is signed.
- A contract offered by a consulting organization may provide too much protection for the consulting firm at the potential expense of a customer. A contract may be ambiguous about responsibility for performance. When a contract uses vague terms, rather than precise, concrete terms about the level of work, quality, responsibility, and support, a customer must be cautious. Customers have found, to their dismay, that when things go wrong, the responsibility of the consulting firm, as outlined in the contract, is limited.
- The financial terms of the assignment must be clearly outlined in the contract. The arrangement may be for time and materials, or it may be a fixed bid. In either event, items such as overtime, travel expenses, and other costs should be agreed upon in writing.
- Although it may seem obvious, one of the items that the customer should pay attention to is that of having the workspace for the consultants ready for them before they arrive. It does happen that consultants show up and they do not have the hardware needed to begin

work. Having the consultants sitting idle for several days while the hardware issues are being resolved is an unnecessary expense.
- As is the case with any transaction involving legal liability, IT managers must consult an attorney.

RESPONSIBILITIES OF CONSULTANTS

Consulting assignments should be built on strong relationships between customers and consulting firms. A consultant's objective is to obtain the business. This should be done on the basis of values that can be very clearly articulated. Consultants are responsible to customers for the following:

- Taking the time and effort to clearly understand the needs of the customer
- Honestly evaluating their ability to provide the caliber of people required to successfully complete a project
- Clearly and accurately reporting, in a timely manner, to customers on the status of a project
- Candidly raising issues of concern
- Making certain that their employees have strong work ethics and provide a fair value for their expense to customers
- Ensuring that customer expectations are met and, when possible, exceeding those expectations

The list of responsibilities is considerably longer for customers than for consultants because customers bear a heavier burden for a project's outcome. Customers must keep in mind that consultants deal with issues that arise everyday. So, in the event of difficulty, consultants are going, *de facto,* to be in a stronger position.

MANAGING AN ASSIGNMENT

Most consulting firms are ethical and have the best interests of customers as their primary concern, but some firms do not hold these values. When management at a consulting firm changes, the firm's former values may change because they no longer fit the goals of the new management.

Because consultants are brought in to do work that, for whatever reason, is beyond the capability of the customer, consultants enjoy an immediate advantage over their customers. Customers may be vulnerable if their organization does not have experience in managing large IT projects. It may be that the decision has been made to move to a new technology about which no one in the customer's organization has any experience. It may be that the level of pressure is such within the organization that no one pays appropriate attention to the work of the consultants. In any situation where the consultants have a clear advantage, the possibility exists that the advantage may be used to the detriment of the customer.

Customers have to guard against being in a position where consultants are the only ones with knowledge about how to maintain the applications once the consultants have developed them. Examples exist of situations where consultants have been at a customer site in excess of five years, doing essentially the same work, because none of the customer's employees understand how the system works. Falling into such a situation is a failure on the part of IT management.

If consultants fulfill their obligations to a project but do not transfer project knowledge to members of the customer's staff, the consultants have not completed their assignment. Any consulting assignment should include a transfer of knowledge from consultants to employees of the customer.

Sometimes, consultants are assigned to handle all cutting-edge or advance technology and members of the IT staff are given more mundane work. This arrangement is not advisable. A better approach is to find a way to involve members of IT in areas of a project where they can develop new skills and gain experience. A major reason that IT employees leave an organization is because they are not given opportunities to develop new experience and skills. By allowing only consultants to gain experience with new technology, IT management may inadvertently make their personnel look for these opportunities with other organizations.

THIRD-PARTY ASSISTANCE

One way to mitigate concern about managing consultants is hiring a third-party expert, who accepts responsibility to manage the consultants. This approach can be a sound business move. Nevertheless, responsibility for project outcome still rests with the customer. Such an expert must be able to deal effectively with consultants and should be compensated on the basis of the consultant's performance.

Although using a third-party manager may be viewed as additional overhead, it can substantially benefit a project. Because consultants are hired to provide skills that the customer does not possess, IT management may have difficulty in determining whether the consultants are delivering what they are contracted to deliver. A third-party expert can make this determination and judge the quality of the consultants' work.

A third-party manager is in an excellent position to verify that project knowledge transfers from consultants to members of the IT staff. Completing that transfer should be the responsibility of a third-party manager, who should develop a plan for this transfer and present the plan to IT management for approval. A third party can also bring a higher level of objectivity to the issues that are certain to arise; as the work moves forward, it will not have a particular turf to defend.

Using a third-party manager does not have to complicate IT's management of a project. IT managers should find someone who has the required experience and have that person serve as liaison between the customer and the consulting organization. An expert can be valuable to IT management by simply posing appropriate questions about the project to consultants. Raising these questions forces consultants to use care in providing answers. A third party can also help level the playing field between the customer and the consulting organization.

A third-party arrangement does not have to be full-time. A third party can conduct periodic reviews. When such an assignment is not full-time, a customer and the third-party manager must be specific about meeting with consultants. Although having the third party available on a full-time basis is more effective, one working part-time can also considerably benefit a project.

CONCLUSION

Many IT consulting ventures work out with both parties pleased at project's end. No matter what the outcome may be, however, final responsibility must be borne by the IT customer. Ideally, the process should be seen as a partnership where IT and the consultants, working together, provide solutions. When the process works well, it is possible to deliver results that exceed expectations.

From the start of a project, IT and consultants must agree on a set of deliverables due at the project's end. There also has to be agreement about the deliverable's level of quality. From the beginning, a strong partnership must be developed between the IT organization and the consulting group. The partnership must be focused on the customer's needs.

Capable consultants, working on clear assignments, strongly managed by the customer, can yield a good return on the customer's investment. A lack of strong consultant management, or allowing hostility to arise between members of the IT department and the consultants, can quickly create an environment for failure.

Chapter 29

How to Manage Outsourcing for Best Results

Douglas B. Hoyt

Outsourcing is often compared to a marriage. Each is a relationship in which both sides can benefit substantially. Yet both relationships have inevitable friction and conflicts. The key to success in both affiliations is for the parties to keep in mind the interests and desires of the other, and to try to please each other, and to resolve conflicts in a civilized way. The one difference is that marriages are intended to continue "until death do us part," whereas all outsourcing contracts have defined termination dates, which of course can be extended.

This chapter discusses the plans and actions computer operations managers, and others, must take to make an outsourcing relationship work smoothly and with maximum benefits for the client, as well as for the service vendor. There are always difficulties in these relationships — conflicts, obstacles, misunderstandings, and changed circumstances. These types of difficulties must be anticipated and approaches created for coping with them successfully. With careful planning and management, outsourcing can be a source of savings and other competitive advantages; some sloppily planned and managed outsourcing have been disasters.

TREND TO OUTSOURCING

Eastman Kodak was an early pioneer in the outsourcing movement. In 1989, Kodak contracted with Integrated Systems Solutions Corporation (ISSC), IBM's services branch, to do the computer work that Kodak had been performing at four of its facilities. Then in 1994, Xerox signed a 10-year outsourcing contract for $4.1 billion with Electronic Data Systems Corp. (EDS) to do a major portion of its computer work. AMTRAK expects

0-8493-1190-X/02/$0.00+$1.50
© 2002 by CRC Press LLC

to save $100 million over a 10-year period from its outsourcing arrangement.

Those are three examples of the well-publicized movement to outsourcing as a business strategy. It has been estimated that 80 percent of information systems work will be done by contractors by the year 2000.

WHAT TO AND NOT TO OUTSOURCE

Outsourcing has proven effective in accomplishing several goals: to reduce costs, to generate cash, to focus management's attention on the organization's prime purposes, to take advantage of an outsider's expertise, and to help expand globally. Functions inappropriate for outsourcing are systems work necessary to monitor the outsourcing vendor, a system that is part of a competitive advantage, and outsourcing that could expose key proprietary and confidential information.

TIPS FOR WORKING WITH THE CONTRACTOR

There are certain steps that can be taken at the beginning to establish a basis for working together constructively and cooperatively. Clear responsibilities for liaison are essential, regular meetings are helpful, and avoiding misunderstandings is important, yet having a mechanism for dispute resolution is essential.

Spirit of Partnership

Outsourcing arrangements work best when there is a basic feeling of trust and cooperation between the client and vendor. Truly, both should be working to accomplish common goals wherein each benefits in its own way. Both sides should gain substantially from the relationship. However, if conflicts dominate the relationship, lawyers probably get involved to protect what they see as their individual side's rights, and the original goal of mutual gain and benefit is not achieved.

Liaison Staff

One person should be appointed as chief liaison representative for the client in dealing with the outsourcing vendor on a continuous basis. Liaison individuals should have the authority to act for their employers and should be the normal route of communications between client and vendor, particularly for complaints. Therefore, the liaison person must be knowledgeable about the technology involved, be a diplomat, yet be able to be firm in monitoring and demanding proper performance from the vendor. The liaison officer must also be of unquestioned loyalty to the clients' interests (many systems technicians may see their best future career opportunities with an outsourcing services firm), yet see that the vendor's legitimate interests are respected.

The outsourcing contractor should be asked to set up a liaison counterpart, and both client and vendor should clearly define their liaison representatives' responsibilities and *modi operandi.*

The liaison function may vary in size and scope depending on the circumstances. McDonnell Douglas has a group of 15 to 25 employees managing its relationship with Integrated Systems Solutions Corporation (ISSC), IBM's services branch, with which it has a $3 billion outsourcing contract. Hughes Electronics has a staff of 50 to oversee the work of its outsourcer, Computer Systems Corporation (CSC), in its $1.5 billion outsourcing contract covering 7 years, and is pleased with the way the relationship is working out.

Meetings

The spirit of working together can be strengthened by frequent meetings between representatives of the client and vendor on topics of interest to either party or to both. Having such meetings on an ad hoc basis, or perhaps regularly, under the guidance of the liaison representatives can get problems under control before they get out of hand, and foster an understanding of people on both sides about the interests and activities of the other parties, thereby encouraging a friendly and cooperative relationship and a feeling of participation, which are important factors leading to the success of the relationship.

Avoiding Misunderstandings

The best way to avoid misunderstandings is to have a contract clearly describing the work to be done and the standards of performance expected, and covering all the contingencies that are considered as possible to occur. But even with a well drawn up contract, there will be events that have not been anticipated, or one party may construe a part of the contract to mean something different from the other party's interpretation.

Resolving Conflicts

There are three general approaches to conflict resolution other than legal action, which it is recommended be avoided at all costs. They are:

- A conflict resolution committee
- Referring the matter to higher executive levels
- Arbitration or mediation

The conflict resolution committee should probably be co-chaired by the two liaison representatives, with specialists added based on the nature of the issue, such as whether it is an accounting or technical matter.

If the committee cannot bring the matter to a compromise or other solution, it can be referred up the executive ladder — say to the vice president level, then to the CEOs — to resolve. This process sometimes can settle the matter quickly. However, it often takes valuable executives' time away from their main functions, time they would take in researching and negotiating the issue.

Taking the conflict to arbitration or mediation is far superior to court action. Using the established processes of the American Arbitration Association can resolve issues faster, cheaper, and easier than suing, engenders less hostility, and can even be done without attorneys.

MANAGING THE TRANSITION TO OUTSOURCING

Making Detailed Plans

The key to a successful transition is a carefully and thoroughly drawn up plan listing all the events that must take place and their timing, including equipment transfers, data and software transfers, people transfers, and who (client and vendor people) is going to do what. Hopefully, much of the transition process has been spelled out in the contract; but even so, there are further details and dates to be made more specific, such as people's names instead of job names, and actual dates instead of time periods.

The transition is a time for the people on both sides to become acquainted with each other. Full discussion and conversations are encouraged during this period to try to establish working relationships that will help in the continuing operation of the contract. The liaison representatives of the client and the vendor should take the lead in coordinating the design of the transition plans, as they will take a major role in their implementation.

Running Systems in Parallel

Running the old system concurrently and in parallel with the new outsourced approach is the best way to confirm the validity of the new way of processing a system. Sometimes, it may be unduly expensive to run the whole system in parallel, and it may be possible to accomplish the purpose of parallel processing by doing it in part, say putting through 1000 of a total of 10,000 orders, which may be sufficient to verify the correctness of the outsourced process. Of course, some outsourced work is for systems that are new and have never been done before, in which case no parallel operation is possible.

Monitoring and Evaluating Contractor's Work

To achieve the client's desired results requires, first of all, to clearly define what known facts will be considered satisfactory, then to get feedback on how the actual performance compares to established standards, and finally to motivate the vendor to conform to or exceed the defined expected results.

Establishing Standards and Managing Expectations

All outsourcing contracts should not only define what work will be done by the outsourcing vendor, but what results are expected and how they will be measured. In order processing, for example, the contract might define the turnaround time from input to output, the maximum percent of errors that would be acceptable, and the cost to the client if the vendor has some control of that. For an outsourced help desk function, the standard might specify the maximum response time, the percent that needs referral to a second technician, and feedback from the users as to their satisfaction with the results.

While these performance standards should be in the contract, as the work gets underway, there may arise additional factors to be considered and adjustments and clarifications that need to be made to keep the standards practical and current. The refinements should be negotiated between the liaison representatives and others concerned, with the agreed new terms put in writing to confirm the agreement and to inform all concerned about them. Since the contracts often run for several years, the changing needs of the client, such as new products and new markets, and changing vendor conditions, such as new hardware or software or location, frequently create the need for revisions to the expectation results.

Performance Reports

It is essential to arrange for some report to be made regularly on each feature of the performance standards so that the outsourcing vendor's results requirements will be measured. Regular and prompt reports should be made by the vendor of items for which a performance standard has been established, measurable or not. Some of the reports will be by-products of other data processing functions, most will come from the vendor, but some may originate from the client, such as reports from users about their help desk performance. The liaison representative is a logical person to be responsible for coordinating, compiling, and disseminating the performance results.

Some aspects of contract requirements cannot readily be checked by reports. For example, keeping proprietary information confidential is a matter that can be verified only by keeping full communication with the right people, discreetly looking for possible breaches and diplomatically looking into anything noticed that raises suspicions.

Motivating Vendor to Conform

If the vendor's payments are tied to the performance results, that provision can be a principal motivating factor for the contractor to accomplish the outcome the client wants. Of course, having the vendor sharing the rewards and risks is a worthy plan where the circumstances make such an arrangement practical. It can make the vendor feel more like a partner than a contractor, and that spirit is desirable. Or, the contract may specify financial penalties when the vendor does not meet specified performance standards, generally a desirable type of provision.

The time to make terms for sharing the rewards and risks is when the contract is being negotiated; however, such an arrangement can be negotiated as an amendment to the original contract if both sides can see that it is to their benefit.

Whether or not the contract provides for the vendor's payments to be tied in to its performance criteria, it is essential for the performance report results to be communicated regularly and systematically to the client's management. The contractor should be thanked for meeting or exceeding set standards, and must be reminded of situations where the results criteria have not been met. If the performance is less than satisfactory a few times and the vendor is not brought to account, the contractor will not be motivated to hit the target. Thus, it is important to let the vendor know that the client is aware of the deficiencies and expects them to take corrective measures. Careful records of the deficiency and copies of the reminder notices are important to keep, so that if the situation becomes a larger issue, the historical facts are documented for reference in discussions and negotiations about corrective action.

The client has one advantage in its pressures to the contractor to meet performance requirements. Outside service firms, for business reasons, are anxious to please their clients so that contract renewal can be achieved. Therefore, a request for improved performance should normally be met with respectful responses or negotiations to resolve the matter. If a contractor is seriously and repeatedly deficient in its compliance, the ultimate threat is to terminate the contract, which is the last resort and an undesirable conclusion for both parties; terminations under hostile circumstances can hurt the client as well as the vendor, since they inevitably cause disruption and the difficulties of moving the work back in-house or to another vendor under unpleasant circumstances.

HOW TO HANDLE EMPLOYEES WHEN DOWNSIZING

One of the most difficult parts of outsourcing and other types of downsizing is to manage the human relations aspects so that morale and loyalty are preserved and that the best employees are retained. Unfortunately, transferring employees out or letting them go inevitably strains the feelings of the other employees, and this section shows some of the tactics that can minimize the negative results of downsizing and even, sometimes, leave the new organization stronger than it was before.

Downsizing Methods

Downsizing is a major part of, indeed one purpose of, nearly all outsourcing programs. Cost reduction is an objective of most outsourcing, and that reduction is primarily in terms of fewer employees.

But there are a variety of ways that downsizing can be accomplished without outsourcing. One currently popular approach is reengineering, which consists of methodically examining the operating processes of an organization by analyzing the types and numbers of employees needed for each function as well as developing better approaches for performing these processes. Another downsizing method is to make "across the board" cuts, say 10 percent of each department; this approach, which is used to hastily meet a budget crisis, is generally not recommended as it usually makes cuts in the wrong places.

In the data processing arena, many companies have been able to reduce staff by converting mainframe systems to client/servers, by adopting CASE methods for programming, and other methods for accomplishing the work goals with fewer employees.

Inevitable Anxiety and Resentment

Anxiety is an inevitable result of uncertainty. When a situation arises that will involve letting employees go, or requested to be considered for employment by an outsourcing services firm, it results in anxiety for those affected. These employees' source of livelihood is put in limbo until the situation is resolved, even though the sources of their income may be improved under the new arrangement. Unfortunately, the uncertainty and resentment caused by downsizing usually also results in the lowering of morale of the employees who remain.

There are several general principles reviewed below for taking steps to minimize the disruption from downsizing, to maximize the morale and loyalty of the remaining employees, and to help to retain the employees the client wants.

Explain Process at Earliest Opportunity

The timing of the announcement of a downsizing plan to the employees concerned is a difficult decision, and usually not a perfect one. The plan should be explained before the rumors become prevalent. It can obviously be disconcerting for an employee to learn first of a downsizing plan from the newspapers.

While the plan must be discussed in advance with key employees who need to be consulted in preparing the structure of the downsizing effort, the planning phase should be as short as possible because, once the plan is known by top people confidentially, leaks and rumors almost inevitably follow.

Boeing's announcement in 1993 that it would reduce its workforce by nearly 20 percent over $1\,1/2$ years was received without any special alarm by its employees. The reason for the calm acceptance was that Boeing had made a point of revealing over the previous period that sales in the aerospace industry had been at a low level and that drastic corrective action was in order.

Explain Openly the Business Reasons for the Change

When the downsizing plan is announced, the important matters to emphasize and clarify are the business reasons for making the change and the fairness features of the plan for the employees.

There has been enough downsizing in recent years that it has become an accepted fact of life to most people. It has become recognized that in the evolving intensity of global competition, companies must often make major cost reduction efforts to beat or stay even with competitors. The real reasons for the decision to lessen staff can be to reduce a downward profit trend, to meet known cost levels of competitors, to generate cash for an important new venture, or some other of the many possible business considerations. These business reasons should be explained so that all concerned are made aware of the valid and logical necessity of the downsizing plan. It should be made clear how the downsizing program will make the organization stronger so that departing employees will understand the logic and reasonableness of the effort and remaining employees will feel more secure.

The fairness of the plan structure as explained should include the general terms of a financial package and career assistance for those that will leave, and the benefits of working for a computer service firm for those employees who may be made available for employment with the outsourcing vendor. The plan may give choices to some employees, making it somewhat voluntary, such as having them decide whether to accept a severance package or transfer to some alternative positions.

All of this open discussion of the business reasons and fairness will not eliminate some bitterness and lowering of morale. But done well, it should keep those disadvantages to a minimum.

Get Help from Human Resources and Legal Staff

When Philadelphia Newspapers, Inc. planned a downsizing effort in 1993, based on moving from its mainframe to client/servers, the unions threatened to walk out. The downsizing program had to be deferred until the labor dispute was resolved. That delay indicates the value of securing counsel and advice from legal and human relations specialists.

The human resources staff should participate closely in the planning of the downsizing steps. It is their job to be skilled in the handling of employee relations matters, especially those involving intense emotional feelings. Therefore, human resources' advice and guidance should be sought in laying out the plan. However, the execution is a line responsibility; that is, it is the line manager's proper role to make the announcements to the groups affected and, ultimately, to explain to each individual how the plan affects him or her.

The legal staff should also be consulted in designing the downsizing plan and the separation packages. Their advice is needed to make sure of compliance with the Employee Retirement Income Security Act (ERISA), the Consolidated Omnibus Budget Reconciliation Act (COBRA), union agreements, and other legal requirements.

Assess Individual Employee's Loyalty

Decisions regarding which employees are to remain and which are to be let go should be based mostly on their skills in relation to the client's needs. But the employee's loyalty to the employer is also an important factor in that decision even though there is no objective way to measure that loyalty. At best, loyalty can be judged by intuition, but there can be signs such as cooperative behavior, expressions of bitterness, and general demeanor indicating acceptance of management's decisions and plans.

When downsizing is a part of an outsourcing arrangement and some of the client's employees are to be employed by the services vendor, employees who are more loyal to their computer specialty than to their current employer may prefer to join the computer service firm rather than stay in an organization in which computer operations are not the primary function.

But loyalty can be a double-edged sword. Some employees who may not be the best qualified may feign loyalty, sensing the severe competition for survival in a downsizing situation. Their attempts to please may be appreciated, but should be tempered with a balanced evaluation of the employee's worth.

Encourage Valued Employees to Stay

Once it is known, from announcements or rumor, that a downsizing program is underway, some of the better employees may feel it is a good time to seek greener pastures. The employees whom the employer needs or wants to retain because of their skills and loyalty assessment, should be encouraged to stay. This may involve giving assurances as to future plans, possibly a pay increase because of added responsibilities, bonuses, or other financial incentives. These assurances are important particularly because of the general negative atmosphere that is generated by the downsizing, including lowered morale and anxiety due to the uncertainties involved.

Preach Loyalty Rationale Continuously

To those employees who will be retained, management should continuously be explaining the goals of the organization, why the prospects are good for reaching those goals, and how the individual employees fit into the plans and are wanted to help achieve those goals. These efforts are necessary to bolster the morale and offset the feelings of bitterness and resentment that are inevitable among some of the employees who are retained after seeing many of their associates leave, even though they may be given generous departure packages.

After downsizing, it is natural for remaining employees to feel insecure, anxious, depressed, and even resentful. Open communications can help. It is well to continue discussing the place of the downsizing in the organization's overall goals, and to seek employee views and help in planning how the work can best be done under the post-downsizing environment. Let employees vent their feelings without being recriminated for doing so. Such communication can foster a renewed feeling of trust and sense of value.

Offer Reasonable Severance Terms

It is essential for the public relations well-being of the organization to offer fair and generous settlements to employees who are asked or encouraged to leave. Such settlements may include provisions such as a cash amount based on the years of service, earlier pension starting dates, and career guidance and support.

The cash settlement is intended primarily to support the person until he or she is able to locate another position (though some have urged stock options instead of cash so that the ex-employee may share in increased profits from the downsizing). The earlier pension can be given by adding, say, 5 years to the employee's actual age to enable him or her to achieve a retirement pension earlier than would be available otherwise. The outplacement assistance is usually provided by a consultant who guides the ex-employee in the techniques for seeking a new position and may also provide some of the resumé preparation and phone and office services helpful to the job seeker.

All these separation assistance tools help the organization's management to feel and say properly that it is doing what it reasonably can to help those who are put in a difficult position by the downsizing program, often due to no fault of their own.

Try to Give Choices Between Favorable Options. To whatever extent possible, it is wise to build into the severance arrangement choices for the employees so that the employees feel that there is a voluntary element in the plan and that they are not being forced unilaterally into their new status. For example, at a downsizing program at Sea-Land Service, many employees were offered a generous severance package, but given the choice of remaining with the company, which would try to, but not guarantee to, find them a lower-level position with the company if the package was rejected. With this choice, no employees left Sea-Land without the severance package.

SECURITY

The data in the hands of an outsourcing service may be the lifeblood of the client organization. It is, therefore, essential for the client's management to make sure that there are adequate backup copies of the operating data that the vendor possesses. This can often be accomplished by securing from the vendor current copies of the data so that operations could be continued should a disaster — like a flood, earthquake, or fire — destroy the client's data at the location of the outsourcing service. If the client relies on backup data that the vendor has arranged, such as with a firm like the Iron Mountain Depository or Comdisco, then the client must periodically audit those extra copies to verify that they are current, complete, and properly secured. However, even if the vendor does maintain an extra data security copy off-site, by keeping its own backup copy, the client is in a better position to terminate the vendor and resume its own work or use a new contractor. The backup data discussed here must include copies of the current software needed to run the other data.

The other major security concern is the exposure of proprietary information through the outsourcing vendor. Of course, the restrictions on the use of key business and technical data should be spelled out in the outsourcing contract. Whether they are or not, it behooves the client to check on the proper handling of information in the hands of the vendor, by observation, inquiry, and other means. If the contract does not spell out security requirements sufficiently, they should be discussed with and agreed to between the client and vendor, with the terms put in writing, in effect, as a supplement to the contract.

HOW TO TERMINATE A CONTRACT

The contract terms have much to do with how the contract is terminated, and there are may different reasons for ending a contract that affect how it should be done. A major factor in making a smooth transition to whatever the new arrangement will be is to prepare a careful plan and schedule of the items and events involved. Finally, both client and vendor may wish to renew the contract; but then there are always adjustments and improvements to make over the previous terms and features.

Terminating a contract before its scheduled end because of problems or changed circumstances cannot be done easily or quickly. It takes time to reestablish IS operations in-house or transfer the work to another contract service vendor. Therefore, if and when problems occur or conditions change, it is generally best to negotiate appropriate revised arrangements with the vendor rather than choose an early separation.

Reasons for Terminating

There are many reasons for terminating outsourcing contracts. One reason may be that the contract period is finished (though if the arrangement has worked well, a renewal would be the logical outcome). It may be that the client or the vendor has become dissatisfied for one reason or another and wants out. A good reason is that another vendor, possibly with some advanced technology, has offered terms that could save more money and provide specialized benefits. Or possibly, the client's needs have changed in terms of product or territory, or an acquisition or merger was made that has caused the vendor's services to be unsuitable.

Planning and Scheduling Termination

The transition to setting up the outsourcing arrangement required listing the myriad of details that had to be taken care of; a careful plan listing the equipment, software, and personnel changes to be made; and scheduling the events in a logical fashion. The termination process requires a similar listing of the hardware, software, and people changes and a time schedule for the events to take place. The scheduling process may be aided by Gantt or PERT charts, which help to identify the actions needed, their sequence, and the steps to follow up to keep the schedule on track.

The written or charted schedule also helps in coordinating the steps with the service contractor who, of course, must agree with the plan and cooperate to make it successful. There should be some guidelines about the termination steps in the contract, but they are never enough to be a working schedule at the time of the transition. Hopefully, the contract will set an elapsed period for the termination process that is ample enough to make it a smooth transition. If not specified in the contract, the pricing of the services in the termination period must be negotiated as one of the early steps.

RENEWING A CONTRACT

Long before the contract termination date, the computer services manager and others should be evaluating whether some other vendor might do the work better, whether the client has come to believe that it can do the outsourced work more advantageously in-house, or whether the contract should be renewed. If the decision is to renew, then the client should analyze in what ways the arrangement could be improved and whether a more advantageous price could be obtained, and begin to negotiate a revised contract — hopefully to the benefit of both the service firm and the client. The new contract should also reflect the many circumstances that undoubtedly have changed since the original contract was written, such as new technology used by the vendor and new products, customer groups, or geographical territories for the client.

SOURCES OF GUIDANCE AND SUPPORT

The operation and managing of an outsourcing or other downsizing program are matters in which it is helpful to talk with others who have been or are managing similar plans for their organizations. Informal meetings with peers in other such organizations about common problems can be a source of ideas and a feeling of support. There is considerable literature on these subjects; one thorough and pertinent source is *Winning the Outsourcing Game: Making the Best Deals and Making Them Work* by Janet Butler (Auerbach Publications, 2000).

Many organizations do buy, for a fee, the advice of experts who have experience in managing outsourcing and downsizing programs. These sources include the Outsourcing Institute and a variety of consulting firms.

The Outsourcing Institute

The Outsourcing Institute Inc. (www.outsourcing.com) is a for-profit membership group to which both outsourcing users and vendors belong. Membership is free.

Consultants

Consultants, especially consulting arms of large public accounting firms, have been engaged to advise and counsel on whether and what to contract out, vendors to select, and how to negotiate and manage outsourced work.

Firms like Anderson and PricewaterhouseCoopers provide such advisory assistance, though their fees range from $250 per hour to much higher.

The leading consulting associations can also refer inquiries to members, who can provide outsourcing vendor advisory services. These include:

- Institute of Management Consultants (IMC): www.imcusa.com
- The Association of Management Consulting Firms (ACME): www.amcf.org
- Independent Computer Consultants Association (ICCA): www.ica.org

Consultants' capabilities can also be researched through the Internet via Management Consultant Network International, Inc. (MCNI), reached via www.mcninet.com.

CASE EXAMPLE: SEA-LAND SERVICE

As reported in the November 1993 issue of *Personnel Journal*, Sea-Land Service, a major cargo-shipping company based in New Jersey, in 1989 determined that its modest profits were due to excess staffing that had developed over the years. To overcome its inefficiency, the company decided, after careful planning, to redefine all jobs by analyzing what functions and how many people were really necessary for operating the business. By comparing the skills and abilities of its employees with its analytically determined staff guidelines, from CEO on down, the company was able to reduce its employee number by 800, or 15 percent. The restructuring of its organization eliminated five levels in its organizational hierarchy. These downsizing changes enabled the company to reduce operating expenses by $300 million and increase revenues 30 percent to $3.3 billion and increase profits by 35 percent to $151 million. All this improvement took place during a period of intense competition in this global industry.

The plan was designed to be as fair as possible by giving employees reasonable choices, with those choices being voluntary. Employees whose new positions would be two or more levels lower, or who lived over 50 miles from work, were offered severance packages and outplacement services. Those who turned down the severance arrangement would be helped in relocating within the company, though doing so made them forfeit the severance benefits. In the end, no one was laid off without benefits.

RECOMMENDED COURSE OF ACTION

The following points are highlights of the actions a computer operations manager should take to oversee and manage the work of outsourcing service vendors:

- Establish a relationship of cooperative partnership with the outsourcing vendor.
- When obstacles and conflicts occur, resolve them rather than fight about them.
- Even though there is trust and respect between client and vendor, monitor performance and demand results that were contracted.
- Select and rely on a strong liaison representation to coordinate relations with the contracting services vendor.
- Make careful and detailed plans for the steps to transfer the work to the outsourcing vendor and, at termination, to transfer the work to another vendor or in-house.
- Make parallel runs, if possible, with each change.
- Explain the downsizing reasons to employees — clearly, openly, and promptly — and reinforce those explanations regularly.
- Keep current copies of computer data and software in-house.

Chapter 30

Outsourcing as a Means of Improving Process Maturity: An Approach for More Rapidly Moving up the Capability Maturity Model

Brian Keane

Because it can take years to progress to higher levels within the Capability Maturity Model (CMM), many organizations are outsourcing. Outsourcing is an approach for improving productivity and lowering costs by contracting the support or development of one or more software applications to a software services firm. Productivity and quality objectives can be aligned with the CMM and structured into an outsourcing contract.

Software services providers can be significantly effective in assisting the move up the CMM. This effectiveness is gained through the tight management controls, formal processes, and constant measurements that are the hallmarks of organizations high in CMM. IS managers can use outsourcing as a means for obtaining and implementing "best-in-class" processes in their organizations.

Most IS organizations are level 1 organizations — far from the level of flexibility required for today's competitive business environment. Even with the CMM providing guidelines for process improvements, lower-level organizations find it difficult to implement new processes and advance from their current level. Process reengineering of any kind is undoubtedly challenging, and in an IS organization it can be even more difficult. In fact, it can take years to progress from one level of maturity to the next, and the move from level 1 to level 2 requires the most commitment, effort, and expertise.

Outsourcing is a viable method for introducing and more quickly institutionalizing new processes within an IS organization. This section of the chapter provides background on outsourcing and discusses how outsourcing can be used to accelerate the implementation of process improvements. The discussion focuses on application outsourcing — contracting a software services firm to manage and be accountable for one or more software applications — as an example of the processes and methods that are available to IS organizations. In this presentation, highlights from the methodology of Keane for application management are included to illustrate the environment and processes required to move up the CMM.

A Note on Terminology. *Outsourcing* is a term used to describe the contractual transfer of an internal corporate function to an external service provider. Typical IS functions that may be outsourced include data center operations, help desk operations, new application development projects, and maintenance and support for applications. The term outsourcing is reserved for situations where the service provider supplies its processes and takes direct responsibility for the daily operations of specific portions of the IS requirements of a corporation according to a predefined level of service. This mixture of processes, expertise, and accountability is the foundation for the major benefits that can be gained from outsourcing. In this chapter, supplemental staffing is not considered a form of outsourcing.

OUTSOURCING AND THE CMM

When measured on the CMM scale of maturity, the best outsourcers rank quite high. While a consulting company may be successful in an occasional outsourcing engagement through excellent staffing, it cannot provide reliable and predictable levels of service, quality, and profitability across multiple projects without a well-managed set of outsourcing processes documented in a methodology. Highly experienced outsourcers develop a set of world-class processes that they customize and apply to each of their projects. The experience of the outsourcer over many projects allows it to select and combine the best and most effective practices from many organizations. These procedures are documented within the methodology of the outsourcer and are used to train its staff. Since outsourcers tightly manage their projects, process usage is enforced. By using the same processes from project to project, the outsourcer is able to shift its consultants as needed between projects.

IS organizations at the lower end of the CMM need years of effort and massive cultural change to achieve the level of process maturity present in a best-in-class outsourcer. Fortunately, IS organizations can take advantage of the knowledge and experience of the outsourcer to move them up the scale of maturity faster than is possible through other means. Outsourcing engagements offer IS organizations a number of powerful benefits.

Access to Best-in-Class Processes

A top outsourcer will have a separate team that manages its outsourcing processes. This team is responsible for maintaining and continuously improving the processes of the organization using the experiences from all of its ongoing projects. As a result, the processes of the outsourcer evolve far faster than those of most IS organizations. Since the livelihood of the outsourcer is based on its ability to provide its services at maximum efficiency, the outsourcer has considerable incentive to improve its process effectiveness.

Ability to Watch the Procedures in Action

Implementing an outsourcing project within the IS organization provides staff members with the ability to watch the new processes and tools in action. This enables side-by-side comparisons of existing IS processes against those used by the outsourcer. Any doubts or misgivings about the value of more efficient processes will be dispelled by this exercise.

Hands-on Training

Any large-scale outsourcer will have well-prepared training materials, skilled trainers, and training facilities to prepare its own staff for outsourcing assignments. These resources can be applied to training internal staff. IS staff members can supplement their learning by working alongside the outsourcer staff on an actual project.

A Means to Overcome Cultural Resistance

Often, the required cultural change is the most difficult obstacle to overcome. The current practices of the IS organization are heavily ingrained in its staff members, and they often strongly resist changes to the status quo. An interesting paradox is that this resistance vanishes if a staff member takes a new job in a new company. The staff member expects to learn and assimilate new procedures as part of the job move. It is far easier to add staff members successfully to an existing process environment than it is to change the process environment of existing staff members. Outsourcers take advantage of this phenomenon when staffing their outsourcing projects. By putting the process environment in place at the start of the outsourcing project and transitioning staff into the environment, the outsourcer avoids the resistance that occurs when IS organizations attempt to change. The same principle can be applied within the IS organization by allowing the outsourcer to set up the project environment and then transferring IS staff to new assignments within the project.

KEY COMPONENTS OF A SUCCESSFUL OUTSOURCER

Selecting an outsourcer to assist the IS organization in moving up the CMM is different from selecting an outsourcer strictly for assuming responsibility for a given function. The outsourcing project must be performed on site, and it requires an outsourcer with the experience and desire to share its methods. These requirements preclude offshore outsourcing organizations. Some outsourcers will consider their practices proprietary and will be unwilling to transfer knowledge to the IS organization. The IS organization must find an outsourcer that is willing and able to provide its procedures and the required training. Since claiming expertise is easier than providing expertise, the IS organization must evaluate the claims of each outsourcer carefully for accuracy before selecting a vendor.

The list that follows provides information about the key components of the service offering of a successful outsourcer. IS organizations should consider these components in detail when evaluating outsourcers.

Project Management Experience

Large-scale project management experience is one of the most important characteristics of a successful outsourcer. If the outsourcer does not have a solid track record of achievement, all of the other components in this list are suspect. For example, the methodology of the outsourcer represents the codification of this knowledge. If the outsourcer has limited experience, how strong can the methodology be? While experience in managing ongoing outsourcing projects is crucial, experience in managing the implementation and transition into a new project is especially important when using outsourcing to move up the CMM.

Methodology

The methodology of the outsourcer documents its processes and methods. The methodology describes which processes are used, how those processes are implemented, how they are used during project operation, and how they are managed. It is the primary training and reference document for the project. IS organizations should review the methodology in great detail. The methodology describes how the IS organization will operate if the project is successful. The evaluators must ensure that the methodology meets their long-term requirements and is sufficiently complete to serve as a meaningful training tool. The methodology must support the processes required to move up the CMM. It must also include the supporting metrics, quality reviews, and process improvement activities to ensure that the processes are used effectively.

Central Support Team

A central support team is needed to maintain the methodology and capture best practices from multiple projects. Such teams are a primary vehicle for building continuous improvements into the methodology. The team receives project metrics from each ongoing project and assists in conducting management reviews of project quality. The existence of a central support team is indicative of the commitment of the outsourcer to its practice and to the ideals expressed in the CMM.

Experienced Staff

While training courses are valuable, actual project experience is even more important. A successful outsourcer will have staff members who have worked on multiple outsourcing engagements. These staff members know how to implement the processes in the methodology in a variety of circumstances.

Training Materials

Examining the quality of the training materials of the outsourcer is another good method for determining its value in a process improvement effort. Lack of good-quality training materials indicates poor training on the part of the outsourcer and casts doubts on the experience of its staff. Good training materials will be highly tuned from use on multiple assignments and will provide a strong foundation for training IS staff members.

A MODEL FOR AN APPLICATION MANAGEMENT METHODOLOGY

Highlights of the Keane application management methodology (AMM) are offered below as an example of a methodology that supports the environment and processes required to move up the CMM. The AMM is customized to fit the needs of individual organizations; however, the fundamentals remain the same.

Project Management Processes. These processes manage ongoing project operations, personnel issues, and project performance to level of service agreement commitments. There are three major groups of processes in this category: project management, level of service management, and training.

Customer Assistance Processes. The customer assistance function ensures that user support is based on centralized and common practices. This approach enables fast response to requests, management controls on workload, and a collection point for project performance metrics.

Project Operation Processes. These processes include those needed to execute the tasks necessary to implement scheduled application maintenance and enhancement projects. They include processes for the estimation, prioritization, specification, and programming of project tasks.

Asset Management Processes. Asset management processes ensure the integrity of client application assets and effective project management through release management and configuration management. Application assets include source code, load modules, documentation, test cases, and other application components.

Production Control Processes. These processes ensure the quality of project deliverables and the integrity of the client's production environment. They include processes for system testing, acceptance testing, production turnover, and project close.

Operational Improvement Processes. These processes identify methods to improve project operations and implement continuous quality improvements. They embody the principles of continuous process improvement as defined by the CMM. Metrics from all project tasks and from process operations are continuously monitored to identify opportunities for improvement.

Management Review Processes. These processes sit above all phases of an outsourcing project. They define the methods used by project management, client management, and Keane management to audit and review the quality of project performance regularly.

IMPLEMENTING AN OUTSOURCING PROJECT

When an IS organization decides to pursue an application outsourcing project, there are many activities that must occur to prepare the environment for outsourcing. Similarly, when a project is completed, there are activities to wind down operations and return the project to the IS organization. As a result, outsourcing projects are usually organized into four distinct phases.

Phase I: Planning and Definition

This is the initial phase of the application outsourcing engagement. This phase evaluates the existing environment to develop a complete inventory of project assets and determine the types of improvements necessary to set up the project. A level of service agreement is created to document the project performance commitments, and a transition plan is created to begin the assumption of project responsibilities.

Phase II: Transition In

This phase addresses the turnover of the project to the application management team. In some cases, Keane introduces its employees to the application environment, whereas, in other cases, Keane acquires client employees to form the application management team. During this phase, depending on the team makeup, members either focus on acquiring the business and technical knowledge necessary to support the application(s) or they focus on learning and implementing the Keane process model. Team members also begin high-priority improvement activities. At the end of this phase, the application management team has full responsibility for the project, and the processes of the project are fully implemented and operational.

Phase III: Project Operations

This phase covers most of the outsourcing engagement. The application management team is totally responsible for the support of all aspects of the outsourced applications following the standards agreed upon in the level of service agreement. In addition to supporting the daily support activities for the application(s), the project team also focuses its attention on increasing its efficiency at supporting the project. The team will implement any necessary procedural and technical improvements in the early stages of this phase to reap the benefits over the life of the project.

Phase IV: Transition Out

This is the final phase of the outsourcing project where the outsourcing team returns control of the application(s) to the IS organization. As part of the transition, the IS staffers are trained in the new processes and tools that were established during the project. At the end of the transition out, the IS organization is supporting the application(s) in the new, higher-level operational environment.

CONCLUSION

Businesses are finding that strong processes are critical to their efforts to improve organizational flexibility. This chapter was developed to provide insight into how process improvements can help IS organizations face the challenges of a growing application portfolio, new technology shifts, and an increasingly fast-paced business environment.

The CMM is an excellent vehicle for assessing the quality of existing processes and determining the steps needed to improve those processes.

Organizations can use the model to identify deficiencies, adopt practices, and meet specific goals through evolutionary steps. The CMM does not require any specific software technology, organizational structure, life-cycle model, or set of documents. In addition, unlike other mechanisms for establishing processes, the CMM can be used to create an organization where processes are not only defined, but practiced, shared, and continuously improved.

Moving up the CMM is not without its challenges, especially for lower-level organizations. Once processes are redesigned, it is much more critical, and difficult, to get the practices adopted throughout the organization. Under continued pressures and project deadlines, IS professionals do not have the time to familiarize themselves with newly defined procedures. As a result, the adoption of new practices is slow and, in some cases, impossible. Because it can take years to overcome such barriers and progress from one level of the maturity model to the next, organizations are forming outsourcing agreements with vendors that are willing to transfer their processes.

Outsourcing is a valuable tool for IS organizations seeking to accelerate their move up the CMM. The following section details some of the services a major software services firm provides to assist clients with their process improvement objectives.

IS Productivity Assessments (ISPA)

Before attempting to improve their process maturity, IS organizations need to understand their current situation. Through a detailed assessment of the IS organization, IS managers can ascertain where improvements are needed, determine which improvements would provide the greatest value, and establish a baseline from which to measure future improvements.

Keane offers a comprehensive evaluation of an IS organization through its ISPA service. This service is based on the principle that productivity is ultimately a synthesis of people, processes, and technology. An ISPA goes beyond typical process maturity evaluations by including people and technology factors in its evaluation. Evaluations of issues such as application software quality and staff training enable Keane to develop an improvement strategy that will maximize the benefits of the recommended process improvements. This strategy is documented, along with the current status of the IS organization, in a complete report that also includes a project plan for implementing the recommended improvements.

Outsource Full Responsibility to Keane

This is the traditional outsourcing model. The IS organization increases its process maturity by outsourcing areas of low maturity. This arrangement allows the IS organization to concentrate its resources on its strengths.

Keane takes responsibility for all aspects of the project, including staffing and process improvements. Keane operates the project following CMM principles, as contained in its AMM, and the corporation receives the benefits that ensue from more mature processes.

Outsource and Transition

This method is similar to the outsourcing service described above, except that the application(s) is transitioned back to the IS organization after the new project environment has been put into place. This method is useful for overcoming cultural barriers to change. Keane takes responsibility for the project using its own staff. The project team members implement the Keane process model and operate the project until all processes are fully tuned. At that stage, the IS organization can continue to outsource or it can reassume responsibility for the project. During the transition-out period, project team members fully train the IS staff members in all aspects of the project and the new processes. Cultural resistance is reduced by effectively moving IS staff members into a new assignment rather than attempting to change familiar processes on their current assignment. The IS organization can use its newly trained and experienced staff members to seed other projects in its portfolio.

Outsource a Pilot to Keane

A pilot project is used as a proof of concept. Keane assumes responsibility for the project and fully implements its outsourcing model. The IS organization observes the process and can compare its operations against those used by Keane. It enables the IS organization to see precisely how the new processes will operate in its environment. When the organization is ready, it may decide to outsource additional projects, or it may seek assistance from Keane to implement the model for internal IS projects. This method provides the IS organization with the methodology, staff, and training necessary to improve its processes successfully. The pilot project provides a demonstration of the benefits that can be gained when the new processes are fully implemented across the organization.

Section 5
Managing Special Projects

Chapter 31
The Role of Project Management in Knowledge Management
Ralph L. Kliem

Knowledge management (KM) involves collecting, organizing, and distributing knowledge that is accumulated over a period of time for the purposes of improving and increasing a company's competitive edge. This knowledge is more than mere facts and data. It is information and experience collected and applied to achieve the overall goals of a company.

Surveys by IT research firms reveal the popularity of KM. For example, a survey of 500 professionals by the Delphi Group revealed that more than 50 percent of the respondents have begun implementing KM, and more than 80 percent saw it as a major contribution to their companies.[1] According to Dataquest Inc., KM grew from a $2.7 billion market in 1997 to a $5 billion one in the year 2000.[2] Several advantages have been attributed to KM, and include:

- Dealing with "gray" situations with greater confidence
- Encouraging greater collaboration among employees
- Identifying best practices
- Improving the capacity for product and process innovation
- Increasing the competencies of existing employees
- Minimizing the negative impacts of employee turnover
- Responding cost-effectively to rapidly changing environments

A KM project is implementing knowledge management disciplines, tools, and techniques to build a system that will achieve specific goals and objectives. The challenge, of course, is to collect, organize, and distribute knowledge to achieve goals and objectives that are often as vague

0-8493-1190-X/02/$0.00+$1.50

as the definition of KM. This can lead to scope creep and overlooking customer wants and, ultimately, wreak havoc on cost, quality, or schedule performance.

The vagueness surrounding KM, in general, manifests itself via a survey of 100 IT managers by *Informationweek*. Forty-five percent of the respondents said that their IT management did not have a clear understanding of KM or did not know; 56 percent of the respondents said of the company's senior management did not know.[3] All this leads to one simple conclusion: the opportunity for knowledge management projects ending in failure is great.

The challenge, then, is to ensure that KM projects are completed in a timely, efficient, and effective manner. Project management is the way for doing just that.

PROJECT MANAGEMENT

Project management is applying concepts, tools, and techniques for completing projects on time and within budget while simultaneously meeting the customer's needs. It requires implementing four basic processes of project management:

1. *Planning* is deciding in advance what a project will accomplish, determining the exact steps to accomplish it, and identifying when to begin and end each step.
2. *Organizing* is using resources efficiently and effectively while executing the plan.
3. *Controlling* is determining how well the plan is being implemented.
4. *Leading* is motivating people to achieve the goals of a project.

KM makes an excellent candidate for project management, considering the track record of other information technology (IT) projects. Most projects fail for a variety of reasons, including:

- Incremental expansion of scope
- Lack of meaningful schedules
- Miscommunications
- Poor teaming
- Poor understanding of requirements
- Unrealistic estimates
- Unrealistic plans
- Vague definition of goals

Of course, the list is endless. The point is that KM projects are prime candidates for applying project management. Coupled with the results of the past and vagueness surrounding knowledge management, project management becomes even more imperative for project success.

Exhibit 1. Elements of a Typical SOW

Element	Example
Introduction	The purpose and scope of the system
Constraints (schedule, budget, quality)	The cost for developing and implementing the KM system and its date of completion
Responsibilities	Responsibilities for knowledge capture and tool selection
Requirements	Customer providing subject matter experts
Deliverables	Repository, training, documentation
Signatures	Project manager, project champions, customer's requirements

Planning

Planning involves performing these critical steps:

- Preparing a statement of work (SOW)
- Developing a work breakdown structure (WBS)
- Estimating time and costs
- Preparing schedules
- Performing risk management

Preparing a Statement of Work. Also called a SOW, this document is a contract between the project manager building the KM system and its recipient, or customer. From a KM perspective, the customer is often within the user community and the project team comes primarily from the IT organization.

Considering the vagueness surrounding KM, a SOW makes good sense and can preclude a host of misunderstandings surrounding the functionality of a KM system and responsibilities for performing specific tasks. A well-written, definitive SOW provides a meaningful basis for planning a KM project. A typical SOW consists of the elements shown in Exhibit 1.

Developing a Work Breakdown Structure. Also called a WBS, the work breakdown structure is a top-down, general-to-specific hierarchical listing of components of a KM system and their respective tasks to complete. An effective WBS reaches a level of detail that enables development of a meaningful schedule, makes valuable assessments of progress, and ensures completeness of the tasks. A heuristic is that the lowest level of tasks in a WBS cannot exceed 80 hours to complete, or the equivalent of two weeks of work for a full-time equivalent. A sample portion of a WBS is presented in Exhibit 2.

Estimating Time and Costs. The real value of a definitive WBS is its use in estimating the time and costs for a KM project. It provides the level of granularity that allows for "rollups" to different levels of tracking and monitoring.

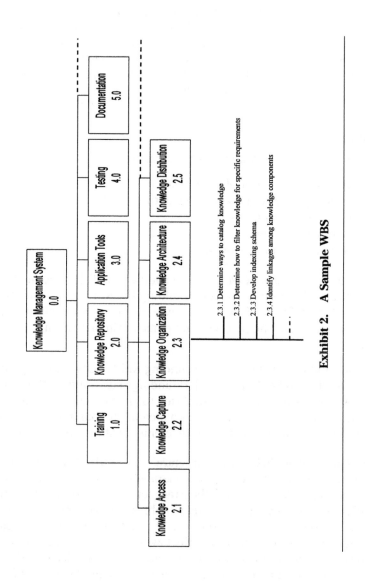

Exhibit 2. A Sample WBS

The estimating for time should involve the application of the three-point estimate. This approach can reduce the dramatic influences of extreme optimism and pessimism that often accompany estimates. Hence, the three-point estimate reduces the tendency to exaggerate. The best approach for applying this estimating approach is having the individuals who perform the tasks do the estimating. The people assigned, however, are often not available, so the project manager must make the initial estimates. Regardless, the three variables for each task to consider are the:

1. Most pessimistic, which is the time required to complete a task under the worst conditions
2. Most optimistic, which is the time required to complete a task under ideal conditions
3. Most likely, which is the time required to complete a task under normal conditions

The three variables are plugged into a formula to derive the expected time:

$$\text{Expected Time} = \frac{\text{Most Pessimistic} + 4\,(\text{Most Likely}) + \text{Most Optimistic}}{6}$$

Example: $\dfrac{144 \text{ hours} + 4\,(60 \text{ Hours}) + 50}{6} = 72.33 \text{ hours}$

The expected time is then adjusted by a percent to account for interruptions, absences, and other nonproductive times not related to performing the tasks:

Example: $72.33 \times 1.07 = 77.39 \text{ hours}$

After estimating, the estimator for each task translates the revised expected time into flow time to develop schedules. The time is normally divided into eight-hour units:

Example: $\dfrac{77.39}{8} = 9.7 \text{ hours}$

With time estimates, the project manager can then calculate costs using the hours. Often, a burdened rate is used for labor and indirect costs that may be added to the task.

Preparing Schedules. The combination of the SOW, WBS, and estimates provides the basis for developing a meaningful, integrated schedule for the KM project. The SOW provides the mandatory dates; the WBS provides the listing of the tasks to perform; and the estimates provide the length of time to perform each task.

The schedule is first developed by identifying the dependencies, or logical sequence, among the tasks and then applying the flow times for each one. The eventual result is the calculation of four dates for each task:

1. Early start, which is the earliest time that a task can start
2. Early finish, which is the earliest time that a task can finish
3. Late start, which is the latest time that a task can start
4. Late finish, which is the latest time a task can finish

The above dates are important because they not only indicate the flexibility available for starting and completing tasks, called float, but, *in toto,* identify the critical path. The critical path in the network diagram is the longest path, following from left to right, and does not allow for flexibility in the schedule. A slide in the critical path will, consequently, result in a slide in finishing the project on time. Exhibit 3 is part of a network diagram for a KM project.

Performing Risk Management. Because KM projects face many variables, risk management is absolutely essential. Like all projects, some risks have a higher probability of occurrence and a greater level of impact than others. The project manager who performs a risk management can increase the likelihood of project success by identifying the necessary measures that need to be established to respond to certain risks affecting cost, schedule, and quality. Here are some risks that many KM projects can face and that can impact cost, schedule, and quality:

- Failure to obtain management buy-in
- Failure to tie the KM system into the overall strategic direction of the company
- Inability to get employees to share knowledge
- Lack of detailed requirements
- Lack of integration among development tools

Organizing

Having good plans is necessary but of little use without an infrastructure to execute them. A project infrastructure consists of many elements, such as a team organization, responsibility matrix, project manual, meetings, and software.

Team Organization. Assembling a group of people and calling it a team are not enough. Structure is necessary to capture the energy and synergy created and to channel both in the right direction. Because KM is still in its infancy and requires the participation of many specialists, it is important to identify clear responsibilities and reporting relationships. A simple organization chart, such as the one shown in Exhibit 4, can help clarify responsibilities and reporting relationships.

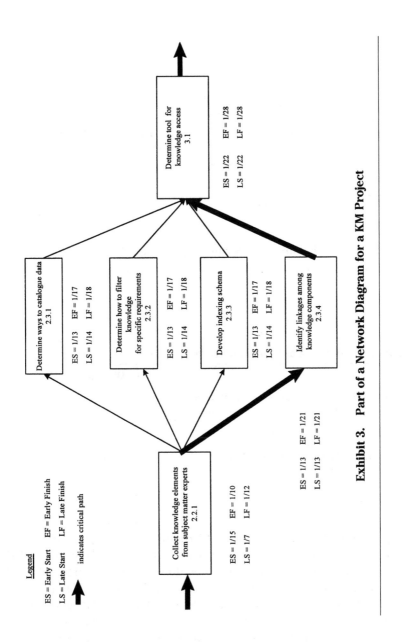

Legend

ES = Early Start   EF = Early Finish
LS = Late Start   LF = Late Finish

↑ indicates critical path

Collect knowledge elements from subject matter experts
2.2.1

ES = 1/15   EF = 1/10
LS = 1/7   LF = 1/12

Determine ways to catalogue data
2.3.1

ES = 1/13   EF = 1/17
LS = 1/14   LF = 1/18

Determine how to filter knowledge for specific requirements
2.3.2

ES = 1/13   EF = 1/17
LS = 1/14   LF = 1/18

Develop indexing schema
2.3.3

ES = 1/13   EF = 1/17
LS = 1/14   LF = 1/18

Identify linkages among knowledge components
2.3.4

ES = 1/13   EF = 1/21
LS = 1/13   LF = 1/21

Determine tool for knowledge access
3.1

ES = 1/22   EF = 1/28
LS = 1/22   LF = 1/28

Exhibit 3. Part of a Network Diagram for a KM Project

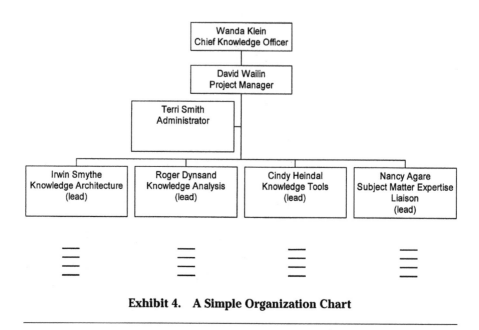

Exhibit 4.   A Simple Organization Chart

Exhibit 5.   Example of a Responsibility Matrix

		Smith	Watson	Henricks	Garcia
2.3.1	Determine ways to catalogue knowledge	P	S		
2.3.2	Determine how to filter knowledge for specific requirements		P	S	S
2.3.3	Develop indexing schema	S		P	
2.3.4	Identify linkages among knowledge components		S	S	P

Legend: P = Primary; S = Secondary

Responsibility Matrix. The WBS and resource allocation provide the basis for constructing a responsibility matrix. The matrix is a chart that shows the relationship of the work to be done and the participants on the project. The advantages of the matrix are that it communicates responsibilities for performing specific tasks and identifies their levels of involvement. Project managers can elect to parse out the matrix, meaning that a person receives only that portion of the tasks he or she is responsible for completing, or it can be distributed in its entirety to everyone. Exhibit 5 is an example of a responsibility matrix.

Project Manual. Everyone on a project needs access to certain data to complete it successfully. If the information is not readily available, participants consume time and energy finding it and, consequently, reduce their efficiency and effectiveness. One way to ensure the availability of the necessary information is to create a project manual in electronic or hard copy form. Exhibit 6 is an outline of a typical project manual.

Meetings. For a KM project, there are three basic types of meetings: checkpoint review, status review, and staff. Checkpoint review meetings are held at a major milestone point in the schedule, such as capturing knowledge from subject matter experts. The purpose is to determine how well the project progressed, what went and did not go well, and whether to proceed. Status review meetings are held regularly. The purpose is to collect and assess status on the performance of the project of cost, schedule, and quality basis, such as meeting a major milestone date in the schedule. The staff meeting, too, is held regularly with the project team and selected invitees. The purpose is to discuss issues and share information, such as technical challenges in building the KM system.

Software. As a project increases in size, so does the complexity in managing it. Good software can help deal with complexity. Software might include a spreadsheet, a word processing program, or a sophisticated project management package such as Microsoft Project for Windows and Primavera Project Planner. It is important to note, however, that project software will not guarantee success but can help achieve success. Regardless of the type or size of a project, if the project manager does not know how to use the software or populates databases with bogus data, then the likelihood of success drops dramatically. Software must be applied in a manner that maximizes payback and minimizes waste.

Controlling

Regardless of the thoroughness of a plan, exercising control is absolutely necessary to bring a KM project to a successful conclusion. Controlling involves performing these four fundamental actions:

1. Status collection and assessment
2. Tracking and monitoring
3. Contingency planning
4. Replanning

Status Collection and Assessment. Having a plan in place is one thing; executing it efficiently and effectively is another. Status collection is gathering data on cost, schedule, and quality and then transforming that data into information — that is, something meaningful. The information is then used to assess progress to date *vis-à-vis* the plan. The key activities for assessing performance are identifying and evaluating variance. Variance is the difference between what should happen up to a point in time and what has actually occurred. A negative assessment is typically one that misses a key schedule date or cost target; a positive assessment is meeting a key schedule or cost target.

For KM projects, status and assessment are critical. The ambiguity of project goals requires keeping a pulse on performance by raising two key questions: where are we *and* are we going in the right direction? Answering these two questions will decrease the likelihood of having a runaway project.

Tracking and Monitoring. Good status collection and assessment require looking at the past and anticipating the future. Tracking is looking at past performance; that is, what has occurred. Monitoring is looking into the future using the past. Both tracking and monitoring provide the link between the past and future to understand how well the project is progressing. Both, closely intertwined with status collection and assessment, are very important for KM projects because they help answer two more fundamental questions: where have we been *and* where are we heading?

Contingency Planning. Good risk management requires good contingency planning; that is, developing ways to respond to specific scenarios.

Contingency plans offer several advantages, to include responding in a proactive rather reactive way to a given situation, furthering progress according to plan, and instilling in team members a confidence in the eventual success of the project. Obviously, not all scenarios can be identified in advance and under certain circumstances that can require the next activity — replanning.

Replanning. Sometimes, nothing can be done other than to replan the project. That requires developing a new SOW, WBS, estimates, schedules, and reorganization. A severe budget cut or a technological snafu may require overhauling everything. The best contingency planning in the world will not make a difference. Replanning, however, should not occur unless absolutely necessary because it may mean a large loss in investment of time, money, and energy. As a project moves down its life cycle, the losses become larger.

Leading

In its basic form, leading is motivating people to achieve the goals and objectives of a project by:

- Providing a vision
- Communicating
- Maintaining direction
- Motivating
- Being supportive
- Building a team

Leading actually occurs throughout the life cycle of a project. It is required during planning, organizing, and controlling.

Providing a Vision. Without a vision, a KM project is heading for disaster. A vision is a description of what will be in the future. It gives a sense of purpose and direction. The SOW provides the basis for generating a vision because it describes the final result of the project. The challenge for developing a vision and keeping people focused on it is a particular challenge to KM projects. Knowledge management in general is a vague concept, and the description of the elements in a KM system can be difficult due to the changing, multifaceted technology it involves and the business environment in which it finds itself.

Communicating. The best vision and plans mean little if no one knows about their existence and any changes to them. Project managers are at the hub of a KM project, thereby serving as the communications center for a project. Their use of tools, such as the project manual and status review meetings, enable and enhance communicating. However, good communication must be ongoing and widespread to prove useful.

On a KM project, communication is absolutely critical. The involvement of many specialized disciplines and representatives from various organizations necessitate that communication continues. Otherwise, project failure is inevitable because the opportunities for operating "in the dark" and going in different directions increase. Everyone must follow the same vision and plan.

Motivating. People on a project must be emotionally committed to the vision of the project or they will not provide a significant contribution. It becomes even more important, especially in a matrix environment, because the project manager lacks any functional control over people. The difficulty in motivating is further complicated by the subject matter. Project managers on KM projects, therefore, must continually keep the fire burning among their team members.

Being Supportive. KM projects require extensive coordination when using tools and applying knowledge. These projects face many obstacles that can impede project success — from obtaining hard-to-find software to political interference. Leadership necessitates supporting the team's needs to achieve success. Because KM projects are by nature lengthy and complex undertakings, project managers must facilitate task execution.

Building a Team Atmosphere. As the complexity of projects increases, so does participation in the number of disciplines and people. KM projects are no exception. An effort is required not just to assemble specialists, but also to encourage commitment toward cooperation in achieving the vision. Project team, sponsor, and customer must work together and have ownership in the project's outcome.

KM IS THE FUTURE

From reading IT literature, it is safe to predict that interest in KM will grow. More and more companies are building KM applications that will play an integral role in their performance. As the number of KM systems increase, so will the challenges in implementing a successful KM project. Like other IT development projects of the past, KM projects will produce some great results — but also some equally great disasters. It is because of the desire to achieve the former and avoid the latter that project management will play an important role in building KM systems.

Notes

1. *KM World,* May 25, 1998.
2. *Interactive Week,* December 8, 1997.
3. *Informationweek,* March 16, 1998.

Chapter 32
Managing Development in the Era of Large Complex Systems
Hugh W. Ryan

To many of us, it appears that every move toward making technology simpler has been matched by a corresponding move toward increased complexity. This is a prime paradox of IT today: on the one hand, technology for the business user has become dramatically simpler as end users have become shielded from complexity; on the other hand, the actual development of systems architectures and business solutions has become far more complex.

Distributed computing environments and architectures that span the enterprise have meant that our IT work is no longer a point solution for one department or division of a company. In most cases today, a systems development effort takes place with greater expectations that it will have a significant impact on the enterprise's book of business.

Where there is greater potential impact, there is also greater potential risk. Companies are making substantial investments in their technologies; they expect to see business value from that investment quicker; and they expect that the solution that is delivered will be robust enough to serve as a transition platform as technological change continues to compress years into months.

GROWTH IN PROJECT SCOPE

The new complexity of systems development can be viewed in several ways. First, one finds that more people are now involved in development than one saw either in the mainframe development days or in the early years of client/server. Frequently, projects today may involve anywhere from 100 to 500 people, and this figure will continue to increase until thousand-person projects become common over the next several years.

Second, the number of years required to develop the more complex business solution has also increased. Enterprisewide solutions, delivered over several releases, may require three to five years, or more, to bring all aspects to fruition. This, in turn, adds additional complexities. For example, with longer development periods, the chances are good that management may go through at least one change during the course of the development project. If the project has not been careful to communicate and gain sponsorship at many different management levels, a change in management may put the investment at risk.

The New Development Environment

This new systems development environment is what this author's firm has come to call "large complex systems" (LCS). It is an environment where the solution:

- Requires many years to develop
- Requires a hundred or more people to be involved
- Is expected to have a significant business benefit
- Has both a high potential value *and* a high potential risk

Management Strategies

The author has recently completed a year-long field review that looked in some detail at some of his firm's largest complex systems development efforts. Based on a set of going-in positions about the challenges of such efforts, extensive interviews were held with personnel at many different levels of the projects. From these interviews, definite repeated patterns about these projects began to emerge, and it became clear that it is possible to set forth a number of factors necessary for a successful implementation of a large complex systems effort. Although a full treatment of all these factors is outside the scope of a single chapter, the focus here is on several that have to do with new ways of leading and managing a large complex systems effort:

- Business vision
- Testing and program management
- Phased-release rollout plan

BUSINESS VISION

A vision of a new way of doing business that will result from the large complex systems (LCS) development is critical to the success of the LCS. Although intuition, as well as prevailing business management thinking, would indicate this is so, it was important to see the real benefit of business visions played out.

For example, one major project studied was one for a global stock exchange. There, the business vision was an integral part of the project — a crisp articulation of the eight essential capabilities that the final system was to provide. It was integrated into the project training and displayed in all essential documents of the project. Most important, all projects within the larger engagement had to be tied back to the vision and justified according to how they contributed to the realization of that vision.

Another development effort at a national financial institution also began with a business vision and a rollout plan that clearly delivered the long-term vision in a sequence of steps. The business vision and rollout plans have served as the basis of work since they were created. The vision deals with the concept of a "model bank" — a consistent set of processes and systems that permits customers around the country to get a standard high quality of service, and also permits employees to move within the company without having to learn new processes. The vision is owned by the senior management of the bank, and communicated to all employees in powerful yet simple ways.

Changes in management can frequently have a negative effect on the power of a business vision. For this reason, it is essential that the business vision be held by more than one individual. On a large complex system built in the U.K., for example, there were several management personnel changes over the years required for the complete development. The key to success here was ensuring that at any given time, there was a set of senior management personnel committed to the effort. As natural career progression took these people to other roles, there was always another core set coming in who continued to own the vision and push it forward.

TESTING AND PROGRAM MANAGEMENT

An LCS effort consists of a set of projects with many interdependencies. Many of these interdependencies can be rather subtle, but all of them must work. The traditional approach for determining whether "things work" is systems testing.

Everyone knows that traditional testing works well for a single application. However, for an LCS with many projects and many interdependencies, the systems testing approach comes up against some real limitations. Experience in these efforts is showing that it is not reasonable to expect a single project leader to define, design, and execute all the tests that are needed to verify that the LCS works as a whole. It is not the responsibility of individual projects to test the LCS release as a whole. An architecture group typically does not have the application skills and user contacts to undertake the testing. In other words, the testing of a large complex system as a whole, using traditional approaches, is an undertaking that has no clear owner.

This creates a dilemma. Program management is not positioned to underwrite the quality of the timely delivery of an LCS effort. Individual project leaders cannot be expected to underwrite the quality of the LCS as a whole. At most, they can underwrite that their project works with its primary interfaces. An intense need today, therefore, is to develop the means to underwrite the quality and timeliness of an LCS release as a whole.

In practice, successful LCS efforts have found a way to resolve the dilemma. This approach, as it turns out, is actually a synthesis of program management and what is called the "V-model" testing strategy. This new synthesis in LCS engagements is called engineering management.

Engineering management adds a testing responsibility to traditional program management. This testing role is charged with validating and verifying that the LCS effort works as a whole, as a system of systems, to meet user expectations of a release of an LCS. For example, it will test that when all the online applications are running as a whole, online response time, reliability, and availability meet service-level agreements (SLAs). Individual projects can be expected to have confirmed that they meet their SLAs. The projects often, however, cannot confirm that they continue to meet SLAs when the entire LCS release runs. They do not have access to the rest of the LCS release. They may find it difficult or impossible to create a high transaction volume with multiple LCS applications running in a production-like environment.

PHASED-RELEASE ROLLOUT PLAN

Finally, one of the critical success factors with LCS development involves a move away from a single-release rollout strategy and toward a phased-release plan. Only one of the projects reviewed had attempted to use a big-bang strategy and, even in this case, it became apparent that the approach would prove problematic as the conversion approached. The effort encountered significant delays as it reworked the release plan and moved instead to the view that a phased release was most desirable.

The remaining projects followed a phased delivery. The phased-release approach serves a number of functions:

- *Reduced risk.* Using a number of releases with partial functionality can reduce the risk of implementation. At the global stock exchange, for example, initial discussions with the company's management were key in moving from the riskier single-release approach and toward a phased rollout, although the phased approach appeared to delay the benefits of the system. The balance was the reduced risk of achieving the benefits.

- *Early verification.* A phased approach permits early verification by business users of essential components as they work with the system in their business. From the review work conducted, it appears that a first release tends to take from 18 to 24 months. Subsequent releases tend to occur in the range of 6 to 12 months after earlier phases. This is in contrast to a more typical three- to five-year development that a single-release approach may require. The result of the iterations is that the user has worked with the system and provided verification of the value of the system.

- *Ability to make mid-course corrections.* Inherent in the release approach is the ability to review the overall situation as the releases are rolled out and thereby to make mid-course changes. As noted, an LCS effort can go on for many years, during which time a company and its business environment can go through a great deal of change. The release strategy can provide the means to deal with the changes in a controlled manner. It can also address issues in a long systems development where for periods of time the design must be "frozen."

- *Closer user involvement.* Business impact can be seen faster when rollouts are provided to the user earlier through iterations. This allows the user to build up experience with and support for the system, rather than facing a sudden conversion at the end of a large development.

The downside of a phased rollout strategy is the significant increase in development cost. To this author's knowledge, there are no widely accepted estimates of the increase in cost caused by the phased-release approach. However, there have been some evaluations that showed more than a 50 percent increase in costs when a multiple-release strategy was compared to a single release. This would seem to suggest not going with a multiple-release strategy. The trade-off is the very high risk of failure in a single release, combined with the benefits noted above of a multiple release.

The points discussed above are key to understanding the value of a release strategy. Phased releases allow a company to reduce risk, increase buy-in, and build a system that is closer to the company's business needs. The lower apparent costs may make a "big bang" approach appear desirable, but the hidden costs and greater risks may prove unacceptable in the longer term. It is vital that management involved in this decision carefully weighs the costs and risks of either approach.

CONCLUSION

When beginning the review of large complex systems, the author's first thought was that the most important thing to do was simply to figure out how to eliminate the complexity. Based on the two years of review, the author is convinced that eliminating the complexity is not possible. One needs to accept complexity as a part of the systems development world for the future. The size of projects that affect the enterprise as a whole tends to be large and it will continue to increase. A project that affects the entire enterprise will increase complexity. Only when one accepts the complexity can one come to grips with managing that complexity.

Finally, today's business environment — with its increasing focus on business partners, virtual enterprises, and the global span of business — makes complexity a reality that cannot be overcome. Delivering quality solutions in this environment must start with a recognition that complexity is inescapable. From that point, then one initiates a set of strategies to manage the complexity and risk. There is no "silver bullet" in these strategies. The three points discussed in this article are examples of such strategies. Each one of them is necessary; but none of them alone is sufficient to guarantee success. From a base of well-defined and -directed strategies, managing the ongoing complexity must become the focus on management in such large complex systems.

Chapter 33
Developing IT Projects on a Pay-for-Performance Basis

John P. Murray

A constant lament within organizations relative to the performance of the information technology (IT) department is a high level of dissatisfaction with the delivery of IT projects. Too often, that dissatisfaction, on some level, is justified. The reality, as often happens when things go wrong, is that some of the causes of the problems relative to IT project delivery tend to be obscured. Given its high visibility, coupled with the basic responsibility for the project, IT will always take the hardest hit when a project experiences difficulty. Of course, the fact is that in most cases, everyone involved with the project (business area project team members as well as members of the IT staff and sometimes members of the senior staff) probably should share some level of responsibility for the failure.

If the problem were simply that of a failure on the part of IT to provide a high level of project development, the solution would be easy: simply replace the people in the IT department. Sometimes, that is the problem and replacing some IT people brings a partial solution. Generally, however, the failures of IT development projects are the result of a combination of factors, of which IT is going to be one — but certainly not the only one.

Considering the empirical evidence with regard to the movement to improved IT project development success, it can be argued that it is time to try some new approaches. Historically, most of the approaches that have been used to make progress in the delivery and quality of IT projects have focused on the introduction of more precise management methods or on technology-based approaches. One approach that has not been given very much attention, but which is worth trying, is that of changing the way IT development teams are compensated for their work.

This chapter explores the benefits that can be obtained from addressing the topic of improved IT project delivery through the process of tying financial incentives directly to improvements in the delivery of IT projects. In reality, there are no silver bullets. However, in thinking through the issues involved, the idea of specific financial rewards tied to clearly defined results, holds sufficient promise to encourage organizations to given the topic careful consideration.

SOME CAUSES OF THE DISAPPOINTMENT WITH IT PROJECT DELIVERY

IT development projects fail for any variety of reasons. Usually, those failures are not the result of a single circumstance, but the result of a combination of causes. Some of those causes include:

- Poor project planning
- A lack of well-done project requirements and specifications
- Inadequate project funding
- A failure of appropriate senior management involvement and support for the project
- Limited involvement on the part of the people who have requested the project.
- A failure to accept proper "ownership" for the project
- The use of inappropriate technology
- The assumption of excessive project risk
- An inability to develop an appropriate sense of urgency among the members of the project team
- Instances of distraction with other business needs on the part of members of the project team

The preceding is not intended to be a comprehensive list of the causes of IT project difficulties. What is intended is to illustrate that IT project difficulties can arise from many causes and from many areas. It also demonstrates that technology is not always the cause of the difficulties. It is safe to speculate that, more often than not, the technology is not the primary cause of IT project difficulty.

Although many approaches have been used to address the issue of IT project failure, the results have been uneven. Some organizations have made progress in some of the problem areas; some have had success in other problem areas; and some have had success in a number of areas. However, it must be admitted from an overall perspective, that few organizations have enjoyed high levels of consistent IT project development success. Very few organizations have been able to sustain high IT project development levels over a long period of time.

CONSIDERING A NEW APPROACH TO IMPROVING IT PROJECT DELIVERY

Given that the various approaches to improve IT project development have not been wholly successful, it is time to consider new approaches. One of those approaches is to rethink the way people are rewarded for their work on development projects. An unfortunate aspect of IT project work is that because it has not been as successful as it should, less than strong performance in that area has become accepted in many organizations. That circumstance has generated a situation in which people are not particularly surprised when IT development projects fail to meet expectations. Over time, a lowering of expectations results in a lowering of performance.

The dilemma here is that, despite the expenditure of considerable amounts of time, energy, and money, not only has the goal of improved IT project delivery not been met, but in many organizations the expectations associated with that delivery have fallen. The high incidence of IT project failure and the associated costs, both hard and soft, mandate attempting new methods to improve the situation.

One aspect of that lowering of expectations and performance is that, although the work on a particular project may be viewed as less than successful, there is seldom any penalty imposed on the members of the project team. Yes, managers do from time to time face termination if the situation is sufficiently difficult. On occasion, people may be chastised for poor performance; but on balance, little in the way of pain comes from a failure to meet project expectations.

However, it is also the case that when good work is done, when IT projects are delivered in a professional manner, that good work is not always recognized. It does occur that a project can come in early, it can be under budget, it can meet all the requirements and specifications, it can exceed the expectations of the IT customers, and the team members may receive a "thank you." Although the work has been exceedingly well done, the paychecks of the team members are probably not going to be any larger than normal. They were, after all, only doing their job, right?

One of the problems associated with the lack of a concrete distinction — other than some probably minor level of praise or criticism — between well-done IT project work and poorly done work is that over time the incentive to push for improved performance is diminished. Doing IT projects well, in addition to having strong management, the right technology, and the appropriate tools, requires a strong commitment to the project. In addition, there must be a willingness to work hard and to assume a reasonable level of risk. When the financial rewards are the same for success or something less than success, it is difficult to motivate people to make a strong commitment, to work hard, and to take risks.

Think about the typical reality of project work. When it is discovered that a project is falling behind schedule, a common occurrence, usually some attempts will be made to bring the work back on schedule. However, too often, the answer is to extend the due date of the project and at the same time open up a new project phase (phase two) to reduce some of the deliverable in the current phase. Usually, in such a situation, the organization's senior management will approve the approach, in part because that approach has been used in the past. Sadly, no one will be too surprised by the delay.

If no distinction exists between the monetary reward for doing good work or for poor work (the reality in many IT departments), there is going to be little incentive to strive for higher project quality or to meet tight delivery dates. An argument can be raised that good people will, regardless of monetary considerations, strive for higher quality work. While that assumption has merit, it does not seem to work quite that way in the real world of IT project development and delivery.

TYING MONETARY REWARDS TO PROJECT PERFORMANCE

Given that people pay attention to what they are rewarded for, it follows that changing the compensation system would change the focus of those working on the project. If the focus on the improved delivery of higher quality IT development projects can be sharpened, it is reasonable to believe that the results will be improved. No one could successfully dispute the contention that the level of IT delivery of projects needs to improve in many organizations. Developing a different compensation approach and giving it a fair trial is worth serious consideration.

Why doesn't the argument that compensation incentives aside, good people will strive to do good work pertain to IT project development? The answers can be found in several project development circumstances. First, most IT project efforts consist of a team of people. To assume that all the people on the team are going to be well-motivated and highly interested in striving to produce high-quality work would be unrealistic.

Second, too often at least some of the IT project team members will have to deal with a dual set of responsibilities. Where team members are assigned to the project, but are also expected to continue their normal duties (or at least some aspects of their normal duties) during the life of the project, problems are certain to arise. Dealing with those other duties, because the reality is that handling those duties is what their performance is going to be judged upon, is likely to remain their first priority. That situation is often reinforced by subtle or overt signals from the employees' manager. The message often is that the work on the IT development project carries less importance than other duties.

Finally, IT projects often come to rely upon several key people to bring them to completion. It is not unusual to see projects where, part way through the effort, one or two of those key people decide to leave the project and as a result, difficulties quickly mount. The issue for those people is often that the project is clearly in trouble and now is the time to move on. That circumstance, coupled with a likely more attractive salary offer from someone else, is often enough to encourage a search for new opportunities. Now, the situation is that an IT project in difficulty has to struggle to find new leadership.

So what happens is that the organization has a disrupted IT project team. In addition, the project team members understand that the outcome of the project, well done or not, is not going to have any particular effect on their compensation. It will also be understood that a poorly done IT project is probably not going to have an adverse effect on any career opportunities in the future. Understanding that scenario, it may be a bit easier to understand one of the causes of IT project failure.

A key component in IT project development success is that of focus. To succeed at project development a strong focus has to be brought to bear and it has to be maintained throughout the life of the project. Because focus is a key component in project success and because, as has been shown, project teams tend to be structured with a limited focus on the project, it follows that a sharpened focus, maintained throughout the project, will bring increased rewards. When a clear, substantial system of financial rewards is in place and is tied to the delivery of high-quality IT projects, the focus on those projects is going to improve. If the potential rewards are sufficiently attractive, that improvement in focus can be dramatic.

COMPENSATION PLAN GUIDELINES

To make the process of increasing financial incentives for increased IT project delivery quality a practical approach, a specific set of criteria must be tied to the process. In addition, the administration of the process must be seen as being fair and consistent. Items that must be in place prior to beginning the implementation plan include:

1. *A method that can be used to objectively and consistently measure the results of the particular project compared to the original project specifications.* Where an incentive plan is to be used, there will have to be a high level of precision in the development of the project budget and corresponding time frames. The goal here has to be to come away with realistic estimates. As the compensation incentive plan gains favor, there could be a tendency to "pad" project estimates and time frames. What is likely to occur is an attempt to enhance the probability of project success and, as a result, increase the chance

for additional income, by building in longer time estimates than would be considered reasonable.

One way to counter the padding of estimates is to have them reviewed by a competent, uninvolved third party. Understanding that such a person is going to review the project estimates will help reduce the tendency to pad the estimates. In any event, the use of a third party will provide sound benefits in coming to reasonable project time estimates.

The idea relative to project estimates is that they should be realistic, yet they should, in order to be met, require the project team members to increase their effort. A part of the process is going to be evolutionary, in that as projects are developed under the system, empirical data can be gathered to assist in developing a more precise set of estimating guidelines in the future. Care will need to be taken to make certain not to allow an environment to be built where anyone — employees or management — feels that the other group comes away with an unfair advantage.

One of the ancillary benefits to be found in the project development compensation approach will be that, because an increased emphasis is going to have to be placed on the development of project estimates, over time that process is going to become much more precise. When people understand the relationship between sound project estimates and their additional compensation, they are going to be very careful about the estimates they develop. In addition, they are going to look for tools and techniques that will strengthen the estimating processes. As a result, confidence in the ability of IT to accurately size projects early in the development cycle is going to grow.

2. *The development of a scale for additional compensation, based on agreed-upon performance for each project.* At the onset, one of the criteria with regard to the topic of compensation should be to recognize the importance of flexibility. Until some experience has been gained, whatever is decided about compensation should be seen as being subject to change.

A key issue is that the compensation plan should be sufficiently generous (within the framework of a high level of performance) to make the plan attractive to the participants. The purpose of the plan is to drive for improvement in reducing the time required to deliver IT projects and, at the same time, to improve the quality of those projects. In reality, that goal would no doubt be seen as all but impossible in many organizations. When significant rewards can be obtained for meeting those goals, the probability of realizing those goals is going to greatly increase.

AN EXAMPLE OF AN IT PROJECT COMPENSATION APPROACH

One example of the structuring of a compensation plan might be as follows.

1. A medium-sized project is estimated to require 14 months of effort, a total staffing level (from all areas, IT, and business sections) of 18 people, and a total budget of 3 1/2 million dollars. In addition, as a reasonable precaution, this project carries a contingency fund of ten percent, or $300,000.
2. Each member of the project team is assured, provided all conditions of the incentive program are met, a bonus of $7500. Those goals include:
   a. Meeting the 14-month timeframe to complete the project. Meeting the timeframe precludes the shifting of any part of the original project into a follow-on phase.
   b. Total project expense cannot, if the incentive rules are to be met, exceed the estimate of 3 1/2 million dollars.
   c. The quality of the project must meet the established and agreed-upon quality standards that were set at the beginning of the project.

It will be understood, as a part of the original agreement with the project team, that determination of the success of the project will be made by an independent third party. That determination will be based on the agreed-upon project time, function, and quality criteria of the project that were established at the onset of the project.

3. In this example, if the project meets the incentive standards set for the project, the total bonus expense will be 18 x $7500.00, which equals $135,000.00. Success with this project will mean that the project will be delivered on time, on budget, and in accord with the established quality standards. Although paying the incentives will increase the expense of the project by $135,000 that can be considered to be a small price to pay for a project of that size delivered on time, on budget, and at a high level of quality.
4. There are two other aspects to the example that should be recognized. One is that the total expense of the project, even with the incentive payments, is going to be less than that estimated if the project had run over and the contingency fund had to be used to complete the project. The other is that when completed, the project will have been fully completed. It is by no means uncommon to see IT projects, as they move through the development cycle, and begin to fall behind schedule, broken into "phases." What happens is that some portion of the work in the original project is shifted to phase two, or perhaps phase three, in order that some aspects of the original project can be moved to production.

In developing the incentive plan, every full-time member of the project team, whether from the IT or the internal customer areas, should participate in the plan. The incentive shares should be exactly the same for everyone on the project. Providing equal shares to everyone involved will build a strong sense of teamwork. In addition, as the project moves forward, the team should have the option to remove any member of the team (through a vote by team members) deemed not to be making an adequate contribution to the project.

One of the pluses of the inclusion of all team members in the incentive plan is, obviously, to ensure a strong focus on the project. Another plus is that it will be clear that, in order to share in the incentive plan, everyone is going to have to make a strong commitment to the success of the project and to work hard to meet the project goals. When the team focuses on the incentive to do the work well and on time, peer pressure is going to correct any difficulties associated with a lack of commitment on the part of an individual team member.

That increased project focus, particularly on the part of people in the business areas is bound to have a positive effect. One of the problems with IT project development is that of involvement in the project of those who request the project. Too often, the feeling outside IT is that the project is an IT project and those who requested the project have limited responsibility with the work or, with the results of the project. Moving to a clear financial incentive for everyone involved to pay appropriate attention and to help push the project can only be good for everyone.

It should be made clear that the installation and use of the IT project incentive plan is to reward people for going beyond the normal effort to make projects succeed. That being the case, people should understand that if they do not meet the standards established for the incentive plan, they will not be faced with the prospect of having their regular salaries or benefits reduced. Moving to the incentive plan should be based on the positive position of encouraging people to raise the performance bar, not as a potential club to change behavior. Indeed, if the incentive plan works as proposed, then over time, behavior is going to change; but those changes will come voluntarily — from the employees — rather than being forced on them by management.

The process must be clearly understood by the organization's senior management and must be supported by that group. In order to gain the required approval, it is going to be mandatory that the senior management group be fully informed of the plan, why it is being recommended, how it will work, and the potential pitfalls associated with changing the way IT projects are funded.

MOVING TO THE NEW APPROACH

When the criteria for the IT project development project incentive plan have been identified, documented, and approved by senior management, the next step is to begin to install the process. Moving to the process should be done in a careful, controlled manner. To begin, a project should be selected as the pilot for initiating the plan. As with any pilot, the goal is to prove the feasibility of the process with a successful implementation. Whoever assumes responsibility for the project must do everything possible to ensure that the pilot will be a success.

As with any pilot approach, the first project under the new compensation incentive plan must be very carefully managed and controlled. Two goals should be considered in developing the pilot. First, it will be important to have the pilot succeed in order to convince those with doubts that the process has merit. The reality here is that this is going to be a plan to sell the concept, and whatever needs to be done to strengthen the probable success of the sale should be done. Toward that end, the project selected should be small enough so that it can be easily managed. Another advantage to starting with a small project is that it will not require an excessive amount of time to come to conclusions about the value of the process.

Second, the employees who take part in the pilot must be convinced of the merit of the plan. They must also be enthusiastic about the potential value of the approach and be willing to work hard to make the pilot succeed. Obviously, the selection of the people to participate in the pilot should be very carefully managed.

Although this will be the first attempt to use the incentive plan, it is going to be critical that as much work as possible is completed on the details of the approach to be used prior to beginning the pilot. Given that this is going to be the first time the incentive plan is used, it will be impossible to cover every detail. However, taking the time to think through the issues associated with the process, and addressing as many of those issues as possible at the onset, represents the correct approach. There will be items to be adjusted, added, or corrected at the conclusion of the pilot. That adjusting process will no doubt continue through other projects as more is understood about what works and what does not work; but the more that can be addressed prior to the introduction of the pilot, the better for everyone.

THE BENEFITS OF THE APPROACH

A number of benefits are going to accrue from the use of the incentive plan. Some of those benefits are going to be easy to quantify — hard benefits. Some of the benefits are going to be more difficult to quantify — soft benefits, but they are also going to be important and should be recognized. It will help to identify benefits in both categories.

Hard Benefits

- A reduction in the expense and time associated with the development of IT projects, and the ability to move IT projects through the development cycles at an increased pace
- The ability, as the result of the process, to produce more IT project work without a concomitant increase in the size of the IT staff
- Increased, measurable levels of IT project quality, including an improved understanding of the project in those areas that have requested the work
- Over time, an improved willingness on the part of the organization's senior managers to support new IT initiatives

Soft Benefits

- An increase in the overall level of the work, and the quality of that work, produced by the IT department
- Improved morale within the IT department (This is will occur for two reasons; of course, the opportunity to obtain additional income is going to be a positive factor. Also, as the process gains acceptance, the performance bar is going to be raised. As people see that by properly focusing on the project, they are able to accomplish more and they can take more satisfaction in their work, they will be motivated to reach higher levels of performance.)
- A probable lowering of IT personnel turnover as the benefits of the process come to be understood (People like to do good work, and to gain a feeling of satisfaction from the work they do, as the level of IT performance rises, people who might have left are going to be encouraged to remain.)
- Increased teamwork and communication between the IT department and those for whom the department does development work
- Improved levels of IT service throughout the organization
- An increase in the levels of IT service to the customers of the organization

DEALING WITH THE CULTURAL ISSUES

Considerations about moving to an IT project development incentive program should include careful thought about the cultural issues involved in making the transition. Going to this new approach means change. Whenever change is introduced within an organization, it brings out issues that will have to be recognized and resolved. Many of the issues associated with a new compensation approach to the development of IT applications projects have been identified in this portfolio. That is not to imply that additional issues will not arise; every culture is different and each presents its set of unique concerns.

The salient concern, relative to the cultural changes involved, is to develop an awareness that they will create some level of discord and that as they arise, they need to be addressed. Those concerns that are raised should be given a fair hearing and carefully considered. Much of what is going to be done here will probably be new to the organization, and as such it should be recognized that it will require time and some adjustments to come to a sound approach.

One of the cultural issues certain to arise is that of the fairness of providing people working on IT development projects an opportunity to earn additional income. This is going to have to be explained within the context of why they are being given additional consideration for what might be considered "normal" work. One way to address this issue is to explain the benefits that are going to accrue to the organization if the plan is put in place and it succeeds. Another way to help this situation is to develop a process that will, if the plan proves workable and is adopted, allow others an opportunity to join projects in the future.

As has been indicated, an underlying issue with the plan is that the project team, in order to obtain the additional income, is going to have to put forth extra effort to meet its goals. As people come to understand that getting the additional payments requires extra effort — in some cases, considerable extra effort — some of them are going to lose interest in becoming involved.

There will be some element of inherent unfairness in moving to a compensation incentive program. However, if doing so makes good business sense, the plan should be put in place. The difficulties associated with some level of employee discontent at the onset are going to be more than overcome by the eventual success of the process.

An important key to dealing with the cultural issues is for management to be as candid and as fair about the process as possible. When disagreements arise, if the managers are willing to take people through the logic of the plan and answer any and all questions as fully as possible, they will have discharged their responsibility. At that point, the onus for accepting or rejecting the process resides with the employee.

CONCLUSION

If the correct environment is developed, the right people are chosen to participate, and the compensation incentive plan is well-managed, it can produce benefits (perhaps significant benefits) for the entire organization.

Putting the plan in place, overcoming whatever difficulties may arise, and documenting the result will take time and patience. Several versions of the process might have to be tried to find the best approach for a particular organization.

The potential payoffs within the plan: improving the quality of IT projects, bringing those projects to completion on time, and within the original budget, should be seen as of paramount importance to the IT department and to the organization. Achieving those rewards is worth the effort required. They are also worth enduring any cultural strains that may have to be faced and overcome in order to reach the desired goals.

The subject of changing IT development project compensation should be considered on the basis of risk versus reward. Using that approach, a favorable argument can be quickly developed that balancing the risk (the approach fails) against the reward (significant improvements in IT project management), there is no reason not to move to a changed compensation plan. New ways must be found to improve the IT project development process; going to a new compensation approach represents a sound way to move toward that improved environment.

Chapter 34
The Pitfalls of Client/Server Development Projects

Paul Cullen

The management of client/server projects involves unique pitfalls within traditional systems development categories. This chapter addresses the unique characteristics of client/server development projects within the following categories:

- Defining/documenting business requirements
- Determining hardware/software/network requirements
- Estimating
- Project tracking
- Defining tasks
- Estimating hours required
- Estimating percentage of completion
- Timekeeping
- Issue tracking
- Developing skills with technology and tools
- Security
- Testing/QA process
- Developing documentation
- Organizational stability
- Prototyping/usability
- Sign-offs and approval

DEFINING AND DOCUMENTING BUSINESS REQUIREMENTS

As with a traditional development project, documenting requirements should be the start of a client/server development project. It is here that the user requirements are defined as a basis for the project estimate and cost benefit analysis. The requirements document should be detailed and include input screens, processing cycles, and output reports. The database design should also be included, defining data relationships. Not only is defining/documenting business requirements important for estimating the initial effort of the project, it is also critical for determining changes in scope and determining what "done" is. Many times what is casually reviewed at the start of a project becomes critically important in determining a project's completion. Typical elements of a requirements document include:

- Objective of the project/system
- Business requirements
- Input/output requirements
- Affected business area
- Processing requirements
- Security requirements
- Data or file handling requirements
- Organizational impacts
- Documentation requirements

It is difficult for an auditor to determine if the all requirements are comprehensive and adequately defined. However, at a minimum, the auditor should verify that the requirements are defined at a sufficient level of detail and that there is appropriate user management authorization.

DETERMINING HARDWARE, SOFTWARE, AND NETWORK REQUIREMENTS

Once user requirements are defined, hardware/software/network requirements can be established. These requirements are used to determine the processing platform and networking for the system. Factors that determine the appropriate platform(s) are existing/strategic network infrastructure, number of concurrent users, size of the database, and volume of transactions. There is typically no "right" platform to use and many IS personnel have differing opinions. In addition, vendors are always announcing new releases with new features, making it difficult to distinguish existing product features versus vaporware. Beware of technologies and methodologies that introduce new terms and vernaculars that provide a smoke screen for poor project management and lack of expertise. Hopefully, a best approach is chosen considering cost, systems performance, and ease of development. Typically, the requirements are documented in an architecture document that include:

- Business requirements
- Tactical considerations
- Strategic considerations
- Interfaces with other systems

No one hardware/software platform will "fit" all applications, just as a hammer alone will not build a house. However, no small part of the platform choice should be what platforms the developers are familiar with. Familiarity with the platforms chosen will improve the accuracy of the estimates and help ensure that "system killer" problems will not be encountered later. It is too risky to use unproven technologies as a platform for large development projects.

A potential bottleneck with client/server systems is the network capacity and traffic between the user workstation and the server. Many times, these systems are expected to perform over wide area networks (WANs) that may not provide consistent network response times.

ESTIMATING

One use of the project estimate is to determine whether management wants to fund the project based on a cost/benefit analysis. Obviously, if the estimates are not accurate, management cannot make good decisions on whether they want to do the project, assign people to tasks, or plan on when deliverables will be available. Essentially, without goods estimates, project managers cannot manage. Factors that go into good estimates are:

- *Experience with the hardware/software/network/development tools:* If the developers are not experienced with the platforms/tools, management should realize that the estimate is probably not very good and be ready to spend much more on the project and expect delays.
- *Familiarity with the requirements:* Were the developers involved in the requirements definition? If not, again the estimate is probably not very good; and be ready to spend much more on the project and expect delays.
- *Existing systems:* Is the new application a rewrite of existing systems where the reports and data requirements are defined? If so, the estimate may be pretty accurate. Otherwise, additional effort may be required to re-do the system to meet user requirements.

Hopefully, a track record of similar development efforts can be used to provide a reality check for the estimates. This can also be used as a control for managing developers who may be padding their estimates. A confidence factor or range should be a part of this estimate. This would give management a best-case and worst-case scenario. This would allow management the ability to decide not to do the project if it might be too expensive or likely not meet deadlines. A final pitfall to watch out for is a target date set by senior management to be committed to by the project team. If a top-down target date is set, there is pressure on the development staff to "back into" estimates that are not based on what is required or pressure to not have estimates at all.

PROJECT TRACKING

As with all development projects, essential to avoiding or managing client/server development pitfalls is effective project management. The elements listed below are used to identify where the project is, what is left, and the amount of effort remaining.

- *Defining tasks:* Development tasks should be defined at a size that is small enough to be easily tracked and meaningful. The project manager can effectively manage a project if there are specific deliverables with clearly defined hours and frequent due dates. Large tasks with ambiguous deliverables make it difficult to know if the project is in trouble in time to effectively manage the pitfalls. Task interdependencies and assignment of responsibilities are particularly important for projects with multiple related teams where it may be difficult to determine who is responsible for what.
- *Estimating hours required:* This should be done by someone who is experienced with what is required — hopefully the developer that will be performing the task. This would provide some ownership or commitment to task completion.
- *Estimating percentage of completion:* This can be an inaccurate guess if based on the amount of work that has already been expended to complete a task. It should be based on defined deliverables such as number of tasks, screens, or reports completed.
- *Timekeeping:* Timekeeping is frequently not used effectively. Many developers do not regularly record their time or keep an accurate estimate of the hours spent. This makes it difficult to determine the project status. In addition, the failure to record all hours for this project may cause other projects to be underestimated if the recorded hours are used for future estimates.

ISSUE TRACKING

Issue tracking can be used to refine project requirements by documenting and resolving decisions that were not contemplated during the original requirements definition. The issues log is also a good vehicle for tracking outstanding problems and ensuring that they are resolved before the system is implemented into production. A common pitfall with client/server systems is the lack of stability due to software incompatibilities, network errors, and weaknesses with the database handling concurrent updates. Issues should be weighted in severity from "show stoppers" to "nice enhancements" to prioritize the development effort. The owning user of the system should be the one to determine if an issue has been resolved, as there as a tendency for developers to claim resolution prematurely. As with any problem log, the issue log should contain who identified the issue, the date the issue was identified and communicated, severity, a description of the issue, and if resolved, the resolution text. This can also serve as an audit trail of the decisions made.

Issues should be retained after they are resolved to be used for future trending. Trend analysis should be performed to track training issues, as well as problems with hardware, operating systems software, and other application software. If each error is logged, the issues log can also be used to track the overall stability of the system. The issues log can be used to diagnose problems by pinpointing the situations where the problem occurred. The problem information can also be useful in obtaining vendor assistance in problem resolution by providing clear evidence of correlation between problems and vendor products.

DEVELOPING SKILLS WITH TECHNOLOGY AND TOOLS

On-the-job training is not the way to learn new client/server development tools and techniques. A developer should certainly take classroom or computer-based training (CBT). However, developers should not embark on large-scale projects without first having successfully completed small projects. This would reduce project risk by allowing the developers to prove themselves on a smaller scale and give them the ability to more accurately estimate the effort involved. Project managers should also be trained in managing progressively larger projects focusing on multiple teams, task interdependencies, and multiple users.

On larger projects with new technologies, there can be many people with different levels of expertise attempting to make decisions. There are many levels of knowledge. This can range from what a person read in a magazine, to what they heard from someone else, to what they know from training, to what they know from working with a system or past development experience.

The first three levels of knowledge are fairly weak but pretty common. People's roles should be managed, based on a recognition of their level of knowledge to ensure that tasks are appropriately assigned, estimates are reliable, as well as that the decisions made and directions taken are sound. Reference checks should be made for new employees and outside consultants who claim to be "experts" to verify their level of expertise.

SECURITY

A successful security implementation can be difficult in a client/server environment due to the many processing layers that must be secured:

- *Client workstation.* Historically, this has been a personal computer that has weak controls restricting who has access to programs and files. However, with the introduction of operating systems such as Microsoft's Windows NT Workstation, the controls available are rivaling the level of security available on a mainframe.
- *Application.* This level of security typically controls the menus and fields that a user is able to access. The levels of access are typically read, update, and delete.
- *Network.* This deals with securing activity on the network. Tools such as network sniffers are available to read and alter data that is transmitted over the network. There are typically two types of network controls used to prevent inappropriate disclosure or alteration of data. The first is restricting access to segments or areas of a network. This is usually done with firewall systems or screening routers that restrict traffic based on source and destination addresses. Internet connections should be controlled by firewalls. The other method for securing network traffic is encryption. This prevents the ability to read or alter data going across the network. At a minimum, passwords should be encrypted.
- *Server.* Servers typically control who can log on to the network and who can access databases and files on the network. Server security is the most common type of security used in a local area network. Access to the network is typically controlled through a userid and corresponding password. Access to files is then granted based on the assigned user or group id. Most servers provide for logging security administration and violation activity. In large client/server systems, a mainframe is performing the server function.
- *Database.* The database system can also perform security functions, requiring a userid and password and then assigning access to data based on the user or group id. In addition, databases can log security administration and violation activity.

Coordinating multiple levels of security is difficult, and many systems introduce security weaknesses by ignoring access controls on certain platforms or scripting logons on platforms that can be easily circumvented. Another typical problem with client/server systems is that they are cumbersome, requiring multiple logons with multiple userids and passwords.

Ideally, the application should be designed with a single sign-on that controls access on the application, workstation, server, and database systems, along with network controls that restrict access to the appropriate segments of the network and encrypt sensitive traffic.

TESTING

While the elements of the traditional quality assurance/testing process apply to the client/server environment, this environment contains unique challenges requiring more rigorous testing although developers may not take testing as seriously because it is "only a PC system." The client/server systems development process should include test plans with expected result, actual result, and disposition of differences. If the system requirements have been well defined, they can be used to develop the test plans. Testing should include all platforms, as well as the interfaces between them and the ability to handle concurrent users. In addition to handling multiple updates through concurrent connections, many client/server systems include the ability to operate without a direct network connection through database synchronization using a process called replication. This requires unique testing steps to verify that replicated additions, updates, or deletions are handled correctly through the replication process as well as working with the system operating in a multiple-user mode. Concurrent updates to databases (two people attempting to update the same record at the same time) can create database conflicts. How the system handles conflicts should be documented and managed by the application software or manual procedures.

Poor response time is often an issue with client/server systems. Bottlenecks can be corrected by increasing network capacity, tuning database queries, or optimizing the database design.

Client/server change management also creates unique challenges with version control. Programming code is typically distributed across multiple platforms as well as embedded within databases. While PC version control packages are frequently used, change management systems that include source/object synchronization are not as sophisticated as the systems used in the mainframe environment.

DEVELOPING DOCUMENTATION

While the goal of a client/server system is to be user friendly and provide online help functions, these systems should additionally have the traditional types of documentation available to operate, maintain, and use the system. The documentation requirements should include the following:

- System overview
- User instructions/transaction codes
- System flowcharts
- System interfaces
- Processing function, organization and brief description of programs.
- File descriptions/dataset characteristics (database design if applicable)
- Security and control requirements of system, and implementation of those requirements in the system

- File backup and retention requirements
- User errors and messages

Documentation requirements should be included in the project plan, as well as contracts if working with an outside vendor.

ORGANIZATIONAL STABILITY

Reorganizations and staff turnover are difficult to manage, particularly in large organizations. These impacts can easily kill a project. A good project manager will anticipate the possibility of losing team members before the "two weeks notice" is given. Obviously, management should do what they can to retain key people. However, losing staff is inevitable — especially if staff is trained on "hot technologies" that are very marketable. Things that can be done to reduce the impact of staff changes are:

- *Training:* ensuring that enough people on the staff are knowledgeable with the technologies to assure that the team is not overly reliant on any one person. This could also be used to help manage personnel who are resistant to change and do not want to deal with it.
- *Establishing backups:* identifying who could fill a person's position, what it would take to get the individual up to speed, and implementing a plan before it is required. It may make sense to have designated backup individuals write parts of the system to ensure that they have the skills necessary to support it.
- *Mentoring:* identifying opportunities for more senior individuals to assist others by answering questions, assisting with reasoning, and working through problems.
- *Programming standards:* covers how code is to be written and documented to ensure that it can be supported by others.
- *Code reviews:* involves reviewing systems as they are developed to ensure that they are logically written, understandable by others, and adhere to the documentation standards.
- *Maintenance screens:* should be built to enable the modification of key system functions/parameters without programmer intervention.

PROTOTYPING

Prototyping can be useful for screen design and helpful in determining user needs. However, documentation should exist over and above the prototype. Prototyping should not be used as an excuse for not following a systems development methodology. It is crucial that the developers are involved in the requirements definition phase, as the assumptions used in the requirements definition are critical in developing the estimate. With the development of middleware, object-oriented coding, and computer-assisted software engineering (CASE) tools, it is some times difficult to determine if business requirements have in fact been adequately defined. It is crucial that project managers and auditors are certain that the development team can articulate the system requirements in "plain English" to be assured that deliverables are understood.

Prototyping is often done in cycles or iterations. It is necessary to document what will be delivered in an iteration and when it will be delivered to manage user expectations as well as avoid project slippage by pushing deliverables into future iterations.

If the client/server system is being developed to replace an existing legacy system, hopefully users of the existing system will be involved in the prototype review. In addition, user representatives who understand the workflow and are good at assessing usability should also be included.

SIGN-OFFS AND APPROVAL

Sign-offs and approval should be obtained at least at the following points of a project:

- *At the start of a project,* preferably to begin an estimate of what the project will take to complete.
- *At the completion of the requirements definition and prior to development* with an estimate of what the development effort will take in terms of development personnel, user personnel, money required for equipment, etc., as well as the timelines and task plans required to complete the project. This should be in sufficient detail to define the scope of the project, track the percentage of completion, and determine when key people need to be involved. If working with a vendor, this should be a contract.
- *At the completion of significant deliverables* to ensure that:
  - users are getting what they asked for when it was supposed to be delivered
  - the system has been tested to assure that it is performing and functioning correctly
  - the system has been developed according to programming standards and it can be supported
- *At the completion of the project* to ensure that deliverables match what was defined at the start of the project. Invariably, once the system is developed, it will be different than what the user wanted or what the developer thought the user communicated. In some cases, this begins the argument over who pays for the changes. Usually this is where it is evident that it was critical to clearly articulate and document requirements at the start of the project. Beware of the introduction of the term "phases" at the end of the project that was not mentioned at the project's beginning.

CONCLUSION

It is not easy to manage projects that are dependent on complex client/server systems. Technical problems may occur that "kill a system" that have nothing to do with project management. However, project management controls can be introduced that mitigate the risks of these problems. While auditing project management controls diverges from the traditional audit approach, corporate resources can be saved by escalating to senior management situations where these controls are not in place. As previously discussed, the most important controls to watch out for include:

- Experience with the technology and similar projects
- Adequately defining and documenting user requirements
- Accurate estimating and establishing realistic target dates
- Tracking progress and issues
- Implementing effective security
- Effectively documenting and testing the system
- Obtaining user approval

If these controls are in place, the project manager and auditors have some assurance that the risks associated with client/server pitfalls are being effectively managed.

Chapter 35
Using Project Management to Build an IT Help Desk

Ralph L. Kliem

Information technology (IT) organizations are under pressure to operate cheaper but also faster and better. At the same time, they must satisfy business objectives or meet requirements described in service level agreements as users employ complex information technology (e.g., client/server tools) in unique environments (e.g., virtual offices).

To meet these demands, many IT organizations are setting up a help desk to which users can direct inquiries and problems, ranging from training to network management. Many of these services are becoming automated in response to users' needs for a fast, meaningful response. Yet an effective help desk is more than an automated tool. It requires a complete infrastructure to support it and to provide those services that cannot be automated. It is important, therefore, to build a help desk that consolidates and coordinates its tools and services to meet demands.

This need becomes even more important as the growth of help desks will climb steadily. Some help desk experts believe the market for help desk tools will quadruple by the end of this century. In addition, the market for outsourcing help desk development is expected to climb as the result of a failure to deliver services and contain development costs.

HELP DESK DEFINED

A help desk, of course, is a centralized place that people can direct their inquiries for answers and problems for resolution. Depending on the size of the organization and the role of the help desk, it requires both application software and a supporting infrastructure. Typically, an IT help desk addresses queries and problems dealing with technological and business

0-8493-1190-X/02/$0.00+$1.50

process issues. A help desk uses automated and manual approaches to handle queries and problems.

If an IT help desk fails to meet the criteria of speed, reliability, and service, it will fail. The larger the organization to support and the greater the array of services to provide makes project management essential for providing a help desk that users will want to contact and receive rapid, reliable responses.

CRITERIA FOR A PROJECT

Building a help desk meets all the criteria for being a project. It has a fixed end date for completion. It has a defined end product (e.g., fully operational help desk with specific services). It requires a sequence of tasks that must be completed before becoming operational. Finally, it consumes money, especially for labor and tools. Depending on the magnitude of the help desk, the total development cost can range from several thousands to millions of dollars.

SIX FUNCTIONS OF PROJECT MANAGEMENT

Building a help desk is a project that requires laying the groundwork for its successful completion. This involves performing six key, basic functions: leading, defining, planning, organizing, controlling, and closing.

Leading is motivating people to perform in a manner that contributes towards meeting or exceeding project goals and objectives. It is the only function that occurs throughout the life cycle of a help desk project. It requires not only doing the right things but doing them continuously, from project inception to completion. Leading is also required during the execution of all the other project management functions.

Defining is identifying what the help desk project must accomplish. It requires pinpointing the overall goal(s) of the project, its specific objectives, the major players and their responsibilities, and any significant constraints.

Planning is developing a path to achieve the goal(s) and objectives of the project. It requires determining in advance who must do what and when.

Organizing is setting up an infrastructure that efficiently and effectively executes the plan to achieve project goals and objectives. The idea is to maximize the output of resources with minimum investment via communication and coordination.

Controlling is tracking (looking at the past) and monitoring (projecting into the future). It requires ensuring that the project has, is, and will achieve the project's goal(s) and objectives according to the plan.

Closing is completing a project in a manner that minimizes waste and maximizes effort as well as provide lessons for future projects.

Leading

Building a help desk uniquely requires project managers to exercise leadership. It involves a broad array of players: senior and mid-level executives, supervisors, end users, and IT technical experts, just to name a few. Project managers must motivate all of their players to provide information, expertise, time, and effort. Without that leadership, acceptance of the help desk will be difficult and can result in project failure, whether from a cost, schedule, or quality perspective.

Exercising leadership on help desk projects is even more difficult in a general business environment that is constantly changing, from markets to organizational structures. In addition, help desk projects face challenges of high staff turnover, shortage of people with the requisite technical expertise, and unyielding customer demands for good, reliable service. These circumstances challenge the leadership skills of even the best project managers.

It is important for project managers of help desk projects to perform the basic skills of leadership.

Communicating Regularly. Setting up an IT help desk requires the participation of a large number of people with unique skills. Often, these people work independently and isolated. It is important that project managers ensure that communication flows among all the participants, horizontally and vertically.

Encouraging Teaming. Because many people on a help desk project are specialists who work independently, the feeling of being a member of a team is difficult to acquire.

Project managers must work to encourage greater interaction so that synergy is generated and directed towards accomplishing the goals of the project. Otherwise, the esprit de corps of the team suffers and, consequently, the output.

Facilitating Performance. Team members working on a help desk project are more than likely supporting other projects. They can find themselves facing conflicting priorities. Such conflicts can interfere with their productivity. Project managers must work to resolve these conflicts and other impediments to productivity.

Keeping Focus on the Vision. A tendency on help desk projects, like all projects in general, is to stray away from the vision. Scope creep, for example, is a common occurrence on a help desk project because of the tendency to

Exhibit 1. Outline of the Statement of Work (SOW)

Section	Example
Introduction	The causes for the help desk project and a description of the customers
Scope	The specific services that the help desk will and maybe will not provide
Goal and objectives	The minimum level of services to provide and their priorities
Assumptions	The anticipated levels of support from internal functional management and expectations from customers
Resources	The required skills for performing the tasks of the project, such as specific PC application programming, knowledge of call management systems, and problem management
Schedule	Major milestones, including the project completion date
Budget	The total cost of the project, broken by phase or deliverable
Approvers	The signers of the SOW

increase the services that the help desk will provide. Project managers keep everyone concentrating on the vision, not expanding it.

Defining

For a help desk project to start off successfully, it is important to know its basic who, what, when, where, why, and how. The medium for accomplishing this is the statement of work (SOW).

The SOW is a document that captures all that information at a high level. It lays the groundwork for effectively and efficiently managing the project, throughout its life cycle. It also serves as an excellent communications tool between the help desk development team and the customers.

The SOW is especially useful for help desk projects. The customer, expectations, and deliverables often are vague concepts and remain ill-defined. Just the draft of a SOW helps to define more clearly all three, thereby avoiding problems later in the life cycle of the project. Exhibit 1 is an outline of the SOW with accompanying examples for each section.

After completing the SOW, project managers can develop a project announcement that declares the formation of the project. The project sponsor signs the memo, which communicates the name of the project, goal(s), completion date, and any other information deemed important.

The project announcement serves two primary purposes. First, it gives visibility to the project. Second, it communicates that senior management is behind the project.

Work Breakdown Structure

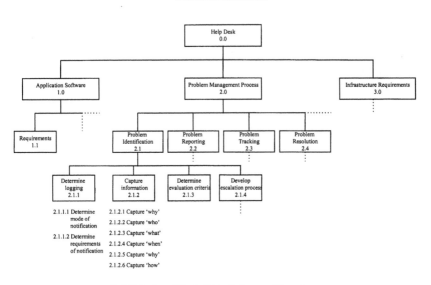

Exhibit 2.   Work Breakdown Structure

Planning

After the SOW and the project announcement comes the project plan. It involves several actions.

Building the Work Breakdown Structure (WBS). The deliverables (e.g., products or services) that make up the help desk are defined in Exhibit 2. It has a top-down, broad-to-specific, hierarchical structure to it, showing the deliverables at the top and the tasks to build them towards the bottom.

Each leg of the WBS can vary in depth and content. It is preferable to explore each leg in sufficient detail so that progress eventually can be tracked meaningfully.

Some common items to include in a WBS for a help desk project are:

• Application development and maintenance
• Asset management
• Call/service request management
• Escalation criteria
• Evaluation criteria
• Metrics
• Problem management
• Procedures
• Processes

Exhibit 3. Responsibility Matrix

Task		Smith	James	Valdez	Ludlock
2.1.1.1	Determine mode of notification	P	S		S
2.1.1.2	Determine requirements of notification	P	S		S
2.1.2.1	Capture "why" data		S	P	
2.1.2.2	Capture "who" data		S	P	
2.1.2.3	Capture "when" data		S	P	
2.1.2.4	Capture "what" data		S	P	
2.1.2.5	Capture "where" data		S	P	
2.1.2.6	Capture "how" data		S	P	

Note: P = Primary responsibility; S = Support responsibility.

- Resources
- Security
- Service support requirements
- Systems management
- Tools
- Tracking and reporting
- Training
- Workflow

Assigning Resources. After preparing the WBS, the next action is to determine the skills required to complete each task. The assignment of skills is done at the lowest level of the WBS; the lowest level is called the work package level. It is at this level that tracking schedule performance is done.

Project managers, of course, consider more than skill to perform each task. They must look at the personality, training, and experience requirements to complete a specific task. When assigning more than one person to a task, they should also designate one primary person to be held accountable for results. In the end, project managers should produce a responsibility matrix, as shown in Exhibit 3.

On a help desk project, two sets of skills are critical for an IT help desk to succeed: technical and people. Technical skills, for example, deal with building applications. People skills, for example, deal with how to interact with team members and customers. Unfortunately, it is rare to find both sets of skills in one individual. Yet both are essential for the success of all IT projects in general and especially help desk ones. The latter must provide technical expertise while at the same time provide a service to the customer. Assignments, therefore, must weigh carefully the requirements for both sets of skills.

Exhibit 4. Estimating Time and Flowtime

Most Optimistic = 48 Hours

Most Likely = 84 Hours

Most Pessimistic = 124 Hours

Expected Time = [48 + 4(84) + 200]/6 = 97 hours (approx.)

Non-productive time = 10 percent
$\qquad$ 97 × 1.10 = 107 hours (approx.)

Convert to flowtime, assuming 8 hours per day

107/8 = 13 days (approx.)

Estimating the Time to Complete Each Task and Convert It to Flow Time. With the resources now assigned at the work package level, the next action is to estimate the time to complete each task and convert the numbers to flow time. The estimates will be important to calculate schedule dates and costs as well as employ people efficiently.

A reliable but effective estimating method is the three-point estimating technique, as illustrated in Exhibit 4. It involves determining three estimates to perform a task: most pessimistic (the time required to complete a task under worst conditions); most optimistic (the time required to complete a task under best conditions); and the most likely (the time required to complete a task under normal conditions). The result is an expected time. The expected time is then further adjusted for nonproductive time (e.g., interruptions) and, subsequently, converted to flow time.

Developing a Network Diagram. Using the lower level tasks in the WBS, the next action is to illustrate the relationship between them in a network diagram (Exhibit 5). In other words, the network diagram shows the dependencies among tasks, reflecting which one starts and ends first, second, and so on. The network diagram is useful for calculating dates for each task and, consequently, the entire project.

The network diagram is an excellent tool for managing help desk projects. The projects involve a complex array of tasks that are both technical and business in nature. The diagram provides a roadmap to follow to ensure that both sets of tasks are coordinated well by the time the help desk is open to the customer.

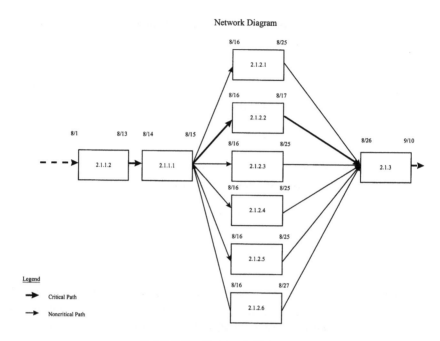

Exhibit 5.   Network Diagram

Calculating the Start and End Dates for Each Task. With the flow time now available for each task and the dependencies identified, the next action is to calculate two sets of start and stop dates for each task and, consequently, the entire project: early start date is the earliest time to begin a task; early finish date is the earliest time to complete a task; late start is the latest time to start a task; and late finish is the latest time to complete a task.

The early late and start dates are calculated by moving through the network diagram from left to right, using the relationships between the tasks and their respective flow times. The late start and finish dates are calculated by moving from right to left in the network diagram.

Both sets of dates are important for determining the critical path. Tasks on the critical path have matching early and late start and stop dates, thereby indicating no opportunity to let those tasks slide. If they do slide then completing the project on time is impossible unless corrective action is taken. Another characteristic of tasks on the critical path is that they occupy the longest path in the diagram.

The network diagram works best for managing the details of a project. Under some circumstances, such as reporting to upper management, a simpler, easier to understand schedule is preferable. Exhibit 6 displays a

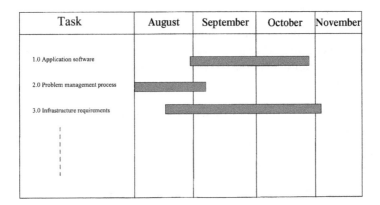

Task	August	September	October	November
1.0 Application software				
2.0 Problem management process				
3.0 Infrastructure requirements				

Exhibit 6.   Bar (Gantt) Chart

schedule called a bar or Gantt chart. It does not show the dependencies and only shows the early start and finish dates.

Organizing

Communication and infrastructure are two key elements in organizing a help desk project. Both ensure that the project is executed according to plan efficiently and effectively.

Communication. This element has two parts: documentation and meetings.

Documentation entails developing any material that proves useful for managing the project. Typical documentation includes forms (e.g., time collection), reports (e.g., status report), procedures (e.g., change control), and reference material.

Often this documentation is collected and then filed in project history files. These files serve as a repository of information about the history of the project, from inception to completion. This information can prove useful for analyzing problems and learning from experience.

Meetings are of three basic types: checkpoint review, status review, and staff.

A checkpoint review meeting is held after completing a major milestone (e.g., completion of a phase). Its purpose is to learn from the experience up to a specific point in time and decide whether to proceed.

A status review meeting is held regularly to determine progress against the project plan, from a cost, schedule, and quality perspective. It is preferable to collect status prior to the meeting so people can discuss issues intelligently.

A staff meeting also is held regularly. Its purpose is to share information and experiences. Often times, the staff and status review meetings are held together in the same session to reduce the number of meetings and the time spent in them.

Infrastructure. This element deals with applying resources in a manner that maximizes output. One approach is to set up a project organization, which is reflected in an organizational chart. The organizational chart should provide a reporting structure and clarify roles and responsibilities. The organization should incorporate basic management principles, such as span of control, unity of direction, and accountability.

Another approach is to publish a responsibility matrix as discussed earlier. The matrix helps to clarify responsibilities and the extent of involvement. Publication breeds commitment because it gives visibility.

Still another effective approach is to establish a project office. Depending on the project's size, of course, the project office is a place for holding meetings, storing documentation, and displaying information. A good way to display information is to set up a visibility wall or even a room to display plans, architecture, and other key information of the project. The wall or room then turns the project office into an effective communications as well as administrative center.

Team members and customers of help desk projects will find the visibility wall or room useful. With plots or diagrams on display, they can see the overall structure of the help desk center, its services, its procedures, and the impact on the business.

Controlling

It is rare that a project proceeds according to plan throughout its life cycle. Frequently, variances from the plan will occur, either from a cost, schedule, or quality perspective. Keeping a pulse on the project, therefore, is critical to ensure adherence to the plans. This involves performing the following four actions.

Collecting Status Data. This action will occur just prior to or during status review meetings. Data should come from the people responsible for their respective tasks.

Assessing Performance. After collecting and compiling the status data, determine whether a variance or deviation from the plan has occurred and its criticality. The variance will come from one or more of three areas: cost, schedule, or quality. For cost and schedule, project management software can help determine the impact of a variance.

Taking Corrective Action. If a variance appears, the next action is to decide whether to take corrective action. Corrective action might entail working overtime to get back on schedule or pursuing a complete replanning effort for the help desk project.

Managing Changes. With movement, goes an old saying, comes change. A project environment constantly is moving and changing. Project managers must deal intelligently with those changes; otherwise, they constantly will fight fires. It is important, therefore, for project managers to establish an infrastructure to capture, prioritize, evaluate, and dispose changes. This action involves going beyond using configuration management software. It also deals with organizational and behavioral changes, something help desk projects must continually reconcile with their development plan.

Closing

All projects end for many reasons. They may last so long that they lose their relevancy to the customer. They may lose their funding. They may have achieved their goal(s). Whatever the reason, it is important to close as efficiently as possible while remaining effective to the very end. It also means learning from the performance so that history does or does not repeat itself on similar projects in the future.

When closing a project, therefore, it is important to perform several actions.

Converting Data into Information. Throughout a project, if organized well, it will accumulate data. This data must be converted into information. This information is useful to track performance and identify what did and did not go well. With this information, project managers can determine the overall success or failure of the project. It also enables preparing the lessons learned.

Preparing the Lessons Learned. This document captures the key experiences of the project team so that future projects can capitalize on what to do and not to do. The lessons learned should cover business and technical topics.

Releasing People. Although keeping an inventory of people to handle contingencies provides a comfort level, it is more efficient to retain only the necessary individuals to complete remaining tasks. Having too many nonproductive people adds unnecessary costs and lowers the productivity of the people with remaining work. It also prevents people from working on other projects that could use their skills.

CONCLUSION

Building an IT help desk was once seen as a dead-end route for IT professionals. Today, just the opposite is the prevalent viewpoint. A help desk serves as an information hub for answering questions and solving problems that are business and technical in nature. It is imperative, therefore, that a help desk project results in an organization that provides timely, meaningful services to its customers. Project management is the tool to ensure that occurs.

Chapter 36

Leveraging Developed Software: Organizational Implications

Hal H. Green
Ray Walker

Leveraging is the reusability or portability of application software across multiple business sites. The extent to which an application can remain unchanged as it is installed and made operational at each location is referred to as leverageability.

Leveraging can reduce the cost of acquiring and maintaining application software. However, the ultimate measure of leveraging is the resulting business benefit — the cost of delivering a working capability from site to site across an enterprise.

Whether a manufacturer chooses an off-the-shelf or custom software solution, achieving leveraging requires the cooperation of multiple sites, beginning with the initial phases of the process. In downsized companies and companies with greater decentralization of decision making, this type of businesswide effort can become difficult. This is especially true when the application is not necessarily a supply-chain-level application but one affecting more directly the manufacturing process.

ASSESSING PREPAREDNESS FOR LEVERAGING

Where a leveraging opportunity exists, limiting the scope of the target sites to a common business, product type/configuration, or other shared interest may mitigate some of the management challenges to leveraging. This strategy constrains the leveraging activity to sites that are likely to benefit most. These sites are likely to be willing to compromise on functional requirements to realize the reduced costs of acquiring and supporting the leveraged application.

Analysis Team Responsibilities

Leverageability of software is affected by the initial choice of platforms. Ideally, the application should result from a rigorous data and function modeling phase that clearly depicts the natural systems of the sites. All too often hardware, operating systems, and database platforms are the decisions that precede, shape, and limit the follow-on choices. As is the case for all good design practice, business requirements should drive technical architecture, not the other way around.

If a solid data and function model exists for each site, the choice of acquiring or developing software becomes clearer. When an off-the-shelf application exists serving most of the business needs, then the choice becomes a selection between vendors' offerings relative to the specification. When no commercial offering exists on the market that satisfies the site information model, then new development or modification of some existing software is the obvious choice. In either case, the following questions are germane to understanding the number of sites that can apply the application to be acquired or developed:

- Will changes in product or the manufacturing differences affect the applications?
- How do manufacturing business practices change from site to site?
- What type of process control or I/O systems exist at each site?
- What hardware, system software, and networking protocols exist at each site?
- Do the user communities differ at each site with respect to their information needs?
- What user communities should be interviewed to assess requirements?
- What type of training or follow-on consulting must be provided to make the application effective at each site?
- Who will be responsible for first-line support at each site once the application is commissioned?

Answers to these and a host of other questions should be captured as part of the deliverables that result from the analysis process. Once the architecture vis-á-vis the applications is known, the quality and location of sites to be included in the analysis can be selected.

Exhibit 1 presents an overview of the process of requirements analysis or documenting the common specification across the target business. In Exhibit 1, leveraged resources represent the analysis team responsible for designing and delivering the application across multiple sites. Site resources consist of two groups:

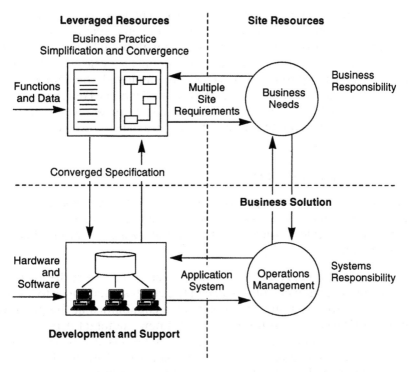

Exhibit 1. **Roles and Responsibilities Model for Leveraged Software Development and Support**

1. *The user community:* Users provide the business objectives and needs.
2. *The IS community:* IS maps the effect of systems on manufacturing operations.

The analysis team captures information needs across multiple sites. In a manufacturing context, information needs may be similar to these examples:

- Amount of product waste on yield on each line by shift
- Statistics of key process/quality parameters
- Recipe or formulary for each product
- Trend of selected process values over time

A successful modeling effort results in a shared specification that enjoys system independence in that it describes what the business does, not simply "how" it does it. The use of a shared data and functional model is an effective means of creating a living specification that reflects the information needs of the business.

Data and functional models resulting from analysis can also be used to complete development. Whether the design team elects to purchase off-the-shelf application components or to develop custom software, the model-based specification is useful. Whether full life cycle computer-aided software engineering tools or 4GL tools are employed, the data and functional specification are foundational to the applications. Fourth-generation client/server tools that allow decoupling of client processes from the database server can be effectively used to capture user screen requirements during prototyping.

ORGANIZING FOR LEVERAGING

Leveraging is a business objective, originating from a purposeful decision to provide common solutions across numerous manufacturing sites. Leveraging begins, therefore, with the affected organizations sharing this business objective.

Businesses that enjoy a culture where ideas germinate at the lower levels of the organization can offer some of the greatest challenges to leveraging. These businesses often build strong IS capabilities at the plant and manufacturing sites to support and build new manufacturing software applications. For such organizations, their strength is also their weakness when it comes to leveraging applications software. Overcoming the cultural and organizational barriers at a site to a businesswide or corporatewide convergence effort or solution can become a serious hurdle to the planner and analyst. One means of mitigating this problem is the use of a leveraged application work group that represents the various sites.

Leveraged Application Work Groups

The leveraged application work group is responsible for capturing the business benefits that accrue across multiple manufacturing sites during the definition, development, and deployment of an application. The work group is composed of representatives from each business or site that derives benefit from the application, as well as a project engineer or analyst and a sponsor from the corporate staff function that is held accountable for the success of the program.

The work group is formed soon after an individual business unit or site requests development of a new manufacturing application. Additional sites and business units are solicited for membership in the work group by distributing a brief description of the application and anticipated benefits from deployment across multiple sites. A project engineer or analyst is assigned to draft a detailed specification that is then reviewed and upgraded by the work group. Upon reconciliation of all the requested modifications to the specification, the document is reviewed with the application supplier. The supplier provides a proposal for developing the application (functional design concepts, cost, and schedule).

Funding from each site and business unit for the development of the application is a key component in the success of leveraging software. Funding from multiple sources reduces the cost for each individual site.

Upon delivery of the application analysis and detailed design documents from the supplier, the application work group reviews the design and decides what modifications or scope changes are required. The work group is responsible for making certain that the final design will bring the maximum benefit across the different sites.

The application work group decides which site is appropriate for piloting the application. Selection of the first site is important because the lessons learned at this site will be the basis for deployment at additional sites. After installation at several sites, the work group compiles all the installation lessons and benefit information. A best practices/implementation guide is compiled for rollout at multiple sites.

A communications bulletin is distributed to all the business units and sites for potential reuse of the application. This communication alerts sites considering development of a similar or redundant application.

DELIVERING LEVERAGED APPLICATIONS

If as a result of the analysis and design it is determined that an off-the-shelf package exists to provide the desired solution, the construction phase assumes the characteristics of a rollout. Key considerations revolve not around code development but around applying the packaged software in the target sites. Key concerns are as follows:

- Integration with existing systems (if necessary)
- Database population plans
- Interfaces with I/O devices
- Any necessary modifications of the off-the-shelf software
- User training
- Ongoing support

The use of pilot or prototype systems is encouraged as a means of continuing to align user expectations for leveraging the application. Working pilots in plants are an excellent means of identifying potential benefits of the application if a solid base case is first established for comparison. Pilots serve as a platform for technical and performance evaluations while providing a test bed for the user community before full implementation or rollout.

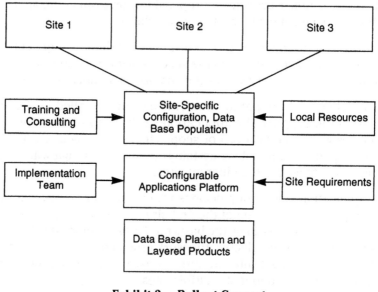

Exhibit 2.   Rollout Concept

Planning the Applications Platform

The analyst and designers must plan for leveraging from the initial phases of the project. Common database platforms, common user interfaces, and even common I/O drivers are not sufficient to realize the full benefits from leveraging. Exhibit 2 presents an overview of an applications platform and illustrates delivery of leveraged applications.

Beginning with the database, standards should be set around database configuration. If the database engine is relational, then the data model becomes the common basis of configuration. If the database is part of a real-time process control system, then standards could include tag naming conventions, data types, screens, process icons, trends, and SPC charts.

Layered over the database engine are the applications that will operate on data in the database. The applications should be sufficiently complete that only database population need occur once the systems are delivered to the site. This means meta-data is known and fixed. Similarly, user screens are complete and ready to work out of the box. Process control systems that use configurable graphical user interfaces are a convenience and a luxury if uniquely configured for each site.

Common graphical user interface screens with generic capabilities from site to site offer greater economy to create and less cost to support. Where graphical screens are being leveraged across multiple sites, there is usually sufficient economy created by the leveraging approach to produce higher-quality graphics. The quality of the delivered applications should rise with leveraging.

Ideally, applications can be made operational quickly once hardware and system-level software are operational. A factory acceptance test should be performed where the complete system is staged, integrated, and checked out before rollout.

CONCLUSION

There are organizational implications in any effort to leverage software effectively. Leveraged software development and support requires the cooperation of multiple sites beginning with the initial phases of the process.

It is also appropriate to point out that the business model for leveraging software, reviewed in this chapter, implies fewer contributors to the effort. The need to have a different system integrator provide development or application programming per site is diminished, if not eliminated. The leveraged application work group is likely to find that the applications can be made operational with a small dedicated team systematically moving from site to site.

Chapter 37
Managing Legacy Assets

Christopher Slee
Malcolm Slovin

To discuss the legacy issue is to raise fundamental questions about how the Information Systems (IS) organization optimizes the use of information technology (IT) in the business. Instead of viewing legacy applications in purely technological terms, managers must look at the processes that generated these applications in such a way to make them problematic. This shift in perspective requires that legacy issues be understood within a larger business context.

In reality, IS is simply a microcosm of larger economic forces. Today's businesses are striving to respond to rapid change by creating flexible, modular business processes that can be quickly implemented and reengineered as necessary. To support these types of processes, IS organizations are moving beyond traditional transaction processing into new areas and deploying rapid development and client/server architectures. But if the IS function is merely trying to learn to perform systems development with new technologies, it is missing the larger challenge.

Although emerging technologies such as objects, client/server, and the Internet bring exciting opportunities to create new types of business solutions, it is legacy systems that hold the major key to future success. Legacy applications dominate IS resources, represent trillions of dollars of investment, and present the leading obstacle in more than half of reengineering efforts. In many cases, the IS organization itself is a legacy issue, tied to mainframes and old-world processes in a time of rapid change. Faster business change and faster technology change challenge IS managers to integrate business-driven development with legacy perspectives, processes, applications, and infrastructures.

THE LEGACY CHALLENGE

Recent estimates show that the current installed base of mission-critical legacy applications would cost $3 trillion to replace. Because of the magnitude

0-8493-1190-X/02/$0.00+$1.50
© 2002 by CRC Press LLC

of these expenditures and their business impact, IS organizations must move carefully yet decisively. Even basic maintenance of legacy systems costs huge sums of money, leaving managers with only a small fraction of their budget for critically important new applications.

These cost pressures will intensify in the future for three main reasons: first, CEO have invested in Information Technology for many years and are demanding accountability for results; second, budget increases have been limited to the rate of inflation for most of the recent past; and third, in an increasingly competitive world, companies continue to demand cost reductions and better returns on investment from every segment of the business. As a result, several challenges confront the IS organization:

- At least 80 percent of most IS budgets is spent on legacy systems, with a declining residue left for new development. At the same time, each new application is more complicated, costing more to develop and maintain.
- Because much of the focus of legacy maintenance is on corrections, minor enhancements, and preventing catastrophe, legacy investments quickly reach a point of decreasing marginal utility: each additional dollar buys fewer and fewer benefits, especially when compared with each dollar spent on new solutions to business problems.
- The accelerated pace of technological change means that systems are superseded more rapidly than they were when technologies were more stable.
- As Exhibit 1 illustrates, too much of the effort expended on legacy systems is fundamentally non-value-added; studies show that more than 50 percent of the effort is devoted to understanding a legacy application and then retesting the application after a change.
- As a result of the intensive effort made to change a legacy application, about 25 percent of legacy time is spent on testing. A more intelligent, planned, and focused approach should provide adequate testing with less effort.
- This year's new application becomes next year's legacy, typically increasing the installed base of legacy systems that must be maintained.

These challenges have several implications for IS managers. Managers must break the cycle of an ever-increasing yet fractured installed base that drives an ever-larger annual maintenance expense. New systems have to be funded by gains in IT productivity and an accumulation of small cost savings rather than by increasing infusions of corporate capital. As with many business reengineering efforts, IS transformation will have to be quickly self-funding.

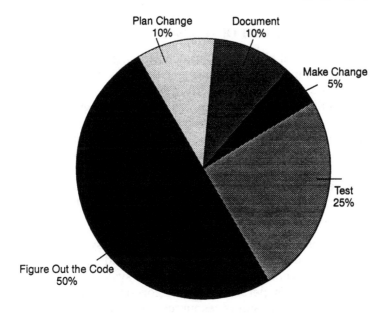

Exhibit 1. **Legacy Maintenance** (From GUIDE Study on Legacy Maintenance.)

IMPROVING LEGACY MANAGEMENT

These pressures all point to better legacy management as the key to the future of the IS function. IS managers and their staffs should improve their approaches to the legacy issue — the applications, the organization, and the linkage to the business — both to increase the value derived from legacy assets and to free up resources for supporting new applications.

Instead of viewing the so-called legacy problem as a monolith — and despairing that it cannot be defeated, only dented — some IS managers are reframing the legacy issue and helping to drive the strategic integration of business performance and IT. They have begun to address the legacy puzzle with the following series of phased responses:

- Focusing on portfolio management by developing a comprehensive understanding of and strategy for IT assets and investment that relates both legacy and new assets to business processes and the business value derived from each element
- Embracing the challenge of hybrid computing and working to recover value from legacy assets by converting and interfacing the old and new architectures concurrently running in most companies
- Transforming the IS function with legacy considerations in the forefront, which involves rethinking the day-to-day processes and procedures that support the evolution of IT assets and essentially means reengineering IS itself

PORTFOLIO MANAGEMENT OF IT ASSETS

Yesterday's sequential planning approach, which provided the IS function with sufficiently long lead times to meet business objectives, no longer exists in today's rapidly changing business world. Although business change drives the integration of process and technology, ineffective communications are causing the gap between business strategy and IS delivery to continue to widen. As IT becomes a major engine of change, it redefines what is strategically possible and gets further embedded into every business process, including electronic commerce, computer-integrated manufacturing, investment program trading, and supply chain optimization. The future of IT therefore requires a holistic understanding of business strategy and processes.

In stark contrast, many decisions regarding legacy systems are episodic, tentative, and trapped in a pattern of inertial spending. To address these tendencies, IS managers should evaluate legacy systems in much the same way as sales territories, personnel, or the corporate image are evaluated. Looking at IT assets as business resources provides IS managers with two main evaluation criteria:

1. How effectively does a given system or suite of applications support business objectives?
2. How efficiently does the system perform its support tasks?

This orientation highlights a pair of key points. First, both business and technical perspectives are necessary to assess a portfolio. Business objectives are derived from evolving business processes and evolving strategy, and this can be a difficult process. IT assets are mapped against these objectives and evaluated using a comprehensive set of metrics. Second, the portfolio must be examined in meaningful pieces. Individual elements of the portfolio fit together like puzzle pieces to support a critical business area or process. Even though individual elements may appear to be valuable, the overall business results may be considerably weaker because of critical shortcomings in the way the various parts fit together.

The results of this assessment are then mapped within a grid called the 4R portfolio assessment matrix (Exhibit 2).

The 4R Portfolio Assessment Matrix

The 4R portfolio assessment matrix contains four categories with suggested actions — the four Rs — that guide decisions. Sorting assets into a differentiated portfolio reduces the magnitude of the legacy problem with a strategy of divide and conquer. IS managers who understand the relative scale, size, and investment in each of the applications acquire insights that guide future action.

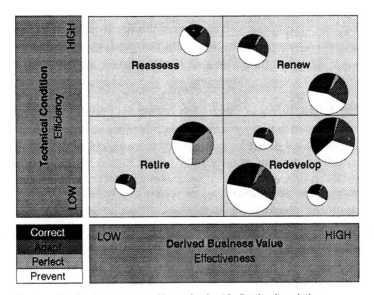

Each application is represented by a pie chart indicating its relative size, value, and the recommended allocation of future resources.

Exhibit 2.   Portfolio Assessment Matrix

Category 1: Low Business Value, Low Technical Condition; Action: Retire. If a system performs a function of questionable value unsatisfactorily, why is it running in the first place? These systems, which constitute about 25 percent of the North American legacy base, are excellent candidates for early retirement or benign neglect. If they must be kept alive, IS managers should consider installing a graphical user interface on top of the character-based screen. Selective system improvement is another option, but only if the cost can be justified with business results.

Category 2: Low Business Value, High Technical Condition; Action: Reassess. IS managers should reassess why a high-performance system is contributing so little to the business. These systems, only about five percent of the installed base, may not have been well justified with an adequate case for action. Alternatively, over time a justification may have become outdated. In other cases, rollout may have been mishandled. IS managers should consider moving these assets to more critical applications if they still are capable of providing business value and to a phased retirement if they are not.

Category 3: High Business Value, Low Technical Condition; Action: Redevelop. About half of legacy systems fall into this category. These systems may require pampering; yet the business still depends on them. IS managers should strive to maintain business support, retain asset value, and improve functionality where appropriate — all while reducing cost. This can be done in many ways, for example, by extracting business rules from operational systems, developing value-based cases for action that support replacement, or developing a strategy for gradually substituting new functionality for old.

Category 4: High Business Value, High Technical Condition; Action: Renew.
About 20 percent of legacy systems are in this ideal asset state of delivering tangible business value and being in good technical condition. It is an unfortunate truth that most applications started off in this quadrant or were targeted to start in this quadrant but have since fallen out of it. The organizational mission regarding these systems is to preserve asset value by allowing them to migrate forward as business goals and technologies change.

After assessment, IS managers can look beyond the immediate and see the problems with legacy systems as products of root causes. Rather than viewing legacy applications as fragile and redundant, the IS function can move to extend the useful life of these legacy assets. By addressing the causes of these problems — which are often not technical issues — IS managers can move to prevent the all-too-rapid decline in business value and technical condition experienced with most applications.

Institutionalizing Portfolio Management

For all of its benefits, portfolio assessment as a one-time event will not deliver lasting gains. Although it identifies some improvement opportunities that IS managers should act on promptly, over time a one-time assessment rapidly degrades into architectural shelfware. Instead, portfolio assessment must be the first step in a process that lets IS managers continually manage the portfolio by reevaluating the linkage between IT assets and the evolution of business needs. The life span of current technologies is a fraction of that of mainframes; expecting an assessment to drive a three-year plan inevitably leads to mounting questions about its relevance and growing disappointment with its effectiveness.

A well-structured portfolio assessment should lay the groundwork for this ongoing management approach. In addition to the 4R profile, the assessment should address other key questions:

- How do end-user and formal IS-supported solutions interact?
- How do current IT assets support fundamental business goals and processes?
- What is the transition and development approach for each application in the portfolio?
- What is the life cycle condition and investment posture for each application?

- How does the applications strategy fit with the technical infrastructure?
- Where should IS focus its spending?

Answering these questions provides the foundation for a new relationship that aligns the IS function and its business partners around business goals. Portfolio assessment becomes the first step in a fundamental shift away from the previous pattern by the IS function of responding to a stream of requests and associated expenses driven by demands for change to existing systems or proposals. Instead, the IS function builds anew toward managing the evolution of a series of IT assets. In this new approach, IS managers evaluate changes against the state of IT assets and the business processes they support.

The assessment itself represents a high-level plan for the development of IT assets; at the very highest level, it is a conceptual architecture for the corporation. A relevant parallel to this high-level plan is found in the model used for citywide planning and construction. Allowing for adaptations resulting from the intangible nature of computing, business processes, portfolio strategy, technical infrastructure, and code inspections all have simple equivalents in the basic planning and construction disciplines of the model (e.g., zoning plan, infrastructure plan, design approval, various permits, code inspections, and maintenance regulations). What the IS function typically lacks is the discipline of the process, the role of a city planning department, and the maintenance regulations for ongoing upkeep.

ADJUSTING TO HYBRID COMPUTING

Some IS organizations narrowly view the legacy challenge primarily in technical terms. In these times of hybrid computing, IS managers must navigate between sharply contrasting world views: relational versus hierarchical, flexible versus rigid, object-based versus procedural, distributed versus centralized, open versus closed. The days of the single paradigm are gone, and the accelerating pace of business and technological change requires the IS function to accommodate multiple architectures, languages, and platforms. In response, successful companies are rethinking their fundamental approaches to integration, planning systematic value recovery from legacy assets, and devising comprehensive transition strategies.

Rethinking Integration

Legacy Overintegration. The typical business application has increased in size by an astounding 5,400 percent since the start of the 1980s. A typical mission-critical integrated application has grown to include 1.2 million lines of code — assembled by stringing together what would have been 20 different applications 15 years ago. These numbers begin to illustrate the challenge posed by legacy overintegration.

Spaghetti code — the dominant challenge 15 to 20 years ago — has been replaced by spaghetti integration. Many architectures present numerous opportunities for uncontrolled interactions among applications, programs, code, and data. Structured programming — a widely accepted step forward over spaghetti code — offers some lessons for spaghetti integration. It stresses tight cohesion (i.e., keeping highly related functions together) and loose coupling (i.e., minimal connections between functions).

Unfortunately, in most cases of spaghetti integration and integrated shared databases, the opposite is true. Legacy applications are usually characterized by loose cohesion, with functional logic such as product edits and customer data sprinkled through numerous programs and applications. The applications are tightly coupled both through shared databases, redundant databases, and interface files and through uncontrolled interactions between numerous fields in countless programs.

Shifting to Component Architectures. Component architectures replace shared data integration with tight cohesion and controlled coupling — practices that have much in common with object-oriented design and analysis. These architectures shift the focus to standardized interfaces and construction guidelines. In addition, communications mechanisms based on the use of components complement the traditional focus on applications and data. Component architectures use such items as desktop integration, a software message bus, remote data access, and data warehouses as building blocks to help applications cooperate through standardized interfaces.

Although the idea of components is readily understandable in terms of new development, it can also be applied to legacy applications. Some organizations are now viewing these applications as reusable components that can be incorporated into new development using object-oriented techniques. Building on component-based message-driven architectures, IS professionals can use a variety of techniques to avoid plunging into the heart of legacy systems and forcing in new levels of complexity. Many of these techniques are now becoming well established, as the following sections on value recovery and transition strategies will discuss.

The shift to component architectures also supports two concrete commitments — reuse and maintainability — that increase the value of IT assets. Reuse increases the value of an asset by reducing future development costs. Maintainability increases value by allowing an asset to evolve as the business changes. Both significantly reduce costs by focusing investment on fewer, more flexible assets. Breaking applications into controllable, standardized components is as important to maintainability as it is to reuse.

Recovering Value from Legacy Assets

Legacy applications are storehouses of immense business value, even if that value can be extremely difficult to exploit. The value can be classified as falling into one of three main areas: data, processing logic, and business rules.

Fortunately, new strategies, techniques, and tools are emerging that let IS managers and their staffs reengineer, recondition, coexist with, or extract value from existing applications. These approaches also move legacy assets closer to the architectures that underlie new development.

Transition Strategies for Legacy Assets

Several fundamental techniques are now emerging as the basis of a value recovery program in a hybrid environment. As the following sections illustrate, most of these tactics rely on breaking large applications into smaller components and then reengineering or reconditioning them.

- *Reverse Engineering* — Automated tools help raise a system to a higher level of abstraction by, for example, deriving a system specification or requirements model from existing code and data. This technique may create a new baseline for incorporating enhancements and enabling future code regeneration. It also facilitates traditional maintenance by enhancing developers' understanding of the system.
- *Package (i.e., Components)* — Standard COTS (commercial off-the-shelf) packages such as word processors, spreadsheets, work-flow engines, and graphics libraries can provide critical components for hybrid solutions.
- *Components* — Partitioning legacy systems or legacy programs into smaller components lets IS staff phase out or replace a system one piece at a time. Some code analysis tools help with this task, but the conceptual commitment to modularity and reuse is more important than particular tools.
- *Rationalization and Restructuring* — Cleaning up existing code by eliminating redundancy, instituting standards, improving structure, and updating documentation simplifies maintenance and enhancement. This is frequently the first step in a legacy strategy.
- *Conversion and Rehosting* — Rehosting involves moving legacy applications — untouched — onto client/server platforms. This approach not only promises potentially lower costs but also enables multiple application components to be more seamlessly integrated into a solution for the business user.

- *Architectural Layers* — Layering separates the various components of an application, such as presentation/user interface, application logic, data access level, and communications.
- *Wrappering* — Creating a software wrapper to encapsulate and modularize legacy components enables them to coexist and communicate with object-oriented components. A function server lets the legacy code send and receive object-oriented messages. In this way, wrappering positions legacy code to provide continuing value and to be reused in future systems.
- *Forward Regeneration* — Automated tools help developers regenerate code based on modified higher-level abstractions rather than modifying the code directly. This technique may be used after reverse engineering, or if the original system was developed through code generation.
- *Surround* — Creating additional functionality and data components around the legacy system, but without modifying the system itself, allows legacy components to be phased out as the surrounding components supplant the legacy functions.
- *Data Warehouse* — Whereas surround strategies put new functionality in front of legacy systems and integrate at the desktop level, warehouses integrate the data behind legacy applications.
- *Maintenance and Enhancement* — As the section on transforming the IS organization will illustrate, leading practitioners are rethinking the traditional approach to managing the evolution of legacy assets even in the areas of maintenance and enhancement.
- *New Development* — Best-practice models and capability maturity assessment help chart a course to better results and productivity in new applications development.
- *Package Replacement* — Software packages often replace a legacy system, especially if it is used for nondifferentiating basic support applications. COTS application packages may also be used in a surround approach.
- *Outsourcing: Long-Term or Transitional* — Because it can be cost-effective under the right circumstances to identify a clearly definable task and outsource it, IS managers should consider outsourcers in the enhancement, redevelopment, or replacement phases of a legacy strategy.

These transition techniques are certainly not stand-alone mechanisms. Not only is there overlap among the various techniques, but they also interact with each other to produce more finely tuned results. IS managers should carefully assess the techniques in a given situation as part of the overall project plan.

TRANSFORMING THE IS ORGANIZATION

Once the IS organization is committed to developing a system of architectural components, IS managers face the task of transforming the way the IS function itself interacts with the legacy portfolio. Because IS managers have relatively stagnant budgets, improvements must be rapidly self-funding. Such improvements result from five sources:

1. Better alignment of business and IS goals and strategies
2. Better partnering between the business and IS communities
3. Better management and technical processes within the IS organization
4. Better skills, practices, tools, and techniques at the developer level
5. Continuous enhancement of IS capabilities

Transformation of the IS organization centers on managing user demand, legacy systems evolution, and IS resources. There is a tendency to accept the behavior of an IS organization as yet another legacy rather than to challenge old assumptions and reshape managerial approaches. The IS function must fundamentally rethink and reengineer itself in the same way that many organizations are reengineering business processes.

IS management has traditionally focused on significant technology changes that cause work processes, skills, and understanding to lag until they are reshaped. Recent examples of such change include client/server technology, object orientation, and multimedia. The fundamental issues of IS transformation, however, relate to commonly accepted practices and beliefs — in other words, to the culture within IS itself.

IS Cultural Change

Craft-Based Development. Much IS activity is still conducted in the cultural equivalent of a preindustrial craft. Methods are personal and unstandardized, private knowledge confers power, and success or failure is not readily determined. At worst, code is written in idiosyncratic ways by employees who must be retained to update their personal handiwork, trapping other developers because nobody else supposedly understands that system. Finally, a member of the guild can only be understood and therefore judged by another craftsperson, who is hesitant to criticize co-members. For example, even though formal peer review is proven as the most cost-effective method for preventing and eliminating coding errors, few IS developers inspect each other's work.

A growing body of evidence highlights the severity of this problem. Recent experiments involving personal software production found that some programmers with at least five years of experience injected hundreds of defects per thousand lines of code, with a worst case of more than 1,100.

413

Fundamental lessons from the quality movement imply that the cost of finding and reworking all these defects must be enormous. Most IS professionals do not recognize the scale of the problem, and most IS organizations lack the metrics to quantify it. Even more startling is the improvement that results after three months of using personal metrics: the same programmers who injected hundreds of defects per thousand lines of code improved their delivered quality by a factor of from five to ten.

Moving to the Age of Engineering. Much of legacy management requires IS organizations to move software maintenance and development from craft work into the age of engineering. Mary Shaw of the Carnegie Mellon University Software Engineering Institute has developed a useful model of this transition for several other professional engineering disciplines (Exhibit 3). In an engineered approach, standards of performance are shared and transferred, patterns of work are made more methodical, and components are interchanged and reused.

Because this mode of thinking represents a dramatic change in the mind-set of the IS organization, opposition to the software engineering perspective can be widespread. IS managers are challenged to foster recognition by the IS organization of the need for change and to reinvent methods and priorities in accordance with the engineering culture.

Managing the Change Process

Most changes to existing systems are processed in a highly inefficient manner; they take approximately four times as long as a change made during new development. IS organizations pressured to respond to business units often attempt the quick fix. Developers routinely enter complex software systems and perform minor fixes (often generating a stream of so-called fix-on-fix errors before completing the job). They then proceed to another task without leaving a record of what they did. The conceptual integrity of the original design, the documentation, and the implemented system itself rapidly degrade as repeated quick-fix alterations build up like electronic scar tissue. Such systems are inevitably difficult to understand and maintain.

Once again, some organizations are fundamentally rethinking their approach by treating the installed base more like packaged software, which means that change requests are rationalized and managed. These organizations have replaced the quick-fix cycle with an iterative enhancement approach that achieves the following significant benefits (Exhibit 4):

- They gain a broader perspective of a series of minor changes.
- They resist demand for expensive tinkering that delivers little business benefit.

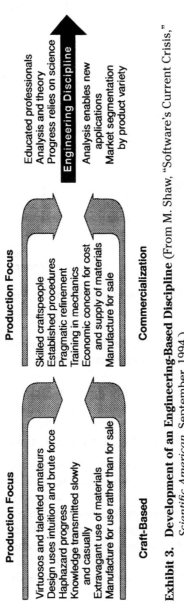

Exhibit 3. Development of an Engineering-Based Discipline (From M. Shaw, "Software's Current Crisis," *Scientific American*, September, 1994.)

415

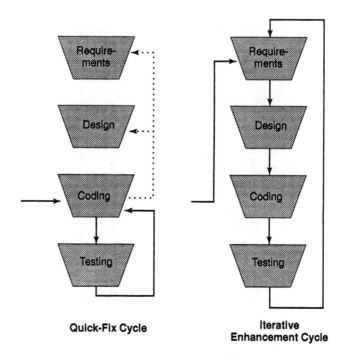

Quick-Fix Cycle

**Iterative
Enhancement Cycle**

Exhibit 4.   Quick-Fix and Iterative Enhancement Cycles

- They develop a more efficient approach to maintenance because they reduce the 50 percent of maintenance time that is spent understanding the current application.
- They use advanced techniques such as workshops, business process reviews, and prototyping to ensure that the right problem is being solved.
- They protect the integrity of design and documentation.

Through this approach, business and IS partners exert a far greater level of control and address the real business and technical issue. A formal oversight body or change review board joins business sponsors and process owners with IS portfolio managers. The board maintains a long-range focus (built around the 4R portfolio assessment) and avoids being caught up in the daily routine of change requests. Significant changes obviously require board approval, but even minor adaptations and fixes undergo some less formal scrutiny. Any contemplated change requires the answers to several questions:

- To what degree is the requested change compatible with the original design?
- To what degree is the change necessary?

- How much will the change enhance the system? Does the benefit justify the cost? Is the change compatible with the strategic plan?
- Is the change within budget limits?
- How critical is the change compared with others in the backlog?
- How soon will business payback be realized?
- Are there combinations of changes that generate economies of scale or other synergies?

After these questions are answered, the organization then classifies changes, groups requests by urgency and business benefit, and establishes a review process to schedule changes by priority, cost-effectiveness, and appropriateness for overall legacy strategy. Urgent tasks — such as those associated with a system failure — are performed more quickly when the system is well documented and skilled people are available. Minor changes with no strong business case are grouped and implemented in a planned release to optimize the maintenance process.

Once a regular schedule of updates and releases is established, business users rely on organized batches of changes, plan the introduction of change into the business, and see the portfolio as a business asset from a long-term rather than a moment-to-moment perspective. Reducing the time IS personnel spend each day on possibly redundant or ill-advised system changes frees them for more types of work.

The Case for Metrics

What would business be like without a profit-and-loss statement? What would baseball be like without earned run averages and on-base percentages? For most organizations, the lack of legacy metrics is only partially a matter of technical and methodological issues; it may be a prototypical example of the challenge posed by organizational culture.

Although many organizations thus find it difficult to maintain a history of their projects, estimates, and actuals, other organizations do commit to measurement programs and reap dividends. The results of these programs are striking. For example, a recent report on 500 IS organizations found that between 25 and 30 percent (even up to 60 percent) of effort in the few organizations that succeeded in instituting a metrics program is focused on corrective actions on an installed system (in classic quality terms, this is pure rework).

A growing body of support for metrics is originating outside the IS organization in the product and embedded software communities within the business. These outside customers will not return for more poor-quality software. Thus, the issue of metrics is best understood as being fundamentally a cultural conflict and a managerial challenge within IS. The main issue is that as long as solid knowledge about past performance is impossible to find, reliable assessments of future performance remain out of reach. As the following sections indicate, many categories of legacy activity lend themselves to accurate measurement.

Product Measurements. How many lines of code were generated, changed, reengineered? How many function points were delivered or modified? How many defects were embedded along the way and how many errors were discovered before delivery? After delivery?

How well do the products satisfy customer needs? How well does a given system add value to or enable a business process?

Process Measurements. How many hours were devoted to which projects in the past 12 months? How many of those were direct, indirect, and managerial? What funds were expended where and when? How much time was spent adding value to the application? What were the cycle times? When was testing performed and how effective was it? What kind of work was being performed?

The following four categories have been suggested for maintenance work: corrective (i.e., fixing mistakes), adaptive (i.e., keeping up with external regulations and changes in technology), perfective (i.e., changing user requirements or performance), and preventive (i.e., enhancing maintainability and reliability).

Organizational Performance. How well does the IS organization compare with industry standards such as the Software Engineering Institute maturity model? How does the IS organization satisfy its customers? How well is IS delivering value and responding to needs?

Once a system of metrics is in place, managing users, legacy systems, and IS people becomes more straightforward. Without metrics, management remains a matter of educated guesswork. Some of America's most admired corporations — such as Motorola and Hewlett Packard — have recognized the urgency of the issue and are driving metrics throughout their organizations.

RECOMMENDED COURSE OF ACTION

What has come to be known as the legacy problem is not only a matter of today's inheritance of yesterday's assets. Tomorrow's legacy must be considered as well. If today's IS organizations use the same procurement and maintenance processes, handle the same customers using the same change control and architectural approaches, and then have to cope with four or five times as many technology choices, they cannot expect anything better five years down the road. One might even argue that the legacy situation of five years from now will be an order of magnitude worse than it is today.

As with any major reengineering effort, issues of politics and culture are significant. Traditional wisdom on integration has left a legacy of complexity. This inheritance must be managed in a world where the IS function no longer has the monopoly franchise on rapidly changing information technology. These challenges create the need for IS managers both to reengineer IS itself and to provide the leadership and understanding critical to rethinking perspectives and driving the change.

Legacy is not an episodic, one-time hangover from the days of the mainframe. Legacy is the ongoing challenge of leveraging evolving IS assets in the era of hybrid computing.

Section 6

Measuring and Improving Project Management Success

Chapter 38
Facilitating Your Way to Project Success

Nancy Settle-Murphy
Caroline Thornton

This chapter describes four common time wasters that undermine IS projects and discusses how to avoid them by using facilitated workshops with key team members and sponsors. A checklist to help project managers make the most of facilitated team communications is included, as well as guidelines for deciding when to use a facilitator and choosing whom to hire (see Exhibit 1).

The enterprisewide project you have been leading has been declared "a complete success" by your business sponsors. End users report they have never experienced such a leap in productivity and quality in such a short time. You have helped your manager become a hero in the eyes of the CFO: Not only is your project on time, but you have managed to deliver the promised results at 80 percent of budgeted cost. Your competition orders a top-notch headhunting firm to "offer whatever it takes" to lure you over to its side so you can duplicate your astounding success. For most project managers, this scenario might sound like science fiction. But it does not have to.

THE UNIQUE DEMANDS OF A LARGE-SCALE IT PROJECT

Few organizations within a typical company can compete with IT for missing deadlines so reliably, and with such prominence. Is it that the IT profession simply draws those with exceptionally poor time management skills? Or that a badge of honor for IT project managers is awarded for setting particularly unrealistic delivery dates? Or do IT managers just enjoy being heckled by disgruntled end users?

In fact, IT managers are probably no more or less inherently efficient than their business counterparts. Nor is their ability to estimate time realistically or keep track of costs any less well honed. Rather, it is the very nature of large-scale IT projects that makes it so difficult continually to meet deadlines, work within budget constraints, and please business sponsors:

0-8493-1190-X/02/$0.00+$1.50
© 2002 by CRC Press LLC

Exhibit 1. How to Select a Facilitator

Not just anyone can pull off the successful facilitation of an IT project kickoff. Important qualities and attributes include
- Trained and skilled in group facilitation techniques
- Seen as impartial and not vested in outcome of session
- Regarded as able to lead all team members fairly
- Excellent communications skills — particularly listening and paraphrasing
- Is politically "wise"
- Plays a dedicated role
- Has time to prepare adequately; is not "added in" at the last moment
- Can effectively deal with tough issues likely to arise
- Understands when digression from agenda is likely to produce positive results

- Many enterprisewide IT projects are seen by business managers as a panacea to solve a critical business problem — creating a heightened sense of urgency and pressure.
- IT projects tend to run in the double-digit millions of dollars, thus commanding particularly close scrutiny and criticism.
- Business sponsors often lack an understanding of realistic time frames and resource requirements, particularly when they insist on making changes midstream.
- A shortage of IT talent often means that several business units within a company compete fiercely for available resources, with no corporatewide process for setting IT investment priorities.
- IT organizations and their business counterparts often have an uneasy partnership, where they find it difficult to understand how they can best collaborate for mutual success.

FOUR LEADING PROJECT "SINKHOLES"

Most time wasted on IT projects can be traced to four major reasons:

1. Vague or conflicting project definition and scope
2. Lack of clearly articulated expectations
3. Competing (and shifting) priorities
4. No process established for problem resolution and feedback

Through careful planning and clear and continuous communications, these trip wires can usually be avoided. At worst, they can be quickly overcome with minimal damage.

The secret? Facilitated workshops where team members and business sponsors can openly hash out differences, identify potential conflicts, and agree on key aspects such as project scope, deliverables, and dependencies (see Exhibit 2).

Exhibit 2. Steps to Workshop Success

Step	Outcome
Secure the commitment of executive sponsors, both within IT and with the business side	• Sponsors more likely to personally participate at appropriate intervals • Visible management support engenders enthusiastic participation
Involve at least a few team members in the creation of the workshop agenda	• Identifies issues that may have been missed • Fosters a greater sense of commitment to the workshop results
Communicate how and why facilitated sessions will play a critical role in the success of the project	• Establishes facilitated sessions as important components of a successful project • Sets expectations that everyone will make time to contribute
Identify and invite participants and include representative example of stakeholder groups that lie outside of the project team, such as business sponsors, HR, and marketing	• Diverse perspectives can enrich results • Upfront involvement can secure early commitment from important supporters
Create and distribute a preparation package (executive project overview document), which includes workshop objectives, scope, a carefully timed agenda and expected deliverables — along with any pre-reading that will increase the value of face-to-face meeting time	• Sets realistic expectations • Members can more fully contribute to all conversations • Provides chance to revalidate participant list
Assign dedicated roles for each workshop: facilitator and document manager	• Ensures that objectives are met in time frame allotted • Output will be made available for immediate distribution
Arrange for logistics conducive to creating an open, supportive environment (e.g., space, refreshments, ambiance)	• A team that's comfortable and well-fed is more likely to contribute to the best of its ability

In the pages that follow, you will read about a major project under way at Cenemex, a fictitious company that is about to roll out a new enterprise resource planning (ERP) application affecting all 5,000 employees in 16 countries.

KICKING OFF THE PROJECT WITH A BANG

Like so many other major IT projects, the Cenemex ERP project falls prey to every single one of the four "favorite" leading project time wasters. We will first see the project as it unfolds without the benefit of facilitated sessions.

Exhibit 3.   Recovery Workshop Agenda

AGENDA FOR DAY ONE

8:00 A.M.	Continental Breakfast	
8:30	Introductions/Overview/Agenda	
8:45	Kickoff by Executive Sponsors	
9:00	TEAM NORMS	(Establish rules of conduct for the team)
9:30	PROJECT DEFINITION	(Non-negotiable factors: define Charter, Scope, Exclusions)
10:30	Break	
10:45	REALITY CHECK — evaluate existing plan	

       1. Completed
       2. Under way but not complete
       3. Under way and in jeopardy
       4. Not started
       5. "Major concerns"

12:15 P.M.	Lunch
1:00	REVISED PROJECT PLAN

       1. Project charter, scope, and phases
       2. Schedule and key deliverables
       3. Dependencies and/or competing priorities

2:30	Break

       4. Team roles and responsibilities
       5. Priority-setting mechanism
       6. Executive committee project involvement

4:50	SUMMARY and FEEDBACK
5:00	Close

AGENDA FOR DAY TWO

8:00 A.M.	Continental Breakfast	
8:30	REVIEW MATERIALS FROM DAY ONE	(Confirm and edit the document)
9:30	CRITICAL SUCCESS FACTORS	
10:00	Break	
10:15	CONTINGENCY PLANNING	
11:15	COMMUNICATION PLAN	

       (a) Project team
       (b) Executive committee

12:15 P.M.	Lunch
1:00	(c) Business units

       (d) External stakeholders
       (e) "Other communication factors"

2:30	Break
2:45	PROBLEM-RESOLUTION PROCESS

Exhibit 3. Recovery Workshop Agenda (Continued)

3:15	ACTION PLAN
	– next 30 days
	– next 60 days
4:00	WORKSHOP REVIEW
	Log any Action items and prepare summary
4:30	PRESENTATION TO EXECUTIVE SPONSOR(S)
4:50	Feedback and acknowledgments
5:00	Close

Then we will explore how facilitated working sessions can help keep the project firmly on track as Dave organizes and delivers a much-needed "Project Recovery Workshop" (see Exhibit 3).

Dave Doyle, ERP project manager, has been with Cenemex for five years, all of it in corporate IT. He has earned the respect of CIO Belinda King, a fast-track executive who has been with the company just under two years. Belinda knows that a successful outcome of this ERP project will place her firmly in the running for an executive VP slot within the next 18 months.

Of the 14 full-time corporate IT project team members, about half are highly technical and work independently on most projects. The other half is split roughly between seasoned project managers and individual contributors who spend most of their time as part of project teams. In addition to the core team members, another eight to 12 field IT professionals make up the "extended" team.

The project, slated to last between 18 and 24 months, has been blessed by the executive committee members, who have high hopes that a successful ERP will provide the competitive advantages they need to sustain profitability. Belinda had persuaded them that for a $22M investment, Cenemex could expect to see dramatic reductions in manufacturing and distribution costs, significant increases in revenue, and a 50 percent decrease in the "time to order" to "time to cash."

With help from Belinda and one of the more senior project team members, Dave pulls together a two-day project kickoff meeting. His overall objective: To get the project off to a smooth start by agreeing on fundamentals such as project goals, scope, roles and responsibilities, and critical success factors. He would also like to use this off-site session as an opportunity for team-building, given that some of the team members have not worked well together in the past.

Included are the core team members, four of the remote IT team members, and two consultants from the systems integration company that will participate in the early stages of the project.

427

TIME WASTER 1: VAGUE OR CONFLICTING PROJECT DEFINITION AND SCOPE

Once Belinda rallies the troops with a rousing introduction, she leaves Dave to run the rest of the meeting. After leading group introductions and making welcoming comments, Dave gets down to business by reviewing the project definition and scope. This part, he had guessed, would be the easiest. After all, everyone had received a copy of the project plan proposal that Belinda had presented to the executive committee.

The 15 minutes that he has mentally allotted to this part soon expands into a heated three-hour discussion. Among the questions that emerge (one often over another): How was this related to other past and current projects? How could an ERP application really deliver the kind of benefits quantified in Belinda's proposal? Was this project not going to be just like the one that poor Joe tried to launch a couple of years ago (the one that cost him his job)? Who determined when the project would be "complete"? Is this scope realistic for this group to achieve in the agreed-upon time frame?

After allowing this conversation to run on through lunchtime, Dave throws up his hands and asserts that the scope as written in the project proposal was the one they were going to live with. End of story. As they break for lunch, team members express varying degrees of frustration, confusion, anger, and resignation. Most leave feeling that their questions and concerns had gone unheard, and that they will have far less influence in the project than they had hoped.

Among the likely results: Team members will tune out the rest of the meeting. Most are likely to disengage from the project before it starts. Without a clear agreement about what the project will accomplish or include, the scope will continually expand and contract, wreaking havoc with the schedule, leaving team members vulnerable to accusations of slipped deadlines and missed expectations. Changes will be requested, and without criteria regarding what belongs and what does not, the project is likely to grind to a halt at several junctures along the way (see Exhibit 4).

TIME WASTER 2: LACK OF CLEARLY ARTICULATED EXPECTATIONS

Two months after the now-infamous kickoff meeting, Dave feels that despite a rocky start, the project seems to be running pretty smoothly. Few people have aired any issues at the biweekly team meetings and even fewer have reported any problems to him. Most team members say they are on target to meet agreed-upon milestones.

Exhibit 4. When to Bring in an External Facilitator

- No one on the team is regarded as neutral and able to demonstrate impartiality
- Project team members all need to participate fully in the working session
- Issues are likely to be contentious and will require an expert who can deflect problems and keep the group focuses
- A sense of urgency makes it imperative that sessions are planned and delivered rapidly
- There is recognition that a trained facilitator can get more out of the team than any existing members

One day, as Dave is passing through the cafeteria, he catches wind of a spirited conversation a few team members are having at a table in a far corner. He is stunned by what he hears:

- "My deliverables are complete for this month. Now I can take it easy for the next week or two ..."
- "How can you say that? I'm depending on you to complete a whole host of other deliverables before I can make any progress. You're not even *close* to finishing!"
- "Hey, no one ever told me I was responsible for those things. As far as I am concerned, someone else is doing all of that."
- "Well, who do you *think* is working on it?"
- "To tell you the truth, I don't know. Ask me if I care."
- "You know something? I don't think any of us really knows exactly what the other one is doing. Wouldn't you think that Dave would be concerned?"
- "Nah. He's just happy he can tell Belinda that everything is going just fine. I think the guy's oblivious to what we're really doing — or *not* doing."

His knees turning to jelly, Dave makes his way back to his office and does a quick calculation of how much time has been lost with team members waiting on missed deliverables, which are apparently not on *anyone's* radar screen. Then he realizes that this cafeteria conversation included only three project team members. Would he have to multiply the time lost by three or four, if all members feel the same way?

TIME WASTER 3: COMPETING PRIORITIES

As the project chugs along in fits and spurts, more demands are placed on team members as business priorities change. In some cases, the business sponsor for the ERP project is adding new requirements to list that is now so long, the project time could literally double as a result. Since no one has said anything to the contrary, the business sponsor is fully expecting all requirements to be fulfilled.

At the same time, business sponsors of other projects are complaining loudly that their needs are going unmet. They insist on stealing "just a little" time from ERP project team members to get their own projects on track. Because the ERP project team is "virtual" in nature, many members actually report directly to the business units that fund them. They agree to devote some time to their business units over the coming months. In most cases these agreements are tacit. Dave is unaware that he has lost up to a day a week from many key team members.

When Belinda asks Dave for a project update, he confesses that they are way behind schedule. When pressed for a reason, Dave scratches his head. He allows that the project scope has expanded somewhat, but that none of his team members had raised any red flags as a result. He also acknowledges that some of his team members may be spending time on other projects, but he thought this time was negligible.

Belinda keeps her anger in check as she suggests to Dave that he and the team regroup immediately and pinpoint all problems that are causing these delays and develop action plans to solve these problems. She wants a report by the end of the week.

TIME WASTER 4: NO PROCESSES OR TOOLS FOR PROBLEM RESOLUTION

Dave calls an emergency team meeting that afternoon. A few of the team members are off site with their business managers. He begins by blowing off some pent-up steam, which takes the team by surprise. After all, Dave has not voiced any concern about the schedule slips so far. Posting the original project schedule on the wall, he uses red ink to show how far they were from their milestones. He turns to the team and asks them why they thought they had fallen so badly behind.

He hears a chorus of replies:

- "The scope kept changing and we never knew when to say 'no'."
- "We had different ideas about who does what, and some things haven't been getting done."
- "The guy I report to had some really critical problems only I could help solve."
- "We figured you didn't have a problem with what we were doing."

Dave is once again shocked by what he hears. He realizes his team members are right and that he needs to quickly demonstrate leadership.

"Okay," he says. "I hear you. And I *am* sorry I didn't hear you long before this. We haven't had great communications and I accept responsibility for that. Now, how can we work together to get this project going back in the right direction? I have promised that I would give Belinda an action plan for getting on track by the end of the week. Now, who has some ideas?"

Team members look around the table. Some shrug. Others blink. None knows how bullish they can be in making recommendations. The team has never established precedence for surfacing or tackling problems. All wait for Dave to take the lead. And he waits for someone else.

HOW FACILITATED SESSIONS CAN AVERT PROJECT SINKHOLES

Can a single facilitated session, even if executed superbly, help overcome all of these project time wasters? Probably not. But if planned and implemented thoughtfully, a "project jump-start" session, combined with ongoing facilitated meetings, can address many of these issues before they have a chance to grow into full-blown problems.

Why is a facilitated session so important? A facilitated session:

- Establishes a structured, formal forum for two-way communications
- Accelerates problem resolution and clarifies likely areas of confusion up front
- Provides an environment where all team members can contribute ideas and raise questions
- Ensures that the team meets critical objectives in the allotted time
- Uses session output as a communication vehicle to inform all interested project stakeholders

"RECOVERY WORKSHOP" GETS PROJECT BACK ON TRACK

Dave knows he needs to act fast to save the project — and quite possibly, his career — from imminent disaster. He calls for a two-day emergency session starting tomorrow at 8 A.M. sharp and adjourns the meeting to prepare.

He enlists the help of Sally McGuire, an ace facilitator from Human Resources, who drops everything to bail out Dave, an old friend who has helped her in the past.

Together, they review the steps Dave needs to take, along with the intended outcome. Given the urgent nature of Dave's "Project Recovery Workshop," he must compress these steps into just a few hours, rather than the few days that would typically be needed.

Exhibit 5. Workshop Overview Document

RECOVERY WORKSHOP

PURPOSE: To evaluate the current ERP project environment and build a revised project plan and processes to ensure successful completion

SCOPE

- Team members
- Project definition — nondefinition factors
- Reality check (Where are we now?)
- Revised Project Plan
  - Schedule and deliverables
  - Dependencies
  - Roles and responsibilities
  - Priority-setting mechanism
  - Executive committee involvement
- Critical Success Factors
- Contingency Plan
- Communication Plan
  - (a) Within the project team
  - (b) For executive committee
  - (c) To business units
  - (d) To external stakeholders
- Problem-resolution process
- Next Steps (Action plan for 30 days and 60 days)

Exclusions: War Stories
　　　　　　References to specific individuals

DELIVERABLES

- Every member of the team will contribute to and agree to support the Revised Project Plan.
- Each individual on the project team will know how key processes are to be managed (such as priority setting, contingency planning, communication, problem resolution).
- There will be a clear Action Plan to move forward from this session.

ASSUMPTIONS

- The project deadline is fixed; no further time extension is possible.
- The current budget is approved; the Revised Project Plan is not expected to increase the cost of implementing ERP.
- The selected vendor is contracted to deliver the product; no alternatives will be considered.
- The skills required to complete this project exist in the current team members.

Exhibit 5. Workshop Overview Document (Continued)

TEAM MEMBERS

- Dave Doyle
- 14 full-time team members
- 6 of the "extended" IT professionals
- 1 vendor rep
- 2 business reps (HR and Marketing)
- 1 document manager
- 1 (trained and experienced) facilitator

---

1. Dave meets informally with a few key team members and solicits their input regarding what elements they consider most critical for a successful project recovery workshop. Based on these conversations, Dave creates a draft agenda (see Exhibit 3).

2. He sits down with Belinda and with the key business sponsor for the ERP project and works with them to map out an executive project overview document (Exhibit 5), ensuring that they agree with the workshop objectives and the agenda. Dave secures their commitment to kick off the session, reviewing key points and assigning each a precise time slot.

3. Based on the objectives, Dave realizes that he should include not only the core team members and all remote team members, but also one or two representatives from key business units. He also realizes that because he himself must contribute fully to the discussions, he needs a skilled facilitator to keep the meeting on track and ensure that objectives are met. Sally has already agreed to perform this role. He also needs a document manager whose job is to capture and communicate all workshop output. Dave taps a newly minted junior project leader for the task.

4. Dave sends each participant an e-mail, which includes the workshop overview document as well as a personal message, underscoring how important this workshop will be to the success of the project. This session will also set the stage for more such sessions as an important forum for ongoing communication. He attaches the project proposal Belinda had created for the executive committee, as well as a memo from the CEO, discussing how vital this project is for the success of the company.

5. Dave asks his administrative assistant to arrange for a comfortable working space removed from the office, with plenty of light, a U-shaped table, lots of flip charts and wall space, and adjustable temperature settings. His assistant also arranges for copies of all needed documents and audiovisual equipment and supplies.

6. At 8 A.M. the next day, Dave welcomes the team and relaxes perceptibly as Belinda and the business sponsor kick off the day with an inspiring vision of what Cenemex can become with the new ERP application. Looking around the room at his newly energized team, Dave knows that he can count on Sally to capitalize on the momentum and lead the team on the first step of a successful recovery.

CONCLUSION

Even the most well-planned project can be derailed. Sometimes the factors lie beyond the ability of the project team to control, such as a sudden downsizing of budget or staff, or a last-minute "critical" business requirement that *must* be accommodated.

But just as often, project derailments can be avoided by the project team. One key: a facilitated launch workshop where members reach consensus of vital project elements, such as scope, responsibilities, problem-solving process, dependencies and risks, and process for managing changes. This way, all team members quickly reach a shared understanding of the desired end state, as well as the "journey" they will be taking together to get there. Issues can be deflected and areas of confusion can be resolved. This kickoff session models the kind of open communications forum the team can expect to partake in for the duration of the project.

Such facilitated sessions should not begin and end with the project kickoff. (And with good planning and open communications, a "recovery workshop" should not be needed.) Many project team meetings would benefit from facilitated sessions, especially when problems need to be resolved, teamwide commitment or agreement is needed, or well-informed decisions must be made quickly.

A relatively small amount of time allocated early in the project life cycle can pay huge dividends later. Establishing structured, facilitated workshops helps ensure that team members work interactively and build shared comprehension and commitment throughout the project.

With the appropriate people, tools, and processes in place, project management can actually be fun. Team members and the project manager will gain confidence, enhance their professional reputations, and deliver results that actually make a difference.

Chapter 39

Reducing IT Project Complexity

John P. Murray

The pressures that drive IT project complexity are numerous. IT application project complexity is generated from a variety of sources. It can be taken as an IT project precept that virtually every project will increase in complexity once it has been approved. Two basic issues tend to drive the increase in complexity. First, IT projects are generally approved for development before all the ramifications of what is to be delivered from the project are clearly understood. For whatever reason, there is always an urgency to set a completion date for the project, regardless of how limited the information concerning the scope of the project. Second, once approved, IT projects are too often seen as opportunities to load on any number of ancillary items which, while they may be of benefit, do not justify extending project development time and associated risk. This second item can be considered as a cost/benefit issue — namely, that the benefits to be gained from adding on items are usually not justified by the additional risk those items pose to the project.

The typical pattern is that everyone involved in an application development project will be found to have contributed to the pressure to enlarge the project and, as a result, add to its vulnerability. Factors such as attempting to gain as much functionality as possible, to correct existing business problems in other production applications, and to incorporate new business practices are often seen as plausible reasons within the business units to encourage project growth. From the IT side, there is interest in using new development software; in moving to more sophisticated operating systems, communications techniques, and hardware; or trying new development methods. Within the senior management group, there is an interest in improving the organization's competitive position within its industry, in taking advantage of an opportunity to move to a higher level of customer service, and, often, in an assumed ability to reduce expense.

Given the levels of interest in the perceived benefits of the project and the pressure from several areas to expand features and functions, it is easy to understand why IT development applications often increase in complexity as their design moves forward. It is important to recognize the relationship between project growth and increased levels of project complexity and risk. Unfortunately, it is too often the case that that relationship, if indeed it is understood, tends to be forgotten as the project moves forward. People typically get caught up in the euphoria associated with the excitement of a new development project, and, as a result, a march begins to load up the project. It is often assumed that a little more here and a little more there will not add much to the project. Although that may be the case with individual items, combined, those items can lead to considerable difficulty.

A typical development scenario often follows a pattern in which a business need is identified and an approach to accommodate the need through the development of an IT application is proposed, taken to senior management, and approved. Almost without fail, once the project concept has been approved, the expansion process begins. Small changes are often presented as being necessary to the improvement of the business issues being addressed by the project. Or, it may be that items are proposed that are not entirely necessary for the business needs to be addressed, but because they are small, or appear to be small and therefore will not require much in the way of time or resources, they are added to the project. The result is a cumulative process that in a short time has added a considerable amount of burden to the project. Usually, although the items have been added, the original project completion date remains the same.

From the IT side of the project, comes a push to include technology items that, while not necessary to address the business issues of the application, may be nice to have or may form the basis for moving the organization to some new level of technology. Or, worst case, using the technology may be good for the resumes of individuals within the IT department. For example, the project may be seen as an opportunity to move to the use of object-oriented technology, which has not been used before within the IT department. That proposition is likely to be prefaced with a statement such as "this would be an ideal project to get us into the object world." At that point, several salient questions should be raised. First, what are the business benefits to be found in the use of object-oriented technology and second, how much will the level of project risk be raised by using the technology?

It may be that the project does provide a strong opportunity to move to object technology, and it may be that doing so is in the best interest of the organization. The important issue here should not be seen as the need for movement to a new technology but rather, is this the right time and the right project in which to learn object technology. Too often, perhaps because of their size and complexity, new technology approaches are attached to large IT projects. Taking that approach is almost a guarantee of serious project difficulty. The best place to begin that learning is with a small, noncritical project in which time can be taken to learn and dealing with mistakes will not jeopardize the entire organization.

THE TRADE-OFF BETWEEN ADDED VALUE AND INCREASED PROJECT COMPLEXITY

The question to ask, relative not only to the use of new technology or approaches but to any other project encumbrances, is How will this, in terms of lengthening the project or adding complexity, affect the project? If the answer is that the effect will be negative or the answer is not clear, caution should be exercised with regard to opening the project to include those additional items. The argument should not be allowed to move to the validity of the requests or their value. It should be recognized that the proposed additions to the project would all probably be beneficial. The issue is what, in terms of time and complexity, will those items add to the project. The focus must be on the balance between adding the requested items whatever they may be and the potential cost in terms of project risk associated with accommodating those requests.

In thinking about adding new technology, it is important to keep in mind that either little is really understood about the technology, or that the levels of IT time and effort needed to get it to work are going to be underestimated. In dealing with medium to large IT development projects, given their inherent complexity, adding a technology learning curve portends difficulty for the project.

Given that the probability of success with IT applications projects can be increased if the complexity of those projects is reduced, taking an approach of developing more but smaller IT applications should be accorded serious consideration. Assume that a request for an IT application project is made and the request is approved for investigation. After the analysis of the request, it is found that the project as proposed will require 3,000 hours of effort to complete.

The duration of the project has been established as eight months. Although the time estimated to complete the project at this point in the development cycle is probably arbitrary, that estimate is likely to be seen as absolute. That circumstance, quite common in the development of IT projects, represents another negative aspect of project development that adds to the level of risk. Although the setting of arbitrary project completion dates present serious project complications, that is a topic beyond the scope of this chapter other than to acknowledge it as a negative factor.

Subsequent to approval, a project team is assembled and work begins on the project. As that work moves forward, requests begin to arise for additional functions within the project. Given the business needs being addressed by the project and the benefits to be derived from the expansion of the project, the levels of staffing to complete the new requirements are approved. At this point, the completion date may be moved out to accommodate the additional work, or, it may be assumed that by adding staff, the completion date need not be adjusted. In terms of outlining the increased needs of the project, adding the needed staff, and in at least attempting to reset the completion date, the project team has done the right things. What has not been done correctly and what will bring about difficulty is that the project team has not, in this situation, considered the increased complexity that has been layered into the project. The assumption is that adding staff and adjusting the completion date will cover the requirement to add features and functions.

In this example, the project team, even though it has considered the need for additional resources and time to handle the project expansion, has put itself in an unfortunate position. By not recognizing the issues of the expansion and increased complexity of the project as they relate to potential difficulty, if not serious problems, the team has set itself up for, at the least, disappointment. Too often as a project expands and it becomes clear that the project is experiencing difficulty, the focus moves to the issue of adding people and time to meet the project goals. While that is an appropriate focus, it is only a partial focus in that the factors of project expansion and its related additional complexity must also be considered in the analysis. In reality, adding people to the project, whether at the beginning of the project or after it has been determined that the project is in difficulty may be an apparently easy answer to the problem, but it may be the wrong answer. Adding more people to the project increases the level of effort associated with the issue of project management and coordination and, as a result, adds to overall project complexity.

The correct way to handle the issues involved in the example would have been, in addition to calling for more staff and time to meet the new project demands, to present and push for the option of dividing the project into more manageable components. That process might have been to structure the project into smaller components (phases), to break the work into separate projects, or to reduce the scope of the project. Finding the right answer would depend on the circumstances, but the concern should have been with avoiding undue size and, as a corollary, complexity.

It is of course correct that reducing the size of the project or breaking it into phases would cause the potential benefits associated with the project to be reduced or delayed. Every organization must make decisions about the acceptable size and risk of IT projects. However, in many instances the belief that smaller is better represents a pragmatic approach. Many large, well-intended IT applications projects have floundered. Some of those projects have been scaled back and salvaged, but others, after considerable cost and organizational stress, have been abandoned.

DETERMINING PROJECT DEVELOPMENT TOLERANCE WITHIN THE ORGANIZATION

Every organization has a particular level of IT application project development tolerance. The level within a given organization depends on a number of items throughout the organization. One approach to improving the IT development project process is to come to an understanding about the practical manageable size of IT applications projects within a particular organization. That determination can be made through a review of past projects. Reviewing the results of past IT applications development projects provides information that can be used to develop success or failure trends, which in turn, can be analyzed with reference to project size.

Some type of criteria must be developed by which to judge project "success" or "failure." Those criteria will vary within organizations, depending on those factors that are considered important within the organization. The key with regard to any single criterion used to make the judgements is that it should be seen as a reasonable measure within the organization. In addition, the criteria cannot be allowed to become cumbersome or complex. The goal here must be to select a set of basic components that will provide not the definitive answer but rather a guideline as to the probable success of a given project based upon past experience within the organization. Where that probability suggests that the project is likely to fail, adjustments must be made to bring project size, time, and complexity to a level that will provide a higher probability of success.

As an example, assume that during the past three years, the IT department has worked on 125 projects. During that time, an average of 700 development hours have been devoted to those projects, for a total of 87,500 hours. In doing an analysis of the 125 projects, it is found that, under the criteria developed for determining success or failure, 18 projects fall into the failure classification. Of those 18 projects, 14 have exceeded 900 hours of development time and again, using the success or failure criteria, all 14 projects carried a high level of complexity. In addition, only three projects taking more than 800 hours have been brought to a successful conclusion during the past three years.

At this point, what the analysis shows is that, within this organization, projects that exceed 900 hours of development time are prone to failure. The result of that analysis indicates that IT development projects in excess of 900 hours of effort seem to be beyond the management capabilities of the IT department. Another fact developed from the analysis showed that over the three-year period, three IT project managers had, regardless of the size or complexity of the project, always brought their projects in on time, within budget, and in accord with the project requirements.

Several quick conclusions can be drawn from the analysis. First, it is probably not in the interest of the organization to consider any applications development projects that approach or exceed 900 hours of effort. Second, several project managers are, in spite of the development environment, able to bring projects to a successful conclusion. Two conclusions can be drawn about the role of those project managers. First, those project managers should be assigned to the largest, most complex projects within the organization. Second, further study should be done to determine why those managers are successful.

Where the analysis is carefully done and the criteria used to judge success or failure are reasonable and consistent, patterns of IT project development success and failure can be identified. Done correctly, the analysis of prior applications projects should provide information about the optimum level of project size and complexity with regard to probable success. That should not be seen to imply that whatever that level is it is the best that can be accomplished. What it means is that for the present, a ceiling on project size can be determined. Remaining under that ceiling can bring about an immediate improvement in the management of projects, but it should also be seen as setting the base for moving to new practices that will allow that ceiling to be raised.

So, the analysis meets two requirements. It provides a guideline as to the limits of project size and associated complexity within the organization. It also provides the basis for moving forward to bring about changes within the organization, particularly within the IT department, that will lead to the ability in the future to handle larger, more complex applications projects.

In the example used, several conclusions can be drawn that can be used to identify IT project development problem areas and to begin to develop plans to raise the levels of development success within the IT department. The material drawn from the analysis in the example shows that in the past, the organization got into trouble when project size exceeded 900 hours of effort. In thinking about that hour range, it should be kept in mind that not only are the hours a factor, but as the size of a project grows, the complexity of that project also grows. An inherent linkage exists between project size and complexity, and they have to be considered as inseparable when examining the causes of project failure.

With regard to size and complexity, the analysis also shows that they do not appear to be negative factors in the development of projects if the management of those projects is under the direction of one of the several strong project managers. It would be beneficial to pursue the reasons why some managers appear to do well regardless of the size or complexity of their projects. Determining what those managers are doing correctly and then applying their management techniques to the manner in which other projects are managed could bring significant benefits to the organization.

EXAMPLES OF THE FACTORS THAT ADD TO IT APPLICATIONS COMPLEXITY

Complexity, when it applies to IT projects, is going to be found in a number of areas. Some of the more prominent areas include the following situations:

- The scope of the project exceeds the ability of the organization to handle the work. In other words, the expectations of the people involved (IT and or business people) are unrealistic given the levels of resources and project development experience within the organization. It sometimes happens that an organization will recognize that it is in over its head and, in an attempt to improve the management of the project, will go outside for assistance. Doing so can be another way that the complexity associated with the project will increase.
- There is an extensive use of new (either to the IT department or the industry) technology which is deemed as critical to the success of the project.
- The business issues to be addressed by the project are either new to the organization or not well understood within it.
- The organization finds itself the victim of a vendor who promotes a series of application packages that are beyond the capacity of the organization to effectively manage. Another aspect of that phenomenon can be that the packages offered by the vendor do not deliver what had been expected and, as a result, a considerable amount of custom work has to be completed to obtain the needed results.
- The issue of project "scope creep" is not properly managed. Although a serious hindrance to successful IT project management, scope creep tends to be a common factor in the development of IT projects. Scope creep is just what the name implies — the size of the project is allowed to expand as the project moves forward. The problem here, as previously stated, is that project size relates to increased project complexity, so when scope creep is tolerated, additional complexity is likewise tolerated.

RECOGNIZING THE COORDINATION DANGERS INHERENT IN OVERLY COMPLEX IT PROJECTS

As development projects grow, the number of the factors involved in the successful completion of the project and the complexity of those factors also grows. The problem is not limited to the issue of managing the identified project components along a specified project management time line. That effort, particularly with a large project, will present significant difficulty by itself; the problem becomes much more pronounced because of increases in the external connections to the project that will require close management.

Those connections include items such as the transfer of data between existing systems and the new applications. To complicate matters, that data may be in different formats in the different systems. There may also be timing issues in terms of when data needed from one system to another is going to be updated in order to provide current information. Developing the planning for the various interactions and making certain that the data contained in the data streams are and remain current and correct can pose considerable management challenges. The task becomes more complex, because people responsible for those ancillary systems may not feel a sense of urgency about doing the work required for the support of the new applications. That is not necessarily to imply that the people do not care; it may be that, given their normal workload, accommodating the needs of the new system will not have a high priority. Obviously, delays in progress with the ancillary systems will have a waterfall effect on the development project, which will translate into delay and additional expense.

Another way to look at the issue of the connections to other systems is to consider the growth of the number of people involved as the project enlarges. It is possible that the total number of people involved might grow by a factor of three or four, or more with really large projects. As the number of people involved grows, the coordination and communication issues within the development project can become extremely difficult to manage. In that environment, not only is the risk of failure going to rise, the costs associated with attempting to manage the coordination and communications aspects are also going to rise.

Staying with the theme of the difficulties inherent in project growth, it must be recognized that beyond the increased difficulties associated with coordination and communication, the exposure to risk increases as a corollary of the growth. For example, a project of moderate size might involve six or seven key participants to take it to a successful conclusion. With a full-time project manager, the issues of coordination and control among the key group of participants can be fairly easily managed. Assume that the project grows and now, rather than six or seven key participants, the number rises to 14 or 15.

In the foregoing scenario, the number of connections relative to moving the project forward has grown considerably. The project manager is now faced with two to two-and-a-half times more people who will have to be included in dealing with project issues and decisions. That growth is very likely to require an additional project manager, so the cost of the project is going to be increased. Cost is not the only issue. While another project manager will help to lighten the load, the issue of coordination and communication between the two project managers must be recognized and managed.

The increase in the number of connections as the project grows will not be limited to the people-associated problems; the apparently simple issues associated with the coordination of all the aspects of the project will expand rapidly. There will be additional hardware issues, and there may be the issue of dealing with different systems, data formats, and operating systems and the timing and use of testing to handle the work being done in the different areas can become major items. Making certain that everything needed is available at the appropriate time now becomes a much larger task than it was before the project grew.

Issues associated with the testing phases of the project development process grow dramatically as the scope and complexity of the project expands. What that means in practical terms is that more attention must be paid to the management of the testing processes and to the verification of the testing results. For example, assume that a test is run in one set of programs within the project and changes are required to the programs to correct testing errors. Although those programs are correct, the changes to the application have created the need to make changes in several other applications within the project. So the issue becomes not only one of appropriate unit testing, but also of carrying the testing changes to other areas of the project. Again, the issues of coordination and communication are of serious concern. The issue is not limited to large complex projects; it is common in many IT projects. However, what raises the level of concern in large projects is that the change environment becomes much more difficult to manage.

TAKING STEPS TO CONTROL IT PROJECT COMPLEXITY

Discipline must be seen as a critical success factor in any IT development project. When dealing with the issue of the control of IT project complexity, the work can be made considerably easier if an appropriate level of discipline is a component of the development process. The importance of discipline as it relates to project success has to be recognized, and its application must be consistent throughout the entire development process.

Moving to a higher level of discipline, particularly in organizations where it has been lacking, can be a difficult task. Attempting to improve the discipline associated with maintaining and controlling the size and complexity of IT applications projects is not easy. Adopting a more disciplined project management approach is likely to open the IT department to charges of being unwilling to provide higher levels of service, of being uncooperative, and of lacking a sense of customer service. In organizations in which there is already a level of hostility between the IT department and other sections within the organization, attempting to raise the level of IT project development will increase that hostility.

When it comes to the issue of project discipline, one of the duties of those who have responsibility for the eventual success of the project must be to very carefully assess the size and complexity of what is being proposed within the project. Although there is a natural tendency to want to accommodate any and all requests for features and functions within a particular system, that tendency must be modified by the reality of the possible. Accommodating every request should not be the goal of the project; rather the goal should be to deliver a reasonable set of functions and features on time and within budget. If project discipline is in place at the beginning of the project, and is consistently maintained throughout the project, the eventual result is much more likely to be what everyone had expected. When that occurs, everyone benefits.

Assessing proposed IT development projects in terms of the size, features, and functions to be delivered within the established project funding and schedule should be seen as being a joint effort between the IT department and those business units in which the new applications will be used. To be effective, the work associated with coming to a realistic project size cannot be done through a process in which the members of the IT department attempt to mandate project size. The approach has to be to include every area that has an interest in the ultimate result of the project and to work out a compromise that comes as close as possible to meeting the needs of all the areas. Those needs must be met within the context of maintaining reasonable project size and complexity.

What constitutes "reasonable" project size and complexity? There will be a different answer to that question for every organization and every project. Each time an IT project is proposed, except for small projects, the issue of reasonableness is going to have to carefully considered. Taking the time to make that consideration should be seen as one component of improved project management discipline.

It is understandable, given the pressure on everyone involved to deliver more function and features at an increasingly rapid pace, to want to be as responsive as possible. The apparent way to do that is to include as much as possible into a single project. That issue can be compounded by the need for various features and the very real possibility that, if they are not included in the current project, the opportunity to get them may simply be lost. Where the need is recognized, along with the often real situation that *now* may be the only time to obtain the particular features, it is very difficult to resist loading as much into the project as possible. However, the important question here has to do with the probability that the project, having grown too large to effectively manage, will fail, and nothing (or perhaps very little) will be delivered.

Having come to a realistic assessment of what can be delivered in terms of IT projects within an organization, IT management has both an obligation and a duty to set and hold the line on project size and complexity. If developing the project in phases or as several or even a series of smaller projects makes good business sense, that route should be taken. The idea has to be to assist the organization to avoid making project mistakes.

CONCLUSION

Although IT projects are inherently complex and difficult to manage, and the larger and more complex the project the more difficult effective management becomes, steps can be taken to mitigate the potential difficulties associated with IT projects. To begin, there must be an awareness within the IT department that project size and complexity represent the primary factors with regard to project success or failure. Organizations must come to some level of understanding as to what the particular culture can successfully absorb in regard to project size. When that understanding has been reached, everyone involved has to be willing to cooperate to make certain that proposed projects do not exceed a size and complexity that presents a reasonable chance for success.

Restraining the natural tendency to add as much function and as many features as possible onto every new IT project must be seen as a discipline that must be accommodated within the organization. The goal has to be one of balance, between obtaining the most value possible from the project while avoiding a risk of failure that is too high for the organization. One of the problems is that in many organizations, the ability of the IT department to meet the needs of the organization has been constrained by the use of arbitrary IT funding levels. Those funding levels are usually too low, and the result is that IT cannot meet the business needs of the organization. Where that circumstance has existed over a period of years, the result is often to try to gain at least some of the needed business items through IT project overloading.

An important aspect of making the changes needed to reduce the risk of IT project failure must be to recognize the cultural issues involved in dealing with the problem. Making the needed changes is going to have to be a joint effort between all areas involved in IT projects. In order to begin the process, IT management should provide the needed leadership. Preparing and presenting factual information highlighting existing IT project development approaches that lead to difficulty, coupled with a factual analysis of the level of development capability within the organization, constitutes the first step in moving to improvement.

The next and more difficult step is going to be to "sell" the benefits of making needed changes throughout the organization. Doing that, as is the case with any cultural change, will not be quick or easy, but IT managers should see making it happen as one of their mandates. In many organizations, developing a case that the current processes are not working will not be difficult. Using that case as the basis of a presentation to senior management for support to begin to take a different approach to the way IT projects are considered and structured within the organization should provide support for needed changes. Where there is a clear, well-presented review of the facts, coupled with a well-developed plan to move to improvements, the probability of the support of senior management will be high.

Chapter 40
Designing an Effective Project Management Office

Leigh Hardy and Tom Chaudhuri

An organization setting up or developing a project management office (PMO) must necessarily consider a range of dimensions and responsibilities such as those discussed in this chapter. In many cases, organizations unsystematically grapple with the design process. This chapter proposes that a group setting up a PMO can shortcut the process of designing a PMO, that will match the requirements and priorities of their organizations, by systematically evaluating the dimensions listed herein and adopting the design options that best meet their needs.

As the move to "manage by projects" becomes more popular in organizations, there is also a move to set up PMOs to support project management. The role of these PMOs is diverse and varied, but commonly includes setting standards and methodologies for project management. Often, this role is expanded to include aspects of project human resource management and sometimes to include responsibility for the execution of projects.

Confronted with the task of setting up a project office, the responsible executive or group must define the roles and responsibilities of the office. Some authors have identified several types of project office design such as the PMO as repository of project management knowledge, or the project office as a functional group responsible for managing projects. However, these models oversimplify the variety of designs that are possible. This chapter contends that there is an almost limitless variety of possible designs.

A framework is presented for designing a project office that is appropriate to the needs of an organization. A number of key dimensions and responsibilities that should be considered are identified. These have been subdivided into: organizational factors; human resource responsibilities; responsibilities for setting project management standards; project execution responsibilities; and strategic responsibilities. These dimensions and responsibilities are discussed in terms of the choices that are available, and the reasons for adopting a particular design. This chapter takes the position that there is no one ideal design for a PMO and that the design of a PMO within an organization should (and will) evolve over time as the organizational requirements and priorities change and the organization's project maturity and competencies change.

ORGANIZATIONAL FACTORS

A starting point in setting up and designing a project management office is establishing the organizational role and power of the office. Some of these organizational factors may be mandated by the executive or group setting up the office, but frequently they are refined as a PMO evolves. These factors are pivotal to the roles and responsibilities of a PMO. The following are some of the core design factors to be addressed in establishing and designing a PMO.

Reporting Arrangements

The reporting relationship of a PMO is an important factor in establishing the power and potential roles of a PMO. A variety of reporting arrangements is possible. A PMO can be set up as an independent group reporting directly to a president or executive committee. This potentially provides the office with considerable power and independence. Alternatively, a PMO can report to an executive within a functional department. This provides a lesser degree of independence but may still provide the group with considerable power. The reporting arrangement can be at lower levels; but in these cases, the role of the PMO generally becomes more restricted to particular areas of an organization's operations.

In addition to the external reporting arrangements, there are a variety of possible internal reporting arrangements that may impact the roles of a PMO. For example, in geographically dispersed organizations, there are benefits in establishing separate PMOs. These PMOs may report locally but be affiliated with the other PMOs or report to a central PMO. Matrix reporting relationships are also common.

Organizational Positioning

PMOs can be established as stand-alone groups or can be part of a functional group such as information technology (IT) or operations. Typically, a PMO will be positioned in a functional group with prime ownership for projects. For example, in financial institutions that are heavily reliant on information technology and its development, PMOs are often located in the IT areas. This has the benefit of bringing a PMO close to the project execution areas; however, there can be a downside when the PMO is seen to be too heavily influenced by the functional group in which it is located. Broadening the reporting arrangement to a cross-functional steering committee can overcome this concern.

Projects in Scope

There is a wide variation in the scope of projects for which a PMO can have responsibility. PMO responsibilities can include all the projects undertaken by an organization; all the projects undertaken by a particular functional group such as IT; or projects of a certain type. The scope of responsibility should be closely aligned to an organization's needs. Typically, when PMOs are first established, scope is restricted within an organization. This is often part of a "prove yourself" strategy as organizations assess the value of a structured approach to project management. PMOs may be established to progress particular organizational priorities. For example, many organizations set up PMOs to oversee and implement special projects. Similarly, PMOs have been set up to support organizational transformation projects or to facilitate organizational acquisitions. Projects in scope typically evolve over time to reflect changing organizational strategies and also organizational project management maturity.

Ownership of Resources

A PMO can operate as an independent group with a mandate to oversee and influence projects but without direct control of projects. In these cases, a PMO can be quite small in size. Alternatively, a PMO can "own" the staff who undertake projects. This could be restricted to owning an organization's project managers but could extend as far as owning an organization's total pool of project resources. All these models have been adopted. The choice depends on the expected extent of direct involvement in projects.

A Permanent or Temporary Office

A PMO can be set up either as a temporary or permanent office. A temporary office may be set up to manage a particular group of projects. For example, a number of organizations set up PMOs to overview their Year 2000 initiatives. Other examples include managing an acquisition or managing a major organizational transformation project. The motivation for a temporary office is to support a set of projects with a fixed duration. A permanent office is suited to supporting an organization's projects on an ongoing basis.

Although an organization may initially adopt the temporary model, the value demonstrated and the infrastructure established often lead to the PMO being given expanded responsibilities and a continued mandate.

Size and Budget

In addition to the direct ownership of project resources, budget and staff resources are fundamental organizational factors to be addressed. Clearly, the staff and budget need to be increased as the responsibilities and capabilities of a PMO are expanded.

HUMAN RESOURCE RESPONSIBILITIES

A PMO can have a broad range of human resource-related responsibilities. These responsibilities can range from no responsibility for human resources to a role where a PMO takes on a wide range of human resource responsibilities for project resources. These expansive roles can occur both in the case when project resources report directly to a PMO and in cases where resources report independently to different functional groups. Potential human resource responsibilities of a PMO include the following.

Recruitment and Selection

A PMO can have responsibility for recruiting and selecting project staff. This may be restricted to a narrow group of positions such as project managers or it could include a broad cross-section of project resources. Recruiting and selecting staff provides an opportunity to have a significant impact on the project management culture of an organization, to ensure that skills acquired align with projects in scope, and to shortcut the development of project management skills.

Training and Certification

PMOs can take on the role of providing project management training to organizational staff. They may do this by providing this training themselves or they may facilitate this through outside vendors. In these cases, the role generally would include the selection of vendors. Responsibilities can also include the certification of project managers.

A PMO may set minimum standards that staff must achieve to be selected or promoted as project managers, or set a project management accreditation path within the organization. For example, an organization may agree that only externally accredited project managers be designated as project managers. Training and certification provide a PMO with significant opportunity to develop and promote project management skills.

Appraisal and Promotion

Appraisal of project managers often provides challenges that are not present in the traditional hierarchical organization. Project managers often move between projects and consequently between different sponsors and managers. This makes it difficult for consistency and comprehensiveness of appraisal. A PMO can play a central role in the appraisal process by providing appropriate templates and guidelines and acting as a coordinating point to obtain and combine appraisals from a variety of managers. This role can be expanded to being responsible for making or recommending promotions. The need for these roles increases as the movement of project managers across diverse projects increases.

Providing Resources to Projects

A role that PMOs can fill is to coordinate the provision of resources to projects. This could be restricted to the allocation of project managers, but could extend to providing entire project teams. As the size of an organization and its project resource pool increases, there is an increased need to systematically manage resources. This includes both managing availability and competencies. For example, in a large IT group where there may be hundreds of employees with a diverse set of skills, it is important to know when staff are available and the skills that the staff have in order to make the most effective use of resources. This facilitates the alignment of resources and requirements and the minimization of idle resources. A role that PMOs have provided is to maintain a project resource repository and to use this to manage the allocation of project resources. In a resource pool with hundreds or even thousands of resources, this becomes a major undertaking. Even in a smaller resource group, the uncertainty associated with project execution and competing priorities in an organization can make this a daunting task.

Time Recording

A PMO can have the responsibility for managing a time recording system. This role may include selecting the time recording tool and tracking time spent. This may also include analyzing staff utilization or time to be charged to a client, utilization against budget, etc. These roles are most relevant in large organizations and organizations where staff time is billed to the department being served.

Career Planning

A PMO can have the role of supporting the career planning of an organization's project resources. This role can be linked to other human resource responsibilities such as recruitment, training, certification, appraisal, and resource allocation. A PMO, by monitoring and administering these factors, can potentially play a significant role in career planning — both from an organization's and an individual's perspective. This has value, both in supporting individual growth and in building organizational capability.

Personnel Administration

Personnel administration, such as managing holiday schedules and sick leave, administering salaries and bonuses, etc., can be a role for which a PMO is responsible. Reasons for having a PMO undertake these roles include freeing project and program managers from these day-to-day responsibilities to better focus their efforts on project execution.

External Vendor Management

PMOs are frequently exposed to a variety of external vendors due to the central role they play in a variety of projects. These may include recruitment agencies, service providers, hardware and software vendors, management consultants, etc. The multiple exposures that come from these interactions may place PMOs in a position where they are best able to manage the relationships with these vendors.

Counseling and Mentoring

A PMO may provide either formal or informal counseling and mentoring to project resources. This role can be especially useful to support new project management staff, such as when an organization is establishing project management or new staff are recruited.

RESPONSIBILITIES FOR SETTING PROJECT MANAGEMENT STANDARDS

Establishing project management standards is a common role for PMOs. This set of responsibilities provides the opportunity for a PMO to influence how an organization undertakes projects. These responsibilities help to set the organizational infrastructure for projects. This can provide both a direct and an indirect influence on projects.

Setting Project Management Methodologies

This role can include either, or both, defining project execution standards and defining project life cycle standards. The former relates to setting parameters for items such as documentation, reporting, sign-offs, issue management, etc. The latter relates to defining, usually at a high level, the sequence of activities a project will go through (e.g., requirements gathering, design, prototyping, sign-off, building, testing, and roll-out).

Defining the methodologies to be used by projects is a powerful force in influencing how an organization undertakes its projects. It is thus often a key responsibility given to a PMO when an organization expects a PMO to have a major impact on improving its project execution.

Providing Templates

This responsibility links closely to setting methodologies. By providing templates for project activities such as chartering, status reporting, risk assessment, budgeting, issue management, and post-implementation reviews, a PMO can have a very direct impact on how projects are managed. Templates can provide very explicit direction on what processes are to be followed. This enables an organization that is new to project management to quickly put standard processes in place.

Providing Project Management Tools

Providing tools has both a direct and an indirect impact on how projects are managed. Tools can range from templates (discussed above), to "off-the-shelf" project management software, to customized project management tools.

Providing Repositories

Another potential responsibility for a PMO is to set up and maintain project repositories. These can include shared computer directories for storing project documentation such as status reports and budgets; directories for maintaining all project documentation; and a central source of "best practice" project process and deliverables. A recent trend in this area is to establish Web or intranet sites.

PROJECT EXECUTION RESPONSIBILITIES

Responsibilities for project execution or delivery are closely tied to ownership of resources. A PMO that "owns resources," typically project managers or a project resource group, generally takes on much of the responsibility for delivering projects. A PMO that has responsibility for project execution will require expertise in the range of project management knowledge areas and project management processes. Many PMOs do not have this direct responsibility. Their responsibilities are more indirect, focused on supporting and building project management capability by influence. However, even in these cases, PMOs typically will have responsibility for some key processes.

Risk and Issue Management

A PMO can be given a comprehensive risk management role. This may vary from setting the standard for risk management processes to actually facilitating or conducting project risk management. Reasons to make this a PMO, rather than project, responsibility can include introducing independence, introducing greater cross-project input, and building specialty expertise.

Issue management, like risk management, responsibility can be moved to a PMO from a project. Reasons for this are similar to those for moving risk management.

Impact and Change Management

Responsibility for assessing impacts of projects on their stakeholders — customers, employees, and shareholders — can be given to a PMO. A PMO as a focus for project activity can be in a good position to be able to understand the impacts of projects, both on each other and on stakeholders. For example, a PMO may be able to overview the impacts of quite separate initiatives on employees because of its vantage point. Individual projects may not have the same ability to assess these impacts. Similarly, analyzing and understanding the organizational changes that projects cause can be a responsibility particularly suited to a PMO. The potential for a PMO to have a useful role in managing impacts and changes increases as an organization's size and project portfolio grow.

Communication

The exposure of a PMO to multiple projects places it in a good position to both manage communication among projects, and between projects and other parts of the organization. This role may extend to providing executive updates on projects to an executive group. Communication can be mediated either by direct communication such as by providing newsletters and presentations, or indirectly by providing access to project repositories such as shared directories or intranet sites. These roles become more important for larger organizations or organizations with many projects. In these cases, a PMO has the potential to provide a summarized and focused overview of projects.

Project Auditing

A major potential role for PMOs is auditing the application of project management standards. This may be done to all projects or may focus on particular "high importance" projects. This may be done by formal assessment or it may be an ongoing oversight role of a PMO. Some organizations use their regular internal audit processes, but others choose to use their PMOs due to the project management expertise that these groups may have.

Focus on Major or Special Projects

A variant on the role of a PMO in project execution is giving a PMO execution responsibility for a selected group of projects. This could include major projects, projects requiring special attention such as politically sensitive projects, or groups of related projects.

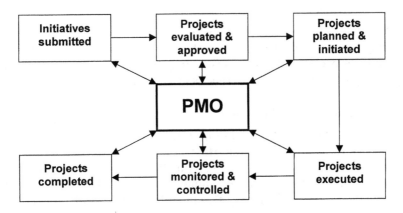

Exhibit 1. Potential Central Role of a PMO in the Project Initiation and Execution Life Cycle

RESPONSIBILITIES FOR BUSINESS STRATEGY

In organizations such as those in the communication and financial sectors, which have an ongoing major investment in technology, and others where project-related expenditures consume a major part of the discretionary budget, PMOs are ideally situated to take on an expanded strategic role. As shown in Exhibit 1, PMOs, by their involvement in many aspects of projects, are in a unique position to take on a central role in the project life cycle.

This central role, plus exposure to the life cycle of multiple projects from initiation and planning to execution and closing, places PMOs in a unique position to take a major strategic role in organizations. The strategic responsibilities of a PMO can potentially include the following.

Collection of Initiatives

A PMO can act as a central point for the gathering of initiative proposals. This role can include the provision of templates and guidelines to assist those submitting proposals.

Project Evaluation

PMOs can be a central point for project planning. This would include the evaluation of proposals against various criteria. These criteria could include evaluation of factors such as costs, benefits, strategic fit, stakeholder impacts, risk assessments, resource impacts and availability, and relationships with existing projects and schedules.

Project Prioritization

The PMO role can also include the prioritization of the proposals received. This may be from a cost/benefit or other financial perspective, but may also include prioritization by assessing project resource availability, project impact evaluations, and risk assessments.

Project Planning and Scheduling

PMOs can play a key role in planning individual projects by providing appropriate tools and templates. However, because of their exposure to multiple projects, PMOs are in an ideal position to coordinate projects and entire programs. Projects may be planned and scheduled by coordinating tasks and dependencies, but may also include resource and impact considerations.

Project Approval and Funding

An extension of the prioritization and scheduling role is the formal approval and funding role. A PMO cannot replace other organizational groups in planning or managing an organization's discretionary budgets and activities. However, they are ideally positioned to coordinate and facilitate these processes.

Project Monitoring and Controlling

Once projects have commenced, a PMO can take on the role of monitoring project progress. This is already a common role of PMOs. By implementing and reviewing regular status reporting, a PMO is able to monitor elements such as cost, resource utilization, timing, and progress against plan. This information provides a basis for exercising control over projects. Remedial action can be taken on projects that are failing to meet cost and other plan targets.

Project Portfolio Management

An extension of the monitoring and controlling role is the management of the portfolio of projects. A delay, or speedy progress, in one project may provide opportunities for other projects. Similarly, monitoring a portfolio of projects enables rapid response to changing organizational priorities; resources can be moved from one initiative to another, or scope or time priorities can be adjusted.

AN EXAMPLE OF APPLYING DESIGN PRINCIPLES

Exhibit 2 provides a number of common design alternatives for the factors discussed above. The checklist enables a rapid evaluation of factors that should be considered in designing a project management office. The

Exhibit 2.   Design Alternatives for a Project Management Office

Design Factors	Alternatives
Organizational Factors	
• Reporting arrangements	• To CEO, to a functional head, to a steering committee, to a subunit head
• Organizational positioning	• Stand-alone, in a functional department
• Projects in scope	• All, major, specific type (e.g., merger), one department or business unit's projects
• Ownership of resources	• PMO leaders, all project managers, all project resources
• A permanent or temporary office	• Permanent, temporary
• Size and budget	• From just PMO specific costs and resources to all project resources and costs
Human Resource Responsibilities	
• Recruitment and selection	• Project managers, specialist staff, all project resources
• Training and certification	• Internal training, training vendor management, standard setting, accreditation
• Appraisal and promotion	• Provide templates for project management staff, facilitate process, coordinate
• Providing resources to projects	• Provide project managers, provide teams, provide all project resources, maintain repositories
• Time recording	• Implement, manage, analyze
• Career planning	• Support individuals, support organization
• Personnel administration	• Manage vacations, sick leave, salaries, bonuses
• External vendor management	• Manage recruitment agencies, service providers, consultants, hardware and software suppliers
• Counseling and mentoring	• Formal, informal, new project resources, all project resources
Responsibilities for Setting Project Management Standards	
• Setting project management methodologies	• Define project management and project life cycle standards, define methodologies/processes to be used
• Providing templates	• Charters, status reports, risk assessments, budgets, issue logs, post-implementation reviews
• Providing project management tools	• Templates, software tools, intranet sites
• Providing repositories	• Computer directories, project documentation, best practices, project deliverables

Exhibit 2 (continued). Design Alternatives for a Project Management Office

Design Factors	Alternatives
Project Execution Responsibilities	
• Risk and issue management	• Set standards, facilitate, conduct, control
• Impact and change management	• Set standards, facilitate, conduct, control
• Communication	• Among projects, between projects and other parts of the organization, executive updates, newsletters
• Project auditing	• Formal, oversight role, with internal audit or independent
• Focus on major or special projects	• Major, specific type (e.g., merger)
Responsibilities for Business Strategy	
• Collection of initiatives	• Provide standards and templates, facilitate, coordinate or manage
• Project evaluation	• Provide standards and templates, facilitate, coordinate or manage
• Project prioritization	• Provide standards and templates, facilitate, coordinate or manage
• Project planning and scheduling	• Provide standards and templates, facilitate, coordinate or manage
• Project approval and funding	• Provide standards and templates, facilitate, coordinate or manage
• Project monitoring and controlling	• Provide standards and templates, facilitate, coordinate or manage
• Project portfolio management	• Provide standards and templates, facilitate, coordinate or manage

checklist can be used for the initial setup of a PMO or an evaluation of design alternatives as a PMO evolves.

The checklist can be used by considering each of the factors in the left-hand column and inserting the design alternative that meets the business needs of an organization. In many cases, there will be responsibilities that are not required. There are many possible alternative processes for completing the checklist. For example, it could be completed by an executive setting up an office; it could be completed in a workshop setting by a cross-functional group interested in designing a PMO; or it could be used as research tool by a group given the responsibility of designing a PMO.

CONCLUSION

This chapter has discussed a wide variety of factors that should be considered in designing a PMO. Undoubtedly, the list is not comprehensive — in fact, it is unlikely that it could be possible to identify all the factors that could be relevant to all organizations. However, the list does include a major set of factors that are relevant to designing PMOs. Every organization will have its own set of requirements. By considering the factors discussed, an organization has the opportunity to systematically choose a set of design factors that will help it meet its requirements at a given point in time.

The design possibilities for PMOs are almost limitless. A PMO can be designed to have quite restricted responsibilities; or a PMO can be established to have a major role in the planning, controlling, and coordinating of an organization's portfolio of projects and managing its project resources. By systematically evaluating the design possibilities, an organization can quickly choose a design that meets its needs.

Chapter 41
Assessing the Real Costs of a Major System Change

Brian Jeffery

The widespread assumption of the late 1980s that downsizing from mainframes would reduce IS costs for just about any business sparked what has come to be an increasingly confusing debate about the costs of computing. Today, evidence from a wide range of sources challenges this assumption. Users have become increasingly disturbed about the high costs of decentralizing IS resources. There is also a growing realization that the cost structures of mission-critical systems have remarkably little to do with underlying technologies.

As user experiences with major platform changes have shown, no one system is inherently more or less expensive than another. Real costs depend greatly on the applications and workload profiles of individual organizations. Cost profiles vary by industry, by type and size of business, as well as by geographical location.

Underlying hardware and software technologies are also less important than the way the IS department is organized, the quality of IS management and staff, and the efficiency with which IS resources are used, including the effectiveness of cost accounting and control procedures. IS managers who are considering a major system change involving new computing platforms need a better understanding of IS cost structures and how these structures change over time. Lack of understanding of these areas can result in a business applying the wrong solutions to the wrong problems — and wasting a great deal of money.

This chapter discusses the key factors affecting IS costs in any business. It offers IS managers suggestions on how to avoid common mistakes in forecasting the costs of computing and guidelines for using comparisons with other companies to determine real computing costs more effectively.

0-8493-1190-X/02/$0.00+$1.50
© 2002 by CRC Press LLC

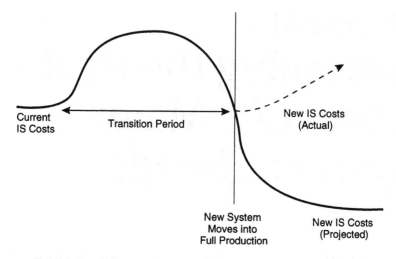

Exhibit 1. U-Curve Effect of a New System on Total IS Costs

COMPOSITION OF IS BUDGETS

The cost of providing IS services to a business involves a wide range of items. These include not only hardware and software acquisitions, but also personnel and their associated costs, along with the costs of maintenance, telecommunications, facilities, supplies, and various other related items and outside services.

A 1993 survey of corporate IS budgets in the United States conducted by Computer Economics, Inc., of Carlsbad, California, found that the largest single IS cost item was personnel (42.1 percent), followed by hardware (28.9 percent), software (11.9 percent), and "other" (17.1 percent). The category of "other" included telecommunications, outside services, supplies, facilities, and miscellaneous items. IS managers should pay particular attention to this category because although the individual items in it may each represent only a fraction of total IS costs, their percentage is far from insignificant. Most of these costs remain the same or increase during major system changes.

Businesses often make the mistake of focusing solely on one-time investment outlays, primarily hardware acquisitions, rather than on longer-term operating costs. This approach inevitably misses the main components of the total IS costs of the company. Organizations that make this mistake are likely to experience a U-curve effect, as illustrated in Exhibit 1. Costs may follow original projections while a new system is in the start-up and test stages, but as soon as the system enters production and handles real workloads, IS spending escalates rapidly as new costs are incurred.

QUANTIFYING PRODUCTION WORKLOADS

In any production environment, a minimum six sets of workload parameters affect the capacity requirements of a system and hence its costs:

1. Numbers of active users
2. Volumes of data generated and used by applications
3. Type, size, and volume of transactions
4. Type, size, and volume of database queries
5. Type, size, and number of documents generated and printed
6. Batch workloads, including data consolidations, backup operations, and production printing

These parameters can vary widely within a company, as well as between different types and sizes of businesses in different industries. As a result, use of standardized, generic measurements for quantifying system performance is one of the most common causes of cost underestimates.

Because there is no such thing as a generic business, any valid computing cost comparisons must be specific to the needs of an individual business organization. Most standardized measurement techniques have little relevance to the performance that will actually be experienced by users in any given production environment.

For example, much of the industry debate about millions of instructions per second (MIPS) is based on a fundamental error. Instruction sets, as well as the complexity and size of instructions, and the system processes that are instructed vary widely between systems. MIPS has no validity in a cross-architecture comparison. In addition, MIPS represents only a measure of CPU performance. In any real production environment, the performance actually experienced by users is influenced by hundreds of different parameters.

Measurements of transaction performance, such as TPC/A, TPC/B, or TPC/C, are based on stylized suites of software and workloads. These rarely correspond to the applications portfolios, transaction volumes, or workload characteristics of a specific business. Variations between different types of transactions have a major effect on capacity requirements, and hence on costs.

The use of any single benchmark is inherently misleading because few production systems handle a single type of workload. Transactions and queries may vary widely from application to application, and the overall processing mix is likely to include batch as well as other types of system operations.

Thus, any cost comparison between different systems should be based on quantified workloads that correspond to the current and future requirements of the business.

Database Query Volumes

Particular attention should be paid to query volumes. Although the effects of transaction and batch workloads are well documented for IS environments, large volumes of user-initiated database queries are a more recent phenomenon. Their effects are still poorly understood in most organizations.

Businesses that move to client/server computing commonly experience annual increases in query volumes of from 30 to 40 percent. Moreover, these types of increases may continue for at least five years. Although most transactions can be measured in kilobytes, queries easily run to megabytes of data. Long, sequential queries generate particularly heavy loading. Thus, once client/server computing comes into large-scale use within an organization, heavier demands are placed on processor, database, and storage capacity.

In many organizations, queries can rapidly dominate computing workloads, with costs exceeding those for supporting online transaction processing applications. IS costs in this type of situation normally go up, not down. It is better to plan for this growth ahead of time.

SERVICE LEVELS

Service levels include response time, availability, hours of operation, and disaster recovery coverage. They are not addressed by generic performance indicators such as MIPS or TPC metrics and are not always visible in workload calculations. However, service levels have a major impact on costs.

Many businesses do not factor in service-level requirements when evaluating different types of systems. The requirements need to be explicitly quantified. All platforms under evaluation should include costs for configurations that will meet the required levels.

Response Time

Response time is the time it takes a system to respond to a user-initiated request for an application or data resource. Decreasing response time generally requires additional investments in processors, storage, I/O, or communications capacity, or (more likely) all of these.

In traditional mainframe-based online transaction processing applications, response time equates to the time required to perform a transaction or display data on a terminal. For more complex IS environments, response time is more likely to be the time required to process a database query, locate and retrieve a file, and deliver a document in electronic or hard-copy form. Delivering fast response time according to these criteria is both more difficult and more expensive than it is for traditional mainframe applications.

Availability

Availability is the absence of outages. Standard performance benchmarks, and even detailed measurements of system performance based on specific workloads, provide no direct insight into availability levels. Such benchmarks do not indicate how prone a system will be to outages, nor what it will cost to prevent outages.

Even in a relatively protected data center environment, outages have a wide range of common causes. These include bugs in system and applications software, hardware and network failures, as well as operator errors. When computing resources are moved closer to end users, user error also becomes a major source of disruptions.

Production environments contain large numbers of interdependent hardware and software components, any of which represents a potential point of failure. Even the most reliable system experiences some failures.

Thus, maintaining high availability levels may require specialized equipment and software, along with procedures to mask the effects of outages from users and enable service to be resumed as rapidly as possible with minimum disruption to applications and loss of data. The less reliable the core system, the more such measures will be necessary.

Availability can be realized at several levels. Subsystem duplexing and resilient system designs have cost premiums. For example, to move from the ability to restart a system within 30 minutes to the ability to restart within a few minutes can increase costs by orders of magnitude.

Hours of Operation

Running multiple shifts or otherwise extending the hours of operation increases staffing requirements. Even if automated operations tools are used, it will usually be necessary to maintain personnel on-site to deal with emergencies.

Disaster Recovery

Disaster recovery coverage requires specialized facilities and procedures to allow service to be resumed for critical applications and data in the event of a catastrophic outage. Depending on the level of coverage, standby processor and storage capacity may be necessary or an external service may be used. Costs can be substantial, even for a relatively small IS installation.

SOFTWARE LOADING

The cost of any system depends greatly on the type of software it runs. In this respect, again, there is no such thing as a generic configuration or cost for any platform. Apart from licenses and software maintenance or support fees, software selections have major implications for system capacity. It is possible for two systems running similar workloads, but equipped with different sets of applications and systems software, to have radically different costs.

For example, large, highly integrated applications can consume substantially more computing resources than a comparable set of individual applications. Complex linkages between and within applications can generate a great deal of overhead. Similarly, certain types of development tools, databases, file systems, and operating systems also generate higher levels of processor, storage, and I/O consumption.

Exhibit 2 contains a representative list of the resource management tools required to cover most or all the functions necessary to ensure the integrity of the computing installation. If these tools are not in place, organizations are likely to run considerable business risks and incur excessive costs. Use of effective management tools is important with any type of workload. It is obligatory when high levels of availability and data integrity are required. In a mainframe-class installation, tools can consume up to 30 percent of total system capacity and license fees can easily run into hundreds of thousands of dollars.

EFFICIENCY OF IS RESOURCE USE

Capacity Utilization. Most computing systems operate at less than maximum capacity most of the time. However, allowance must be made for loading during peak periods. Margins are usually built into capacity planning to prevent performance degradation or data loss when hardware and software facilities begin to be pushed to their limits. If the system is properly managed, unused capacity can be minimized.

When planning costs, IS managers must distinguish between the theoretical and used capacity of a system. Failure to account for this is one of the more frequent causes of cost overruns among users moving to new systems. It may be necessary to add additional capacity to handle peak workloads. For example, properly managed disk storage subsystems may have high levels of occupancy (85 percent and over is the norm in efficient installations). There is a close relationship between data volumes used in applications and actual disk capacity. Inactive data is more frequently

Exhibit 2. A Representative List of Resource Management Tools

System Level
System Management/Administration

Performance Management
Performance Monitoring/Diagnostics
Performance Tuning/Management
Capacity Planning
Applications Optimization

Storage Management
Host Backup/Restore
Hierarchical Storage Management
Disk Management
Disk Defragmentation
Tape Management
Tape Automation
Volume/ File Management

Configuration/Event Management
Configuration Management
Change/Installation Management
Fault Reporting/Management
Problem Tracking/Resolution

Data Management
Database Administration
Security

High Availability
Power/Environmental Monitoring
Disk Mirroring/RAID
Fallover/Restart
Disaster Recovery Planning

Network Management
Operations Management/Control
Change Management
Configuration Management
Problem Management
Resource Monitoring/Accounting
Software Distribution/License Control

Operations
Print/Output Management
Job Rescheduling/Queuing/Restart
Resource Allocation
Workload Management
Load Balancing
Console Management
Automated Operations

Administrative
Resource Accounting/Chargeback
Data Center Reporting
Statistical Analysis/Report Generation

dumped to tape, thus reducing disk capacity requirements and corresponding hardware costs. If a system operates less efficiently, capacity requirements, and hence costs, can be substantially higher even if workloads are the same.

Consolidation, Rationalization, and Automation

Properly applied, the principles of consolidation, rationalization, and automation almost invariably reduce IS costs. Conversely, an organization characterized by diseconomies of scale, unnecessary overlaps and duplications of IS resources, and a prevalence of manual operating procedures will experience significantly higher IS costs than one that is efficiently managed.

For example, in many organizations, numerous applications perform more or less the same function. These applications have few users relative to their CPU and storage capacity utilization, as well as to their license fee costs. Proliferation of databases, networks, and other facilities, along with underutilized operating systems and subsystems, also unnecessarily increase IS costs.

Exhibit 3. Cost Disparities between Best-Practice Data Centers and Industry Averages

	Best Practice	Industry Average	Disparity
Annual Spending per Used MIPS			
Hardware	$51,249	$89,701	1.8
Software	$17,802	$71,440	4.0
Personnel	$41,748	$115,454	2.8
Cost per gigabyte of disk storage per month	$109.91	$272.84	2.5
Cost per printed page	$0.0017	$0.0070	4.1
Total staff per used MIPS	0.70	1.93	

Source: Defense Information Systems Agency, U.S. Department of Defense, 1993.

Requirements for hardware capacity can also be inflated by software versions that contain aged and inefficiently structured code. System loading will be significantly less if these older versions are reengineered or replaced with more efficient alternatives or if system, database, and application tuning procedures are used.

Automation tools can reduce staffing levels, usually by eliminating manual tasks. Properly used, these tools also deliver higher levels of CPU capacity utilization and disk occupancy than would be possible with more labor-intensive scheduling and tuning techniques. A 1993 study commissioned by the U.S. Department of Defense compared key cost items for more efficient best-practice data centers with industry averages. Its results, summarized in Exhibit 3, are consistent with the findings of similar benchmarking studies worldwide.

It should be emphasized that these figures (which are based on used rather than theoretical capacity) compare best-practice organizations with industry averages. Many organizations have cost structures much higher than the averages cited in this study. Capacity utilization, along with the effects of consolidation, rationalization, and automation, suggest that efficiency is in fact the single most important variable in IS costs. Clearly, the best way to reduce IS costs for any platform is to increase the efficiency with which IS resources are used.

APPLICATION LIFE CYCLES

One of the major long-term IS cost items for any business is the staff needed to maintain applications. In this context, maintenance means ongoing changes and enhancements to applications in response to changing user requirements. Even organizations that use packaged software will need personnel to perform these tasks.

468

The typical software application experiences a distinct U-curve pattern of demand for changes and enhancements over time. Demand is relatively high early in the cycle as the application is shaken down. Change and enhancement frequency then decline, before increasing again at a later stage as the application becomes progressively less appropriate for user requirements.

The frequency of application change and enhancement is affected by change in such factors as organizational structures and work patterns. The level may remain low if the business operates in a reasonably stable manner. Because all applications age and eventually become obsolete, increases are inevitable. The main variable is how long this takes, not whether it occurs.

The application life cycle has important implications for IS costs. Once the shake-down phase is completed, a new application usually requires comparatively little application maintenance overhead. However, at some point maintenance requirements usually escalate, and so will the required staffing level.

Measuring application maintenance requirements for limited periods gives a highly misleading impression of long-term costs. Application maintenance costs eventually become excessive if organizations do not redevelop or replace applications on an ongoing basis. Moreover, where most or all of the applications portfolio is aged (which is the case in many less-sophisticated mainframe and minicomputer installations), the IS staff will be dedicated predominantly to maintenance rather than to developing new applications.

As an applications portfolio ages, IS managers face a straightforward choice between spending to develop or reengineer applications or accepting user dissatisfaction with existing applications. Failure to make this choice means an implicit decision in favor of high maintenance costs, user dissatisfaction, and eventually a more radical — and expensive — solution to the problem.

APPLICATIONS DEVELOPMENT VARIABLES

The cost of applications development in any business is a function of two variables:

1. Demand for new applications
2. Productivity of the application developers

Costs will decrease only if there is low demand and high productivity. In most organizations, demand for applications is elastic. As the quality of IS solutions increases, users' demands for applications also increase. This is particularly the case for interactive, user-oriented computing applications. Early in the cycle after a major system change, user demand for these applications can easily reach exponential proportions.

**Exhibit 4. Factors Affecting Applications
Development Productivity**

- Proper Definition of Requirements
- Application/Systems Design
- Applications Characteristics
- Applications Structure/Size
- Underlying Applications Technologies
- Applications Complexity
- Functionality of Tools
- Development Methodology
- Match of Tools to Applications
- Degree of Customization
- Training/Documentation
- Programmer Skills/Motivation
- Project Management
- Management Effectiveness

If this effect is not anticipated, unexpected backlogs are likely to occur. More than a few IS managers who committed to reducing IS costs have been forced to explain to users that it is not possible to meet their requirements. Similarly, the productivity of applications development can vary widely. Some of the major factors affecting applications development productivity are summarized in Exhibit 4.

Development tools are an important part of the equation. Normally, third-generation languages (3GLs) yield the lowest levels of productivity, fourth-generation languages (4GLs) offer incremental improvements, and computer-aided software engineering tools, particularly those using rapid application development methodologies, perform best. Visual programming interfaces and the use of object-oriented architecture can also have significant effects. Productivity, in this context, is normally measured in terms of function points per programmer over time.

Productivity gains are not automatic, however. Tools designed for relatively small, query-intensive applications may not work well for large, mission-critical online transaction processing systems, and vice versa. Matching the proper tool to the application is thus an important factor in productivity. However, IS managers should be wary of vendor claims that the tools will improve productivity and reduce staff costs, unless it can be shown that this has occurred for applications comparable to their own requirements. Increases in productivity can be offset by increases in underlying software complexities (i.e., increases in the number of variables that must be handled during the programming process) and in degrees of customization.

Sophisticated user interfaces, complex distributed computing architectures, and extensive functionality at the workstation level have become common user requirements. However, multiuser applications with these characteristics are relatively difficult to implement and require realistic expectations, careful planning, and strong project management skills. Failure to take these factors into account is the reason for most of the delays and cost overruns associated with client/server initiatives.

New development methodologies and tools may alleviate, but not remove, problem areas. Regardless of the tools and methodologies used, effective requirements definition and management of the applications development process are more likely to be the critical factors in productivity.

TRANSITION COSTS

Costs involved in switching applications and databases from one system to another are commonly underestimated. Many businesses treat transition costs as a secondary issue and give them less scrutiny than capital investment or ongoing operating costs. Even organizations that handle other aspects of the costing process with diligence often tolerate a great deal of vagueness regarding the time and expense required for transition.

This imprecision also extends to many claims of cost savings. Most of the figures quoted by vendors, consultants, and the media refer to purported savings in operating costs, not to net gains after transition outlays. Moreover, operating costs may be artificially low early in the few years following a change precisely because major one-time investments have been made in new hardware and software, with applications that are relatively new and require little maintenance.

Initial Installation of New Hardware and Software

Costs of the initial installation of new hardware and software are comparatively easy to quantify, provided that capacity has been properly estimated using workloads, service levels, and other criteria. If this has not been done, the organization may experience a sharp increase in costs above projected levels during the first year as the new system comes into production and actual requirements become apparent.

One-Time Services Outlays

Some one-time services outlays are usually required as well. These may range from large-scale conversions of applications and data, to the recabling of data centers and end-user environments, to retraining of IS and user personnel, along with the installation and assurance of system and applications software.

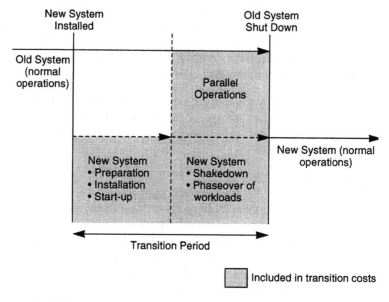

Exhibit 5. Measurement Periods for Comparative Costing

Many organizations use generic cost data supplied by consultants or vendors. This data can be highly inaccurate for the specific situation. Hard costs should be obtained to provide more precise data for planning purposes.

Length of the Transition Period

The length of the transition period has a major impact on costs. The actual time taken depends greatly on several factors. Organizations moving to new, relatively untried platforms and technologies need to allow for longer periods to shake down the new system and test its stability in the production environment. Depending on the size and requirements of the organization, as well as application workloads, transitions can take five years or more. A protracted transition period means that operating costs (e.g., software, hardware and software maintenance, personnel, cost of capital) are substantial even before a new system goes into normal operations. Parallel operations costs (i.e., maintaining the existing system in production) can also increase if the transition period is extended.

All these factors make it important that IS managers set precise dates for the transition process, beginning with the start-up of a new system in test mode and ending with the shutdown of the old system. This approach (shown in Exhibit 5) allows for more accurate five-year costing.

COMPANY-TO-COMPANY COMPARISONS

Reliability of Case Studies. For any business considering a major computing systems change, the experiences of others who have made similar changes should, in principle, provide useful input. However, few well-documented case studies exist, and those that do are not always representative. The lack of reliable information is most obvious for mainframe migration patterns.

Organizations that have replaced and removed mainframes entirely fit a distinct profile. In the majority of the cases, these organizations possessed older equipment and aging applications portfolios. Their IS organizations were characterized by lack of previous capital investment, poor management practices, inefficient manual coding techniques for applications development and maintenance, lack of automation, and just about every other factor that leads to excessive IS costs.

All this raises some major questions about comparisons based on case studies. Even where overall savings in IS costs are realized, the savings occur only under specific circumstances, usually because IS costs were abnormally high to begin with. Organizations with higher-quality applications, current hardware, efficient software, and different workloads will have an entirely different cost structure. Cost savings are particularly unlikely in an organization that uses system resources and personnel effectively.

Mainframe replacements are a relatively small percentage compared with the total volume of mainframe procurements. A survey of mainframe migration patterns in the United States in 1993, compiled by Computer Intelligence InfoCorp of La Jolla, California, is particularly revealing (Exhibit 6).

According to the survey data, users of 309X-class systems who acquired new mainframe systems outnumbered those who moved to alternative platforms by more than 20 to 1. If 309X upgrades are included, the figure is 50 to 1. Among 4300-class users, new mainframe acquisitions outnumbered replacements by more than 8 to 1. This figure does not include users who upgraded within 4300 product lines.

The extent of real mainframe replacement appears to be relatively small. The majority of downsizing actions involve moving specific applications from mainframes to smaller platforms, not actually replacing mainframes. This affects the validity of cost-savings claims. Although the cost of individual applications may be lower on new platforms, this does not necessarily mean that overall IS costs were reduced. In many cases, applications are either relatively small or exploit mainframe databases, or both. In addition, transition costs are seldom included in calculations.

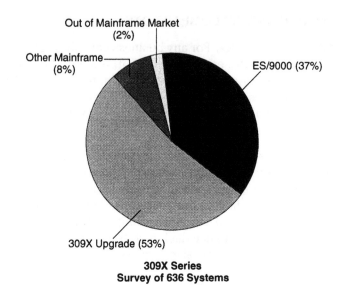

**309X Series
Survey of 636 Systems**

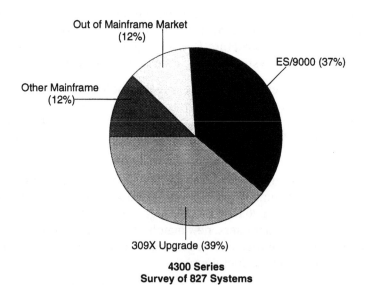

**4300 Series
Survey of 827 Systems**

Exhibit 6.   U.S. Mainframe Migration Patterns in 1993 for 309X and 4300 Series
(From Computer Intelligence InfoCorp, La Jolla, CA, 1993.)

CONCLUSION

One of the enduring ironies of the computer industry is that those who most uncritically and aggressively target IS cost savings are the least likely to achieve their goal. That is because unrealistic perceptions about automatic cost savings or inexpensive platforms often lead to inadequately managed planning and procurement. Preoccupation with technology may mean that major opportunities to achieve real, substantial cost savings through increased operation efficiencies are neglected. Even if real business benefits are achieved, the cost of realizing them is likely to be unnecessarily high.

Only by understanding IS cost structures, and targeting all the variables affecting these structures, can businesses ensure that they will obtain maximum cost-effectiveness from their IS expenditures.

Chapter 42
Information Technology for Project Management Automation

Chang-Yang Lin

Although project management systems have been evolving from mainframe-based, big-iron programs into microcomputer-based, GUI (graphical user interface) programs, they are still in their infancy for enhancing fundamental functions. The fundamental functions and new features that these current project management systems lack include:

- Historical project databases
- Knowledge-based methodologies
- Multimedia-enabling capabilities
- Flexible navigation mechanisms

The significance of these shortcomings is that, without these features, systems are insufficient to facilitate project management automation from the planning phase to the controlling and executing phase. Consequently, the attitude toward a project stays the same: instead of using project management systems, many project managers continue to employ paper and pencil as the principal tools; therefore, project management remains mainly a manual process.

PROJECT MANAGEMENT ACTIVITIES

The main goal of project management is to develop an acceptable information system on schedule and within the allocated budget. Projects usually involve a team of analysts, programmers, technical specialists, and user representatives who work together. Managing projects is the continuing, iterative process by which an analyst plans, controls, and executes tasks

0-8493-1190-X/02/$0.00+$1.50
© 2002 by CRC Press LLC

and resources, and communicates progress and results. Specifically, project management involves the following fundamental activities:

- Planning a project, including:
  - Determining and sequencing the required tasks
  - Estimating the time required for completing the tasks
  - Allocating the staff and resources to perform the tasks
  - Budgeting the tasks
- Controlling the execution of the project, including:
  - Coordinating the tasks and resources according to the plan
  - Monitoring and measuring project progress against the plan
  - Presenting and communicating progress and results with management, team members, and clients

Project Planning

Planning is a critical part of project management. The project plan, resulting from the completion of planning, is the basis for coordinating, measuring, and communicating. Lack of planning has been cited as one of the major factors contributing to the failure of many systems projects. The failure to perform planning partly results from the nature of planning itself:

- Uncertain or unstructured conditions often exist. For example, problems that trigger a development project are usually not understood completely at the early phases of the systems development process.
- Heterogeneous staff possessing various skill levels are common in most organizations.
- Planning techniques (e.g., estimating techniques) are imperfect.

The results are obvious. Some project managers rely primarily on their own experience to perform planning activities because few tools appear to be available for planning. The estimated time required for completing a given task is often highly inaccurate because there is little project data for prediction. The sequence of the tasks is not consistent because project methodology is not standardized and historical project databases are nonexistent. As a consequence, rarely are solid project plans created.

Despite the difficulty in planning, the following steps to improve planning may be considered:

- Establishing the project development methodology for determining and sequencing the development tasks
- Maintaining the historical project databases to support, for example, estimations
- Building knowledge or expert system to assist analysts in resolving such issues as task sequences, personal assignments, and estimation techniques

Project Control

Project control includes coordinating activities and measuring for the execution of the project plan. First, coordinating involves integrating the activities for the ease of interaction among the team members. Creating a cooperative working environment that allows the team members to easily share project information or knowledge is important for the success of the project. Information or knowledge that may be shared includes the entire project plan and the status or progress of the project.

Second, measuring involves tracking and assessing the progress of the project. Without knowledge of individual and team progress, the problems cannot be identified, and the project managers cannot reshuffle the staff or revise the schedule to achieve the goals.

To assist the project team to perform project controlling activities better, the following steps can be taken:

- Gathering project data to support the process management
- Keeping track of the status of tasks, alerting the project manager and team members when tasks are incomplete or resources are not used effectively
- Creating a distributed environment that can coordinate works

Project Communication

Project communication involves reporting, presenting, and accessing. Traditionally, project status, project plans, and other reports are prepared in the forms of text, tables, or graphics on paper using a manual method and a batch-oriented approach. Increasingly, such reports are also available on computers that can be accessed interactively.

Additional features are necessary for effective communication:

- Digitized project information or knowledge to support automated access
- Flexible approaches to access project information or knowledge
- Automated tools for the preparation of project reports, presentations, or demonstrations in multimedia forms

INFORMATION TECHNOLOGY

Historical project databases and knowledge-based project methodology are essential for effective planning, control, and communication. This section identifies and describes specific information technologies that may automate historical project databases, knowledge-based project methodology, and others. Current project management systems are also examined, and the limitations and advantages of these systems are identified.

Current Project Management Systems

Almost all the current products for project management are microcomputer-based GUI programs aimed at both technical project managers and analysts. Examples are Microsoft Project and SuperProject for Windows (by Computer Associates International Inc.). These products are designed to support the process management for single projects consisting of approximately 200 to 500 tasks. Although in their infancy as single-project, single-user, record-keeping systems, these programs are already starting to offer some fundamental functions:

- Simplifying the preparation of CPM, PERT, and Gantt charts
- Generating a simple project plan
- Assigning people and cost resources to tasks
- Reporting project progress
- Answering simple "What-If" questions

These microcomputer-based project management systems, however, lacked sufficient functionality, including:

- Multiproject capabilities
- Support of historical project databases
- Knowledge-based project methodologies
- Advanced decision support functions
- Expert guidance for generating a customized plan

Relational Database Systems

The widespread use of relational database technology and its advantages have been well documented. Such use has been applied mainly to critical business applications in the user department. One essential task in relational technology is to plan an enterprise data model that can support the development of various applications.

Theoretically, the enterprise data model can also be extended to support project management applications in IS departments. However, project data must be planned as an integral part of the enterprise data model. With relational technology, the project database offers many advantages over current, microcomputer-based project management products, including:

- Consistent and friendly data structure
- Openness or connectivity

First relational databases incorporate easy-to-understand tabular structure to store data. A generic data model for project management, shown in Exhibit 1, may be implemented as a relational database in which each of these objects (project, task, assignment, person, time record) is converted into a table. The project database is then viewed as a set of tables that is consistent throughout the organization.

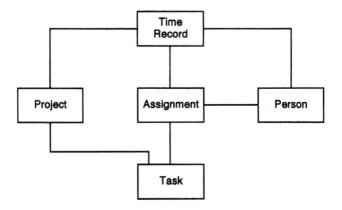

Exhibit 1. Project Data Model

Relational databases also provide an open architecture to support additional functionality involving multiprojects or other non-project-specific systems. For example, a relational project management system may interface with the accounting system, the human resource system, and the financial system to automate charge back, comprehensive resource management, and resource forecasting. This is in contrast with the current microcomputer-based project management systems that can primarily support record-keeping activities typically within a single project.

Relational Database Management System/4GL Development Tools

A relational database management system (RDBMS) has two parts: the back end, which provides the basic data management funcitons, and a set of front ends, which support applications development.

The back-end DBMS is typically equipped with a nonprocedural language that can be used to create, update, and maintain the project database. It also provides concurrent control, recovery support, and data security. Some back ends provide a data dictionary to store metadata about objects and therefore provide a unified view of data. Popular RDBMS products include DB2, Informix, Oracle, Sybase, and Microsoft SQL Server.

The relational front ends constitute a set of facilities for assisting in the process of developing database programs. For the past decade, the front ends have made significant changes to allow for the development of client/server, multiplatform applications.

The front-end tools range from 3GL-like procedural language to nonprocedural database languages, from character-based text modes to object-oriented modes, and from menu-driven 4GLs to graphical 4GLs. These 4GLtype front-end tools support prototyping and have proved to be able to shorten development time significantly. It is expected that the modern front ends are adequate to facilitate the development of the various project management programs, including:

- Transaction programs to request and accept the actual time spent by a person on a specific project
- Data maintenance programs to modify a person's assignment and the projected time for a task
- Decision-support inquiry and project-data reporting programs to generate, for example, a new project plan in response to schedule slippage

Most of the host- or server-based RDBMS have graphical 4GLs (e.g., Informix 4GL, Microsoft Visual Basic, and Sybase Powerbuilder). Some PC-based RDBMS, such as Microsoft Access, Microsoft Visual FoxPro, and Corel Paradox, also provide front-end tools. This means that there are many choices available for automating project management programs in relatively short periods.

Expert, Hypermedia, Relational Technologies

A knowledge-based project methodology should provide, among other functions, a knowledge base about the development methodology and its expert guidance to assist the project manager to derive the first-cut plan and then to customize a plan. The methodology should also provide other types of knowledge bases and their expertlike guidance for selecting the appropriate techniques and tools.

To implement such knowledge-based systems, various information technologies can be employed. For example, hypermedia and expert technology can be used to implement a knowledge base that may be composed of a set of digitized objects. These objects are used to represent knowledge about tasks, phases, techniques, tools, deliverables, skills, and so on. Each of these knowledge-oriented objects is modeled as an independent object that can be further divided into one or more subobjects for the detailed references. The objects may hold text, bit-mapped diagrams, and even animation. Specific rules used to provide guidance for using the project methodologies can also be automated as one component of an expert system.

Besides the above technologies, relational database systems (e.g., DB2 and Oracle) have added hypermedia, object, and knowledge components to make relational DBMSs multimedia capable, object capable, and more intelligent in addition to their standard database management functions. The significance of this development is that relational technology may eventually be able to support project management automation by itself.

Hypermedia Browsing and Relational Query

Hypermedia browsing allows the user to access project databases and knowledge bases in a nonlinear way and may serve as a fundamental navigation mechanism for a project management system. Such a navigation mechanism is interactive and flexible; it can enhance information access in two significant ways. First, it uses a technique known as hypertext to integrate menu items into information. With hypertext, the users can explore the knowledge bases and project databases from one object to the related objects through the embedded menu items. The users can also navigate from one object to other objects through cross-reference links or direct links. Second, it allows text, graphics, images, audio, and video to be combined to form multimedia objects.

Other advanced mechanisms involve a sophisticated query/search technique for flexible and filtered access to project databases. Such mechanisms allow users to see the desired picture of a project, to identify the critical path, and to filter exceptional problems concerning schedules, budgets, or resources. Relational query tools may be used to facilitate the implementation of such advanced mechanisms.

CONCLUSION

This chapter has discussed automation in the context of project management. Although microcomputer-based GUI products for technical project managers and analysts have begun to offer some fundamental functions, they lack sufficient functionality for project management automation from the planning phase to the coordination and execution phase. Three major functions among others that remain difficult to automate are the historical project databases, the knowledge-based project methodologies, and the flexible navigation mechanisms.

Current IT developments are emerging that provide the solutions if they are fully utilized. This chapter identified the specific technologies for project management automation:

- Expert systems, hypermedia, and image/object technology, which can be used to develop the knowledge-based project methodology
- Relational database technology, which can be used to implement the multiproject historical databases and to assist the development of various project management programs
- Multimedia, which can be used to represent knowledge or project data in the forms of text, graphics, images, audio, video, and animation
- Hypertext techniques and relational queries, which can be used to provide a flexible navigation mechanism

Until these technologies are fully incorporated into the systems, project management will remain one of the thorny problems for managers. To alleviate this problem, a new project management system must be planned and built as an integral part of the organizationwide information system. Because relational technology is the best complete technology currently available to support the overall information system, it should be used to implement a project management system.

To better prepare for a new era of relational technology-centered project management automation, the following steps are suggested:

- *Standardizing the project methodology.* A proven project methodology must be chosen. The chosen methodology standardizes project development activities.
- *Planning and building the project database with a RDBMS.* First, the project database must be planned as an integral part of the enterprise data model. Emphasis should be placed on data aggregation and data sharing. Second, the project data can be defined, stored, and maintained with the use of the back end of a relational DBMS.
- *Developing the project management programs with the front-end tools of RDBMS.* The 4GL development tools can be used to facilitate the rapid development of the various project management subsystems including transaction processing, management reporting, and information inquiry.
- *Implementing expert guidance and hypermedia navigation.* These functions may be delayed until RDBMS or other technologies are proved to be capable of implementing them.

Chapter 43
The Project Management Office: A Strategy for Improvement and Success

John P. Murray

As information technology (IT) organizations struggle to deliver applications to their business customers, they are increasingly more open to implementing new approaches to project management. One such approach is using an IT project management office (PMO). A strong PMO can benefit an organization in many ways. The primary benefit is an environment that improves the structure of project management as well as the design, development, and implementation of IT projects.

A PMO is structured to provide a clear path to senior management, whose support for a project can be solicited as needed. A direct track to senior management can quickly and effectively solve disputes that may arise within a project team. A PMO also creates opportunities to introduce new project management tools, concepts, and methods.

A well-managed PMO can help systems developers to:

- Capture and resolve project issues as they appear during the life of the project
- Consider and test out new project management techniques and approaches

Although these activities are not key to successfully delivering a project, they are key in improving project control and quality.

0-8493-1190-X/02/$0.00+$1.50
© 2002 by CRC Press LLC

On many IT projects, management is fragmented. As a result, the assigned project manager cannot exercise sufficient control to ensure project success. Although lines of authority and responsibility are clearly defined, real power over a project resides with someone other than the project manager, the decisions concerning the project may be made on the basis of political or emotional considerations rather than on business ones.

For example, a large order entry project has been approved for an organization. The assigned project manager is a member of the IT department, and it is agreed that the project manager, for the duration of the project, reports to the project sponsor, who is the manager of the order entry department. The project sponsor in turn reports to the vice president of marketing. In this situation, the project sponsor is naturally influenced by the vice president, who has a different agenda than the one agreed upon for the project. As the project moves forward, the vice president pushes for systems features outside the original scope of the project (i.e., "scope creep"). This causes considerable difficulties and threatens failure.

The vice president is not totally committed to the project, although it is important to the marketing department. It is consuming the complete attention of the order entry manager. Over time, the order entry manger understands that the project is second priority to managing the order entry department. To a considerable extent, the project depends on the interests and attitude of the vice president of marketing, and neither the project sponsor nor the project manager is really in charge. In this scenario, which is common for many IT projects, the project manager has limited authority but still carries responsibility for the project. When the project manager tries to shift responsibility, the project sponsor and marketing vice president take umbrage by saying, "We do not understand all the technology-related issues and therefore you cannot expect us to take responsibility."

Project managers charged with a responsibility must have sufficient authority to manage that responsibility. A PMO can ensure a project manager's authority.

IMPROVING PROJECT DEVELOPMENT

IT projects fail for a variety of reasons, and a common one is the lack of proper management focus and structure. Divided loyalties, pressures that lead to scope creep, and vague lines of reporting authority and responsibility — all play their part in IT project failures. When a PMO is correctly established and managed, there is no doubt about who is in charge and who carries responsibility. Of course, a PMO does not eliminate all of the political issues; but when they do arise, they can be directly addressed by a higher level of management in an organization. Because of its structure and placement in an organization, a PMO allows more objectivity to be brought to resolving project issues.

Typically, a PMO is set up with a limited time span. The office is established to manage one, or perhaps several IT projects. When projects are completed, the office is disbanded. As other projects arise, where their size warrants it, a new project management office can be created. A PMO is not needed for all IT projects and is overkill for small projects.

Previous PMOs can be used as models for future IT projects. The tools and techniques used in the past can be reapplied, perhaps on a smaller scale and with adjustments. An organization that uses PMOs can take a more controlled approach to project management. Although many organizations do not value project discipline and control, they are nevertheless keys to success.

A PMO is best suited for large, complex projects, where a number of disparate entities with differing interests must be coordinated and managed. The project manager and project management office have one goal: to succeed. Division of interests and duties is eliminated. Conflicts between IT and its customers can be resolved in a satisfactory manner that does not preclude project success.

OVERCOMING RESISTANCE TO PMOS

In many organizations, a project office is a new concept and therefore faces some level of resistance. Business customers may already be discontent with the IT section because of past projects. Although the goal of a PMO is to improve project delivery, they may doubt this and may view the PMO as one more layer of IT overhead, which cannot improve delivery of IT projects.

Members of the systems development staff may also resist the introduction of a PMO. Employees may view it as an attempt to restrict their creativity in designing, developing, and installing projects. They may also believe that adopting a more formal approach to project management will slow the development process. If the person selected to manage a PMO comes from outside the IT department, some IT employees are likely to be resentful.

Senior managers may be concerned about the value of a PMO. They may object to additional project expense and slower development because of this more formal approach. Also, they may not be willing to be seriously involved in a project.

A project manager and sponsor must recognize that some level of resistance is going to occur. Acknowledging that resistance is the first step in introducing a PMO. If there is resistance at the senior level of the organization, this issue must be the first one addressed. Unless the PMO concept has clear support of senior management, it cannot be viable. An IT manager must develop a strong case for a PMO and be willing to sell the concept to senior management. An outside consulting organization may be brought in to help make the case to senior managers.

Once a PMO has been approved by senior management, members of both IT and business areas must be convinced that the concept is valid. A senior manager should be made the PMO sponsor, one who clearly states upper management's support. Clearly communicating this support reduces resistance throughout an organization.

The purpose and function of a PMO must be carefully explained. Doing a good job of managing the project is difficult enough without the added burden of constantly justifying a PMO. Granted, it takes time and effort to explain the purpose of a PMO and to address questions and concerns. There may be a tendency to attempt to shortcut this process in order to get on with a project. Failing to take advantage of the opportunity to get off to the right start with a PMO is a mistake.

The most effective approach to overcoming resistance is to encourage people to express their concerns. All concerns should be addressed as openly and candidly as possible. It may be virtually impossible to gain complete support in the beginning, but candor about the PMO will make installing it less difficult.

Introducing a PMO creates change and may cause some disruption. In working to overcome resistance, PMO sponsors should not become defensive about the project office concept, but should explain that introducing a PMO is an attempt to improve the IT department's delivery record.

Successfully introducing a PMO is an effort to sell the process to those who are unsure of its value. However, that selling process should not be too difficult in most organizations. Introducing a PMO is typically viewed as IT's acknowledgment that it must improve the manner in which projects are managed and delivered. Having come to the conclusion that improvements are required must, in itself, be seen as positive.

THE ROLE OF A PMO

Simply stated, the role of a PMO is to assume full responsibility for project success. An argument can be raised that project managers have always had that responsibility, which a formal PMO does not change. While a project manager may be charged with this responsibility, it does not always work that way in practice. Political issues or different agendas can get in the way and create project difficulties. A PMO ensures that the person with responsibility for a project also enjoys the authority to manage it and can obtain proper recourse from senior management.

In a PMO, the project manager reports directly to the project sponsor. The project sponsor should be someone who has a vested interest in the project's success. In the previous example, the vice president of marketing is the *de facto* project manager, and such a scenario is much less likely to happen to a PMO project sponsor because the sponsor has direct responsibility. Having that responsibility, the project sponsor is going to pay more attention to the work being done and to making decisions focused on the success of the project. While other agendas are still going to exist, shifting to one of those agendas at the expense of the project is going to reflect poorly on the project sponsor.

A chronic problem with the development of IT projects has been the tendency of people outside the IT department who have requested a particular project to disengage themselves from the project. Too often, the concept of the project team becomes clouded and the IT members of the team find themselves dealing with most of the issues, pushing the project forward and making many critical project decisions in a vacuum. One of the duties of the project manager working within the PMO framework, is to make certain that all team members participate in the project. Again, if needed, the project manager can go to the project sponsor in order to obtain support in refocusing attention on the project.

In essence, the duties of the project manager within the framework of the project office are no different than those of the typical project manager. Those employees who have management responsibilities within the project will report to the project manager. One of the advantages of working within the purview of the PMO is that the project manager will have clear authority over all members of the project team, whether they are within the IT department or in the business areas. As anyone who has dealt with IT projects can readily understand, having that kind of leverage represents a considerable advantage in terms of managing the project.

One of the first steps for the project manager will be to develop the material needed for the successful completion of the project. The significant items involved in the gathering of that material, for any IT project, will include:

- The development of the project charter: the purpose of this document is to identify the specifics of the project. Topics to be covered in the charter would include:
  - The purpose of the project, why it has been approved, the organization of the project team, and the benefits to be obtained from the project
  - The scope of the project
  - Identification of the deliverables associated with the project and also, the identification of those items that are not, within the scope of this project
  - The identification of the project team members and the business units affected by the project

- A review of the roles and responsibilities of the key members of the project team, including the roles of the project manager and the project sponsor.
- A review of the concept of the PMO, its function, and purpose.
- The use of an existing IT system development methodology (SDM). If an SDM does not exist, one will have to be available for the project.
- Development of the project standards, be they coding, testing, quality, or other standards.
- A provision to provide continuing communication to everyone who may have an interest in the progress of the project. That communication process will include timely and accurate project status reports to all interested parties.
- The development of an "issues list," which will provide the ability to capture, track, and resolve issues of concern relative to the project.

SELECTING THE PMO PROJECT MANAGER

The person chosen for the role of project manager must be someone who has strong project management experience and is comfortable with the use of effective project management tools and techniques. It is also a good idea to have the project managed by someone who does not have a vested interest in the project beyond seeing the project completed. In that regard, the more objective the person managing the project can be when issues arise, the better. As the project moves forward, being able to maintain an objective view of the progress being made and the issues that are certain to come up is going to be of benefit to everyone involved in the project.

The issue of project scope creep is also tied to the objectivity of the person managing the project. When the project manager can focus on completing the project in accord with the original requirements, within the project deadlines, without undue concern for political issues, it will be difficult for scope creep to get started. That should not imply that changes or additions will not be allowed once a project begins. Sometimes, there is no choice but to address issues that either were overlooked in the development of the project specifications, or, because of business changes, have to be accommodated within the project. The issue here is that an objective project manager will be able to identify the "nice to have" project add-on requests and to deny those requests without fear of negative personal consequences at some later date.

The project manager must enjoy strong support from the project sponsor. If, after the project gets underway, problems arise between the project sponsor and the project manager, it may be in the best interest of the project to replace one of those individuals. Even with the use of a PMO, there is likely to be some level of project tension. Where tension is generated between the project sponsor and the project manager, the project is going to suffer. It will be better to recognize that the sponsor and the project manager do not make a good team and to correct that situation than to attempt to gloss over the problem.

Once the concept of the PMO has been approved and a project manager appointed, he or she should begin an analysis of the current project management environment within the organization. That analysis should consider the level of apparent project management sophistication within the organization. When considering the sophistication level, the word "apparent" is one to keep in mind. It may be that many good project tools and techniques are in place, but the question should be, "Are those tools and techniques being used in a consistent manner for the development of IT projects?" It does occur that IT organizations sometimes install the tools and techniques required to successfully manage projects and then fail to enforce the consistent use of those tools.

As an example, there may be a set of project management standards in place, but the issue to be resolved is the extent to which those standards are followed throughout the organization. Too often, unless project standards are tightly enforced within the IT department, they are going to be honored more in the breach than in practice. It is not unusual to find IT installations where a clear set of project management practices are in place but, because they are not well enforced, some projects may be developed using the practices and some may not. In some organizations, the project management standards are seen, not as being mandatory, but as a set of guidelines.

Where such a circumstance exists, there is a clear opportunity for the PMO to become a catalyst to move the organization toward an improved project management development environment. While taking on that responsibility may be beyond the defined purview of the role of the PMO, paying attention to the problem can bring added benefit to the organization. Where the project manager has the skill and experience to incorporate those improvements, it is in the best interest of the organization to take a bit of extra time to begin to improve the ways in which the organization manages IT projects.

PROJECT-RELATED ISSUE MANAGEMENT AND RESOLUTION

One of the roles of the PMO should be to install a mechanism to capture and manage all project issues. Absent a formal, managed process to capture and resolve project-related issues, several serious project consequences are likely to arise, including:

- Potentially important project items may be overlooked. It should be seen as certain that those items will create difficulty within the project at some later date.

- The use of a formal process in which project-related issues are analyzed and prioritized will ensure that the most critical issues are identified, addressed, and resolved in a timely manner.
- Absent a formal process of issue identification and prioritization, there will be a tendency to address those items that have the most vocal supporters, rather than those that may have the most impact on the project.
- The use of a formal project issues approach provides a history of those issues, why they occurred, and how they were ultimately addressed.

When an issue management process is put in place by the PMO, some-one must be assigned to oversee the process. That role will include the capture of the items, the publication of those items on a regular basis, reporting of progress against the items, and the final resolution of the items. The process should be seen as transcending the particular project. As the use of an issue resolution process is employed within a number of IT applications projects, the material gathered should be maintained in a database for reference. Over time, the information in that database can be used to develop patterns of project difficulties.

Having knowledge of the types of IT project-related issues and their resolution can prove helpful as the IT department strives to improve the way applications projects are developed and delivered. Over time, it will be seen that projects tend to suffer from a number of the similar problems. Being able to identify the best way to correct those issues when they appear is going to speed project progress and reduce project tension.

THE OPPORTUNITY TO TEST NEW PROJECT MANAGEMENT APPROACHES AND TECHNIQUES

Given that under the PMO, the project manager can concentrate on the management of the project at hand and avoid distractions in other areas, there should be an opportunity to think beyond the traditional IT project boundaries. Some time can be devoted to the consideration of some different approaches to the management of IT projects. A number of sound methods exist that can be successfully used to improve the delivery of IT projects. One of the added value aspects of the PMO should be, as the project moves forward, to consider trying some of those different approaches to manage various aspects of the project.

Whether or not those management approaches should be used within the existing project will depend on a number of factors. Those factors will include the status of the project, relative to meeting its completion date, the willingness of the internal customers and senior management to accept a higher level of risk, and the culture of the organization.

492

In many organizations, the imposition of new or different IT management approaches mid-project is going to represent too much risk. That stance is understandable, particularly in an organization where initiating the PMO concept originally presented some level of difficulty. The project manager must determine whether or not proposing something new during the life of the project is the correct approach.

Although attempting some different project management efforts will increase the risk to the project, where that risk can be appropriately managed, the project manager should be willing to build a case to try some new approaches. Those approaches need not be radical. The idea should be to begin the process of demonstrating the value to the entire organization of moving into new project management areas. Some of those changes are going to succeed, and some are going to fail. However, when the people within the organization come to realize that different project management approaches will produce additional benefits, the risk will prove to have been worthwhile.

CONCLUSION

A primary imperative of a PMO is to raise a project's visibility. A clear and direct line from the project manager to a high-level manager and emphasis on project success greatly increase the chance for actual success. Although responsibility for a project rests with the project manager, in the PMO structure, senior level management shares that responsibility and can positively influence a project.

When a senior manager assumes an important role in project management, many ancillary, unproductive issues that normally arise can be eliminated. People are less willing to raise objections and more likely to avoid conflicts if they know senior management may be involved.

Is a PMO the ultimate IT project management panacea? The answer, of course, is no. No matter what approach is used, managing IT projects successfully involves hard work and risk. However, a properly funded and supported PMO can bring improvement to the process of managing IT projects. Specifically, a PMO can reduce the levels of project tension and risk. There is also an opportunity to begin to set a course for the continued improvement of project management.

When a PMO successfully delivers its first project, customer attitude about IT will begin to change. As people in the IT department, the business units, and at the senior management level begin to understand that higher levels of IT project performance are attainable, support for the PMO and in turn for the IT effort grows. Moving to those higher levels takes time, patience, and persistence, but doing so is worth the effort.

It can be argued that a PMO adds expense to the project. That argument is correct; a PMO is not going to be free. The costs associated with the PMO are going to reach beyond that of dollars. The stress of using new approaches, the effort required to sell, install, and implement the PMO, and the tension associated with the cultural changes brought about by the PMO all have to considered as costs. However, the benefit to be found in the effective use of a PMO quickly negates any concerns about unnecessary additional expense. A PMO is an effective tool to improve the delivery of IT projects. Organizations that adequately fund and support PMOs find they have made the right choice.

Chapter 44
Creating and Implementing a Balanced Measurement Program

Dana T. Edberg

It is still unclear why many information systems (IS) projects continue to fail, and why some succeed. Understanding the reasons for project success or failure, however, provides IS managers the information they need to form actions that enable the IS function to move forward and improve. The best way to gain this necessary knowledge is from a comprehensive IS measurement program.

Measurement is sometimes viewed as an objective in itself rather than as a way of supporting organizational goals. Much of the available advice on the application of measurement to the software development and maintenance process focuses on the intricacies and integrity of specific forms of measurement rather than on understanding the strengths and components of a comprehensive IS measurement program. This chapter focuses on the latter by describing a flexible measurement framework adaptable to specific organizational requirements. The chapter:

- Explores the concept of a measurement program
- Uses the balanced-scorecard structure to develop a framework that serves as a guideline for the measurement procedure[1]
- Divides the measurement procedure into manageable components
- Provides guidelines for the development and successful implementation of a measurement program

0-8493-1190-X/02/$0.00+$1.50
© 2002 by CRC Press LLC

It has been said that the best way to understand the real behavior of software development and maintenance is to institute a measurement program that helps clarify patterns and guides decision making.[2] Measuring key attributes of software development and maintenance reveals behavior patterns that can be analyzed and interpreted to devise methods that better control and improve these functions.

WHAT IS A MEASUREMENT PROGRAM?

A measurement program is designed to help people understand and interpret the processes of an organization. No company, for example, would dream of operating without a way of tracking and analyzing its financial transactions. A financial accounting system is the fundamental data collection process within the financial measurement program of an organization. One measurement used by accountants in this program is the accounts-receivable turnover ratio. This ratio indicates how well assets are used by determining how many times accounts receivable is turned over each year. Calculating this ratio requires a system that collects the net credit sales and the average accounts receivable for the organization.

Although executives would not ask a credit manager to improve operations without first determining the current and potentially optimum accounts-receivable turnover ratios, they frequently ask IS managers to improve operations without any idea about important current and projected data and ratios. Whereas extensive computerized tracking systems support the financial and managerial measurement systems that underlie the operations of an organization, IS managers are left with intuition and guesswork to control their part of the organization. The historical lack of systems to track and analyze key characteristics of the IS function sets the function apart from other aspects of business operations. Cutting costs or enhancing productivity is thus especially problematic in IS because it is usually accomplished without a detailed picture of expected versus current operations.

A measurement program spans the past, present, and future of company operations. Data from past operations is used as a historical baseline to measure present and future processes and projects. Present tasks provide current collection opportunities and data that is analyzed against the historical baseline to guide improvements in future performance. A measurement program thus consolidates data from the past and present to provide the insight that helps IS managers take action for future improvement.

A measurement program requires the formulation of specific, quantifiable metrics. Metrics are quantitative values obtained by measuring characteristics of a system or process. A metric is a piece of information that is analyzed, interpreted, and used to monitor progress toward improvement.

GOALS OF A MEASUREMENT PROGRAM

One of the most frequently asked questions about an IS measurement program is, "What are the best metrics?" A more appropriate question is, "What are the goals of IS and how can they be measured?" Understanding and defining the goals of an IS organization help clarify the metrics that are a part of the measurement program. These goals, and the related goals of the measurement program, must be delineated before the counting begins.

Focusing on goals rather than on metrics is important for several reasons. People notice what is measured in an organization and frequently modify their behavior to make those measurements appear more favorable. Although laboriously counting the number of lines of code written per programmer per day encourages programmers to write more code and results in a lot of code, the code may not solve business problems. Tracking each computer development project and painstakingly updating visibly placed Gantt charts may prod employees to deliver systems on time, but the systems may have many defects that make them difficult to use or maintain. Surveying the satisfaction level of computer users may result in actions that produce happy users, but it could also have the effect of generating a costly and inefficient systems development and maintenance process.

Measurement helps to highlight specific areas in an organization and encourages people to focus their attention and energies on those areas. To leverage this measurement spotlight, IS managers should identify a set of combined goals that achieve the objectives of the organization. Once goals are established, managers should identify specific questions to be answered, which, in turn, leads to the metrics to be collected. This structure is termed the goal/question/metric (G/Q/M) approach.[3]

THE GOAL/QUESTION/METRIC APPROACH

The success of the G/Q/M approach is exemplified by the experience of the Motorola Corporation. Managers at Motorola identified seven goals they believed would improve their systems development organization.[4] For each goal they defined specific questions that needed to be answered to determine whether improvement had occurred. Each question was then defined in terms of an analytical equation, and the variables in the equation were divided into specific metrics that could be collected. For example, one goal was to increase defect containment. The managers defined the following two questions and related metrics to evaluate progress in this area:

> What is the currently known effectiveness of the defect detection process before release?

$$\text{Total defect containment effectiveness} = \frac{\text{prerelease defects}}{\text{prelease defects} + \text{postrelease defect}}$$

What is the currently known containment effectiveness of faults introduced during each constructive phase of software development for a particular software product?
phase I errors

$$\text{Phase containment effectiveness for phase I} = \frac{\text{phase I errors}}{\text{phase I errors} + \text{phase I defects}}$$

Using the G/Q/M approach gave Motorola the opportunity to clarify the semantic use of specific terms such as errors versus defects and the boundaries of given development phases while formulating questions and metrics. (For purposes of clarification, an error is a problem found during testing of the phase in which it was introduced, and a defect is a problem found later than the phase in which it was introduced.) Managers were able to use the information generated from the measurement program to pinpoint errors and defects by software development phase. This information helped them identify areas in the software development process that required changes and to make the needed changes based on information instead of intuition.

WHAT CAN A MEASUREMENT PROGRAM MEASURE?

The complexity of developing and maintaining business systems makes it difficult to isolate the activities and areas for which goals, questions, and metrics should be formed. The balanced scorecard approach to general business measures encourages managers to expand beyond traditional financial metrics and more thoroughly integrate organizational strategy with resulting performance.[5]

The balanced scorecard defines four different perspectives for performance measurement:

- *Financial* — How do we look to shareholders?
- *Internal business* — What must we excel at?
- *Innovation and learning* — Can we continue to improve and create value?
- *Customer* — How do our customers see us?

Although these perspectives were originally defined for measuring an entire organization, they can be translated to the IS world. There they, respectively, are the project, product, process, and performance perspectives.

PERSPECTIVES OF PERFORMANCE MEASUREMENT

Exhibit 1 depicts the importance of the four perspectives to IS measurement. They are discussed in-depth in the following sections.

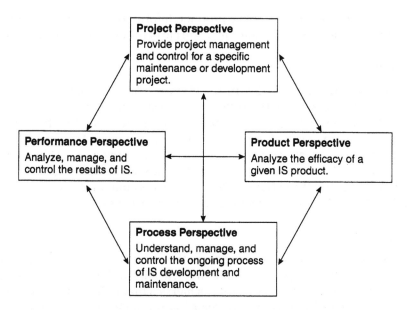

Exhibit 1.   Balanced Scorecard Framework for IS Measurement

Project

The objective of the project perspective is to understand and measure the characteristics of a specific development or maintenance project by focusing on the attributes that make each project unique. Many organizations use a development or maintenance project as the vehicle to gather data concerning personnel effort and costs. Within the project perspective, an IS organization has the opportunity to use this data to create metrics that provide insight into how funds for software development and maintenance are used. What is measured depends on the scope of the project. The attributes of a given project provide information about such factors as personnel utilization, project estimation, and the nontechnical activities associated with a project.

Product

This perspective emphasizes the attributes that differentiate a product from others. The metrics applicable to this perspective are used to understand the growth and progression of a development and maintenance product. It is important to understand the internal scope and attributes of each specific product that composes a system. Managers can use this information to devise new testing procedures, determine individual product defects, or improve the accuracy of product estimation. Because a product frequently lives longer than the project used to create it, product data is gathered over the life of a product. Information generated from the data helps a manager better determine the life expectancy of a given product.

Process

The Software Engineering Institute (SEI) Capability Maturity Model has brought renewed focus to the software development and maintenance process. The process perspective highlights the desire to modify the process used to develop and maintain information systems so that procedures reflect the best practices discovered in the industry and within a given organization. The measures of this perspective consider organizational and human social interactions, as well as the methodological and technical implications of the development/maintenance process.

Performance

The performance perspective measures the outputs of an information system. It encompasses measurements that track both the traditional technical measures of performance as well as metrics that indicate the success of the system as defined by the strategies and policies of an organization. Defining this perspective requires defining system success.

Importance of Balancing the Scorecard

Using the balanced scorecard approach helps IS managers ensure that all aspects of the IS function are appropriately represented in the measurement program. Instead of focusing on a single area, such as personnel productivity for a specific project, the balanced scorecard provides structure from which to view each perspective of IS operations.

Using the scorecard thus helps IS managers delineate critical areas and define appropriate goals, questions, and metrics for each of them. The importance of the perspectives varies across organizations. For example, one company may be more interested in the performance of IS as a whole, whereas another might be more concerned about the productivity of project development activities. The balanced scorecard framework does not attempt to dictate the relative emphasis on each area but instead serves as a guideline for managers during development of specific measurement goals.

Sample Data for IS Metrics

Once an organization decides to implement a measurement program, the problem is usually deciding what not to measure, rather than deciding what to measure. Many organizations collect data for so many different metrics that participants in the measurement program become cynical and the effectiveness of the program is greatly reduced. In other organizations, the problem is to determine what kinds of data are available to be collected. Exhibit 2 lists categories of metrics for each perspective of the balanced scorecard framework, data for potential metrics in each category, and sample metrics. The exhibit is not comprehensive but rather an abbreviated list of possibilities for each perspective of the framework.

As the exhibit indicates, there are more types of data than there is time available to collect them. A measurement program would not be cost-effective if the data necessary to produce all interesting metrics was collected. The best method is to focus on basic metrics such as size, defects, effort, and user satisfaction before moving on to other metrics.

Under the G/Q/M approach, the choice of metrics follows the definition of goals and formulation of specific, answerable questions. To achieve a balanced scorecard of measurement, IS managers must ensure that the metrics selected span each of the four perspectives. If one perspective is not measured, a distorted picture of IS may be the result of the measurement program. Because the balanced scorecard framework is used as a guideline to pinpoint areas for control and subsequent improvement, the implications of such a distortion are enormous.

WHAT MAKES AN EFFECTIVE METRIC?

It is wise to consider the criteria commonly employed to judge the usefulness of proposed metrics before selecting metrics that answer the questions deemed important to the goals of IS. A metric should be:

- *Understandable* — If a metric is difficult to define or interpret, chances are that it will not be used or it will be applied inconsistently.
- *Quantifiable* — Because metrics must be objective, IS managers should strive to reduce the amount of personal influence or judgment that must be attached to a given metric.
- *Cost-Effective* — The value of the information obtained from a measurement procedure must exceed the cost of collecting data, analyzing patterns, interpreting results, and validating correctness. A given metric should be relatively easy to capture and compute, and measurement should not interfere with the actual process of creating and delivering information systems.
- *Proven* — Many proposed metrics appear to have great worth but have not been validated or shown to have value in the drive to improve IS. IS managers should steer clear of metrics that appear overly complex or have not been tested and shown to be consistent or meaningful.
- *High-Impact* — Although some metrics, such as cyclomatic complexity, offer an effective way of predicting testing time and possibly corrective maintenance time, they may not provide enough information to make their collection and calculation worthwhile in all situations. If

Exhibit 2. **Metric Categories, Data, and Samples for the Four Perspectives of IS Performance Measurement**

Category	Sample Data	Sample Metrics
Project Perspective		
Financial, type and scope	Total estimated and actual time and estimated and actual cost per predefined project activity, type (e.g., development, maintenance), estimated and actual project function points	Cost per function point (FP)
Personnel	Experience level, experience type and education of personnel, years using a specific development environment, number of contractor personnel, number of employees	Productivity ratings: time/FP for different levels of experience and education
Methodology	Type(s) used, level of automation, testing techniques, number of models	The metrics for methodology are summarized for the entire software process rather than for a particular project
Interface	Number of meetings, meeting type and length, number of requirements and design changes, pages of documentation, hours of customer training	Percent of time in meetings and by meeting type
Product Perspective		
Financial, type and scope	The same data and metrics used for a project are also applied to a single product; one project could result in many products, or it might take many projects to produce a single product; product measurements exist over the life of the product, whereas project metrics are closed out when the project is completed	
Quality	Number of defects and errors, number of test cases, number of change requests, number of changes, amount of usage, complexity rating, number of reused modules, number of support calls	Number of defects/FP
Results	Business objectives translated into quantitative goals	Inventory percent level
Efficiency	Amount of memory, disk, processor cycles, response time, operator time	Average/peak response time
Process Perspective		
Organization	Number of general meetings, type of meetings, communication methods, hours by activity; amount of office and desk space	Maturity level assessment
Personnel	Data in addition to that gathered for a given project includes vacation days taken, vacation days worked, number of working days, number of employees, number of contractors, number of training days	Metrics in addition to those listed for a given project
Methodology	Gathered by project	Overall productivity by methodology

Exhibit 2. **Metric Categories, Data, and Samples for the Four Perspectives of IS Performance Measurement (Continued)**

Category	Sample Data	Sample Metrics
Performance Perspective		
Satisfaction	User satisfaction survey, number of system users, number of workstations, number of reports generated, number of reports used, number of screens, number of screens viewed, number of help requests	Average time to respond to help requests
Integrity	Number of errors discovered after delivery, number of errors discovered within a selected period of time, error severity	Average number of errors (classified by severity) discovered after delivery

the products being measured have relatively similar levels of complexity, it is more helpful to gather metrics with a more significant impact. For example, it is well documented that one programmer can make a program very complex, whereas another can produce elegant, concise code. The effects of different code on actual testing and correction time, however, pale in comparison to the effects of incomplete or inaccurate design specifications. Therefore, the metric with the most impact in this case relates to the accuracy of design specifications rather than to program complexity.

IMPLEMENTING A MEASUREMENT PROGRAM

Athough use of a measurement program appears to be a rational management approach backed by documented successes, some organizations find implementation a difficult undertaking. Implementing a measurement program is not a trivial task, but rather a significant action requiring management commitment. The two key challenges in implementing a measurement program are time and communication.

Key Challenges

Time. A measurement program is not a quick fix for a broken process with benefits that are quickly realized. Data must be gathered and analyzed over time before the program yields information that people can translate into actions that improve the development and maintenance process. It takes time to create a metric baseline, evaluate the results, and choose appropriate new actions. Then it takes additional time to compare new information about those new actions against the baseline to gauge improvements. Implementation of a measurement program is best viewed as a critical component of long-term continuous improvement.

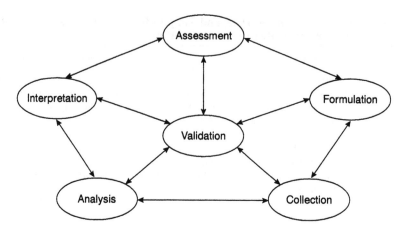

Exhibit 3. Activities of an IS Measurement Program

Communication. Part of making a measurement program work is convincing people that it will lead to organizational improvements. If program participants are not convinced of the importance of the program, chances are the effort will be abandoned before meaningful data is collected and used. If people believe that the results of the measurement program will be used to distribute blame unfairly regarding projects and products, then they will not participate in the program.

A key challenge of program implementation is thus communicating prospective benefits to the diverse audiences that will collect, analyze, interpret, and apply the information. At the same time, the proposed use of the measurement information must be made clear to all participants.

Program Activities

Although the success of a measurement program cannot be guaranteed, IS managers can increase the odds that implementation will prevail by paying attention to the individual activities composing the program. Exhibit 3 shows the activities necessary to implement and maintain an IS measurement program. Each activity is described in the sections that follow.

Assessment. The three primary functions of assessment are:

1. Evaluating the current position of the organization
2. Identifying the goals of a measurement program
3. Establishing specific measurement goals

Since the mid-1980s, formal software process assessments such as those from the SEI and Software Productivity Research (SPR) have been available to evaluate the software development processes of an organization.

Assessment provides a clear picture of the current organizational environment and serves as a starting point from which to gauge future improvements. For example, it would be unreasonable to state that a new development methodology provided increased programmer productivity unless the level of productivity before its implementation was known and documented.

During the assessment phase, it is also important to define the goals of the measurement procedure. Another activity performed during assessment is selling the measurement program to management and IS staff. All participants in the program must understand the relationship between measurement and improvement so that they will support the resulting program.

Formulation. A measurement program requires the formulation of specific, quantifiable questions and metrics to satisfy the program goals. The previously discussed suggestions for choosing appropriate metrics and sample goals/questions/metrics provide a good starting point.

Collection. The collection of specific metrics requires a cost-accounting system aimed at gathering and storing specified attributes that act as input data for the metrics. This process should be automated so that collection takes as little time as possible and the danger of becoming mired in amassing huge amounts of data is avoided. Careful planning in assessment and formulation helps avoid the gathering of too much data.

Analysis. The physical collection of a metric does not, by itself, provide much information that helps in the decision-making process. Just as gross sales do not reveal the financial condition of an organization, the number of function points for a project does not explain how many person-months it will take to produce that project. A metric must be statistically analyzed so that patterns are uncovered, historical baselines are established, and anomalies are identified.

Interpretation. The function of interpretation is to attach meaning to the analysis, in other words, to determine the cause of the patterns that have been identified during analysis and then to prescribe appropriate corrective action. For example, if analysis shows that users are consistently dissatisfied with systems that require an ever-increasing number of user and analyst meetings, then it may not be a good idea to schedule more meetings. A more effective approach is to look for other reasons behind the dissatisfaction. Perhaps the meetings are unproductive, communication skills are ineffective, or business problems are being incorrectly identified. The interpretation of metric analyses furnishes a direction in which to start looking for different problems and solutions.

Validation. As shown in Exhibit 3, validation occurs throughout each phase of the measurement program. It involves asking a set of questions to ensure that the goals of the measurement program are being addressed. For example, the results of the formulation phase should be validated with two key questions:

1. Are we measuring the right attribute?
2. Are we measuring that attribute correctly?

The following scenario illustrates how validation questions are applied. Assume that one of the overall goals of an IS organization is to improve the performance of user support. Using the G/Q/M approach, the IS organization establishes a goal of improving user satisfaction with IS support. A question that supports this goal is, "What is the current level of user satisfaction with IS support?" IS personnel then formulate a questionnaire they believe measures the level of user satisfaction with IS support. The questionnaire is used to collect data, which is analyzed and interpreted.

Analysis shows that there is no relationship between the type, amount, or level of IS support and user satisfaction. Why not? It could be because there is no relationship between user satisfaction and IS support, or because the questionnaire was not measuring user satisfaction with IS support. Validating the questionnaire in the formulation phase helps ensure that it is measuring what it is intended to measure.

Measurement as a Passive Yet Iterative Process

Measurement is a relatively passive process; it is the actions people take because they are being measured and the new procedures that are developed based on the information generated from the measurement program that lead to improvement. The goal of a measurement program is to provide information that can be used for continual improvement of the systems development process and its related products.

Although Exhibit 3 depicts the activities of assessment, formulation, collection, analysis, and interpretation as a sequential, circular process, they are interdependent and not performed sequentially. In the scenario presented in the preceding section, the IS organization found during analysis that the identified metrics were inadequate to determine any patterns. Such a result required validation of the metrics being used and a return to the formulation phase to redefine other metrics that would yield information more relevant to the goals.

MANAGING A MEASUREMENT PROGRAM

A measurement program is a long-term effort requiring the cooperation and coordination of a broad set of participants. One way to support the program is to establish a metrics infrastructure. A metrics infrastructure includes the following:

- A management method
- Data collection procedures
- Ongoing program training

The management method should incorporate an integrated group/committee that performs each of the measurement activities. This group is similar to a conventional project steering committee and includes representatives from general management, IS management, system users, and IS development/maintenance. It differs from a project management group primarily because it survives beyond the implementation of the program. As a long-term, ongoing process, measurement must have a long-term, ongoing management committee.

The management group is critical to the success of a measurement program because it keeps program participants aware of the importance of their activities and provides the broad view necessary to the survival of the program. The committee determines how the program goals evolve over time and serves as a touchstone for their achievement.

It is also beneficial to establish a metrics user group to share experiences and coordinate training. Training is a key element of the metrics infrastructure that should be periodically provided. Training programs encompass data collection, analysis, and interpretation procedures so that project participants understand not only how to collect data, but also how to apply it. The infrastructure should also include tools to automate the collection and analysis phases of measurement, as well as a consolidated database to store all metrics data.

Because the results of a measurement program are not immediately discernible, people must perform many tasks before a visible, attributable outcome is perceived. Training is one way to ensure that all project participants understand the goals and procedures that underlie what may appear, at times, to be a slow process. It also helps to alleviate employee concerns about the application of the measurement program results.

Many of the activities of measurement require the cooperation of diverse groups of people. Even though the concepts of metrics and measurement conjure up an image of required technical expertise, the most appropriate leader for the measurement program is an individual with excellent communication and negotiation skills.

Information about programs used in other companies is helpful during the process of defining program objectives and formulating metrics. The recommended reading list provides a source for gathering this information.

RECOMMENDED COURSE OF ACTION

Each day new articles describe a new practice touted to yield tremendous productivity and efficiency improvements in the IS organization. Some IS managers have discovered that it can take many years to apply the so-called best practices of other organizations recorded in the literature. A measurement program affords IS managers the opportunity to develop local proof of what really works. More important, the information produced from a measurement program helps IS managers better understand and control the process of software development and maintenance.

Creating a custom-tailored measurement program thus provides IS managers with information about the unique behavioral patterns of their organization. In doing so, it helps these managers control their professional destinies as well.

Notes

1. R.S. Kaplan and D.P. Norton, "Using the Balanced Scorecard as a Strategic Management System," *Harvard Business Review,* January-February 1996.
2. L.H. Putnam and W. Myers, *Measures for Excellence,* Englewood Cliffs, NJ: Yourdon Press, 1992, p. 11.
3. V.R. Basili and D.M. Weiss, "A Methodology for Collecting Valid Software Engineering Data," *IEEE Transactions on Software Engineering,* 10, no. 3, 728–738, 1984.
4. M.K. Daskalantonakis, "A Practical View of Software Measurement and Implementation Experiences within Motorola," *IEEE Transactions on Software Engineering,* 18, no. 11, 998–1010, 1992.
5. R.S. Kaplan and D.P. Norton, "The Balanced Scorecard: Measures That Drive Performance," *Harvard Business Review,* January-February, 71–79, 1992.

Bibliography

1. Grady, R.B. *Practical Software Metrics for Project Management and Process Improvement.* Englewood Cliffs, NJ: Prentice-Hall, 1992.
2. Paulish, D.J. and Carleton, A.D. "Case Studies of Software-Process-Improvement Measurement." *IEEE Computer,* September, 50–57, 1994.
3. Putnam, L.H., and Myers, W. *Measures for Excellence,* Englewood Cliffs, NJ: Yourdon Press, 1992.
4. Roche, J. and Jackson, M. "Software Measurement Methods: Recipes for Success?" *Information and Software Technology,* 36, no. 3, 173–189, 1994.

Chapter 45
Software Process Assessment: Building the Foundation for a Mature IS Process

Roger S. Pressman

Managers and technical staff in most companies are all too quick to select new methods and tools and proceed toward modern software engineering practice. The problem is that many of these same managers and technical people have a weak understanding of the development and maintenance process that is currently being applied within their organizations. They proceed without a firm foundation or an understanding of where they are. As a result, new technologies sometimes fail to provide the benefits that are expected.

Companies struggle with software engineering because managers fail to understand that a software engineering approach is one part of a broader total quality management philosophy. Even when this fact is understood, some managers never connect the concept of *kaizen*, or continuous process improvement, to software development activities.

W. Edwards Deming defined quality as striving for excellence in reliability and functions by continuous (process) improvement, supported by statistical analysis of the causes of failure. If an organization wants to improve the quality of its software, thereby enabling information technology to better serve the business, it must focus its attention on improving the process through which software is developed. The starting point is assessment — a look-in-the-mirror approach that enables managers and technical staff to better understand their software development strengths and weaknesses. Process assessment is a first step toward the creation of a viable strategy that will serve as a road map for continuous software process improvement.

0-8493-1190-X/02/$0.00+$1.50
© 2002 by CRC Press LLC

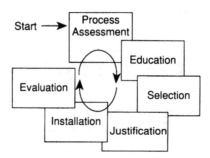

Exhibit 1. A Technology Transition Cycle for Process Improvement

A COMMON SENSE PROCESS IMPROVEMENT STRATEGY

Process assessment is the initial step in a technology transition cycle that spans many process improvement activities. The cycle begins with assessment and encompasses several other activities, as illustrated in Exhibit 1:

- *Education* — Most software managers and developers know relatively little about software engineering. To increase the level of software engineering knowledge, an organization must develop an effective education strategy that is tied to the results of the process assessment and that coordinates training content and timing with immediate project needs so that maximum benefit can be attained.
- *Selection* — Selection defines specific goals and criteria for choosing software engineering procedures, methods, and computer-aided software engineering tools; it leads to the development of a rational mechanism for costing, justifying, and acquiring these important elements of software engineering technology.
- *Justification* — Expenditures for software engineering procedures, methods, education, CASE tools, and associated support activities must be shown to provide a return on investment before money is committed. A justification model is used to demonstrate the bottom-line benefits of process improvement.
- *Installation* — To install software engineering technologies successfully, a transition plan must be devised and executed. The plan defines tasks, responsibilities, milestones, and deliverables and specifies a schedule for getting the work done.
- *Evaluation* — Some managers make changes to improve the development process, select and install new technology, and then stick their heads in the sand, dedicating little time to evaluating whether the technology is working. The evaluation step initiates an ongoing assessment of the CASE/software engineering installation process.

All these steps define transition strategy, and they all depend on a successful process assessment. In the remainder of the chapter, the first step — process assessment — is considered in greater detail.

OBJECTIVES OF A PROCESS ASSESSMENT

Although informal software process audits have been conducted for many years, the use of a formal process assessment is relatively new, and it was not until process assessment was endorsed by the Software Engineering Institute (SEI) that major corporations and government agencies began to adopt the practice.

The term *process assessment* refers to both qualitative and quantitative information gathering. When process assessment is properly conducted, it satisfies its objectives by:

- Providing a framework for an objective examination of the software development practices of an organization
- Indicating technical and management strengths and weaknesses in a way that allows for comparison to industry norms
- Indicating the relative software development maturity of an organization
- Leading to a strategy for process improvement and, indirectly, to the improvement of software quality

Process Attributes

To accomplish these objectives, the process assessment approach should be designed in a way that probes each of the following process attributes:

- Organizational policies that guide the use of software engineering practices
- Training that supports the use of procedures, methods, and tools
- The framework (procedural model) that has been established to define a software engineering process
- Quality assurance (QA) activities for software
- Project management tasks that plan, control, and monitor software work
- Software engineering methods that allow technical staff to build high-quality applications
- CASE tools that support the methods
- Software metrics and measurement that provide insight into the process and its product

STRUCTURE OF A PROCESS ASSESSMENT

Although there are many different process assessment approaches, all have the same basic structure. First, a set of questions that probe process maturity are asked and answered. The questions may focus solely on procedural issues or may delve into the application of software engineering technology. Responses to the assessment questions are evaluated and a process maturity level is computed. The maturity level represents the commitment and adherence of an organization to sound software engineering and QA practices. Finally, the results of the assessment are interpreted and used to develop a process improvement strategy. Interpretation may be global or may target specific process attributes.

Assessment Questions

Assessment questions are designed to enable an assessor (who may be an outside consultant or staff members drawn from the organization undergoing assessment) to gather enough information to understand the software organization, the application of technology within it, and the relative sophistication of the project management framework for applying the technology. An effective software engineering process assessment approach uses three types of questions: qualitative, Boolean, and quantitative.

Qualitative Questions. Questions in this category require a narrative explanation. Some qualitative questions are:

- How are project teams formed? Is a functional or matrix organization used?
- Who are the customers for software within the organization?
- What is the relationship between the customer and the people who develop software? Who initially specifies products with software content? To what degree are software development practices understood by the customer? What communication problems occur between customers and the software engineering organization?
- What is the role of quality assurance, manufacturing, and service organizations with regard to software.
- What are the individual software development tools (available as operating system features and as stand alone functions) used during software development?

Boolean Questions. Questions in this category elicit a yes or no response. Boolean questions are used to assess the following three areas:

- *Design* — Does the software development organization use a specific method for data design? For architectural design? Is procedural design constrained to the use of the structured programming constructs? Is there a defined method for human–computer interface design?
- *Programming and coding* — Is more than 90 percent of code written in a high-order language? Are specific conventions for code documentation defined and used?

- *Testing* — Are specific methods used for test case design? Does test planning begin before code is written? Are the results of testing stored for historical reference? Are there mechanisms for routinely performing regression testing and for ensuring that testing covers all software requirements?

Quantitative Questions. Questions in this category enable an organization to obtain numerical information that can be used in conjunction with software metrics to compute costs and potential payback for new technology. The following information is representative:

- Annual revenue reported by a component
- Annual budget for data processing or IS
- Annual budget for engineering/product-oriented software development
- Annual budget for software-related training
- Annual budget for computer hardware
- Annual budget for software tools (differentiate between hardware and software)
- Number of systems and software practitioners in all application areas
- Number of IS people by job category
- Number of software people working on engineered products and systems
- Current number of outside contractors working on software in-house
- Percentage of software people working on maintenance
- Projected growth or decrease for each aforementioned item

Most assessment questionnaires are organized in a way that probes specific process attributes (e.g., software quality assurance or project management approach); most suggest a grading scheme for responses so that relative strengths and weaknesses can be ascertained; and most address both management and technical topics. The structure of the questionnaire, the types of questions asked, the grading scheme that is proposed, and the usefulness of the results are determined by the overall process assessment model (examples of which are discussed in the section headed "Process Assessment Models").

Response Evaluation

The responses to the assessment questionnaire are evaluated to determine the process maturity level. Although specific evaluation approaches vary, the following steps are common:

- Responses to Boolean questions are used to derive a maturity value. Maturity values may be based on a simple count of yes/no responses, on a specific set of questions that must be answered positively to achieve a given maturity level, or on a weighting scheme that defines the maturity level of an organization that answers a specific question positively.

- Responses to quantitative questions are compared with industry averages, when available. Both quality and productivity data is collected, and compared averages are published in the technical literature.
- Responses to qualitative questions are used to derive additional insight into the current process. By documenting local conditions and constraints, qualitative responses establish a baseline for interpretation.

Interpreting the Results

The maturity values computed from the responses to Boolean assessment questions can provide a means for developing a transition plan for process improvement. Ideally, maturity values are assigned to one of the several process attributes. On the basis of each maturity value, an organization can rank process attributes according to their importance and impact on local efforts to improve process. After priorities have been assigned for process attribute areas, interpretation begins with the goal of developing an organizationally specific set of findings and recommendations. Findings describe specific areas of strength or weakness; recommendations define the actions required to improve the software development process.

PROCESS ASSESSMENT MODELS

A process assessment model defines the overall structure and logistics of the process assessment, the organization and application of assessment questions, the process attributes that are considered during the assessment, and the manner in which process maturity is determined. Assessment models can be broadly categorized as follows:

- Models developed by large companies and originally intended for internal use, such as the Hewlett-Packard Software Quality and Productivity Analysis (SQPA) and the Bell Canada Software Development Capability Assessment Method
- Models developed as an adjunct to consulting services, such as Howard Rubin Associates, R.S. Pressman & Associates, Inc., Software Productivity Research, Inc., and many others
- Models developed by government/industry consortiums such as the Software Engineering Institute Capability Maturity Model, which is the best known of these
- Models packaged as do-it-yourself products for use by any software development organization

In addition, the International Standards Organization (ISO) is currently at work on a standard for software engineering process assessment to ensure compliance to ISO 9000 quality standards. At present, no assessment model meets all of the proposed requirements for the ISO assessment standard.

A detailed discussion of all types of assessment models is beyond the scope of this chapter. However, to provide a further understanding of the assessment approach, two representative assessment models are considered in the following sections.

The SEI Assessment Model

The Software Engineering Institute comprehensive assessment model is predicated on a set of software engineering capabilities that should be present as organizations reach different levels of process maturity. To determine the current state of process maturity of an organization, the SEI uses an assessment questionnaire and a five-point grading scheme. The grading scheme provides a measure of the global effectiveness of the software engineering practices of a company and establishes five process maturity levels:

- *Level 1: Initial* — The software process is characterized as *ad hoc*. Few processes are defined, and success depends on individual effort.
- *Level 2: Repeatable* — Basic project management processes are established to track cost, schedule, and functionality. The necessary process discipline is in place to repeat earlier successes on projects with similar applications.
- *Level 3: Defined* — The software process for both management and engineering activities is documented, standardized, and integrated into an organizationwide software process. This level includes all characteristics defined for level 2.
- *Level 4: Managed* — Detailed measures of the software process and product quality are collected so that both the software process and products are quantitatively controlled. This level includes all characteristics defined for level 3.
- *Level 5: Optimizing* — Continuous process improvement is enabled by quantitative feedback from the process and from testing innovative ideas and technologies. This level includes all characteristics defined for level 4.

To achieve specific levels of process maturity, selected questions from the SEI questionnaire must be answered positively. The SEI has associated key process areas (KPAs) with each of the maturity levels. KPAs describe those software engineering functions that must be present to constitute good practice at a particular level. Across the maturity model 18 KPAs are defined and are mapped into different levels of process maturity. Assessment questions are designed to probe for the existence (or lack) of key practices that reveal whether the goals of a KPA have been achieved.

The SEI approach represents a significant achievement in process assessment, but it has some drawbacks. Although detailed analysis of the assessment questionnaire can lead to an assessment of the efficacy of key process areas and related key practices, the maturity level alone tells little about individual KPAs. The process maturity level is computed in a way that causes a low grade if specific questions are answered negatively, even if other questions that represent reasonable sophistication are answered with a yes. The SEI questionnaire is sometimes criticized for underemphasizing the importance of technology and overemphasizing the importance of policies and standards. Consultants who are accredited assessors are usually needed to provide the additional detail and insight that is missing with the SEI questionnaire alone.

The assessment model proposed by the SEI represents the most comprehensive look in the mirror for the industry. It requires broad-based organizational commitment, an assessment budget in the thousands of dollars, and the presence of accredited assessors to do the work.

The Process Advisor Assessment Model

The Process Advisor assessment model enables self-directed assessment for those organizations that want to begin software engineering technology transition activities without incurring substantial initial expense. Unlike the SEI assessment questionnaire (which contains only Boolean questions), the process advisor model incorporates qualitative, quantitative, and Boolean questions. The qualitative and quantitative assessment questions follow the structure discussed earlier in this chapter. Responses to these questions are assessed using a quasi-expert system that is built into the model. Each response to the questionnaire is compared with a set of typical responses. The quasi-expert system provides a set of inferences that help an organization to develop findings and recommendations based on the response.

Boolean questions address eight process attributes: organizational policies, training, software development process, quality assurance, project management, software engineering methods, computer-aided software engineering tools, and software metrics and measurement. Responses to the Boolean questions generate process attribute grades for each of the eight attributes. These form a process maturity footprint for a software organization.

The process maturity footprint (Exhibit 2) indicates the relative strengths and weaknesses in the process attribute areas and enables an organization to compare itself with common software engineering practice and best practice, which is the level of software engineering practice found

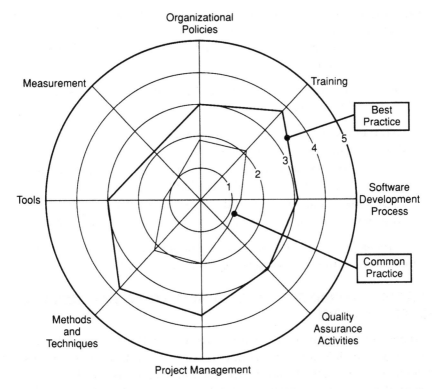

Exhibit 2. A Process Attribute Footprint

in the top 10 to 15 percent of all software development organizations. Process advisor also provides guidance for establishing an education strategy, creating technology selection and justification models, and building an effective transition plan.

PROCESS MATURITY

The majority of assessment models (including the two described in the preceding sections) enable an organization to compute its process maturity. Management must then know how to use this number.

All too often, a senior manager decides that a specific process maturity level should become an organization goal. That is, an organization that currently has a process maturity of 1.0 is chartered with becoming a 3.0 organization within 24 months. Although there is nothing inherently wrong with setting process maturity goals, focusing solely on improving the process maturity value misses the point. The goals of every software development organization should be to improve the quality of the applications it builds, to satisfy its customers and users, and to accomplish work on time. Improving process maturity helps in achieving these goals, but it should not become the goal.

In general, process maturity (and process attribute grades) should be used in the following ways:

- To target areas of strength and weakness
- To raise management consciousness
- To define areas in which further investigation (e.g., assessment meetings with relevant staff) may be needed
- To provide a comparison to industry common and best practice
- To serve as a baseline for reassessment later in the transition life cycle

Using process maturity in these ways, an organization can establish a foundation on which the technology transition plan is built.

DEVELOPING FINDINGS AND RECOMMENDATIONS THAT IMPROVE PROCESS MATURITY

Findings and recommendations are derived from the results of the assessment. However, it is sometimes difficult to interpret the assessment results in a manner that leads to pragmatic recommendations for change. A self-directed assessment approach must provide a set of inference-based guidelines that are tied to different maturity levels for each of the process attributes under assessment. Once the assessment has been completed, the maturity grade for each process attribute is determined. The grade range provides a solid indication of both findings and recommendations. To illustrate inference-based guidelines, the sample findings and recommendations are reproduced from the Process Advisor workbook.

THE SOFTWARE DEVELOPMENT PROCESS

Questions in the software engineering process section of the questionnaire focus on standards as a way to determine whether an organization has codified its approach. Examine the grade and place it in the context of the grade ranges:

Grade Range	Identifier
Below 1.65	E
1.65 to 2.25	D
2.26 to 2.75	C
2.76 to 3.25	B
Above 3.26	A

Interpretation:

- *Grades E and D* — It is unlikely that the organization has developed a written description of its process or defined a process in any explicit manner.
  - *Action:* The organization should create a skeletal framework for software engineering, that is, a set of activities, deliverables, milestones, and QA actions that can be applied as software is being developed. A description of the framework is then needed to solicit comments and recommendations from managers and technical staff. Over time, the framework should be reworked and more detail added until it evolves into a standard.
- *Grades C and B* — The organization has codified many of the activities associated with software development. It is likely that the same approach is applied across different projects and that project planning, control, and software quality assurance are easier to achieve as a result. However, just because standards exist does not mean that the process is effective or properly characterized.
  - *Action:* Each of the standards should be reviewed to determine whether it reflects modern software engineering practice and whether there are aspects that can be streamlined or that do not work well. Time should be spent polling development staff to determine whether the standards are being used as widely as these grade ranges imply. Specific technical areas without standards can be determined by reviewing responses to individual questions. It may be worthwhile to develop a framework approach for a specific technical area (e.g., testing) in a manner similar to that described in the action paragraph for E and D ranges.

QUALITY ASSURANCE ACTIVITIES

Questions in the QA activities section of the process assessment questionnaire explore the emphasis of an organization on documentation, reviews, and other QA functions. Examine the grade and place it in the context of the grade ranges (listed in the previous section). If one or more of the subsection grades are significantly different from the overall section grade, further investigation into that area is warranted.

Interpretation:

- *Grades E and D* — Software quality and the activities needed to ensure it are not a primary focus within the software development organization. Documentation is probably weak, because there are no standard formats to guide developers. Effective reviews are not being conducted and the results of reviews are not applied to improve the process. Software quality assurance is not a formally defined activity.

—*Action:* The organization should develop a plan to improve documentation, reviews, and software quality assurance. Beginning with documents and reviews, the first action is to pick one or two documents and develop a standard format (being brief is best) and then develop a set of review guidelines for them. Over time, the actions can be broadened until most important documents are defined, are being produced, and are being reviewed.

- *Grade C* — The organizational approach to predictable documentation, effective reviews, and basic quality assurance activities is coming together.

  —*Action:* The organization should review responses to each of the subsections to determine which areas need the most improvement. Quality assurance functions are likely to need further improvement; if so, focus on establishing mechanisms for ensuring compliance with documentation and process standards. The organization might also broaden its review approach, if this can be done cost-effectively. At the same time, computer-aided software engineering tools should be employed to create effective documentation in a more productive manner.

- *Grade B* — The organization is at the state of practice in the QA area. However, it may not be using quantitative data to analyze the software engineering process.

  —*Action:* One idea to consider is a fledgling program in statistical QA for software. By first collecting data on defects uncovered through other QA activities, the organization can work to improve methods to reduce defects. It can then acquire tools that will enable the organization to build quality software more effectively.

MANAGING PROCESS ASSESSMENT

The process assessment may be conducted by an internal consulting organization, by outsiders, or in a self-directed fashion. Regardless of the approach that is chosen, the assessment must be coordinated by IS management.

It is vital that management prepare an organization for the process assessment activity before the activity begins. The intent of the assessment, and the benefits to be derived from it, should be communicated to technical managers and staff. The types of assessment data to be collected and the use of assessment data should be thoroughly explained. The results of the assessment should be shared with all participants. All involved must understand that the purpose of the assessment is to establish a basis for process improvement, not to punish or judge technical proficiency.

520

RECOMMENDED COURSE OF ACTION

If an organization is committed to software development process improvement, its first step is to assess the current state of software engineering practice. The IS manager is advised to:

- Set the stage for process improvement by providing preliminary training in software engineering for managers, technical staff, and users. Training should introduce process and technology options, emphasize the benefits of improved software quality, and explain the technology transition cycle.
- Select a local champion to manage the assessment approach from the inside. The local champion should drive the assessment process as well as facilitate those who are conducting the assessment and those who are taking part.
- Select an assessment approach that is appropriate for the organization, its budgets, and its management philosophy. If budgets are limited or outside consultants cannot be used, consider the use of a self-directed assessment model. If consulting budgets are available, hire a competent consulting firm to conduct the assessment. If customer requirements dictate a specific assessment approach (e.g., many government contractors are encouraged to use the Software Engineering Institute assessment),develop a plan that enables that approach to be used.
- Determine the software development process maturity level for the organization. The process maturity level makes it possible to compare the organization with common and best practice in the industry. However, it should not be used to compare internal groups or to force technology transition.
- Examine findings and recommendations derived as a consequence of assessment results to be certain that they accurately reflect the organization. Recommendations must be realistic.
- Begin the development of a transition plan that will lead to software process improvement. The transition plan describes the education strategy, the approach to be taken for selecting process changes and technology upgrades, and the tasks, milestones, and deliverables associated with process and technology installation.

Bibliography

1. Bollinger, T. and McGowan, C. "A Critical Look at Software Capability Evaluations." *IEEE Software,* July 1991.
2. *Capability Maturity Model for Software*, Pittsburgh: Software Engineering Institute, Carnegie Mellon University, 1991.
3. Weber, C.V. et al. "Key Practices of the Capability Maturity Model." CMU/SEI-91-TR-25, ESD-TR-91-25. Pittsburgh: Software Engineering Institute, Carnegie Mellon University, August 1991.

About the Editor

Paul C. Tinnirello is executive vice president and chief information officer for a leading insurance information publishing organization in the financial services industry as well as a consulting editor for Auerbach Publications. He is responsible for all enterprise computing technology, including financial software products and E-commerce development. He holds an undergraduate degree in mathematics from Kean University in Union, New Jersey, and has a Master's degree in computer and informational sciences from the New Jersey Institute of Technology. Tinnirello has been a graduate and undergraduate adjunct instructor at state and local colleges in New Jersey and is a member of the academic advisory board for the College of Computing Sciences at New Jersey Institute of Technology. He has written and published numerous articles on software development and support and continues to present his material at financial services conferences. Tinnirello was a founding member of the Software Management Association and regularly contributes to various computing industry related publications including management trends in the E-commerce business sector. He can be reached by e-mail at paulct@tinnirello.com

Index

Index

Index

Q